ASIAN DEVELOPMENT OUTLOOK 2019 UPDATE

FOSTERING GROWTH AND INCLUSION IN ASIA'S CITIES

SEPTEMBER 2019

ASIAN DEVELOPMENT BANK

ADB

ISBN 978-92-9261-752-3 (print), 978-92-9261-753-0 (electronic)
ISSN 1655-4809
Publication Stock No. FLS190445-3
DOI: http://dx.doi.org/10.22617/FLS190445-3

Notes:
In this publication, "$" refers to US dollars.
ADB recognizes "China" as the People's Republic of China and "Vietnam" as Viet Nam.

Cover design by Anthony Victoria.

Contents

Foreword

Growth in developing Asia remains robust but is now expected to moderate more than forecast in *Asian Development Outlook 2019*. This *Update* projects that the region will grow by 5.4% this year, or 0.3 percentage points below the April forecast, and that growth will edge up to 5.5% next year, or 0.1 points lower than earlier forecast. Excluding high-income newly industrialized economies, the region is expected to grow by 6.0% this year and next. Inflation should pick up slightly but remain subdued.

Downward revisions to the regional growth outlook stem largely from escalating trade tensions, which have affected in particular the more open economies of East and Southeast Asia. Also dampening the growth outlook are deteriorating prospects in the advanced economies and declining investment in developing Asia. In Central Asia and the Pacific, however, increased public spending should support growth higher than forecast in April.

Downside risks to the region's prospects have intensified. The trade conflict may yet intensify, possibly moving beyond tariffs. Evidence already shows it reshaping trade patterns, supply chains, and foreign investment. This *Update* also notes a buildup over the past decade of debt in the region, both public and private, that could erode financial stability and render economies more vulnerable to shocks.

Taking a longer view, this *Update* examines the growing importance of cities in developing Asia. It highlights rapid urbanization in the region and its potential to deliver sustained income and job growth. To function well as labor markets and fulfill their promise, cities need to upgrade their transport systems, plan urban expansion better, and enlarge the supply of adequate and affordable homes. Crucially, cities need to ensure that they are environmentally sustainable. ADB is ready to work with public and private stakeholders alike to harness the potential of cities toward advancing regional development goals.

TAKEHIKO NAKAO
President
Asian Development Bank

Acknowledgments

Asian Development Outlook 2019 Update was prepared by staff of Asian Development Bank (ADB) regional departments and resident missions under the guidance of the Economic Research and Regional Cooperation Department (ERCD). Representatives of these departments met regularly as the Regional Economic Outlook Task Force to coordinate and develop consistent forecasts for the region.

Economists in ERCD, led by Abdul Abiad, director of the Macroeconomics Research Division, coordinated the production of the publication, assisted by Edith Laviña. Technical and research support was provided by Shiela Camingue-Romance, Cindy Castillejos-Petalcorin, Nedelyn Magtibay-Ramos, Rhea Manguiat Molato, Pilipinas Quising, Dennis Sorino, Priscille Villanueva, and Mai Lin Villaruel. Additional research support was provided by Ann Jillian Adona, Emmanuel Alano, Rosa Mia Lasam Arao, Zemma Ardarniel, Kristina Baris, Donald Jay Bertulfo, Janine Elora Lazatin, Jesson Pagaduan, Reizle Jade Platitas, Rene Cris Rivera, and Michael Timbang. Support from Mahinthan J. Mariasingham on the use of the ADB Multi-Region Input–Output Database is much appreciated. Economic editorial advisors Robert Boumphrey, Joshua Greene, Henry Ma, Srinivasa Madhur, Richard Niebuhr, and Reza Vaez-Zadeh made substantive contributions to country chapters and the regional outlook.

A team of economists prepared the theme chapter, led by Rana Hasan, director of the Economic Analysis and Operational Support Division of ERCD. In addition to contributors named in the byline and authors of background papers, the theme chapter benefited from valuable feedback and inputs from Abdul Abiad, Lara Arjan, Bruce Dunn, Hideaki Iwasaki, Robert Guild, James Leather, Thiam Hee Ng, Thomas Panella, Stefan Rau, Norio Saito, Sonia Sandhu, Manoj Sharma, Ramola Naik Singru, Lei Lei Song, Robert Valkovic, Joris van Etten, and Jian Zhuang. Support and guidance from Yasuyuki Sawada, Joseph E. Zveglich, Jr., and Edimon Ginting throughout production is gratefully acknowledged. Renard Teipelke provided editorial advice on the theme chapter. Infographics were created by Rhommell Rico, and map illustrations by Abraham Villanueva and Angel Villarez.

Authors who contributed sections are bylined in each chapter. Subregional coordinators were Kenji Takamiya, Lilia Aleksanyan, and Fatima Catacutan for Central Asia, Akiko Terada-Hagiwara for East Asia, Lei Lei Song and Lani Garnace for South Asia, Thiam Hee Ng and Dulce Zara for Southeast Asia, and Rommel Rabanal and Cara Tinio for the Pacific.

Peter Fredenburg advised on ADB style and English usage. Alvin Tubio handled typesetting and graphics generation, assisted by Heili Ann Bravo, Elenita Pura, and Priscille Villanueva. Art direction for the cover was by Anthony Victoria. Critical support for printing and publishing the report came from the Printing Services Unit of the ADB Office of Administrative Services and the publications and web teams of the ADB Department of Communications. Fermirelyn Cruz, Angel Love Alcantara Roque, and Rhia Bautista-Piamonte provided administrative and secretarial support. The Department of Communications, led by Vicky Tan and Karen Lane, planned and coordinated the dissemination of *Asian Development Outlook 2019 Update*.

Definitions

The economies discussed in *Asian Development Outlook 2019 Update* are classified by major analytic or geographic group. For the purposes of this publication, the following apply:

- **Association of Southeast Asian Nations** comprises Brunei Darussalam, Cambodia, Indonesia, the Lao People's Democratic Republic, Malaysia, Myanmar, the Philippines, Singapore, Thailand, and Viet Nam.
- **Developing Asia** comprises the 45 members of the Asian Development Bank listed below.
- **Newly industrialized economies** comprise Hong Kong, China; the Republic of Korea; Singapore; and Taipei,China.
- **Central Asia** comprises Armenia, Azerbaijan, Georgia, Kazakhstan, the Kyrgyz Republic, Tajikistan, Turkmenistan, and Uzbekistan.
- **East Asia** comprises Hong Kong, China; Mongolia; the People's Republic of China; the Republic of Korea; and Taipei,China.
- **South Asia** comprises Afghanistan, Bangladesh, Bhutan, India, Maldives, Nepal, Pakistan, and Sri Lanka.
- **Southeast Asia** comprises Brunei Darussalam, Cambodia, Indonesia, the Lao People's Democratic Republic, Malaysia, Myanmar, the Philippines, Singapore, Thailand, and Viet Nam.
- **The Pacific** comprises the Cook Islands, the Federated States of Micronesia, Fiji, Kiribati, the Marshall Islands, Nauru, Palau, Papua New Guinea, Samoa, Solomon Islands, Timor-Leste, Tonga, Tuvalu, and Vanuatu.

Unless otherwise specified, the symbol "$" and the word "dollar" refer to US dollars. *Asian Development Outlook 2019 Update* is generally based on data available up to **2 September 2019**.

Abbreviations

ADB	Asian Development Bank
ADO	*Asian Development Outlook*
ASEAN	Association of Southeast Asian Nations
CMAX	ratio proxy for stress in foreign exchange markets
DMC	Asian Development Bank developing member country
FAR	floor area ratio
FDI	foreign direct investment
FSM	Federated States of Micronesia
FY	fiscal year
GDP	gross domestic product
GFC	global financial crisis of 2008–2009
GRUMP	Global Rural–Urban Mapping Project
GST	goods and services tax
IMF	International Monetary Fund
IT	information technology
LAC	Latin America and the Caribbean
Lao PDR	Lao People's Democratic Republic
Libor	London interbank offered rate
LNG	liquefied natural gas
LPR	loan prime rate
LVC	land value capture
M1	money that includes cash and checking accounts
M2	broad money that adds highly liquid accounts to M1
M3	broad money that adds time accounts to M2
mbd	million barrels per day
MLF	medium-term lending facility
NBFC	nonbank financial corporation
NFRK	National Fund of the Republic of Kazakhstan
NGO	nongovernment organization
NIE	newly industrialized economy
NPL	nonperforming loan
NTL	nighttime light satellite imagery
OECD	Organisation for Economic Co-operation and Development
OPEC	Organization of the Petroleum Exporting Countries
PIR	price-to-income ratio
PMI	purchasing managers' index
PNG	Papua New Guinea
PRC	People's Republic of China
PRD	Pearl River Delta
Q	quarter

R&D	research and development
RMI	Republic of the Marshall Islands
ROK	Republic of Korea
SEZ	special economic zone
SMEs	small and medium-sized enterprises
SOE	state-owned enterprise
TOD	transit-oriented development
UN	United Nations
US	United States of America
VAT	value-added tax
WTO	World Trade Organization

ADO 2019 Update—Highlights

Growth in developing Asia is moderating but remains robust. As global trade slows and investment weakens, regional growth forecasts are trimmed from *Asian Development Outlook 2019* by 0.3 percentage points for 2019 and by 0.1 points for 2020. Expansion in the region is projected to slow from 5.9% in 2018 to 5.4% this year, recovering somewhat to 5.5% next year. Excluding high-income newly industrialized economies, regional growth is expected to slow from 6.4% last year to 6.0% this year and next.

Inflation remains benign in the region, but pressure is building slightly as food prices rise. Inflation across developing Asia is forecast at 2.7% this year and next, or 0.2 percentage points up from April forecasts.

Risks tilt to the downside. The trade conflict between the United States and the People's Republic of China could escalate further or even spread beyond trade and the two economies. The risk of deeper malaise in the global economy, and uncertainty over how policy makers around the world will respond to weaker global growth, may stoke volatility in global financial markets. Proliferating private debt in some regional economies could pose another challenge to financial stability.

Developing Asia is urbanizing rapidly, promising job creation and economic growth. However, cities must function well as labor markets if they are to enjoy the economic benefits of agglomeration. This requires sound urban planning, efficient public transport, and affordable housing. As cities expand over municipal boundaries and become more connected with one another through flows of goods, services, and people, better planning coordination is needed at all levels of government.

Yasuyuki Sawada
Chief Economist
Asian Development Bank

Asia girds for prolonged uncertainty

- **Regional growth remains robust but is expected to moderate.** GDP expansion in the region, though still strong, is projected to slow from 5.9% in 2018 to 5.4% this year, then edge back up to 5.5% next year. Revisions to April forecasts in *Asian Development Outlook 2019 (ADO 2019)* are 0.3 percentage points lower for this year and 0.1 points lower for next year. The revisions reflect gloomier prospects for international trade—in part because of re-escalation in the trade conflict between the United States and the People's Republic of China (PRC)—and evidence of slowing growth in the major advanced economies and the PRC, as well as in India and the larger economies in East and Southeast Asia. Excluding newly industrialized economies, growth in developing Asia is forecast to slow from 6.4% in 2018 to 6.0% this year and next.

  » **A slowing trend for growth continued in the first half of 2019.** After slowing from 6.2% in 2017 to 5.9% in 2018, growth decelerated further to 5.4% in the first half of 2019 in the economies of developing Asia that release quarterly GDP data. Exports and investment faltered in many economies across the region, leaving private consumption as the main support for continued growth.

  » **Trade shrank as growth in the advanced economies moderated further.** Worsening uncertainty is driving down aggregate growth in the major advanced economies, which is forecast to moderate from 2.2% in 2018 to 1.7% in 2019 and 1.4% in 2020—in both years 0.2 percentage points lower than envisaged in *ADO 2019*. The euro area and the US will grow somewhat slower than previously projected. Japan surprised on the upside in the first half of 2019 but not enough to prop up demand for regional exports.

  » **Faltering investment in developing Asia could impair future growth.** Along with the weakening trend in trade, the region suffered slower growth in domestic investment. The contribution of investment to GDP growth fell in the first quarter of 2019 and is expected to continue declining throughout this year. Slower domestic investment, if sustained, means less new productive capacity going forward, which has implications for regional growth prospects.

- **The growth outlook varies across the subregions of developing Asia.** Because of the trade slowdown, compounded by a sharp downswing in the electronics cycle, growth forecasts for the PRC and the more open economies in East and Southeast Asia are downgraded. Growth in South Asia is now seen moderating this year as India's economy slows primarily for domestic reasons, such as a pre-election decline in investment and tighter credit conditions. In Central Asia and the Pacific, by contrast, growth prospects improve as public spending continues to stimulate the economy in Kazakhstan and Uzbekistan, and as Papua New Guinea recovers from an earthquake in February 2018.

- **Regional inflation is picking up slightly but remains benign.** Headline inflation will edge up from 2.4% in 2018 to 2.7% in 2019 and 2020—both forecasts upward adjustments by 0.2 percentage points from *ADO 2019*. The revisions come mainly from a buildup of inflationary pressure from higher food prices in the region, particularly in the PRC.

- **The regional current account surplus is rising.** Slower imports are offsetting weakness in exports in many economies in developing Asia. The merchandise trade surplus in the PRC rose in the first half of this year as imports fell more substantially than exports, raising the country's current account surplus. As a result, developing Asia's combined current account surplus is now forecast to increase to the equivalent of 1.1% of regional GDP in 2019, or 0.7 percentage points higher than projected in *ADO 2019*, before resuming its narrowing trend to 0.7% in 2020.

- **The escalating and broadening trade conflict may damage supply chains.** Negotiations broke down in the middle of 2019, prompting a new round of tariff escalations, threats, and nontariff constraints on technology transfer and investment. Bilateral trade data from the first half of 2019 show a decline in trade between the PRC and the US, as well as evidence of trade redirection from the PRC toward other economies in developing Asia. Foreign investment patterns are shifting in tandem with trade redirection.

- **Downside risks to the outlook have intensified.** Further escalation in the US–PRC trade conflict could have repercussions beyond trade. The conflict will likely persist at least into 2020 and could broaden to involve other regional economies. The risk of deeper malaise in the advanced economies has worsened, and there is uncertainty over how policy makers in developing Asia and beyond will respond to weaker global growth. Another downside risk to the forecast stems from proliferating private debt in several economies in developing Asia, which could challenge financial stability, especially in the current environment of high risk from large external shocks.

Debt buildup and financial vulnerability

- **Public and private debt continue to grow in developing Asia.** Since the global financial crisis of 2008–2009, countries in the region have continued to accumulate public debt, partly reflecting countercyclical fiscal stimulus following the crisis and, more recently, some regional governments pushing public investments. The ratio of private debt to GDP has expanded even more rapidly in some economies. The PRC, for example, witnessed rapid growth of corporate debt, while the Republic of Korea, Malaysia, and Thailand have seen household debt grow quickly. In the region as a whole, total debt relative to GDP expanded by about two-thirds in the past decade.

- **Debt that expands too rapidly can harm regional financial stability.** High and rising public debt raises investor concerns about fiscal sustainability and government liquidity and solvency. Further, rapid private debt accumulation can jeopardize the ability of companies and households to service it. The Asian financial crisis of 1997–1998 underlined the damage caused by an unsustainable buildup of private debt. Asian financial sectors and their regulations have strengthened significantly, as is evident in banks' higher capital adequacy, and they weathered the global financial crisis well. But policy makers cannot be complacent in the face of rising debt.

■ **Private debt is significantly linked to financial vulnerability.** New analysis revisits the debt–financial vulnerability nexus using an index of currency stress as a proxy for financial vulnerability. Other things being equal, a country with a ratio of private debt to GDP at the top 25% of the sample suffers 12.6 percentage points more depreciation than a country with low private debt, at the bottom 25%. Further, the adverse effect of private debt on currency stress is more pronounced in emerging markets than in the major advanced economies.

■ **Research supports vigilance against debt buildup, public or private.** Analysis also reveals a significant association, during periods of financial stress, between public debt and financial vulnerability. Further, public debt and private debt are interrelated, as private debt booms and busts may require governments to bail out troubled financial institutions. This suggests that a broader regulatory framework that monitors both public and private debt is warranted.

Outlook by subregion

■ **Growth forecasts for developing Asia are revised down.** Projections for 2019 are downgraded for 17 economies, upgraded for 11, and maintained for 17. The downgrades are concentrated in East, South, and Southeast Asia—which together account for 98% of developing Asia's GDP—while the upgrades are mainly for Central Asia and the Pacific.

■ **East Asia will see deepening economic malaise take its toll.** Affected by global conditions, growth in the subregion is expected to slow from 6.0% in 2018 to 5.5% in 2019 and 5.4% in 2020. Growth in the PRC will slip from 6.6% last year to 6.2% in 2019 and 6.0% in 2020—below previous projections—with increased government spending and a strong housing market partly offsetting the impact of the trade dispute with the US and sluggish manufacturing investment. In Hong Kong, China, recent political tensions, spillover from the trade conflict, and the global electronics downturn will slow growth in 2019 and 2020 well below *ADO 2019* projections. External headwinds lower growth forecasts for the Republic of Korea as well, but in Taipei,China higher government spending will keep growth in line with *ADO 2019* projections. The growth forecast for Mongolia remains unchanged for 2019 with continuing dynamism in mining, but is lowered for 2020 as mining investment moderates. Rising food prices in the PRC will push inflation in East Asia higher than forecast in April, to 2.3% in 2019, easing to 2.1% in 2020.

■ **South Asia's growth momentum has softened.** Growth forecasts are lowered to 6.2% for 2019 and 6.7% for 2020. India's growth forecast for fiscal year 2019 is lowered to 6.5% after growth slowed markedly to 5.0% in the first quarter, April–June. Abrupt declines in manufacturing and investment reflect uncertainty ahead of general elections, subdued lending by banks and other financial institutions, stress in the rural economy, and a weakening external outlook. India is expected to rebound to 7.2% growth in fiscal 2020 and join most other subregional countries in performing at or near their *ADO 2019* growth forecasts for next year. In Pakistan, though, growth in 2020 is now forecast lower as the government implements a comprehensive program of macroeconomic and structural reform to stabilize the economy. For Sri Lanka, 2019 and 2020 growth forecasts are marked down because terror bombings in April 2019 caused tourism to fall sharply. The 2019 South Asia inflation forecast is lowered, largely reflecting unexpectedly low food prices in India, but the forecast for 2020 is maintained.

- **Southeast Asia slows more than earlier anticipated.** The subregional growth forecast is revised down from 4.9% to 4.5% for this year and from 5.0% to 4.7% for next year. Forecasts are downgraded for half of the 10 economies in the subregion and unchanged for the other half. With escalation in the US–PRC trade conflict, weakening global activity and trade, and a downturn in the electronics cycle, a significant export slowdown in the first half of the year hit the whole subregion except Cambodia. Softening domestic investment exacerbated export woes in most larger subregion economies—Indonesia, Malaysia, the Philippines, Singapore, and Thailand—but domestic consumption held up well to cushion the slowdown. The downward revision for growth is paralleled by one for the inflation forecasts.

- **Central Asia is now forecast to accelerate.** Growth forecasts for the subregion are revised up from 4.2% to 4.4% in 2019 and from 4.2% to 4.3% in 2020. Increased government spending has boosted growth in Kazakhstan, while a substantial rise in investment raises prospects for Uzbekistan. These revisions and higher growth projections for Armenia and Azerbaijan more than offset slower growth prospects for Georgia. Growth in 2020 is now projected at 4.3%, revised up from 4.2% on a small upgrade for Kazakhstan and larger ones for Tajikistan and Uzbekistan. The forecast for inflation in 2019 is revised up from 7.8% to 8.0% because cuts to subsidies, rising import prices, foreign exchange shortages, and expansionary credit have stoked inflation in Turkmenistan. This increase offsets—along with higher inflation projections for Georgia and Tajikistan that reflect accelerating prices in the first half of the year—slightly lowered forecasts for Kazakhstan and Uzbekistan. The forecast for subregional inflation in 2020 is raised from 7.2% to 7.4%.

- **The Pacific outlook improves with recovery in its largest economy.** After near-stagnation in 2018, the growth forecast for the subregion in 2019 is revised up to 4.2%, mainly because gas production in Papua New Guinea has outpaced projections, but also with construction expenditure in Solomon Islands and Samoa higher than expected and Nauru suffering less economic decline than predicted. Conversely, tourism downturns require lower growth projections for the Cook Islands and Palau, as does disappointing recovery expenditure for Tonga. Elsewhere, growth forecasts are maintained. The subregional growth forecast for 2020 is downgraded to 2.6% largely because of project delays in Papua New Guinea. Inflation in the subregion is now expected to ease further to 3.4% in 2019, 0.3 percentage points lower than projected earlier. As more benign price pressures are seen to persist into 2020, the subregional projection for inflation next year is reduced to 3.4%.

Fostering growth and inclusion in Asia's cities

Summary

❖ **Developing Asia is urbanizing rapidly.** The number of urban inhabitants in the region has increased from 375 million in 1970 to 1.84 billion in 2017. The urbanization rate is projected to rise from 46% in 2017 to 64% by 2050.

❖ **Urbanization bodes well for economic growth and job creation.** By enabling workers and firms to interact closely, cities generate increases in productivity through several channels, collectively known as agglomeration economies.

❖ **Realizing their promise requires a holistic agenda for cities.** Cities must ensure

  ♦ an efficient multi-modal public transport system;

  ♦ land-use plans and regulations that align with infrastructure investments, promote environmental sustainability and resilience, and are sufficiently flexible to respond to market signals;

  ♦ affordable housing with access to both basic infrastructure and social services such as education and health care.

❖ **Simultaneously, cities must work well together as a system.** Cities are interconnected with one another and with rural areas through flows of goods, services, and people. An efficient urban system requires

  ♦ good connectivity infrastructure between cities and the hinterland and

  ♦ mechanisms for better coordination of spatial and economic planning at various scales—from the city level to city clusters and on to regional and even national levels.

Urbanization in developing Asia

▪ **To understand how cities evolve, comparable data are needed.** Official statistics are typically based on city definitions that differ across countries, and by administrative boundaries that may not match a city's actual footprint. Nighttime satellite imagery and grid population data are combined to assemble a dataset of 1,459 "natural cities" in developing Asia and track their footprint and population from 2000 to 2016. Analysis of this dataset reveals some important features of urbanization in developing Asia that are relevant to policy making.

  » **Natural cities house 34.7% of the population on 2.3% of the land area.** This indicates substantial spatial concentration. From 2000 to 2016, natural city populations grew by an average of 3.3% annually, while the area they cover expanded by almost 5.0% each year. Though cities with populations below 1 million in 2000 have grown at a faster rate than larger cities, the latter still accounted for over half of the absolute increase in the urban population.

  » **As cities expand beyond administrative boundaries, they form clusters.** The urban footprints of many cities have expanded beyond city boundaries, and 476 natural cities that were spatially separated in 1992 had linked up by 2016 to form 124 city clusters. Among the 28 largest city clusters with populations in 2016 greater than 10 million, 19 span two or more top-level administrative divisions such as states or provinces. This necessitates metropolitan approaches to governing urban areas.

■ **Large cities tend to be more productive.** Agglomeration economies arise as workers and firms interact in close physical proximity. Theory suggests that productivity is higher in larger, denser cities because workers are more likely to find jobs that are a good fit, ideas and knowledge are exchanged among individuals and organizations, and resources are more easily shared. Evidence in developing Asia indicates that workers are paid more in larger cities, all else being equal, and that greater city size coincides with higher labor productivity and with firm propensity to undertake research and development and to innovate products and processes.

■ **Some cities fall short of their potential as engines of growth.** Mid-sized cities with weak infrastructure and poor connections with major markets may struggle to realize agglomeration economies. Even major cities may not serve their residents well for lack of affordable housing and transport, or opportunities to acquire skills. Air pollution can pose public health risks, and congestion causes substantive losses to the local economy and residents' well-being.

The city as a labor market

■ **A functional labor market is key to realizing agglomeration economies.** Cities are much more than places of work. However, cities cannot thrive unless they function well as labor markets, connecting both firms and workers. A labor market works best when intracity travel is fast and cheap, firms and households have the flexibility to relocate from one part of a city to another, and real estate is affordable.

■ **Congestion and poor public transport systems impede mobility.** Inadequate mobility within a city fragments the labor market. Especially hard hit are lower-income households residing in remote areas with severely limited access to public transport.

» **Mobility is constrained by severe congestion and scant public transport.** Granular trip data used to measure congestion in 278 natural cities with populations above half a million show there is considerable variation in congestion across cities, with large cities in middle-income countries tending to have the most severe congestion. In 199 cities for which information on public transport was available, 25% of the surveyed trips could not be made by public transport. For the remaining trips, travel duration by public transport including walking time was three times longer than for driving. Finally, the cost of commuting by public transport was found to be high for an average urban resident in developing Asia.

» **A city needs an efficient multimodal public transport system.** The system must combine trains, buses, ride sharing, and less formal services like autorickshaws and jeepneys to improve mobility. Demand-side management may be considered as well to reduce congestion over the longer term. These efforts offer the bonus of helping to tackle air pollution in Asian cities, especially when transport services are provided using clean fuels, such as compressed natural gas.

■ **Land-use planning must support orderly city expansion.** Natural cities in developing Asia expanded geographically from 116 square kilometers in 1992 to 384 square kilometers in 2016. Some of this urban expansion has been unplanned, as demonstrated by declining use of grid layouts and reduced access to arterial grids and even local streets. Poor access can seriously restrict the mobility of residents and fragment a city's labor market. Further, many neighborhoods do not have connections to central water supply and sewerage systems or easy access to schools and hospitals.

   » **Governments should plan for urban expansion.** City growth is sure to continue. Governments must identify likely expansion areas and obtain planning jurisdiction over them. Even if development is not envisioned for some time, land rights for appropriately spaced arterial road grids, public facilities, and open space must be acquired. This lays the foundation for integrated urban planning and provides a template on which actual investments and mixed-use development are implemented.

   » **Some land-use regulations need to be more flexible.** Some regulations can be counterproductive when applied too rigidly. Restrictions on building height, for example, can unnecessarily drive up real estate prices and undercut the effectiveness of investments in public transport such as metro rail and bus rapid transit systems.

■ **Cities need to be environmentally sustainable.** The long-term viability of cities depends crucially on ensuring water sufficiency, reducing air pollution, and protecting against shocks and stresses from disasters. Tackling these challenges requires integrated multisectoral approaches that encompass both land-use planning and transportation. Moving away from car-centric road networks to public transport systems can help reduce air pollution, for instance, and land-use planning has an important role to play in sustaining water security.

■ **Affordable housing requires addressing both supply and demand.** While cities offer higher wages to reward higher productivity, such positive agglomeration effects do not always outweigh high housing prices. A sample of 211 cities in 26 countries found home prices to be severely unaffordable for median-income households in more than 90% of the cities. The problem extends beyond large cities to smaller agglomerations. With affordable housing out of reach, many urban residents settle for inadequate housing with only limited access to safe water and improved sanitation.

   » **Policy can help residents find appropriate, affordable housing.** Governments can offer to low-income groups favorable home finance arrangements such as low-interest loans and, especially for the very poor, provide public housing directly. At the same time, macroprudential policies that govern maximum ratios of debt to income, for example, or of loan to home value are useful tools to keep the housing market from overheating.

   » **Cities need to tackle supply-side constraints on housing supply.** Increased demand for housing can go unanswered because of administrative boundaries and overly restrictive land-use regulations. Cities need to provide ample developable land that is both affordable and offers ready access to basic public amenities and public transportation networks.

Managing the urban system

- **Growth requires vibrancy in all types of cities.** Cities are connected to one another, and to the rural hinterland, through flows of goods, services, and people. They form an urban system. Comprehensive economic growth depends not just on one or two large cities but also on well-functioning market towns that specialize in marketing and distributing agricultural produce, as well as mid-sized cities.

- **Spatial and economic planning need to be better coordinated.** The growing importance of city clusters in developing Asia means that spatial and economic planning must be better coordinated across multiple local government units. Effective systems of metropolitan governance are needed to deliver essential services efficiently and determine land use wisely through decisions on transport hubs, industrial parks, water treatment plants, and solid waste disposal facilities. Further, local governments of individual cities should play greater roles in decisions on economic development. In many countries, economic development is dictated by state or national industrial development agencies without adequate consultation with local governments.

- **Improvement for the whole urban system may harm some locations.** Investments in intercity transport make the urban system more efficient overall but may adversely affect some cities and their hinterland. Similarly, while some small cities benefit from improved connectivity with core cities in a city cluster, others may suffer declines in some lines of business.

- **Public policy affects the spatial distribution of economic activity.** It should be designed with several considerations in mind.

  » **Big cities should draw more on private sector funding.** Big cities have an edge in attracting private investment because agglomeration economies promise high returns. They should be encouraged to draw on the private sector to meet a portion of their own investment finance needs.

  » **Allocations should consider population flows and economic activity.** Many medium-sized cities in the region with populations of 1–5 million, and some smaller cities with populations of at least half a million, continue to attract migrants despite considerable shortcomings in infrastructure and governance. These cities require policy attention and public support.

  » **Government support to lagging areas must be well targeted.** If a location lags for multiple reasons that reinforce one another, a simple tax incentive package is unlikely to attract private investment as intended. It may be more effective to improve its connectivity to major markets and support skills development and industries such as agro-processing and labor-intensive manufacturing. If a small city lags because its young people migrate away to larger centers, the most effective interventions may be ameliorative, such as providing better care for the elderly.

GDP growth rate and inflation, % per year

	Growth rate of GDP					Inflation				
	2018	2019		2020		2018	2019		2020	
		ADO 2019	Update	ADO 2019	Update		ADO 2019	Update	ADO 2019	Update
Central Asia	4.3	4.2	4.4	4.2	4.3	8.3	7.8	8.0	7.2	7.4
Armenia	5.2	4.3	4.8	4.5	4.5	2.5	3.5	3.0	3.2	3.2
Azerbaijan	1.4	2.5	2.6	2.7	2.4	2.3	4.0	3.7	5.0	3.8
Georgia	4.7	5.0	4.7	4.9	4.6	2.6	3.2	4.3	3.0	3.5
Kazakhstan	4.1	3.5	3.7	3.3	3.4	6.0	6.0	5.8	5.5	5.2
Kyrgyz Republic	3.5	4.0	4.0	4.4	4.4	1.5	3.0	2.0	3.5	3.5
Tajikistan	7.3	7.0	7.0	6.5	7.0	5.4	7.5	8.0	7.0	7.5
Turkmenistan	6.2	6.0	6.0	5.8	5.8	13.6	9.0	13.4	8.2	13.0
Uzbekistan	5.1	5.2	5.8	5.5	6.0	17.5	16.0	15.0	14.0	13.0
East Asia	6.0	5.7	5.5	5.5	5.4	2.0	1.8	2.3	1.8	2.1
Hong Kong, China	3.0	2.5	0.3	2.5	1.5	2.4	2.3	2.3	2.3	2.3
Mongolia	6.8	6.7	6.7	6.3	6.1	6.8	8.5	8.5	7.5	7.5
People's Republic of China	6.6	6.3	6.2	6.1	6.0	2.1	1.9	2.6	1.8	2.2
Republic of Korea	2.7	2.5	2.1	2.5	2.4	1.5	1.4	0.7	1.4	1.4
Taipei,China	2.6	2.2	2.2	2.0	2.0	1.3	1.1	0.9	1.2	0.9
South Asia	6.6	6.8	6.2	6.9	6.7	3.6	4.7	4.0	4.9	4.9
Afghanistan	2.7	2.5	2.7	3.0	3.4	0.6	3.0	2.0	4.5	3.5
Bangladesh	7.9	8.0	8.1	8.0	8.0	5.8	5.5	5.5	5.8	5.8
Bhutan	5.5	5.7	5.3	6.0	6.0	3.6	3.8	2.8	4.0	3.5
India	6.8	7.2	6.5	7.3	7.2	3.4	4.3	3.5	4.6	4.0
Maldives	7.6	6.5	6.5	6.3	6.3	-0.1	1.0	1.0	1.5	1.5
Nepal	6.7	6.2	7.1	6.3	6.3	4.2	4.4	4.6	5.1	5.5
Pakistan	5.5	3.9	3.3	3.6	2.8	3.9	7.5	7.3	7.0	12.0
Sri Lanka	3.2	3.6	2.6	3.8	3.5	2.1	3.5	3.0	4.0	3.8
Southeast Asia	5.1	4.9	4.5	5.0	4.7	2.7	2.6	2.3	2.7	2.6
Brunei Darussalam	0.1	1.0	1.0	1.5	1.5	0.1	0.2	0.1	0.2	0.2
Cambodia	7.5	7.0	7.0	6.8	6.8	2.5	2.5	2.2	2.5	2.5
Indonesia	5.2	5.2	5.1	5.3	5.2	3.2	3.2	3.2	3.3	3.3
Lao People's Dem. Rep.	6.3	6.5	6.2	6.5	6.2	2.0	2.0	2.3	2.0	2.3
Malaysia	4.7	4.5	4.5	4.7	4.7	1.0	2.0	1.0	2.7	2.0
Myanmar	6.8	6.6	6.6	6.8	6.8	5.9	6.8	8.0	7.5	7.5
Philippines	6.2	6.4	6.0	6.4	6.2	5.2	3.8	2.6	3.5	3.0
Singapore	3.1	2.6	0.7	2.6	1.4	0.4	0.7	0.7	0.9	0.9
Thailand	4.1	3.9	3.0	3.7	3.2	1.1	1.0	1.0	1.0	1.0
Viet Nam	7.1	6.8	6.8	6.7	6.7	3.5	3.5	3.0	3.8	3.5
The Pacific	0.4	3.5	4.2	3.2	2.6	4.2	3.7	3.4	4.0	3.4
Cook Islands	8.9	6.0	4.2	4.5	4.5	0.4	1.0	-0.2	1.5	1.5
Federated States of Micronesia	0.4	2.7	2.7	2.5	2.5	1.4	0.7	0.7	1.5	1.5
Fiji	3.5	3.2	2.9	3.5	3.2	4.1	3.5	3.5	3.0	3.0
Kiribati	2.3	2.3	2.3	2.3	2.3	2.1	2.3	2.3	2.2	2.2
Marshall Islands	2.5	2.3	2.3	2.2	2.2	0.8	0.5	0.5	1.0	1.0
Nauru	-2.4	-1.0	-0.5	0.1	0.1	3.8	2.5	2.5	2.0	2.0
Palau	1.5	3.0	-0.5	3.0	1.0	2.0	0.5	1.0	1.5	2.0
Papua New Guinea	-0.6	3.7	4.8	3.1	2.1	4.7	4.2	4.0	4.7	3.8
Samoa	-2.2	2.0	2.5	3.0	3.5	3.7	2.0	2.2	1.5	2.0
Solomon Islands	3.8	2.4	2.8	2.3	2.7	3.5	2.5	2.0	2.5	3.0
Timor-Leste	-0.5	4.8	4.8	5.4	5.4	2.2	3.0	1.9	3.3	2.5
Tonga	0.4	2.1	1.6	1.9	2.5	5.3	5.3	3.5	5.3	3.3
Tuvalu	4.3	4.1	4.1	4.4	4.4	1.8	3.4	3.4	3.5	3.5
Vanuatu	3.2	3.0	3.0	2.8	2.8	2.3	2.0	2.0	2.0	2.2
Developing Asia	5.9	5.7	5.4	5.6	5.5	2.4	2.5	2.7	2.5	2.7
Developing Asia excluding the NIEs	6.4	6.2	6.0	6.1	6.0	2.6	2.6	2.9	2.6	2.9

GDP = gross domestic product, NIEs = newly industrialized economies (Hong Kong, China; the Republic of Korea; Singapore; and Taipei,China).

1

ASIA GIRDS FOR PROLONGED UNCERTAINTY

Asia girds for prolonged uncertainty

Developing Asia's strong growth prospects have weakened since Asian Development Outlook 2019 (ADO 2019) was published in April, as global growth slowed, trade tensions escalated, and regional investment weakened. Exports declined with lower demand from the major advanced economies, compounded by the trade conflict between the United States and the People's Republic of China (PRC). Tensions between the two have escalated since May, shaking financial markets. Uncertainty has undermined private investment in the region, leaving domestic consumption as the main support to growth. On the supply side, manufacturing slowed further, with electronics in particular suffering an industry-wide slump. Facing slower growth and muted inflation, many countries have loosened fiscal and monetary policy to support economic activity.

   Regional growth will slow from 5.9% in 2018 to 5.4% in 2019, edging back up to 5.5% next year. Excluding the newly industrialized economies (NIEs), growth will slow to 6.0% this year and next (Figure 1.0.1). Growth in the PRC is expected to decline to 6.2% in 2019 and 6.0% in 2020 under the impact of the trade conflict, while domestic factors will slow growth in India to 6.5% in 2019, recovering to 7.2% in 2020. Regional inflation will rise to 2.7% on higher food prices this year and next but remain well below historical rates. Trade and production redirection in response to the US–PRC trade conflict is already occurring. Downside risks to the region have intensified, with the trade conflict posing the greatest of many risks to global growth and showing no sign of abating. A rise in public and private debt over the past decade leaves the region more vulnerable to shocks.

Figure 1.0.1 GDP growth outlook in developing Asia

Strong growth prospects in developing Asia are dimming.

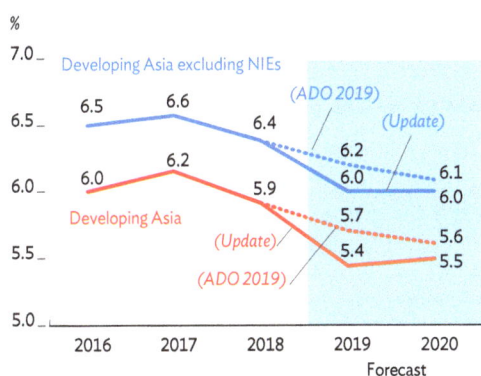

NIEs = newly industrialized economies of Hong Kong, China; Republic of Korea; Singapore; and Taipei,China.
Source: *Asian Development Outlook* database.

This chapter was written by Abdul Abiad, Ann Jillian Adona, Shiela Camingue-Romance, Matteo Lanzafame, Nedelyn Magtibay-Ramos, Valerie Mercer-Blackman, Donghyun Park, Madhavi Pundit, Pilipinas Quising, Irfan Qureshi, Arief Ramayandi (lead), Dennis Sorino, Shu Tian, Michael Timbang, Priscille Villanueva, and Mai Lin Villaruel of the Economic Research and Regional Cooperation Department, ADB, Manila.

1.1 Challenges to Asia's growth

Developing Asia posted strong but moderating growth in the first half of 2019. This continues a trend established in the past 2 years, with growth slowing from 6.2% in 2017 to 5.9% in 2018. In the 11 regional economies with quarterly GDP data, which account for 95% of developing Asia's GDP, growth decelerated to 5.4% in the first 6 months of this year. This moderation came about through a number of factors: weaker global activity and trade, re-escalation of the trade conflict between the US and the PRC, a sharp downturn in the global electronics cycle, and slowing investment in the region.

1.1.1 Global malaise undermines activity

In the advanced economies of the US, the euro area, and Japan, growth slowed from 2.2% in 2018 to 2.0% in the first half of 2019, and growth in the second quarter (Q2) was substantially weaker than in Q1. Within developing Asia, growth in the two largest regional economies edged down: in the PRC from 6.6% in 2018 to 6.3% in the first half of 2019, and in India from 6.8% in fiscal year 2018 (to 31 March 2019) to 5.0% in Q1 of fiscal 2019 (Figure 1.1.1).

Figure 1.1.1 Demand side contributions to growth, selected economies

Consumption supported growth as investment flagged in many countries.

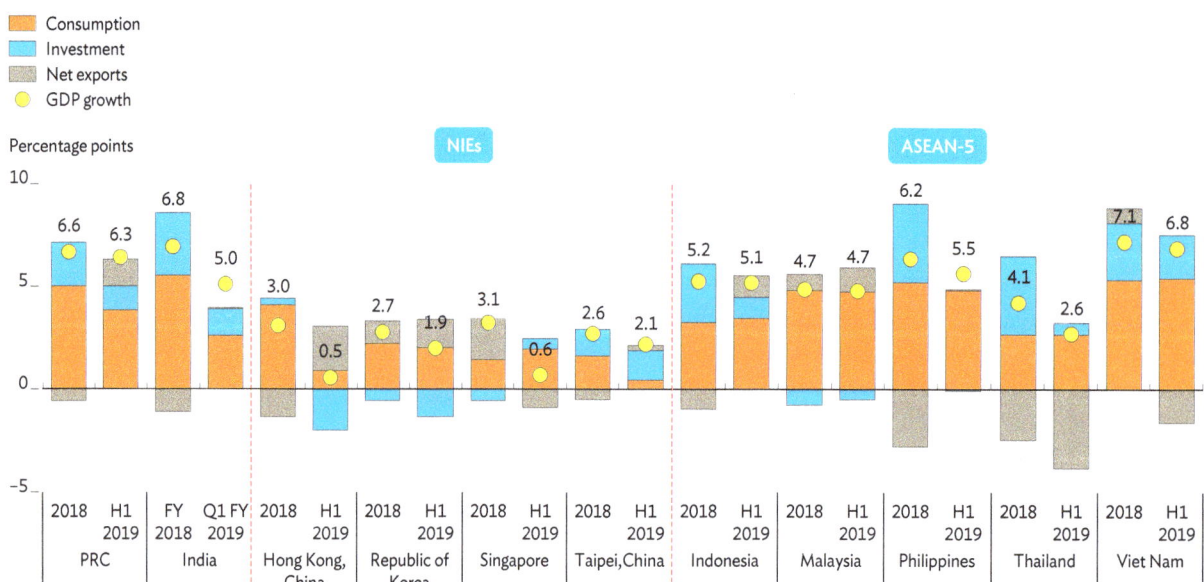

ASEAN = Association of Southeast Asian Nations, FY = fiscal year, H1 = first half, NIEs = newly industrialized economies, PRC = People's Republic of China, Q1 = first quarter.
Note: Excludes statistical discrepancy. For India, 2019 data are for the first quarter (April–June) of fiscal year 2019.
Sources: Haver Analytics (accessed 2 September 2019); ADB estimates.

Slower growth was also observed in the five larger economies of the Association of Southeast Asian Nations (ASEAN-5) and in the NIEs, with the biggest drops recorded in Singapore and Hong Kong, China. In contrast, countries in Central Asia and the Pacific recorded growth in the first half of 2019 that exceeded expectations.

Through much of the region, consumption made up for weakening exports and investment. Net exports subtracted from growth in Singapore, Thailand, and Viet Nam—and in economies where net exports contributed to growth, they did so not because exports accelerated. In fact, exports declined in many countries because of a weak external environment, but imports fell even more steeply. Import decline can reflect weakening investment, and the investment contribution to GDP growth did drop in 8 of the 11 economies with quarterly data. In the PRC, the investment contribution was halved as US tariffs undermined exports and manufacturing prospects. Measures to control imports in Indonesia and a delay in enacting the 2019 budget in the Philippines further curbed investment. In India, the contribution of investment fell substantially because of subdued bank lending and uncertainty ahead of elections in April–May. Relatively robust consumption growth helped keep GDP growth healthy in many countries, though a few suffered somewhat weaker consumption growth as well.

Manufacturing, which had started to weaken in the latter part of 2018, slowed further (Figure 1.1.2). Growth in industrial production declined sharply in the NIEs and ASEAN-5, partly because the trade conflict undermined their exports of intermediate goods to the PRC. The same economies have also been affected by a sharp downturn in the global electronics cycle (Box 1.1.1). A forward-looking indicator of manufacturing activity, the manufacturing purchasing managers' index, has been slipping in recent months and now hovers near the threshold of 50 that separates expansion from slowdown in manufacturing (Table 1.1.1). In the Republic of Korea (ROK) and Taipei,China, the index fell to its lowest in over 2 years, reflecting weak external demand, particularly for electronics. In Southeast Asia, Cambodia and Viet Nam are seeing steady expansion in manufacturing. In India, the only economy in South Asia with a purchasing managers' index, manufacturing output continued to show strength in July.

Financial conditions improved this year but have been subjected to occasional jitters. Major equity markets boomed in Q1, then stabilized throughout Q2 (Figure 1.1.3). The best-performing equity market in Q1 was the PRC, posting a 24% increase, followed by Hong Kong, China and then Viet Nam.

Figure 1.1.2 Growth in industrial production, selected economies

Manufacturing weakened further, particularly in NIEs and the ASEAN-5 countries.

— People's Republic of China
— India
— NIEs
— ASEAN-5
— Developing Asia

% change year on year, 3-month moving average

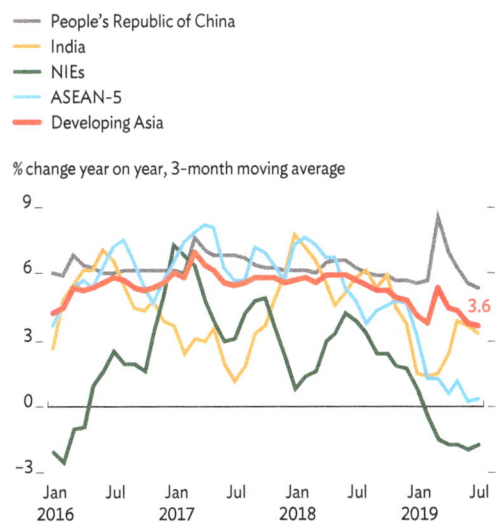

ASEAN-5 = weighted average of Indonesia, Malaysia, the Philippines, Thailand, and Viet Nam, NIEs = weighted average of Hong Kong, China; the Republic of Korea; Singapore; and Taipei,China, Developing Asia = weighted average of the ASEAN-5, India, NIEs, and the People's Republic of China.
Source: Haver Analytics (accessed 2 September 2019).

Box 1.1.1 A downturn in the global electronics cycle and its impact on developing Asia

The electronics industry plays a key role in many economies in developing Asia. It produces semiconductors and other products that depend heavily on them, such as computers and peripherals, telecommunications equipment, and industrial, automotive, and consumer electronics. As panel A of box figure 1 shows, the sector contributes a larger share of value added in developing Asia than in the rest of the world, 3.7% versus 1.6%, with an average of 2.3% for the 22 economies in developing Asia for which data are available. In the PRC, electronics provide 3.8% of GDP. For a few economies in the region—Malaysia, the ROK, Singapore, and Taipei,China—the electronics industry contributes from 6% to almost 16% of GDP.

Moreover, the exports of these economies are highly concentrated in electronics. The industry supplies more than half of gross exports from the Philippines and from Hong Kong, China, for example, while accounting for about 40% of exports from Malaysia; Singapore; Taipei,China; and Viet Nam. Gross exports may overstate the importance of electronics, however, because some economies, such as Singapore and Hong Kong, China, are transshipment points for many electronics products. Panel B of box figure 1 shows that domestic value added in electronics exports comprises almost a quarter of total value added in exports in the PRC and Taipei,China, over 20% in the ROK, and 6%–14% in Indonesia, Malaysia, the Philippines, and Singapore. The average domestic value added in electronics exports as a share of total value added in exports of 22 economies in developing Asia is 5.3%.

Developments in electronics often follow the lead of the industry's semiconductor segment. Virtually all electronic products contain at least one chip—and in many cases multiple chips—so it is natural that the dynamics of the broad electronics industry follow those of semiconductors. Semiconductor products account for 69.5% of all electronics exports from Taipei,China, and shares in exports are similarly high for Singapore at 64.1%, the ROK at 56.7%, Malaysia at 54.7%, the Philippines at 39.8%, and Hong Kong, China at 39.7%. Box figure 2 shows that export growth in electronics correlates very highly with export growth in semiconductors. As such, the global electronics cycle is often monitored by tracking semiconductors, for which comparable data across countries are readily available.

Box figure 1 The importance of electronics for selected economies in developing Asia

Electronics account for a large share of developing Asia's GDP and exports.

----- DMC average

a. Value added in electronics as share of GDP value added, 2017

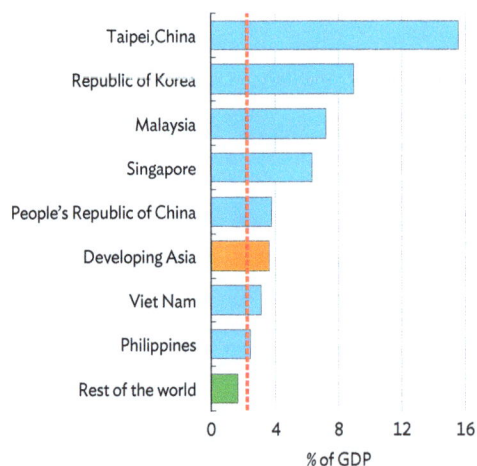

b. Domestic value added in electronics exports as share of total value added in exports, 2017

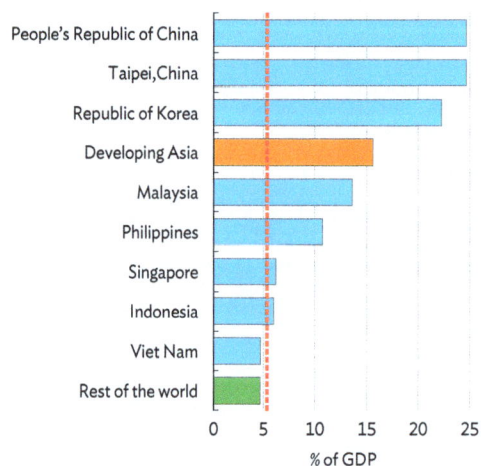

DMC = Asian Development Bank developing member country, GDP = gross domestic product, PRC = People's Republic of China.
Note: The DMC average is a simple average across the 22 DMCs for which data are available.
Source: ADB Multi-regional Input–Output Table database.

continued next page

Box 1.1.1 *Continued*

There is a clear, globally synchronized cycle in semiconductors. Box figure 3 plots semiconductor billings worldwide and across regions from June 2008 to May 2019. Asia and the Pacific contribute nearly three-quarters of semiconductor sales, while the Americas contribute about 17% and Europe 10%. Demand for semiconductor products clearly rises and falls in tandem across different regions, moving through pronounced cycles.

At the end of 2018, semiconductors entered a downcycle, with implications for economies in developing Asia dependent on electronics. Semiconductor sales are driven by sales to consumers of a number of products, in particular smartphones, laptops and other computers, and consumer electronics such as televisions and home appliances. Semiconductor billings declined across all regions, contracting globally by 14.4% year on year as of May 2019. The World Semiconductor Trade Statistics organization forecasts that semiconductor sales will contract by 13.3% in 2019 as a whole—much more than the 3.0% contraction it had expected in April, when *ADO 2019* was published. The electronics downturn will drag on regional activity, particularly in East and Southeast Asia.

Several factors are driving the sharper downturn, which suggests that recovery will be muted. First, rapid growth in the past decade was fueled by first-time buyers of key products such as smartphones in new markets, but many of these markets are nearing saturation—83% for smartphones in the PRC, for example, assuming one per person. Second, consumers no longer replace smartphones and tablets as often as they once did because periodic releases of new models offer only incremental upgrades. Third, the industry had pinned its hopes on a rollout of 5G technology this year, which would enable technologies such as smart manufacturing, autonomous vehicles, and artificial intelligence to drive a new cycle of demand for electronics. The rollout has been delayed, however, by the trade conflict and efforts to restrict exports to Huawei, the largest producer of 5G equipment. Industry experts now expect the 5G rollout to be late next year or 2021.

Box figure 2 Annual growth in exports of electronic goods and semiconductors

Growth in electronics exports correlates highly with growth in semiconductor exports.

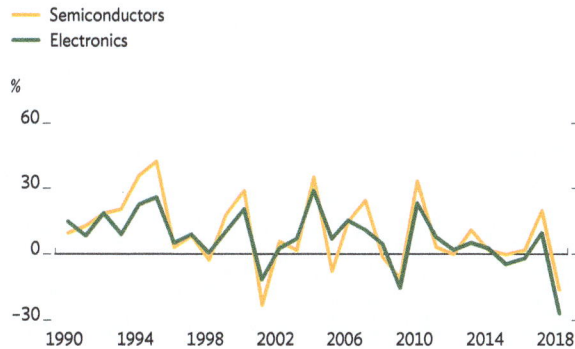

Source: ADB estimates based on data from UN Comtrade database. http://comtrade.un.org (accessed 19 August 2019).

Box figure 3 Semiconductor billings

The global semiconductor cycle is in a downturn.

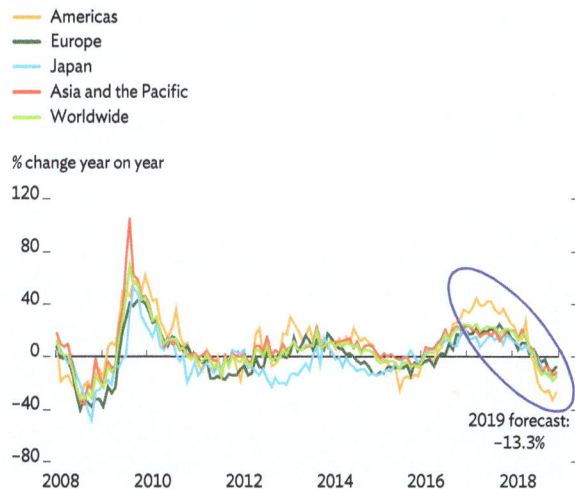

Source: ADB estimates based on data from World Semiconductor Trade Statistics. http:// wsts.tsia.org.tw/ (accessed 19 August 2019).

Table 1.1.1 Markit manufacturing purchasing managers' index, selected economies

Purchasing managers' indexes slipped in recent months, and many are hovering near the threshold.

Economy	2018												2019					
	Q1			Q2			Q3			Q4			Q1			Q2		Q3
India	52.4	52.1	51.0	51.6	51.2	53.1	52.3	51.7	52.2	53.1	54.0	53.2	53.9	54.3	52.6	51.8	52.7	52.1	52.5
Indonesia	49.9	51.4	50.7	51.6	51.7	50.3	50.5	51.9	50.7	50.5	50.4	51.2	49.9	50.1	51.2	50.4	51.6	50.6	49.6
Malaysiaª	53.5	52.9	52.5	51.6	50.6	52.5	52.7	54.2	54.5	52.2	51.2	49.8	50.9	50.6	50.2	52.4	51.8	50.8	50.6
PRC	51.5	51.6	51.0	51.1	51.1	51.0	50.8	50.6	50.0	50.1	50.2	49.7	48.3	49.9	50.8	50.2	50.2	49.4	49.9
Philippines	51.7	50.8	51.5	52.7	53.7	52.9	50.9	51.9	52.0	54.0	54.2	53.2	52.3	51.9	51.5	50.9	51.2	51.3	52.1
Republic of Korea	50.7	50.3	49.1	48.4	48.9	49.8	48.3	49.9	51.3	51.0	48.6	49.8	48.3	47.2	48.8	50.2	48.4	47.5	47.3
Taipei,China	56.9	56.0	55.3	54.8	53.4	54.5	53.1	53.0	50.8	48.7	48.4	47.7	47.5	46.3	49.0	48.2	48.4	45.5	48.1
Thailand	50.6	50.9	49.1	49.5	51.1	50.2	50.1	49.9	50.0	48.9	49.8	50.3	50.2	49.9	50.3	51.0	50.7	50.6	50.3
Viet Nam	53.4	53.5	51.6	52.7	53.9	55.7	54.9	53.7	51.5	53.9	56.5	53.8	51.9	51.2	51.9	52.5	52.0	52.5	52.6

PRC = People's Republic of China, Q = quarter.

ª For Malaysia, the series is adjusted by adding 3 points, as historical experience suggests that values above 47 are consistent with expansion.

Note: Seasonally adjusted. Reddish color indicates contraction (<50). White to green indicates expansion (>50). Data for Q3 is for July only.

Source: CEIC Data Company (accessed 13 August 2019).

However, during periods when trade tensions escalated in May and then again in early August, almost all major Asian equity market indexes experienced synchronized decline. The same pattern was observed in bond markets. Bond spreads for individual countries had been narrowing since January 2019 but shot up in May and early August (Figure 1.1.4).

Following relative stability in early 2019, some regional currencies weakened again in mid-2019 (Figure 1.1.5). Many depreciated against the US dollar through much of 2018, their weakness brought about by continued US Federal Reserve tightening and by reassessment of emerging market risks sparked by problems in Argentina and Turkey. Many regional currencies had stabilized by the end of 2018 and stayed stable through the early part of this year. When signs of slowing activity and rising trade tensions emerged, however, a number of currencies weakened: the ROK won by 8% from January to August 2019; the PRC renminbi, which reached its lowest value since Q2 of 2008; and the Pakistan rupee, which depreciated by more than 10% as the country continued to move to a flexible, market-determined rate. Regional currencies weakened further following a US interest rate cut on 30 July and another round of trade measures in early August. The renminbi weakened beyond CNY7 against the US dollar, and the Indian rupee, Indonesian rupiah, Philippine peso, and ROK won also depreciated.

Figure 1.1.3 Equity indexes, selected Asian economies

After strengthening in early 2019, major Asian equity markets were shaken by re-escalation of trade tensions...

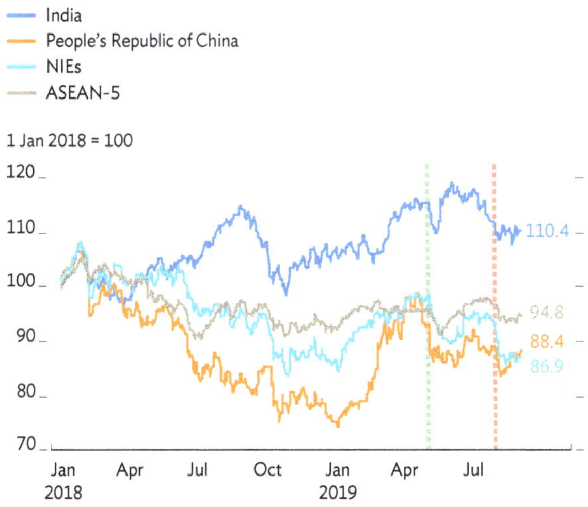

India
People's Republic of China
NIEs
ASEAN-5

1 Jan 2018 = 100

ASEAN-5 = weighted average of Indonesia, Malaysia, the Philippines, Thailand, and Viet Nam, NIEs = weighted average of Hong Kong, China; the Republic of Korea; Singapore; and Taipei,China.

Notes: The green dotted line is 6 May 2019, when the US President tweeted about increased tariffs on $200 billion in imports from the PRC. The red dotted line is 31 July 2019, when the US Federal Reserve cut its rate by 25 basis points, and 1 August 2019, when tariffs on an additional $300 billion of imports from the PRC were announced.

Source: Bloomberg (accessed 2 September 2019).

Figure 1.1.4 JP Morgan EMBI stripped spreads, selected Asian economies

...and bond spreads widened as well with news of the trade conflict.

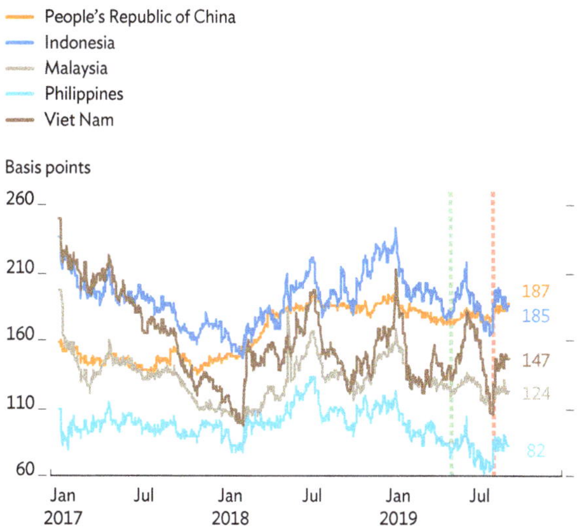

People's Republic of China
Indonesia
Malaysia
Philippines
Viet Nam

Basis points

EMBI = emerging markets bond index.

Notes: Stripped spreads capture yield differences between US and emerging market government debt securities. The green dotted line is 6 May 2019, when the US President tweeted about increased tariffs on $200 billion in imports from the PRC. The red dotted line is 31 July 2019, when the US Federal Reserve cut its rate by 25 basis points, and 1 August 2019, when tariffs on an additional $300 billion of imports from the PRC were announced.

Source: Bloomberg (accessed 2 September 2019).

Figure 1.1.5 Exchange rate against the US dollar, selected economies

Regional currencies were stable in early 2019 until rising trade tensions weakened some of them.

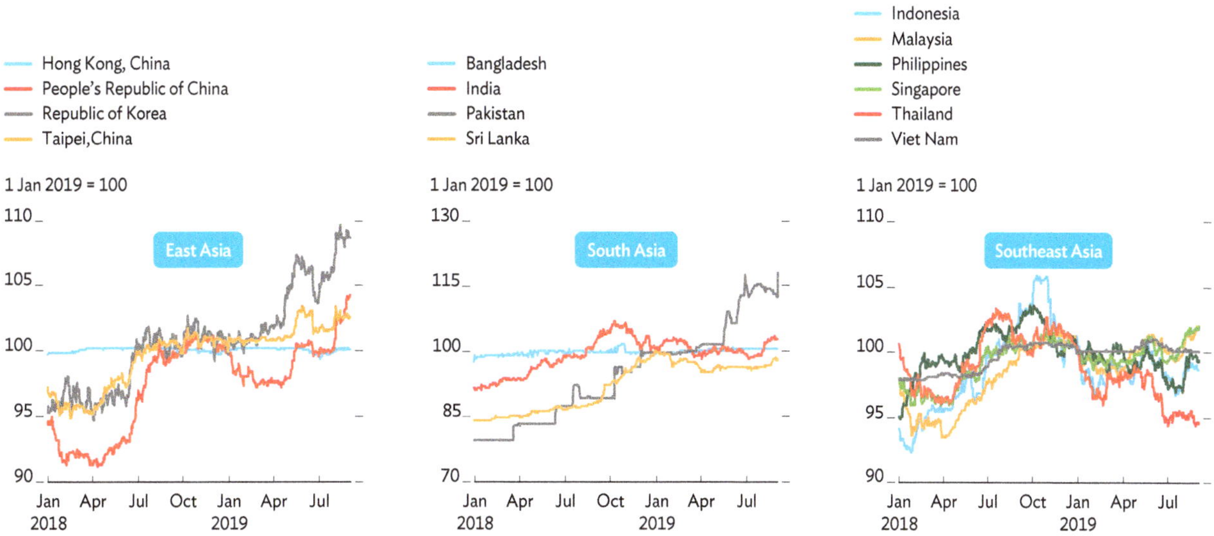

Hong Kong, China
People's Republic of China
Republic of Korea
Taipei,China

Bangladesh
India
Pakistan
Sri Lanka

Indonesia
Malaysia
Philippines
Singapore
Thailand
Viet Nam

Source: Bloomberg (accessed 2 September 2019).

With slower growth and muted inflation, several countries loosened fiscal and monetary policies to support economic activity. August 2019 alone saw expansionary budgets or other fiscal stimulus measures announced in Hong Kong, China; India; Indonesia; the Philippines; and Thailand. Many monetary authorities have cut policy interest rates in step with a more accommodative stance in the advanced economies. Since January, India has cut interest rates four times. Indonesia cut its policy rate by 25 basis points for a second time in August despite the recent weakness in the rupiah. Policy rates declined in most economies in East and Southeast Asia (Table 1.1.2). Easing policy rates seems to be appropriate for some economies under recent conditions (Box 1.1.2). Bucking the trend, Pakistan raised its interest rate as it continued to battle high inflation.

Headline inflation in developing Asia has remained muted so far in 2019, at 2.3% from January to July. Core inflation, which excludes fresh food and energy prices, dipped further below its 10-year average to 2.2% (Figure 1.1.6). The subregion with the highest rate, Central Asia, saw average annual headline inflation slow more than expected, from 4.8% in 2018 to 4.3% in the first 7 months of 2019, with core inflation falling from 5.5% to 5.2%. South and Southeast Asia also recorded drops. East Asia, on the other hand, saw headline inflation accelerate, mainly on higher food prices.

Table 1.1.2 Policy rates, selected economies in developing Asia

With growth and inflation subdued, many monetary authorities loosened policy rates.

Countries	Policy rate as of 13 September 2019		Change from 1 January 2019	
	% per annum	Date of decision	Percentage points	Number of adjustments
Hong Kong, China	2.500	1 August 2019	−0.25	1
India	5.400	7 August 2019	−1.10	4
Indonesia	5.500	22 August 2019	−0.50	2
Kazakhstan	9.000	15 April 2019	−0.25	1
Malaysia	3.000	7 May 2019	−0.25	1
Pakistan	13.250	16 July 2019	2.75	3
Papua New Guinea	6.000	1 July 2019	−0.25	1
People's Republic of China	4.250	20 August 2019	−0.10	1
Philippines	4.250	8 August 2019	−0.50	2
Republic of Korea	1.500	18 July 2019	−0.25	1
Sri Lanka	7.000	23 August 2019	−1.00	2
Taipei,China	1.375	20 June 2019	0.00	0
Thailand	1.500	7 August 2019	−0.25	1
Viet Nam	6.000	13 September 2019	−0.25	1

Sources: Haver Analytics; Capital Economics (both accessed 13 September 2019).

Box 1.1.2 Assessing monetary policy in selected Asian economies

Many Asian countries cut interest rates in 2019 and are deliberating further changes as global risks intensify. Does room exist for future interest rate cuts? The answer depends on whether current monetary policy is appropriate for inflation and growth conditions. This can be assessed by comparing actual interest rates with those derived from a model that estimates how interest rates evolve in response to macroeconomic developments. Actual interest rates were observed from the data. The estimated framework closely followed the specification of Coibion and Gorodnichenko (2011), which suggested that variation in interest rates (r_t) takes into consideration country-specific macroeconomic targets and objectives, such as inflation (π_t), output gap (x_t), and developments in output growth year on year (gy_t):

$$r_t = c + p_1 r_{t-1} + (1 - p_1)(\phi_\pi \pi_t + \phi_x x_t + \phi_{gy} gy_t) + v_t \qquad (1)$$

The lagged term (r_{t-1}) captures the fact that monetary policy actions are implemented gradually. The constant term, c, is the sum of the natural rate of interest and the policy target, such as those set by the central bank for inflation, and v_t is an exogenous monetary policy shock. The actual interest rate relative to this estimated version reveals monetary stance (Basilio 2012).

Monetary policy was assessed for nine Asian economies: India; Indonesia; Malaysia; the PRC; the Philippines; the ROK, Taipei,China; Thailand; and Viet Nam. The start date was Q1 of 2001 and the end date Q2 of 2019.[a] To examine the relevance of various macroeconomic variables, a nonlinear least squares specification similar to Bogdanova and Hofmann (2012) was implemented. The best-fit model for each economy was subsequently identified based on the approach used in Coibion and Gorodnichenko (2011). The estimated coefficients were similar to those presented in Bogdanova and Hofmann (2012).[b] Interest rates were found to be persistent and react to changes in inflation, output gap, and output growth. While the best-fit model depended on country-specific data, the mean estimate of 0.40 for both inflation and output growth, and 0.74 for output gap, hinted at a greater preference for output gap stabilization.

Comparing the extracted interest rate with actual interest rates provided one assessment of current monetary policy. Accordingly, a positive deviation of actual interest rate from the estimated policy rate might be interpreted as tight monetary policy (Basilio 2012). Malaysia, the Philippines,

and Viet Nam shifted from tight monetary policy to a more neutral stance consistent with stable inflation. On the other hand, India seems to have an accommodative stance given current conditions, and the PRC may have some room to reduce interest rates further (box figure).

Box figure Policy rates: actual versus estimated

Some central banks had room for monetary policy easing and used it.

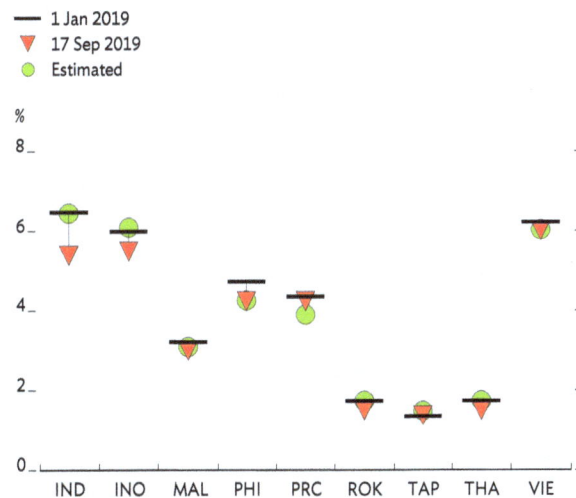

IND = India, INO = Indonesia, MAL = Malaysia, PHI = Philippines, PRC = People's Republic of China, ROK = Republic of Korea, TAP = Taipei,China, THA = Thailand, VIE = Viet Nam.
Sources: Bank for International Settlements; CEIC Data Company; ADB estimates.

[a] Other data start dates were Q1 of 2003 for Viet Nam, Q3 of 2005 for Indonesia, and Q1 of 2002 for India.
[b] More details on the estimated regression coefficients are available in Qureshi and Abesamis (forthcoming).

References:

Basilio, J. R. 2012. Cross-Country Comparison of Taylor-type Rules, Their Patterns and Performances. *Background paper for the BSP International Research Conference on Contemporary Challenges to Monetary Policy.*

Bogdanova, B., and B. Hofmann. 2012. Taylor Rules and Monetary Policy: A Global "Great Deviation"? *BIS Quarterly Review*, September.

Coibion, O. and Y. Gorodnichenko. 2011. Monetary Policy, Trend Inflation, and the Great Moderation: An Alternative Interpretation. *American Economic Review* 101(1).

Qureshi, I. and J. Abesamis. Forthcoming. Assessing Monetary Policy in Selected Asian Economies. *ADB Economics Working Paper Series*. Asian Development Bank.

Figure 1.1.6 Inflation by subregion

Headline and core inflation remained relatively benign in the first 7 months of 2019.

- Central Asia
- East Asia
- South Asia
- Southeast Asia
- Developing Asia

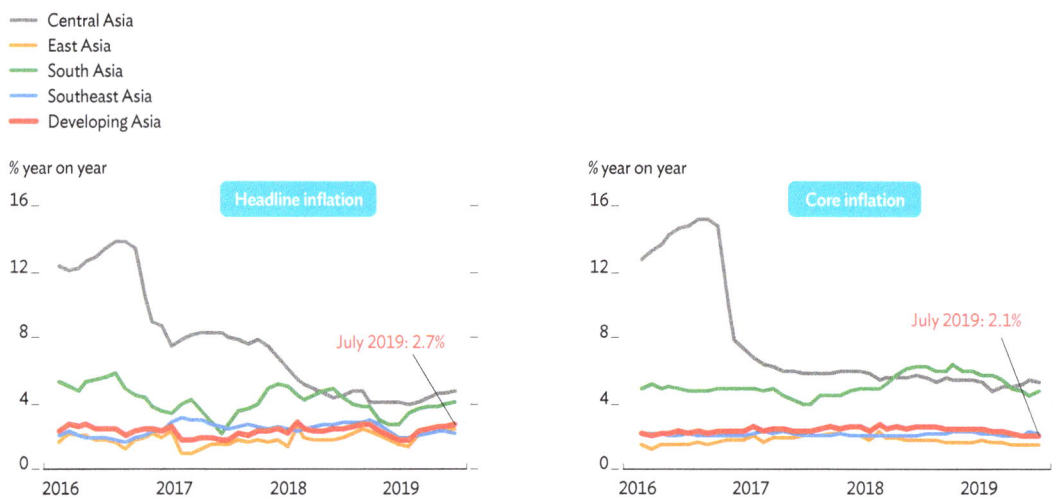

Note: Core inflation excludes fresh food and energy.
Source: CEIC Data Company (accessed 2 September 2019).

1.1.2 Trade conflicts, tech disputes, and supply chain disruptions

The US–PRC trade conflict escalated in mid-2019, with virtually all bilateral merchandise trade becoming subject to a tariff (Figure 1.1.7). Following a truce in December 2018 to allow for bilateral talks, negotiations broke down in May. Since then, a series of measures on both sides has increased the number of products subject to tariffs and has raised rates on goods already taxed. The most recent round of measures, announced in August, will be implemented stepwise in September, October, and December. ADB estimates that, if measures are implemented in October and December as they were in September, 99.3% of US imports from the PRC will be under tariff, with an average tariff rate of 22.2%; and 77.7% of PRC imports from the US will be under tariff, with an average tariff rate of 17.0%. The US and PRC are currently negotiating to head off these additional measures but with little sign of progress thus far.

Measures and threats have arisen separately from the US–PRC conflict. The US revoked zero-duty preferential trade status on $5.6 billion in imports from India. India retaliated with tariff hikes worth $220 million on goods from the US. The economic impact is insignificant for both India and the US, but the damage to trade relations meant more discomfort. Also shaking already weak global business confidence were trade tensions between the US and Mexico over immigration issues; between the US and Europe over aerospace subsidies,

Figure 1.1.7 A chronology of the US–PRC trade conflict, 2018–2019

Escalation has made almost all bilateral imports subject to tariffs this year.

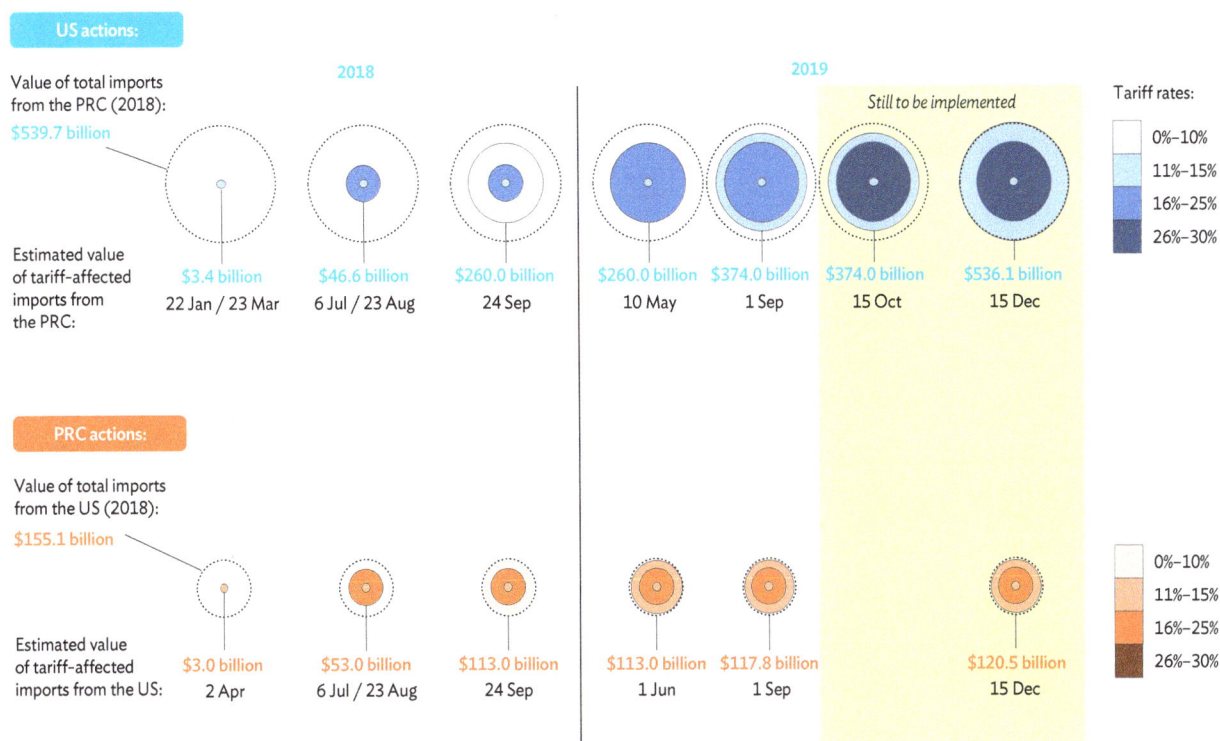

PRC = People's Republic of China, US = United States.

Notes: Bubbles with broken lines show the value of all imports in 2018. Shaded bubbles show the estimated portion affected by tariffs, and shade darkness indicates tariff intensity. Dates refer to when the tariffs took effect. When a range of tariff rates was implemented, as in PRC measures since 24 September 2018, a weighted average tariff rate was calculated.

Source: ADB estimates using data from US Census Bureau, https://usatrade.census.gov/; Haver Analytics; UN Comtrade database, *International Trade Statistics* database; United States Trade Representative, https://ustr.gov; Ministry of Commerce, People's Republic of China, http://english.mofcom.gov.cn (all accessed 13 September 2019).

French tax levies on tech companies, and possible tariffs on autos and auto parts; and between Japan and the ROK over export restrictions.

Measures used and contemplated in the conflict have broadened considerably beyond conventional tariffs. Recent months have seen greater exploration and use of nontariff measures, including investment restrictions, export controls on strategic products, and the targeting of specific companies (Appendix table, page 26). This metamorphosis into what some have called a "technology war" can have widespread implications, affecting innovation in the region.

Bilateral trade data from the first half of 2019 already show impact from the trade conflict. By June 2019, PRC exports to the US that were subject to tariffs had contracted by 30%–40% year on year, and tariff-affected US exports to the PRC had contracted by a similar magnitude (Figure 1.1.8).

Figure 1.1.8 Growth in imports of tariff-affected goods, the US versus the PRC

All tariff-affected imports dropped sharply in 2018, though PRC imports from US recovered somewhat after a temporary truce.

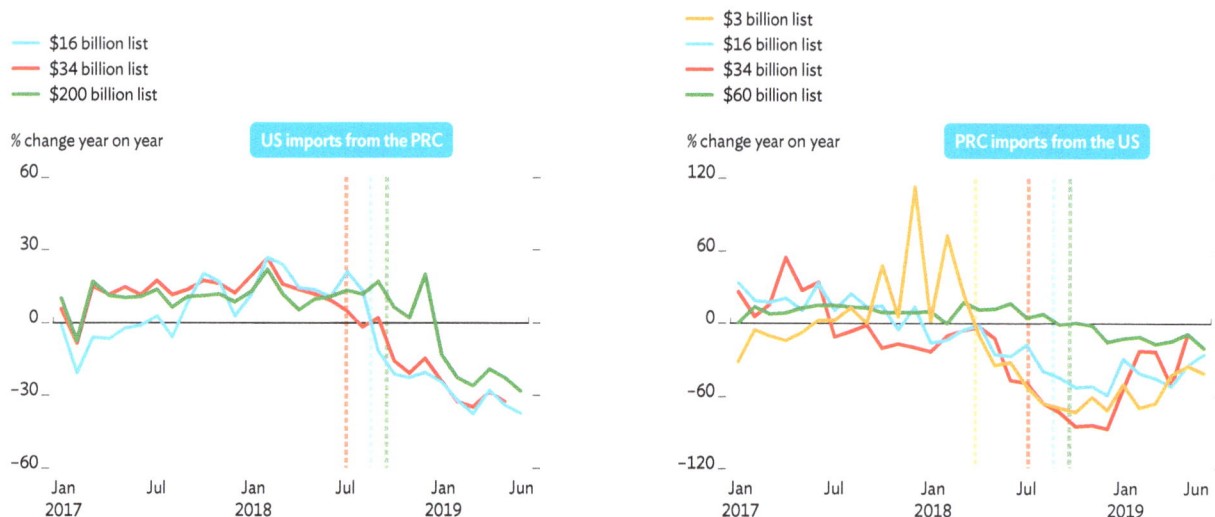

PRC = People's Republic of China, US = United States.

Notes: Broken lines indicate when tariffs went into effect. Left panel: 6 July 2018, 25% on initial $34 billion list; 23 August 2018, 25% on $16 billion list; and 24 September 2018, 10% on $200 billion list, rising to 25% on 10 May 2019. Right panel: 2 April 2018, 15%–25% on $3 billion list; 6 July 2018, 25% on initial $34 billion list; 23 August 2018, 25% on $16 billion list; and 24 September 2018, 10%–25% on $60 billion list, rising to as much as 25% on 10 May 2019.

Source: ADB estimates using data from US Census Bureau. https://usatrade.census.gov (accessed 16 September 2019).

The timing of the decline corresponded closely with the imposition of tariffs, though for some categories of PRC imports from the US there was evidence of frontloading prior to tariff imposition. With demand from the US diminished since tariff imposition, PRC businesses now demand less from suppliers. As a result of this—and also because of weaker domestic investment and consumption—PRC imports have declined from Japanese and other suppliers in developing Asia (Figure 1.1.9).

Recent trade data also provide evidence of trade redirection. In the first 6 months of 2019, US imports from the PRC fell by 12% from the same period in 2018. At the same time, US imports from the rest of developing Asia rose by about 10%, with notably large increases of 33% for Viet Nam; 20% for Taipei,China; and 13% for Bangladesh (Figure 1.1.10). For Viet Nam and Taipei,China, the bulk of the increased exports to the US were electronics and machinery, and for Bangladesh garments. The broader effect of the conflict on global and regional trade volumes is difficult to disentangle from the effects of the slowdown in global activity, the electronics cycle downswing, and deepening uncertainty (partly because businesses do not know when the conflict will end). But, given that production now occurs mostly along global value chains, the ripple effect of the conflict on global trade is likely much stronger than it would have been 2 decades ago.

Figure 1.1.9 PRC imports from Japan and developing Asia

There was a drop in PRC imports from Asian suppliers.

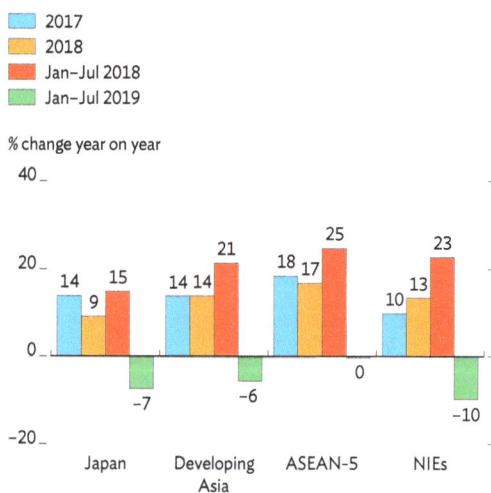

ASEAN-5 = Indonesia, Malaysia, the Philippines, Thailand, and Viet Nam, NIEs = Hong Kong, China; the Republic of Korea; Singapore; and Taipei,China, PRC = People's Republic of China.

Sources: PRC Customs, Haver Analytics (accessed 9 September 2019).

Figure 1.1.10 US imports from selected economies in developing Asia

Trade redirection from the PRC has benefited other economies in developing Asia.

- ■ Agriculture, mining, and quarrying
- ■ Electronics and machinery
- ■ Textile, garments, footwear, and leather
- ■ Others
- — Import growth, % year on year

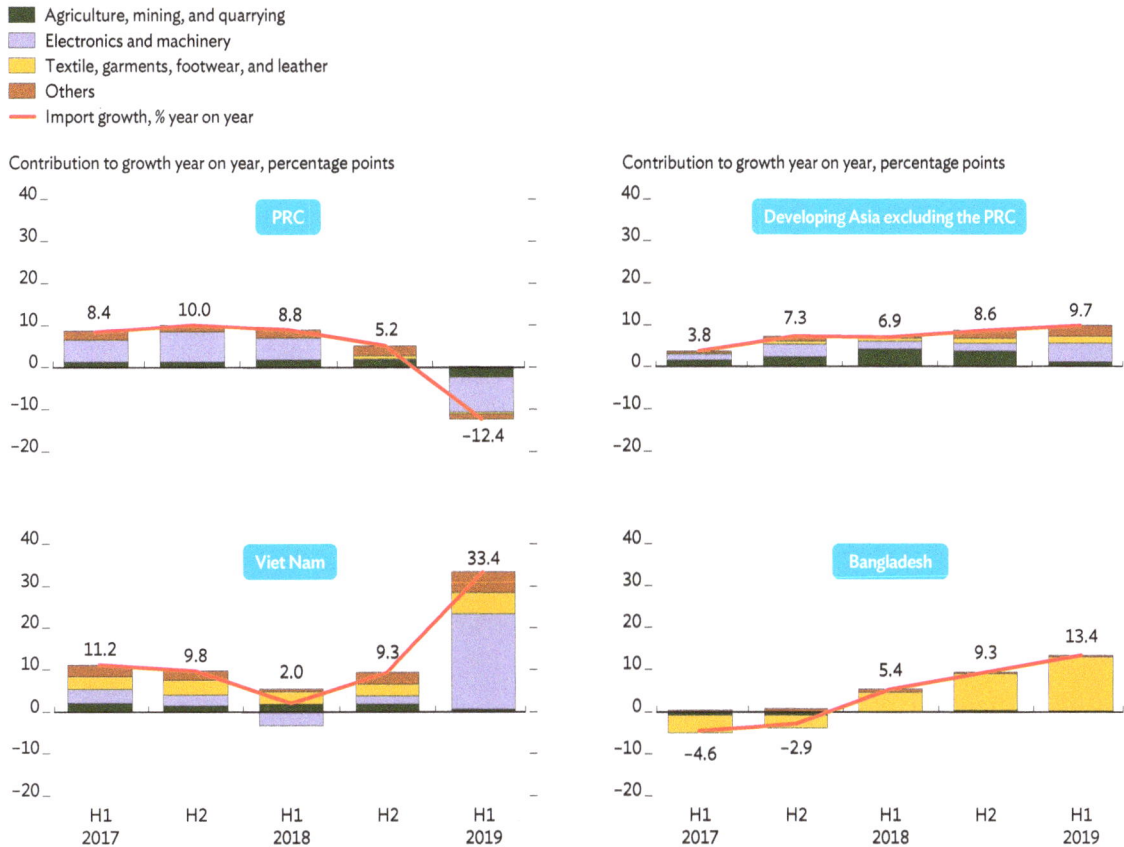

H1 = first half, H2 = second half, PRC = People's Republic of China, US = United States.
Source: ADB estimates using data from US Census Bureau. https://usatrade.census.gov (accessed 16 September 2019).

1.1.3 The outlook for growth dims

Growth in developing Asia is expected to decelerate. In light of declines in global and regional trade and economic activity now evident in the data, regional GDP growth is now projected to slow from 5.9% in 2018 to 5.4% this year before picking up marginally to 5.5% next year. Relative to forecasts published in April in *ADO 2019*, the growth projections are adjusted downward by 0.3 percentage points for this year and 0.1 points for 2020. Excluding the NIEs, developing Asia's growth rate is forecast at 6.0% in both 2019 and 2020, a 0.2-point downward adjustment from *ADO 2019* for this year and 0.1 points for next year.

A weaker outlook for the major advanced economies is one factor behind the downward revision for regional growth. Growth in the three largest advanced economies is seen to moderate from 2.2% in 2018 to 1.7% in 2019 and 1.4% in 2020 (Table 1.1.3 and Annex). The forecasts for both years are 0.2 percentage points lower than in April.

Table 1.1.3 GDP growth in the advanced economies

Growth in the three largest advanced economies is seen moderating this year and next.

	2018	2019		2020	
	Actual	ADO	ADO Update	ADO	ADO Update
Major advanced economies[a]	2.2	1.9	1.7 ↓	1.6	1.4 ↓
United States	2.9	2.4	2.3 ↓	1.9	1.9
Euro area	1.9	1.5	1.0 ↓	1.5	1.0 ↓
Japan	0.8	0.8	1.2 ↑	0.6	0.5 ↓

ADO = Asian Development Outlook, GDP = gross domestic product.

[a] Average growth rates are weighed by gross national income, Atlas method.

Sources: US Department of Commerce, Bureau of Economic Analysis, http://www.bea.gov; Eurostat, http://epp.eurostat.ec.europa.eu; Economic and Social Research Institute of Japan, http://www.esri.cao.go.jp; Consensus Forecasts; Bloomberg; CEIC Data Company; Haver Analytics; ADB estimates.

The downward correction mainly reflects weakening in the euro area, where growth is seen slowing from 1.9% in 2018 to 1.0% in 2019 and 2020 as declining consumer and business sentiment hinder consumption and investment, and as weakness persists in manufacturing. Growth in the US will slow from 2.9% in 2018 to 2.3% in 2019 and 1.9% in 2020 as the lagged effects of monetary tightening in recent years are felt, and as the prospects for the external sector continue to wane. Japan showed some improvement in the first half of 2019, but a consumption tax hike in Q4 of this year may slow activity, as such tax hikes have done in the past.

Weaker domestic demand, particularly slowing investment growth in many countries, is another factor constraining regional growth. As noted in Section 1.1, investment growth is declining in many economies in developing Asia. This pattern is evident in all subregions. In the region as a whole, the contribution of investment to GDP growth is at its lowest in a decade (Figure 1.1.11). In some economies, the reasons for declining investment growth are domestic, such as the delayed passage of the 2019 budget in the Philippines, which constrained public investment, or weaker investment in India in the run-up to elections in April and May. But it also may reflect businesses responding to a less rosy external environment. Since both slowing in the major advanced economies and trade conflict escalation seem likely to continue, the baseline assumption is that the investment growth slowdown witnessed in the first half of 2019 will continue throughout the year. If growth in investment continues to slow, it will likely translate into less productive capacity going forward, which can have discouraging implications for the region's longer-term growth prospects. The main component of domestic demand,

Figure 1.1.11 Investment contribution to GDP growth: developing Asia

The contribution of investment to GDP growth is at its lowest in a decade.

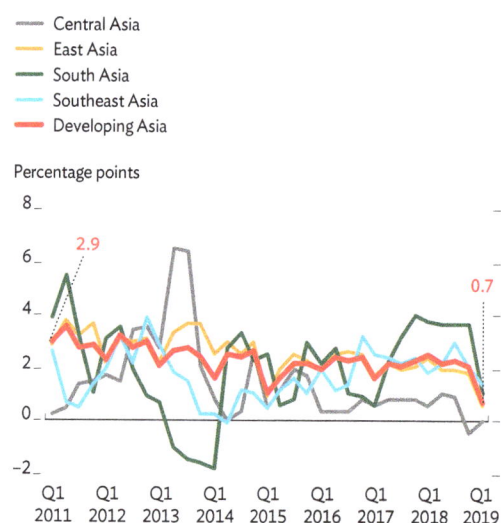

GDP = gross domestic product, Q = quarter.

Notes: Central Asia is represented by Kazakhstan. East Asia includes Hong Kong, China; the People's Republic of China; the Republic of Korea; and Taipei,China. South Asia includes India and Sri Lanka. Southeast Asia includes Indonesia, Malaysia, the Philippines, Singapore, Thailand, and Viet Nam.

Source: ADB estimates using data from Haver Analytics (accessed 31 July 2019).

consumption, should continue to support growth this year and next, though it too is showing some signs of weakening in a few countries, notably India and the PRC.

Growth forecasts for the PRC and the more open economies in East and Southeast Asia are downgraded as global trade slows and the electronics cycle experiences a sharp downswing. The growth forecast for East Asia is revised down from *ADO 2019* by 0.2 percentage points for 2019 to 5.5%, and by 0.1 points for 2020 to 5.4%. Growth in the PRC is expected to slip from 6.6% in 2018 to 6.2% in 2019 and to 6.0% in 2020 as the trade conflict takes its toll on exports and investment. For Hong Kong, China, growth in 2019 is now forecast at 0.3% as the US–PRC trade conflict is compounded by local political tensions. Growth forecasts for the ROK have been revised down substantially because it is strongly affected by the downturn in the electronics cycle—as is Singapore, another NIE for which forecasts are similarly downgraded.

For Southeast Asia as a whole, GDP growth is now forecast lower by 0.4 points to 4.5% for this year and by 0.3 points to 4.7% for 2020. These downward revisions reflect both external and domestic factors. The outlook for Indonesia, the Lao People's Democratic Republic, Malaysia, the Philippines, and Thailand reflects weakening exports and domestic investment, as well as drought-affected agriculture following El Niño. By contrast, the *ADO 2019* growth forecast for Viet Nam is maintained as trade redirection and increased foreign direct investment (FDI) support growth.

Growth in South Asia is softening this year but will pick up next year. Growth forecasts are lowered to 6.2% for 2019 and 6.7% for 2020. India's growth forecast for fiscal year 2019 is lowered to 6.5% after growth slowed markedly to 5.0% in Q1, April–June. Abrupt declines in manufacturing and investment reflected uncertainty ahead of general elections, subdued lending by banks and other financial institutions, stress in the rural economy, and a weakening external outlook. India is expected to rebound to 7.2% growth in fiscal 2020 and join most other subregional countries in performing at or near their *ADO 2019* growth forecasts for next year. In Pakistan, though, growth in 2020 is now forecast lower as the government implements a comprehensive program of macroeconomic and structural reform to stabilize the economy. For Sri Lanka, 2019 and 2020 growth forecasts are marked down because terror bombings in April 2019 caused tourism to fall sharply.

The two subregions that buck the slowing trend and enjoy more buoyant growth prospects, driven mainly by domestic factors, are Central Asia and the Pacific. The 2019 growth forecast for Central Asia improves from 4.2% in *ADO 2019* to 4.4%, building on a pickup in the first half of 2019 in several countries. In Kazakhstan, government spending for social programs and higher outlays for housing and infrastructure construction offset lower oil production. In Uzbekistan, investment was healthy, and in the Kyrgyz Republic, gold production was strong. In Armenia, robust private consumption, especially of services, offset lower government spending. In Azerbaijan, gas production reached a record with full operation commencing at the new Shah Deniz field, which made up for falling oil production. These developments more than offset growth below expectations in Georgia as construction and mining were constrained. Strong growth is expected to continue in 2020 in Kazakhstan, Tajikistan, and Uzbekistan, buoyed by public investment. The 2020 growth forecast for the subregion is therefore revised up from 4.2% to 4.3%.

The 2019 growth projection for the Pacific is raised from 3.5% in April to 4.2%, reflecting improved prospects for Papua New Guinea, Samoa, and Solomon Islands. In Papua New Guinea, recovery from an earthquake in February 2018 benefited growth, as did strong production and exports of liquefied natural gas. In Samoa, higher infrastructure spending and construction for the 2019 Pacific Games boosted growth. Growth projections are lowered, on the other hand, for the Cook Islands and Palau because tourism has underperformed expectations, and for Tonga because of lower reconstruction stimulus. In Timor-Leste, Vanuatu, and the small island economies, growth was broadly in line with *ADO 2019* forecasts. Prospects for 2020 are less sanguine. The forecast for the subregion in 2020 is reduced from 3.2% in April to 2.6% in anticipation of delays affecting major mining projects in Papua New Guinea and of fiscal consolidation in Fiji.

1.1.4 Inflation to remain benign

Regional inflation will pick up slightly but remain below its 10-year average. Headline inflation is seen to rise from 2.4% in 2018 to 2.7% in both 2019 and 2020, reflecting upward adjustments by 0.2 percentage points relative to April projections. The revisions reflect mainly a buildup of inflationary pressures in developing Asia outside of the NIEs, and particularly in the PRC. Excluding the NIEs, inflation is projected to accelerate to 2.9% in 2019 and 2020. Inflation in the region is still comfortably below its 10-year average and remains largely benign. The pickup in inflation this year is unlikely to persist, with core inflation still trending mostly down in line with the global trend. External pressures from international oil and food prices are projected to remain subdued.

Higher inflation this year is driven by food prices, which have risen in the region despite falling globally. As discussed in Box 1.1.3, the trend in food prices across Asia has since mid-2018 diverged from the global trend (Figure 1.1.12).

Figure 1.1.12 Food inflation: developing Asia and the world

Food inflation in developing Asia has been up despite falling global food prices.

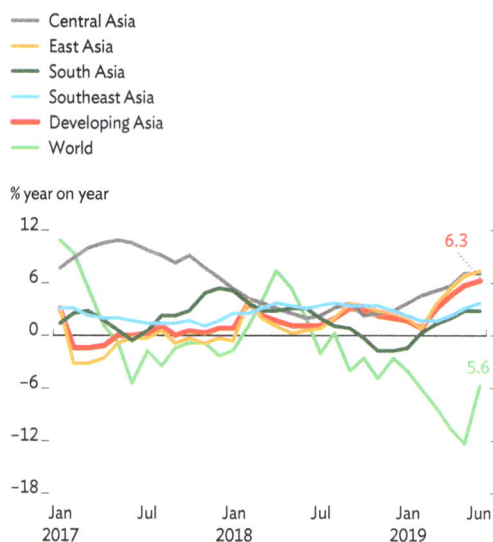

Sources: CEIC Data Company; Haver Analytics; ADB estimates.

Box 1.1.3 What is driving up food price inflation in developing Asia?

Domestic food price inflation trended upward in most Asian economies despite declining food price inflation globally. As of June 2019, food price inflation in developing Asia was running at 4.6% year on year, with the increase evident in all subregions for which data are available. This contrasts with global food price inflation, which declined by 5.6% year on year in June. The current rise in regional food price inflation is still well below the spike observed in 2011, when food price inflation went into double-digit figures and global food price inflation soared to 22.5%. In most economies, current food price inflation is still low by historical standards.

Several factors explain the recent increase in food prices in Asia. First, there are statistical base effects as prices for some foods, notably grain and pulses, fell during most of last year with supply gluts and are now correcting upward. Second, seasonal factors like Ramadan and Eid al-Fitr affect food consumption, which increases during these holidays. Third, currency depreciation in a few economies—especially Georgia, Kazakhstan, and Pakistan—have raised prices for imported food directly and further raised them indirectly through higher prices for imported fuel, fertilizer, and animal feed. Georgia, for example, depends heavily on food imports from Kazakhstan and the Russian Federation, but its currency depreciated by more than 17% against the ruble in the first 7 months of 2019, jacking up prices for wheat flour as well as transportation costs. Similarly, in Uzbekistan, the devaluation of the Uzbekistan sum by 50% against the US dollar in September 2017 increased prices for meat and livestock fodder, which is imported mainly from Kazakhstan.

Outbreaks of African swine fever in Cambodia, the Lao People's Democratic Republic, Mongolia, the PRC, and Viet Nam pushed up meat prices. In the PRC, pork prices have risen by 40% since April. A sharp reduction in the supply of pigs from the PRC affected pork prices in Hong Kong, China, where they soared by 66% in June. With pork prices rising on limited supply, prices for such alternatives as poultry, beef, and seafood also rose on higher demand. In Mongolia, for example, prices for meat and meat products were up by 26% in the first half of 2019, and prices for fish and other seafood were up by 15%.

Apart from the African swine fever, unfavorable weather pushed up domestic food prices. In Nepal, for example, excessive monsoon rains reduced supplies of grain and vegetables. In Thailand, the price index for vegetables rose by 20% in July owing to the low base effect but also to food spoilage caused by erratic weather. In Indonesia, indexes for vegetables, spices, and fruit rose in June and July with an early onset of the dry season. In Uzbekistan, a water shortage in 2018 affected the domestic supply of meat, raising demand for imported livestock and pushing up meat prices in the domestic market.

Domestic policies also played a role. Price hikes for bread and bread products in Uzbekistan are linked to wheat and bread price liberalization that started in 2017 and entailed cuts to farmer subsidies, which raised production costs. In Malaysia, higher commodity prices in 2019 are correcting a slump last year with the removal of a goods and services tax in June 2018.

This analysis confirms the conclusions of several studies on food price movements in Asia. Although international trade and other external factors influence domestic food prices, Asian food markets are only somewhat tenuously connected with the global market. Two factors may limit the influence of world food prices on domestic food prices in Asia. One is subsidies and food price controls that governments use to stabilize prices. The other is government concerns about food security and self-sufficiency, which encourage them to restrict the food trade and protect their farmers. Huh and Park (2013) found that domestic food prices in Asia are largely accounted for by domestic shocks in each economy, especially in the short run. It further found that regional food prices influence domestic Asian food prices more than global food prices do. This finding suggests the presence of strong common components affecting the movement of domestic food prices across Asia: a food culture specific to the region with, for example, the observance of the Islamic festive season, heavy reliance on rice and wheat, similar agricultural and climate conditions, advances in regional economic integration, and similar policy responses to the common regional shocks.

Reference:

Huh, H.-S. and C.-Y. Park. 2013. Examining the Determinants of Food Prices in Developing Asia. *ADB Economics Working Paper Series* No. 370. Asian Development Bank.

While the global food price index is projected to decline in 2019, domestic food prices are forecast to rise in developing Asia. Higher prices for meat, and particularly pork following an outbreak of African swine fever, are one important factor behind the rise in regional food prices. Other factors at play include base effects following bumper crops of grain and pulses last year, as well as seasonal factors like the observance of Ramadan and Eid al-Fitr. Weaker exchange rates have also contributed to higher food price inflation in a few economies, notably Georgia, Kazakhstan, Pakistan, and Sri Lanka.

Inflation is edging up in East Asia but is projected to soften in Southeast Asia. Food price increases pushed up inflation in some economies, but weaker demand has kept core inflation low. In East Asia, inflation is forecast to accelerate from 2.0% in 2018 to 2.3% in 2019, with forecast higher inflation in Mongolia and the PRC, easing to 2.1% in 2020. Higher meat prices on account of the African swine fever pushed up inflation in the PRC and in Hong Kong, China, as did higher food prices and public spending in Mongolia. In the ROK and in Taipei,China, low oil prices and subdued demand have muted inflation, lowering the inflation forecast from April as decelerating core inflation more than compensates for higher food prices. In Southeast Asia, inflation is projected to soften from 2.7% in 2018 to 2.3% in 2019, led by Cambodia, the Philippines, and Viet Nam, before rebounding to 2.6% in 2020.

Inflation in South Asia is expected to remain benign. The subregional inflation projection for 2019 is revised down to 4.0%, mainly reflecting a lower forecast for India with only modest food inflation, and then rise to 4.9% in 2020, as forecast in *ADO 2019*, in large part to reflect a steep rise expected in Pakistan. Inflation this year has been at least no higher than expected in Afghanistan, Bangladesh, Bhutan, India, Maldives, Pakistan, and Sri Lanka and only slightly higher than forecast in Nepal. This *Update* raises the 2020 inflation projection only for Nepal, revised up to 5.5% on a pickup in government expenditure, and for Pakistan, markedly higher at 12.0% in anticipation of planned tariff hikes for domestic utilities, higher taxes, and espccially the lagged impact of currency depreciation.

Average inflation in Central Asia slowed below expectations in the first half of 2019. In the Kyrgyz Republic, inflation turned negative, despite the local currency's depreciation against the US dollar with imports of low-priced food from Uzbekistan. In Kazakhstan, inflation slowed in the first half of 2019 with continuing price controls on utilities, food, and other goods, as well as lower gasoline prices. Yet, the inflation outlook for Central Asia in 2019 is raised from 7.8% forecasted in April to 8.0% in light of offsetting upward revisions for Georgia, Tajikistan, and Turkmenistan. In Turkmenistan, subsidy reform, expansionary credit, foreign exchange shortages, and rising import prices have stoked inflation, prompting substantial upward revisions to forecasts, from 9.0% to 13.4% for 2019 and from 8.2% to 13.0% for 2020. The regional projection for 2020 is thus raised from 7.2% to 7.4%, as expectations of continued double-digit inflation in Turkmenistan and smaller increases in Georgia and Tajikistan offset small downward revisions to inflation projections for Kazakhstan and Uzbekistan.

Average inflation in the Pacific is expected to ease from 4.2% in 2018 to 3.4% in 2019, or 0.3 percentage points lower than the April projection, and to 3.4% in 2020, or 0.6 percentage points lower than forecast in *ADO 2019*. Food prices have been declining in Solomon Islands and Timor-Leste, reflecting lower costs for imported goods. In Tonga, local disruption to food supply in the wake of a cyclone eased fairly quickly, keeping inflation below initial expectations. Benign price pressures are seen to persist through next year, and inflation is expected to be muted further by a weaker economic outlook for Papua New Guinea.

1.1.5 With trade subdued, external balances will improve this year

Trade in developing Asia is expected to remain subdued in 2019. A decline in the global composite purchasing managers' index to below 50 suggests that the outlook for trade in manufactures is grim. Container throughput, another leading indicator for trade, has also declined. With capital goods comprising a larger share of trade than output, weak investment growth to the forecast horizon suggests that trade growth will also remain anemic.

The regional current account surplus is now expected to widen. While regional economies' exports have weakened, their imports have weakened even more. The PRC saw its merchandise trade surplus rise in the first half of this year as its imports fell more substantially than exports. The PRC is now expected to register a current account surplus equal to 1.0% of GDP this year, not the balanced current account forecast in April, pushing the current account surplus in East Asia beyond the April projections. The current account surplus for developing Asia as a whole is now forecast to widen to 1.1% of combined GDP in 2019—0.7 percentage points higher than forecast in the *ADO 2019*—before narrowing to 0.7% of GDP in 2020 (Figure 1.1.13a). Southeast Asia is forecast to see a slight increase in its surplus as the subregion benefits more than others from trade redirection away from the PRC. Meanwhile, the current account deficits that Central and South Asia routinely incur will modestly improve in 2019.

Figure 1.1.13 Current account balance, developing Asia versus the world

The region's current account surplus will widen in 2019...

a. Subregional and regional current account balances

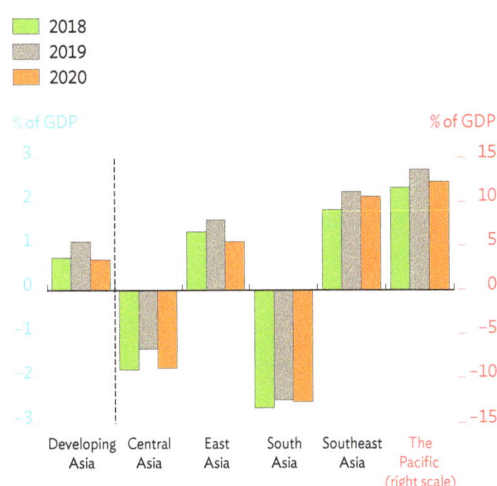

...but its contribution to the global surplus will decline to 2020.

b. Global current account balances

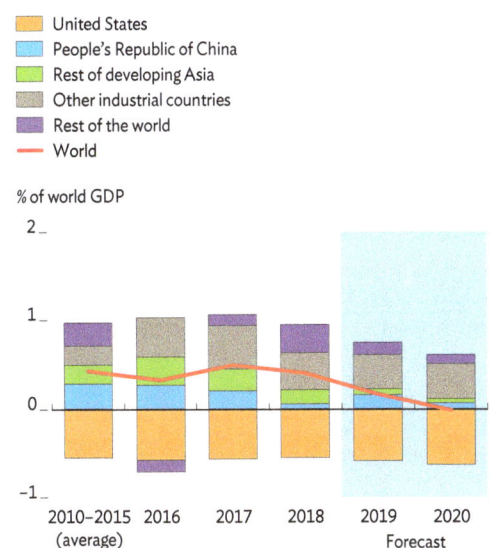

GDP = gross domestic product.
Sources: CEIC Data Company, Haver Analytics (both accessed 2 August 2019), *Asian Development Outlook* database; ADB estimates.

Figure 1.1.14 Impact of the trade conflict on gross domestic product, by scenario

Trade redirection eases conflict impact on global GDP in all scenarios, with net benefits foreseen for developing Asia excluding the PRC.

■ Current
■ Bilateral escalation
■ Auto sector escalation
■ Worse case

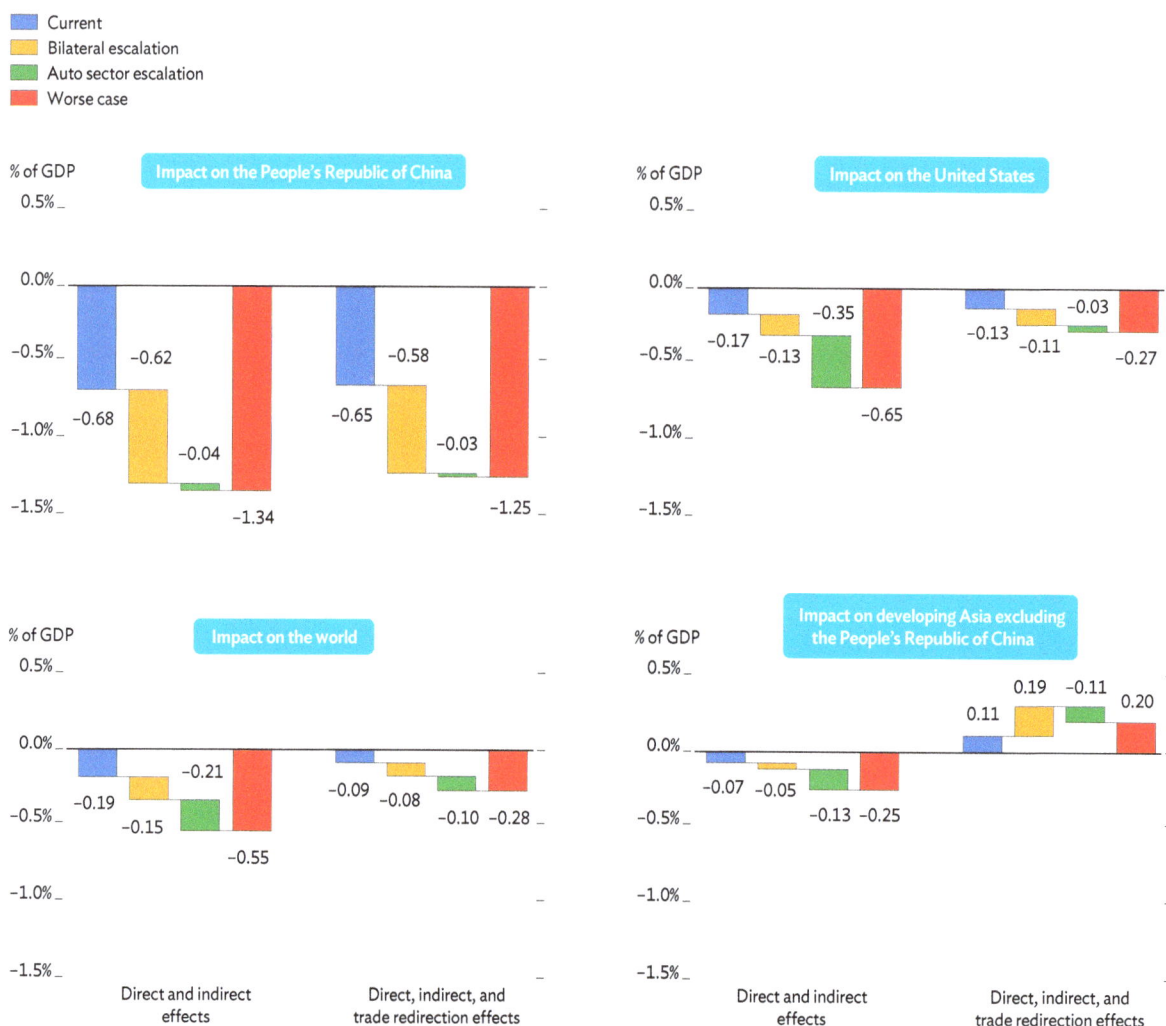

GDP = gross domestic product.

Notes: Blue bars represent the estimated GDP impact under the current scenario, taking into account the tariffs implemented as of 1 September. The yellow bar shows incremental impact potentially brought about by US–PRC trade threats (30% on all bilateral exports), and the green bar shows further incremental impact with escalation in which the US imposes tariffs on all auto and auto parts traded globally. The red bar shows the sum of all the impacts under a worse-case scenario.

Source: ADB estimates using the methodology in Abiad et.al., 2018.

India's trade deficit forecast is narrower than in April, with lower imports because of softer commodity prices and a weakening currency, as well as ongoing credit constraints. In Central Asia, a return to a current account deficit in Kazakhstan will be partly offset by a wider surplus in Azerbaijan and narrower deficits in Turkmenistan and Georgia. The Pacific will widen its current account surplus with recovery in liquefied natural gas production in Papua New Guinea. The declining contribution of the regional current account surplus to global current account balances, already observed in recent years, is expected to continue in 2020 (Figure 1.1.13b).

Updated estimates of the direct impact of the trade conflict show that the PRC will lose even more under the current scenario, while other economies in developing Asia will gain (Figure 1.1.14). The effects of the trade conflict and the redirection of trade and production are expected to extend through 2020 and beyond. Updated estimates show that, under the current scenario, which includes tariffs implemented as of 1 September 2019, the trade conflict will lower the GDP of the PRC by 0.65% over the medium term, relative to a scenario with no trade conflict, and the loss to the US will equal 0.13% of GDP. Recent events require a reassessment of what bilateral escalation may look like. In 2018, when the trade conflict began, the maximum tariff rate considered by the US government was 25%. Now, the US is levying 30% tariffs on some products on 15 October. Therefore, a plausible "bilateral escalation" scenario, which assumes 30% tariffs on all bilateral US–PRC merchandise trade, would shave 1.23% off GDP in the PRC and 0.24% off GDP in the US over the medium term. The effect on developing Asia excluding the PRC would be small but positive with trade redirection, adding 0.11% to GDP. These estimates exclude the effects of nontariff measures described in section 1.1.2, which are harder to quantify.

In a prolonged and intensified trade conflict, the scope for trade and production redirection—and hence potential gain for other economies in developing Asia—increases, particularly in electronics, garments, and related activities (Figure 1.1.15). Model results show negative impacts on diverse sectors in the PRC and the US, including services integrated with affected value chains in the medium term. Under the current scenario, Southeast Asian economies and NIEs are set to gain the most, particularly in machinery, electronics, and related services. Under the worse-case scenario—which adds bilateral escalation and a trade war in auto and auto parts between the US and its trading partners—Viet Nam, Malaysia, and Thailand would be the biggest winners, in that order, largely from redirected electronics, transport equipment, and machinery trade, while Bangladesh and Viet Nam would gain through garment and leather trade. In terms of employment, over 5.0 million jobs in the PRC would be lost, or 0.56% of total employment, while the US would lose 0.2 million jobs, or 0.12% of the total.

Foreign direct investment flows are changing course in tandem with production relocation. Some of the growth in FDI flows into developing Asia, particularly into the ASEAN-5, reflect long-term trends. Certain upstream activities that were located in the PRC are moving down the value chain and relocating to lower-cost sites overseas.

Figure 1.1.15 Net impact of the trade conflict on selected economies, by sector

Estimated gains under the current scenario go to exporters of electronics, automobiles, and garments, and these gains are significantly higher in a worse-case scenario in which all bilateral US and PRC imports pay 30% tariffs and autos and auto parts imports pay 25% globally.

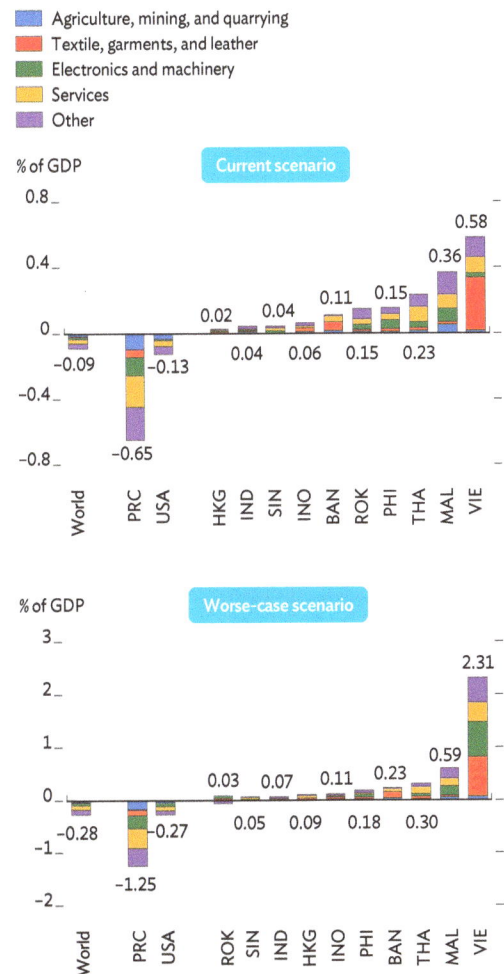

- ▇ Agriculture, mining, and quarrying
- ▇ Textile, garments, and leather
- ▇ Electronics and machinery
- ▇ Services
- ▇ Other

BAN = Bangladesh, GDP = gross domestic product, HKG = Hong Kong, China, IND = India, INO = Indonesia, MAL = Malaysia, PHI = Philippines, PRC = People's Republic of China, ROK = Republic of Korea, SIN = Singapore, THA = Thailand, US = United States, VIE = Viet Nam.

Notes: The current scenario includes all trade measures implemented as of 1 September 2019. Net impact includes direct, indirect, and trade redirection effects, which could take 2–3 years to fully materialize. The worse-case scenario assumes that the US and the PRC impose 30% tariffs on all bilateral imports, the US imposes a 25% tariff on all auto and auto parts globally, and affected partners retaliate tit-for-tat.

Source: ADB estimates using the methodology in Abiad et.al., 2018.

Escalating trade tensions have hastened this trend. Many companies with production in the PRC are considering moving at least some of their production elsewhere to limit exposure. At the same time, continued strong FDI from the PRC, and to some extent from Japan and the US, into developing Asia suggest that close investment ties between the PRC and ASEAN in particular will continue to strengthen. Newly registered FDI in Viet Nam from the PRC—and from Hong Kong, China, which often serves as a conduit for the PRC—rose by 200% year on year in the first 7 months of 2019. In Thailand, FDI applications more than doubled in the first half of 2019 with higher commitments from Japan, its long-running source of investments, and also the PRC. In Malaysia, the value of approved FDI projects in manufacturing, mostly from the US, rose in the first half of 2019 by 80% over the same period in 2018. A big surge in approvals of manufacturing FDI from the PRC had already occurred in the second half of 2018 (Figure 1.1.16).

1.1.6 Risks to the outlook

Downside risks to the regional outlook have intensified. *ADO 2019* assessed risks in April as being tilted to the downside, and some of the risks highlighted there—such as escalation in the US–PRC trade conflict and heightened uncertainty curtailing investment—have come to pass, contributing to the lower forecasts in this *Update*. The risk from additional measures being taken in the US–PRC trade conflict remains, and the conflict may broaden to include other countries. Other risks that hang over the regional outlook include a sharper slowdown in the advanced economies or the PRC, and the potential for delayed or miscalculated policy responses to a slowdown. A rise in debt incurred in the region over the past decade, particularly private debt, leaves some economies more vulnerable to shocks.

A protracted and intensified US–PRC trade war remains the primary risk. With few signs of progress in negotiations beyond agreement to resume talks in October, the trade conflict between the world's two largest economies is likely to linger past 2019 and even intensify further, perhaps taking measures that go beyond tariffs. An additional risk is trade conflict broadening if the US turns its sights on other countries.

The global economy may slow more than forecast, and policy responses are uncertain. A number of shocks could pull global growth down. The United Kingdom is scheduled to leave the European Union on 31 October, but a formal arrangement governing this process has yet to be agreed.

Figure 1.1.16 Value of foreign direct investment projects approved in selected East and Southeast Asian economies, by source

US and PRC investors already plan to relocate some production to other economies in developing Asia.

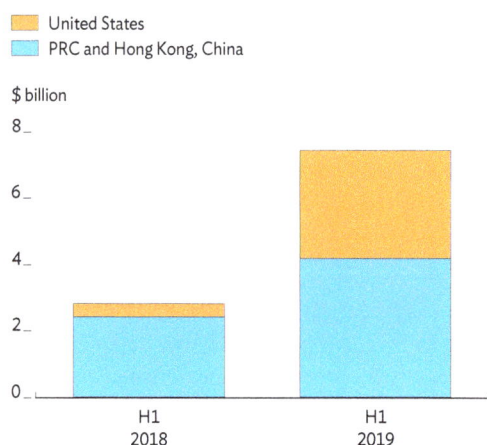

H1 = first half, PRC = People's Republic of China.

Note: Foreign direct investment approvals or commitments in Malaysia (manufacturing only); the Philippines; Taipei,China; and Viet Nam.

Sources: ADB estimates using data from Malaysian Investment Development Authority (https://www.mida.gov.my/home/), Haver Analytics, and CEIC Data Company (all accessed 17 September 2019).

A resulting no-deal Brexit could shock economies in Europe and beyond. In Japan, a consumption tax hike in Q4 of 2019 may slow growth, as similar hikes have in the past, though the government has taken steps to mitigate any slowdown. And, by at least one measure issued by the Federal Reserve Bank of New York, the probability of a recession in the US over the next 12 months has risen substantially (Figure 1.1.17). Geopolitical risks in the Middle East could intensify, triggering a sustained rise in oil prices that would dampen growth. Within developing Asia, the PRC faces a tough challenge as it balances the desire to keep growth strong with the need to rein in financial vulnerability. Uncertainty about how, and how quickly, policy makers will react to weaker growth adds volatility to the global economy.

A decade-long rise in debt leaves economies in the region more vulnerable to shocks. Developing Asia has incurred a steady rise in debt since the global financial crisis of 2008–2009, with most of the increase in private debt. If unchecked, this debt buildup could pose a challenge to financial stability, especially in the current environment of mounting risk from large external shocks.

Figure 1.1.17 Probability of US recession predicted by Treasury spreads 12 months ahead (monthly averages)

The probability of a US recession has risen substantially.

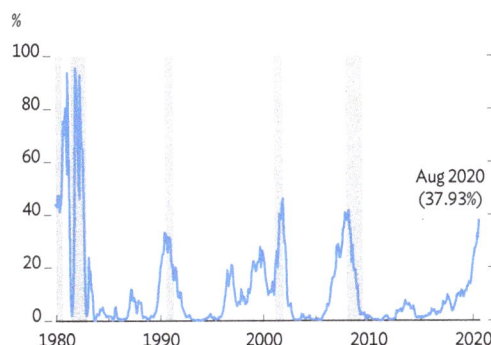

Source: Federal Reserve Bank of New York. https://www. newyorkfed.org/medialibrary/media/research/capital_markets/ allmonth.xls (accessed 17 September 2019).

Appendix table Nontariff measures and threats in the trade conflict

Date	Measure or threat	Impact and current status
15 May 2019	The US President issues an executive order banning US companies from using equipment that the Commerce Department declares a national security risk.[a]	The US Department of Commerce is given sweeping powers to ban technologies considered a national threat. The executive order does not identify any particular company as a threat but is seen as a move mainly against Huawei Technologies Company Limited of the PRC.
15 May 2019	The US Department of Commerce adds Huawei and its affiliates to a Bureau of Industry and Security "entity list."[b]	US companies are banned from selling parts and technology to Huawei without government approval.[c] On 23 July 2019, Huawei announces the layoff of over 600 US workers in its research arm Futurewei in response to being blacklisted.[d]
20 May 2019	Huawei gets a temporary reprieve as the US Commerce Department issues temporary licenses.[e]	Huawei is permitted to keep existing networks and to issue updates to existing phones, tablets, and other devices until 19 August 2019.[f] On that day, the US Commerce Department extends the temporary licenses for 90 days. However, another 46 affiliates of Huawei are added to the entity list, raising the total to more than 100.[g]
31 May 2019	The PRC Ministry of Commerce announces that it will list foreign companies that cut supplies to PRC companies for noncommercial reasons as "unreliable entities."[h]	No announcement is yet made on the specific rules, restrictive measures for listed entities, or the companies on the list. However, the PRC can use the list to retaliate against foreign governments targeting specific PRC companies.[i]
8 June 2019	The PRC announces the establishment of an export control mechanism for sensitive technology using guidelines from a national security law passed in 2015.[j]	This could impose further restrictions on technology exports, in particular military equipment, some encryption technologies, and some dual-use products.[k]
11 June 2018	Visas are shortened for graduate students from the PRC in robotics, aviation, and high-tech manufacturing from 5 years to 1 year, but they remain renewable each year.[l]	On 6 June 2018, a State Department official confirms that embassies and consulates have been instructed to conduct additional screening of students studying in sensitive areas.[m] Processing times for foreign visas are reported to have increased by 46% in the last 2 fiscal years.[n] New enrolment of international students at US graduate schools declines.[o]
25 June 2019	The PRC launches an investigation into FedEx Corporation and whether it undermines the legitimate rights and interests of clients in the PRC.[p]	PRC authorities suspect that FedEx illegally held back over 100 Huawei packages. FedEx denies it and sues the US Commerce Department over the diversion of Huawei packages.[q] The PRC investigation rejects a FedEx claim that it misdelivered Huawei packages to the US.[r]
2 July 2019	The PRC pledges more support for foreign investment and that it "will unswervingly promote opening-up on all fronts." It announces that caps on foreign ownership of financial firms will cease by 2020, a year earlier than previously scheduled.[s]	The PRC State Administration of Foreign Exchange announces on 10 September 2019 the abolition of investment quota restrictions for qualified foreign institutional investors and renminbi-qualified foreign institutional investors.[t]
11 July 2019	The US looks to create a cooperative to boost the domestic production of rare earth elements and compounds amid speculation that the PRC will impose rare earth export controls.[u]	From 2014 to 2017, 80% of US imports of rare earth elements and compounds came from PRC. In 2018, the PRC accounted for 71% of rare earth production globally and for two-fifths of global rare earth reserves.[v] Export controls could affect technological inputs, from thin film resistors and high-end capacitors to pharmaceutical ingredients.
5 August 2019	The US Treasury labels the PRC a currency manipulator.[w]	The action followed the renminbi depreciating past CNY7 to the dollar. The designation allows the US to take "remedial action" such as prohibiting federal government procurement of goods and services from the PRC.

continued next page

Appendix table *Continued*

PRC = People's Republic of China, US = United States.

a https://www.federalregister.gov/documents/2019/05/17/2019-10538/securing-the-information-and-communications-technology-and-services-supply-chain
  (accessed 17 September 2019).

b https://www.commerce.gov/news/press-releases/2019/05/department-commerce-announces-addition-huawei-technologies-co-ltd
  (accessed 17 September 2019).

c Ibid.

d https://uk.reuters.com/article/us-huawei-tech-usa-revenue/huawei-ceo-says-underestimated-impact-of-u-s-ban-sees-revenue-dip-idUKKCN1TI0KL
  (accessed 17 September 2019).

e https://www.commerce.gov/news/press-releases/2019/05/department-commerce-issues-limited-exemptions-huawei-products
  (accessed 17 September 2019).

f Ibid.

g https://www.commerce.gov/news/press-releases/2019/08/department-commerce-adds-dozens-new-huawei-affiliates-entity-list-and
  (accessed 17 September 2019).

h http://english.mofcom.gov.cn/article/counselorsreport/americaandoceanreport/201906/20190602869531.shtml (accessed 17 September 2019).

i https://www.bloomberg.com/news/articles/2019-06-04/understanding-china-s-unreliable-entities-blacklist-quicktake (accessed 17 September 2019).

j https://www.ft.com/content/47562fd6-89f6-11e9-a1c1-51bf8f989972 (accessed 17 September 2019).

k Ibid.

l https://apnews.com/82a98fecee074bfb83731760bfbce515 (accessed 17 September 2019).

m https://www.nytimes.com/2018/07/25/us/politics/visa-restrictions-chinese-students.html (accessed 17 September 2019).

n https://www.aila.org/infonet/aila-policy-brief-uscis-processing-delays (accessed 17 September 2019).

o Okahana, H. and E. Zhou. 2019. *International Graduate Applications and Enrollment: Fall 2018.* Council of Graduate Schools.

p http://www.xinhuanet.com/english/northamerica/2019-06/14/c_138144113.htm (accessed 17 September 2019).

q https://about.van.fedex.com/newsroom/fedex-statement-on-department-of-commerce-litigation/
  (accessed 17 September 2019).

r http://www.xinhuanet.com/english/2019-07/26/c_138259674.htm (accessed 17 September 2019).

s http://www.xinhuanet.com/english/2019-07/02/c_138192530.htm (accessed 17 September 2019).

t https://www.safe.gov.cn/en/2019/0910/1553.html (accessed 17 September 2019).

u https://www.rubio.senate.gov/public/_cache/files/fcea6a9e-6392-415e-a627-938bcd1703a4/07F234F026CA8B3ADB9BFB9C7A46EF3A.re-coop-21st-
  century-manufacturing-act--.pdf (accessed 17 September 2019).

v https://www.usgs.gov/centers/nmic/rare-earths-statistics-and-information (accessed 17 September 2019).

w https://home.treasury.gov/news/press-releases/sm751 (accessed 17 September 2019).

1.2 Debt buildup and financial vulnerability: Evidence from emerging markets

Debt has risen substantially in developing Asia since the global financial crisis (GFC) of 2008–2009. While both private and public debt contributed to the debt buildup, private debt has grown more rapidly. An increase in debt can be healthy, if it reflects the natural process of financial development and the deepening of financial markets. If debt mounts too high and too quickly, though, it can raise concerns about the health and stability of the financial system. Existing research shows that rapid debt buildup can harm the real economy (Mian, Sufi, and Vernier 2017) and exacerbate recessions (Jordà, Schularick, and Taylor 2013, Sutherland and Hoeller 2012). This section presents new empirical analysis that sheds light on the links between debt buildup and financial vulnerability in emerging markets.

1.2.1 Debt buildup in emerging markets since the global financial crisis

Total debt—the sum of public and private debt—took off in developing Asia after 2008 as a pervasive environment of low interest rates following the GFC significantly reduced costs for public and private borrowers alike. The weighted average ratio of total debt to GDP in Asia and the Pacific rose from 131.5% in 2008 to 211.4% in 2017, with the most rapid increase taking place in upper-middle-income economies (Figure 1.2.1). However, developing Asia's debt has fallen since 2017 as some regional governments strove to deleverage. Data for a smaller set of 10 emerging Asian economies, from the Institute of International Finance, show the ratio of total debt to GDP at year end peaked at 267% in 2017, then declined to 255% in 2018, which is still almost a 50% increase (by about 80% of GDP) from the debt level that prevailed prior to the GFC.[1]

Both public debt and private debt contributed to the growth of total debt in developing Asia but with patterns varying across subregions. As a result of countercyclical fiscal stimulus implemented during the GFC, the weighted average ratio of public debt to GDP in developing Asia increased by two-fifths from 2008 to 2017.

Figure 1.2.1 Ratio of debt to GDP in developing Asia

- High income
- Upper-middle income
- Lower-middle income
- Lower income
- Developing Asia

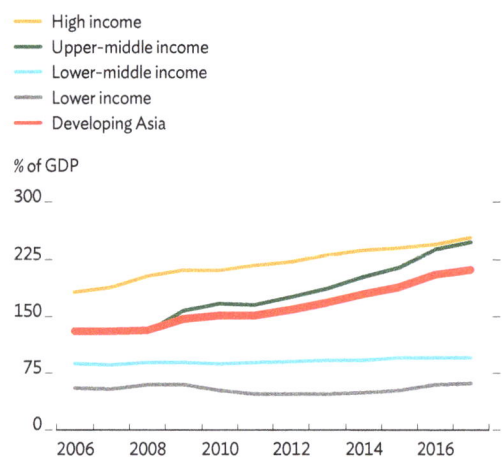

GDP = gross domestic product.

Notes: Aggregates by income classification are weighted averages computed using as weight World Bank gross national income, Atlas method, in current US dollars. Economy income classification is based on World Bank country income classifications by income level, 2017–2018. Malaysia data for 2016 are used in place of missing 2017 data.

Source: ADB estimates using data from the IMF-Global Debt Database (accessed 16 April 2019).

Figure 1.2.2 Public and private debt across subregions in developing Asia

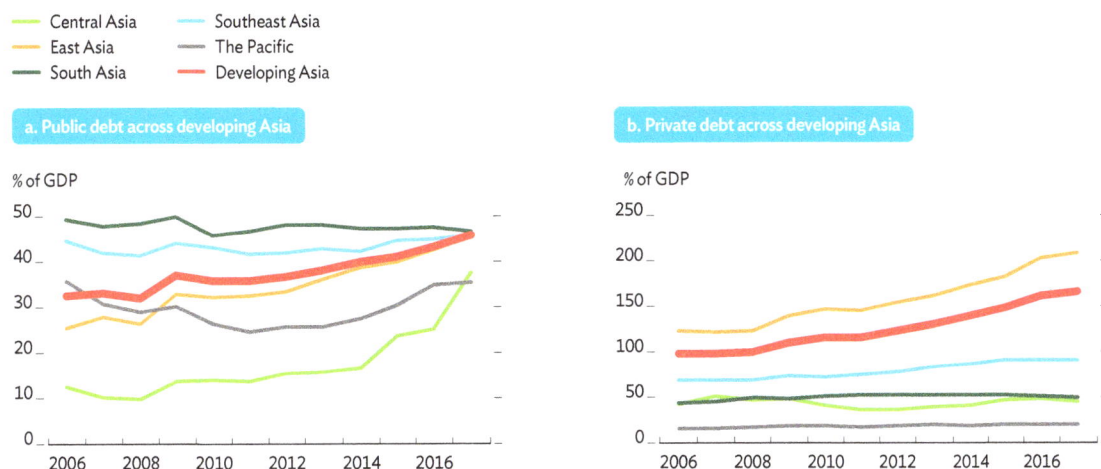

- Central Asia
- East Asia
- South Asia
- Southeast Asia
- The Pacific
- Developing Asia

a. Public debt across developing Asia

% of GDP

b. Private debt across developing Asia

% of GDP

GDP = gross domestic product.

Notes: Subregional aggregates are weighted averages computed using as weight World Bank gross national income, Atlas method, in current US dollars. In Figure 1.2.2b, private data for Malaysia in 2016 is used in place of missing 2017 data.

Source: ADB estimates using data from the IMF-Global Debt Database (accessed 16 April 2019).

While public debt remained relatively stable in South Asia and Southeast Asia at about 45% of subregional GDP, it increased by almost three-fourths in East Asia and more than tripled, albeit from low levels, in Central Asia (Figure 1.2.2a). Much of the increase in Central Asian public debt has occurred since 2015, as governments in the subregion increased public spending and investment in part to offset a downturn in commodity prices.

Developing Asia's private debt expanded at a faster pace than its public debt, growing by two-thirds in the past decade. The buildup of private debt has been most pronounced in East Asia, where debt rose from the equivalent of 123% of GDP in 2008 to 207% in 2017, and most notably in the PRC. More moderate expansion has occurred as well in Southeast Asia, climbing from 68% of GDP to 90% in the same period. In other subregions, private debt remains relatively stable (Figure 1.2.2b).

In terms of composition, expanding private debt shows varying patterns across the region. In the ROK and Thailand, for instance, its growth is driven mainly by household debt expansion, but in some other economies—notably the PRC and Hong Kong, China—both household and corporate debt contribute to private debt expansion (Figure 1.2.3).

Recent data to the end of 2018 suggest that selected economies have continued building up their private debt. According to Institute of International Finance statistics, the ratio of all private debt to GDP in the PRC increased from 148% at the end of 2008 to 238% exactly a decade later, with the ratio of household debt to GDP increasing by 32% and of corporate debt to GDP increasing by 58%. During the sample period, all private debt in Thailand increased by 35%, with household debt contributing 26% of the increase.

Figure 1.2.3 Household debt and nonfinancial corporate debt in selected Asian economies

▢ 2008   ▨ 2017

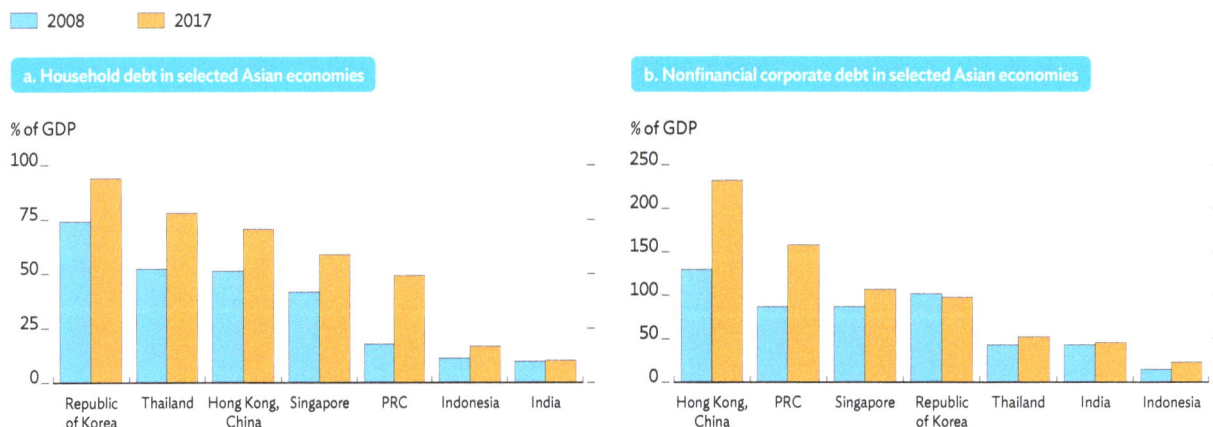

a. Household debt in selected Asian economies

b. Nonfinancial corporate debt in selected Asian economies

GDP = gross domestic product, PRC = People's Republic of China.
Source: IMF–Global Debt Database (accessed 16 April 2019).

1.2.2 What is known about the debt–financial vulnerability nexus?

An accumulation of private and public debt may not necessarily be a problem in itself. Higher private debt can reflect the natural development of the financial sector and financial markets, where household savings set aside to smooth consumption are channeled to finance investment. Alternatively, household borrowing can be welfare enhancing, enabling people to access better housing and to invest in human capital. Public sector borrowing is often required to finance much-needed investment in infrastructure, health care, and education, boosting a country's future productivity.

But a debt buildup that is too rapid and too large may contribute to excessive leverage in inefficient sectors that do not use debt productively, which may drive down the quality of the debt. In addition, rapid debt buildups—sometimes referred to as credit booms—can fuel asset and consumption booms that eventually go bust. In the face of negative shocks such as sharply tightened liquidity, a surprisingly steep slowdown in global growth, or an abrupt reversal of capital flows, asset values may decline sharply. Households and corporations then find it difficult to service their debts, pushing up the rate of nonperforming bank loans and thereby causing liquidity to contract further. Such a vicious cycle poses a systemic risk to the entire financial system and may eventually require a government bailout, which can deepen fiscal deficits and jeopardize public debt sustainability. Rapid expansion of public debt can similarly raise investor concerns about fiscal sustainability and government liquidity and solvency.

Evidence indicates that excess debt buildup can be harmful to the real economy and worsen recessions. Bernardini and Forni (2017) examined the impact of excessive debt buildup on the intensity and duration of recessions and found excess public and private debt alike associated with deeper and longer recessions in emerging markets. Jordà, Schularick, and Taylor (2013) documented that the buildup of excess bank credit exacerbated the severity of subsequent recessions in advanced economies. Das et al. (2010) indicated that excessive public debt could harm financial stability by damaging balance sheets in both the public and the private sector, triggering inflationary-policies and weakening investor confidence. Park, Shin, and Tian (2018) found that private debt buildups could cause larger output declines in emerging economies than in the advanced economies, with corporate debt and household debt both harmful to the real economy.

Less empirical evidence exists on how increases in debt are associated with financial vulnerability and financial crises, especially in developing economies. Adrian and Boyarchenko (2012) developed a dynamic macroeconomic model with procyclical leverage cycles in financial intermediation. It showed that, while leverage fosters output and smooths consumption in normal times, procyclical buildups of leverage worsen forward-looking systematic risks and the probability of crisis.

Bauer and Granziera (2017) examined how the debt level may affect the role of monetary policy tightening in a financial crisis. Using a sample of 18 developed economies, the study found that the ratio of private debt to GDP influenced the probability of financial crisis after monetary tightening. Higher private debt increased the likelihood of financial crisis shortly after unexpected monetary policy tightening. Barrell, Davis, and Pomerantz (2006) evaluated the impact of banking and currency crises on consumption, documenting that high debt levels made financial crises more costly. While most of these studies looked at the link between debt buildup and financial crises, it is also worthwhile to examine how debt buildup links with exchange rate vulnerability. Herz and Tong (2008), for example, showed that debt and currency crises share common drivers in economic fundamentals and established a causal relation with debt crises affecting currency crises. While Herz and Tong (2008) focused on the contagion between currency crises and debt crises by examining causality between the two, this present study contributes to the literature by looking at the effect of private and public debt buildup on financial vulnerability, which is proxied by stress in the foreign exchange market.

1.2.3 Empirical evidence on debt buildup and financial vulnerability

The analysis here, based on Park, Ramayandi, and Tian (forthcoming), empirically analyzes the association between debt buildup and vulnerability in the foreign exchange market. It revisits the debt–stability nexus by using the CMAX ratio as a measurement for stress in the foreign exchange market, which is, in turn, a proxy for financial vulnerability. CMAX is widely used to gauge maximum loss in a financial indicator, such as an equity index or foreign exchange rate, over a specific time horizon (Illing and Liu 2006, Huotari 2015, and Austria 2017, among others). The underlying intuition is that, as debt builds up, investors become more sensitive to vulnerability arising from weak fundamentals and may pull their money out of the country, weakening the currency. The question is to what extent high or rising public and private debt really is an indicator of weak fundamentals. Box 1.2.1 provides the technical description of the analysis.

Here CMAX is the ratio of this month's exchange rate, expressed in US dollars per unit of local currency, relative to the maximum exchange rate over the previous 12 months. A value of 1 indicates that the monthly exchange rate is at its 12-month peak, and a value of 0.7 indicates that the currency has depreciated by 30% from its 12-month peak. The evolution of CMAX is shown in Figure 1.2.4 for different groups of economies. During the GFC of 2008–2009, and when the US started to normalize its monetary stance in 2015, global currencies came under heavy depreciation pressure (Figure 1.2.4a). However, currencies in emerging Asia were more resilient than others during the sample period, suffering smaller losses during periods of currency stress (Figure 1.2.4b). Within developing Asia, Central Asian currencies, particularly the Armenian dram and Kyrgyz som, suffered larger dips in stress periods than did currencies in other subregions, especially during the recent cycle of a strong US dollar that began in 2015 (Figure 1.2.4c). The analysis that follows examines how financial vulnerability, as proxied by dips in CMAX, are associated with public and private debt levels.

The empirical results indicate that higher private debt is associated with greater currency vulnerability (Table 1.2.1). Model specifications 1–3 include private debt and control variables commonly affecting exchange rate stress. The magnitude of the coefficient in model specification 1 suggests that an increase in private debt by 10% of GDP from the sample median value is, on average, associated with an additional 0.9 percentage points in depreciation pressure. In the sample, this means that comparing a country at the 25th percentile of private debt (39% of GDP) to one at the 75th percentile (161% of GDP) shows exchange rate loss 12.6 percentage points larger for the latter. When the stress dummy is included in model specification 2, the results show that, during stress periods, currencies experience an additional 1.7% in depreciation pressure, and those with higher private indebtedness still see a significantly larger loss in currency value.

Box 1.2.1 Econometric analysis of the association between debt buildup and currency stress: Data and empirical methodology

Park, Ramayandi, and Tian (forthcoming) estimated a panel regression using annual data to explore the association between debt buildups and exchange rate stress with this equation:

$$CMAX_{i,t} = \beta_0 + \beta_1 debt_{i,t-1} + \beta_2 debt^2_{i,t-1} \quad (1)$$
$$+ \beta_3 ca_{i,t-1} + \beta_4 inf_{i,t} + \beta_5 ExR_{i,t}$$
$$+ \beta_6 fisb_{i,t-1} + \beta_7 irspread_{i,t} + \beta_8 country_i + u_{i,t}$$

The dependent variable $CMAX_{i,t}$ is calculated as follows. The CMAX indicator for economy i over month m plotted in Figure 1.2.4 is defined in the spirit of Illing and Liu (2006) as below:

$$CMAX_{i,m} = \frac{p_{i,m}}{\max(p_{i,m}) \text{ over the past } 12 \text{ months}} \quad (2)$$

where $p_{i,m}$ denotes the inverted nominal exchange rate (US dollar value per unit of local currency) of country i in month m. Thus, $CMAX_{i,m}$ is the average monthly value compared with the maximum value over the previous 12 months. Dips in CMAX capture periods of relative weakness in a currency. Because some control variables are available only at an annual frequency, $CMAX_{i,m}$ is averaged over each calendar year to get $CMAX_{i,t}$ in each year t. The key independent variable of interest in equation (1), $debt_{i,t-1}$, is debt as a share of GDP of country i at the end of previous year t–1, denoting private debt (loans and debt securities) or government debt, depending on the model specification. The squared term of debt is included to account for possible nonlinearity in this association. Five macroeconomic factors—the current account balance, inflation, the fiscal balance, interest rate spread, and the exchange rate regime—are included as control variables because they are widely believed to affect financial vulnerability, though admittedly many other variables can also affect vulnerability. More specifically, $ca_{i,t-1}$ is the current account balance (expressed as a percentage of GDP), $inf_{i,t}$ is inflation (the annualized consumer price index expressed as a percentage), $ExR_{i,t}$ is the exchange rate

regime (a higher number indicating a more flexible regime), $fisb_{i,t-1}$ is the consolidated fiscal balance (as a percentage of GDP), and $irspread_{i,t}$ is the average month policy rate spread between local market and the US in year t. $country_i$ is a vector of country fixed effects that are included to account for time-invariant country-specific heterogeneities. Finally, $u_{i,t}$ is the error term.

Data on public and private debt as a share of GDP are collected from the International Monetary Fund (IMF) Global Debt database, nominal exchange rates from IMF International Financial Statistics, current account balance and inflation rates from the World Bank's World Development Indicators, and consolidated fiscal balances from CEIC Data Company. The exchange rate regime is defined following the annual fine classification in Ilzetzki, Reinhart, and Rogoff (2017). After matching different variables from all sources, the final panel dataset consists of debt and macroeconomic variables of 59 global economies including 18 emerging Asian economies from 2000 to 2016. The median value of public debt as a share of GDP is 34% and of private debt as a share of GDP, 80%.

To examine whether the impact of debt levels on currency stress may be more pronounced in emerging markets, which tend to have generally weaker fundamentals than advanced economies, a dummy variable for emerging markets (EM) is included. To explore whether debt buildup can contribute to additional currency pressure during periods of currency stress, a dummy variable (Stress) is included that captures three stress periods during the sample period: the GFC of 2008–2009, taper tantrum in 2013, and start of US monetary policy normalization in 2015. The main results of the estimation are presented in Table 1.2.1.

Reference:

Park, D., A. Ramayandi, and S. Tian. Forthcoming. *Debt Buildup and Financial Vulnerability: Evidence from Emerging Markets.* Asian Development Bank.

Model specification 3 shows that private indebtedness relative to GDP induces a greater increase in financial vulnerability in emerging markets than in advanced economies—a 10% higher ratio of private debt to GDP induces an additional 0.6% depreciation pressure in emerging markets relative to the advanced economies.

Figure 1.2.4 Foreign exchange rate CMAX dynamics of different groups of economies

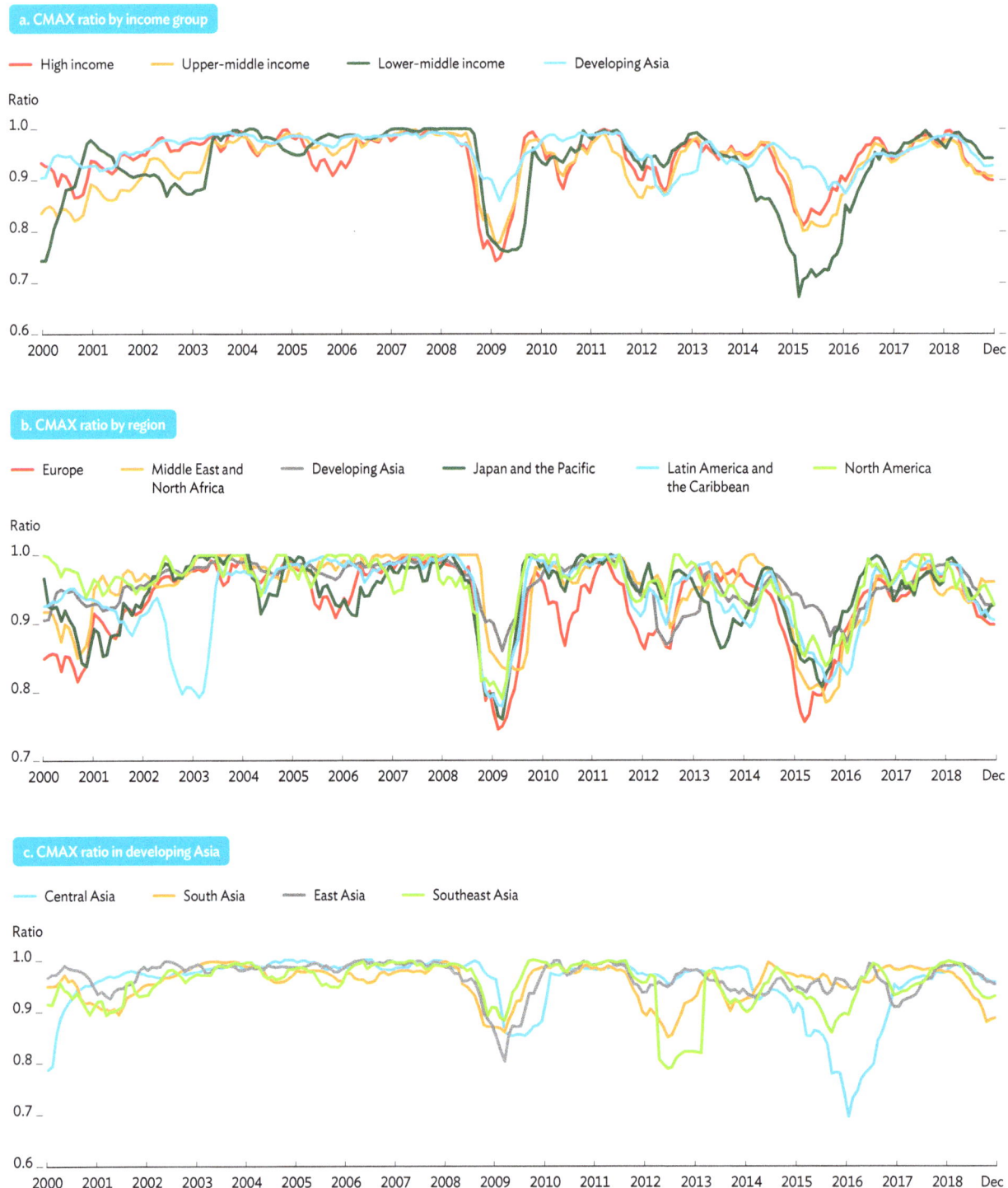

a. CMAX ratio by income group

━━ High income   ━━ Upper-middle income   ━━ Lower-middle income   ━━ Developing Asia

Ratio

b. CMAX ratio by region

━━ Europe   ━━ Middle East and   ━━ Developing Asia   ━━ Japan and the Pacific   ━━ Latin America and   ━━ North America
              North Africa   the Caribbean

Ratio

c. CMAX ratio in developing Asia

━━ Central Asia   ━━ South Asia   ━━ East Asia   ━━ Southeast Asia

Ratio

Notes: CMAX is a ratio for stress in foreign exchange markets. In panel A, each income bracket contains global economies in that income bracket.
Sources: IMF International Financial Statistics and Bloomberg (accessed 19 August 2019).

Table 1.2.1 Private debt, public debt, and financial vulnerability

Dependent variable: CMAX	Private debt			Public debt		
Variables	(1)	(2)	(3)	(4)	(5)	(6)
Debt % of GDP	−0.1108***	−0.0955***	−0.0714***	−0.0532	−0.0469	−0.0909*
	(−4.64)	(−3.77)	(−3.32)	(−1.07)	(−1.02)	(−2.00)
(Debt % of GDP)^2	0.0001***	0.0001***	0.0001**	0.0004	0.0004	0.0004
	(3.81)	(3.09)	(2.58)	(1.41)	(1.45)	(1.37)
Stress = 1		−1.6562***			−1.2577	
		(−2.90)			(−1.45)	
Stress × Debt % of GDP		−0.0038			−0.0361**	
		(−0.94)			(−2.08)	
EM × Debt % of GDP			−0.0622*			0.0599
			(−1.83)			(1.34)
Current account balance % of GDP	0.1495***	0.1486***	0.1447***	0.1929***	0.1884***	0.1907***
	(2.94)	(2.87)	(2.86)	(3.84)	(3.91)	(3.76)
Inflation	0.1134	0.1266	0.1047	0.0091	0.0179	−0.0030
	(0.75)	(0.84)	(0.69)	(0.07)	(0.14)	(−0.02)
Exchange rate regime	−0.4348	−0.4492	−0.4285	−0.4300	−0.4792	−0.4412
	(−1.41)	(−1.48)	(−1.41)	(−1.30)	(−1.50)	(−1.32)
Fiscal balance % of GDP	−0.0795	−0.0337	−0.0990	0.0506	0.0798	0.0229
	(−0.95)	(−0.38)	(−1.20)	(0.50)	(0.80)	(0.23)
Interest rate spread	−0.6697***	−0.6316***	−0.6387***	−0.7085***	−0.6622***	−0.7153***
	(−3.84)	(−3.66)	(−3.75)	(−4.66)	(−4.40)	(−4.64)
Observations	719	719	719	706	706	706
Number of economies	59	59	59	58	58	58
Country fixed effect	YES	YES	YES	YES	YES	YES
F value	13.51	13.59	15.4	8.071	14.76	6.64

EM = emerging market, GDP = gross domestic product.
Notes: Numbers in parenthesis are robust standard errors. *** denotes significance at 0.01, ** at 0.05, and * at 0.10.
Source: Park, Ramayandi, and Tian (forthcoming).

The additional dip in CMAX is 7.6%, when comparing an emerging market economy at the third quartile of the ratio of private debt to GDP relative to one at the first quartile.

Model specifications 4–6 estimate the impact of public debt buildup on foreign exchange CMAX. Model specification 4 shows that, on average, public debt does not have any significant effect on depreciation pressure. However, model specification 5 indicates that public debt undermines currency stability during stress periods. In particular, a 10% higher ratio of public debt to GDP is associated with 0.4% more depreciation pressure. Model specification 6 further shows that public debt buildup does not show any significantly different impact on currency, regardless of whether it is in emerging markets or the major advanced economies. Moreover, most control variables do not exert persistent and significant currency loss pressure, except for the current account balance and the interest rate spread. A better current account performance is associated with less currency stress. A wider interest rate spread, which reflects a higher country risk premium, is associated with more currency stress.

1.2.4 Concluding remarks and policy implications

The new evidence presented here strengthens the case for vigilance against large or rapid debt buildups. The analysis reveals that buildups of both private debt and public debt are significantly associated with financial vulnerability during periods of financial stress. This suggests that policy makers in emerging markets should closely monitor the buildup of both public and private debt, especially in the current global economic environment of slowing growth and high uncertainty.

The results also strengthen the case for shifting from a debt-monitoring framework that narrowly focuses on public debt sustainability to a broader framework that monitors both private and public debt. While excess public debt can jeopardize macroeconomic stability and harm investor sentiment during a period of financial stress, the persistent and significant association between private debt buildup and exchange rate stress points to the need for a broader framework. Private and public debt vulnerabilities are interrelated: when private debt becomes unsustainable for households and corporations, rising rates of nonperforming loans and debt default damage bank balance sheets. This can eventually trigger a liquidity crunch, which may further snowball into government bailouts and fiscal deficits that adversely affect public debt sustainability.

While leverage in itself need not be bad, as it can foster economic activity and smooth consumption, it poses a risk when debt is allocated to unproductive sectors that cannot generate enough cash flow to service it. The risk of debt quality deterioration becomes more pronounced when the buildup is rapid and when economic growth is slowing or negative. Developing Asia has accumulated private debt during the post-GFC era of low interest rates globally, and it now faces a global growth slowdown and a highly uncertain global economic environment. As such, it is advisable for Asian regulators and policy makers to consider macroprudential policies as well as reinforce prudential financial supervision and regulation. This would improve the quality of private debt and mitigate the risk of recession and crisis in the future.

Endnote

1   The 10 emerging markets in Institute of International
     Finance data are the PRC; Hong Kong, China; India;
     Indonesia; Malaysia; the Republic of Korea; Pakistan;
     the Philippines; Singapore; and Thailand.

References

Abiad, A., K. Baris, J. Bernabe, D. Bertulfo, S. Camingue-
     Romance, P. Feliciano, J. M. Mariasingham, and V. Mercer-
     Blackman. 2018. The Impact of Trade Conflict on
     Developing Asia. *ADB Economic Working Paper Series*
     No. 566. Asian Development Bank. https://www.adb.
     org/sites/default/files/publication/471496/ewp-566-
     impacttrade-conflict-asia.pdf.

Adrian, T. and N. Boyarchenko. 2012. Intermediary Leverage
     Cycles and Financial Stability. *Federal Reserve Bank of
     New York Staff Report* No. 567.

Austria, C. P. 2017. Estimating the Extent of Market Herding in
     the Philippine Equities Market. *Bangko Sentral Review 2017.*
     http://www.bsp.gov.ph/downloads/publications/2017/
     BS2017_02.pdf.

Barrell, R., P. Davis, and O. Pomerantz. 2006. Costs of Financial
     Instability, Household-sector Balance Sheets and
     Consumption. *Journal of Financial Stability* 2(2).

Bauer, G. and E. Granziera. 2017. Monetary Policy, Private Debt,
     and Financial Stability Risks. *International Journal of
     Central Banking* 13(3).

Bernardini, M. and L. Forni. 2017. Private and Public Debt:
     Are Emerging Markets at Risk? *IMF Working Paper*
     No. WP/17/61. International Monetary Fund.

Das, U., M. Papapioannou, G. Pedras, F. Ahmed, and J. Surti.
     2010. Managing Public Debt and Its Financial Stability
     Implications. *IMF Working Paper* No. WP/10/280.
     International Monetary Fund.

Herz, B. and H. Tong. 2008. Debt and Currency Crises—
     Complements or Substitutes. *Review of International
     Economics* 16(5).

Huotari, J. 2015. Measuring Financial Stress—A Country
     Specific Stress Index for Finland. *Bank of Finland
     Research Discussion Paper* No. 7/2015. https://ssrn.com/
     abstract=2584378.

Illing, M. and Y. Liu. 2006. Measuring Financial Stress in a
     Developed Country: An Application to Canada. *Journal of
     Financial Stability* 2(3).

Ilzetzki, E., C. Reinhart, and K. Rogoff. 2017. The Country
     Chronologies to Exchange Rate Arrangements into
     the 21st Century: Will the Anchor Currency Hold?
     NBER Working Paper No. 23135.

Jordà, Ò., M. Schularick, and A. M. Taylor. 2013. When Credit Bites Back. *Journal of Money, Credit, and Banking* 45(2).

Mian, A., A. Sufi, and E. Verner. 2017. Household Debt and Business Cycles Worldwide. *Quarterly Journal of Economics* 132.

Park, D., A. Ramayandi, and S. Tian. Forthcoming. *Debt Buildup and Financial Vulnerability: Evidence from Emerging Markets*. Asian Development Bank.

Park, D., K. Shin, and S. Tian. 2018. Household Debt, Corporate Debt, and Economic Growth: Some Empirical Evidence. *ADB Working Paper*. Asian Development Bank.

Sutherland, D. and P. Hoeller. 2012. Debt and Macroeconomic Stability: An Overview of the Literature and Some Empirics. *OECD Economics Department Working Paper* No. 1006. Organisation for Economic Co-operation and Development.

Annex: A worsening global environment

This Update *envisages aggregate growth in the major advanced economies of the United States, the euro area, and Japan slowing more sharply than forecast in* Asian Development Outlook 2019 (ADO 2019). *The combined growth forecasts are revised down from 1.9% to 1.7% for 2019 and from 1.6% to 1.4% for 2020 (Table A1.1). Reescalation of the trade conflict between the US and the People's Republic of China (PRC) and worsening prospects of a no-deal Brexit weigh on business sentiment and investment. A more pronounced growth slowdown is now expected in the euro area, and signs of weakening growth are also seen in the US. Growth in Japan, on the other hand, outperformed expectations in the first half of the year, prompting upward revision of its 2019 growth forecast.*

Table A1.1 Baseline assumptions on the international economy

	2017	2018	2019 ADO 2019	2019 Update	2020 ADO 2019	2020 Update
	Actual					
GDP growth (%)						
Major advanced economies[a]	2.4	2.2	1.9	1.7	1.6	1.4
United States	2.4	2.9	2.4	2.3	1.9	1.9
Euro area	2.7	1.9	1.5	1.0	1.5	1.0
Japan	1.9	0.8	0.8	1.2	0.6	0.5
Prices and inflation						
Brent crude spot prices (average, $/barrel)	54.4	71.2	62.0	65.0	62.0	63.0
Food index (2010 = 100, % change)	0.6	0.3	0.0	-4.0	1.5	1.5
Consumer price index inflation (major advanced economies' average, %)	1.7	2.0	1.9	1.6	1.9	1.7
Interest rates						
United States federal funds rate (average, %)	1.0	1.8	2.6	2.2	2.9	1.9
European Central Bank refinancing rate (average, %)	0.0	0.0	0.0	0.0	0.0	0.0
Bank of Japan overnight call rate (average, %)	-0.1	-0.1	-0.1	-0.1	-0.1	-0.1
$ Libor[b] (%)	1.1	1.8	2.6	2.2	2.9	1.9

ADO = Asian Development Outlook, GDP = gross domestic product.

[a] Average growth rates are weighted by gross national income, Atlas method.

[b] Average London interbank offered rate quotations on 1-month loans.

Sources: US Department of Commerce, Bureau of Economic Analysis, http://www.bea.gov; Eurostat, http://ec.europa.eu/eurostat; Economic and Social Research Institute of Japan, http://www.esri.cao.go.jp; Consensus Forecasts; Bloomberg; CEIC Data Company; Haver Analytics; and the World Bank, Global Commodity Markets, http://www.worldbank.org; ADB estimates.

Recent developments in the major advanced economies

United States

The US economy performed better than expected in the first half of 2019, growing by 3.1% in the first quarter (Q1) and by 2.0% in Q2 in seasonally adjusted annualized terms (as assumed for all quarterly growth rates in this Annex unless otherwise stated). The two quarters yielded growth at 2.6% in the first half of the year. All components of demand contributed positively in Q1, but the main drivers of growth shifted between quarters: Net exports drove growth in Q1 and consumption in Q2. Private investment and net exports contributed to growth in Q1 but subtracted from it in Q2. Meanwhile, consumption growth jumped from 1.1% in Q1 to 4.7% in Q2. Government spending rose significantly in Q2, probably at least enough to cancel drag from net exports (Figure A1.1).

Weakness in the external sector materialized as expected with exports falling by 5.8% in Q2, reversing 4.1% growth in Q1. Prolonged uncertainty in the global economy, continuing trade tensions with the PRC and Mexico, and a strong US dollar all held down trade. Even as exports of goods and services fell substantially in Q2, imports expanded, if only by 0.1%. This further weakened net exports, which deducted 0.7 percentage points from GDP growth in the quarter. Investment also disappointed in Q2, falling by 6.1% and cutting GDP growth by 1.1 percentage points, mainly by drawing down private inventories but also with lower fixed investment, dragged down by lower investment in structures while investment in equipment and intellectual property continued to grow.

Consumption rebounded to contribute 3.1 percentage points to GDP growth in Q2, having contributed 0.8 points in Q1. Strong retail sales reflected rising consumer confidence throughout Q2 as real personal income steadily improved. The rebound was most evident in durable goods, sales of which surged from 0.3% growth in Q1 to 13.0% in Q2. Consumption of other goods was also strong, growing by 6.8% as services grew by 2.8%. Government spending was another substantial contributor in Q2, growing by 4.5%, adding 0.8 percentage points to GDP growth, and thereby compensating for about half of the drag from investment and net exports.

The labor market continued to tighten. From a 62,000 increase in nonfarm jobs in May, employment expanded by 178,000 jobs in June, 159,000 jobs in July, and 130,000 jobs in August as unemployment stayed low at 3.6% in May and at 3.7% in June, July, and August (Figure A1.2).

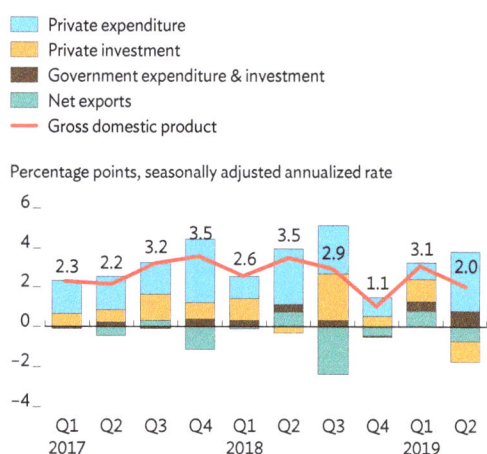

Figure A1.1 Demand-side contributions to growth, United States

- Private expenditure
- Private investment
- Government expenditure & investment
- Net exports
- Gross domestic product

Percentage points, seasonally adjusted annualized rate

Q = quarter.
Sources: US Department of Commerce. Bureau of Economic Analysis. http://www.bea.gov; Haver Analytics (both accessed 15 September 2019).

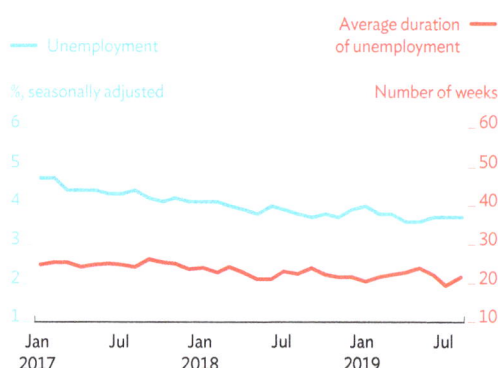

Figure A1.2 Unemployment rate and average duration, United States

— Unemployment

Average duration of unemployment

%, seasonally adjusted   Number of weeks

Source: Haver Analytics (accessed 15 September 2019).

The strong labor market suggests that wage growth will continue, supporting consumption.

However, overall growth is expected to slow, and leading indicators already show weakening economic activity. The composite purchasing managers' index (PMI), having hovered above 55 in the first 5 months of the year, foretelling growth, slid to 54.7 in June, edging toward the threshold of 50 between growth and contraction. The manufacturing PMI slid to 49.1 in August, but a rise in the nonmanufacturing component more than compensated to push the composite PMI back up to 55.6 in August. However, any contribution that fixed investment may make to growth in the coming quarters is expected to be modest. Finally, gloomy global economic prospects and escalation in the US–PRC trade dispute will continue to weigh on the external sector. One important offsetting factor is that consumer confidence and spending remain strong (Figure A1.3). In addition, two major fiscal risk factors evaporated with agreement on 22 July to raise the US debt ceiling and on 2 August to pass the 2020 federal budget.

Inflation eased through Q2, from 2.0% in April to 1.6% in June, but it reaccelerated somewhat to 1.8% in July. Core inflation remained near 2.0%, though slowly creeping up in June and July (Figure A1.4). Citing persistently low inflation and the gloomy global economic outlook, the US Federal Reserve cut the federal funds rate by 25 basis points in July and September, the first sequence of cuts since 2015, following steady interest rate increases. The Fed is expected to keep its policy rate unchanged for the rest of the year. It may cut the rate by another 25 basis points early next year.

GDP growth in the US is now projected at 2.3% in 2019, or 0.1 percentage points lower than in *ADO 2019*, with the forecast for 2020 unchanged at 1.9%. Inflation is now seen at a more moderate 1.9% in 2019 and 2.1% in 2020. Risks to growth projections continue to be mostly on the downside and have worsened since *ADO 2019* was published in April as trade tensions with the PRC intensified again. Further, various indicators, including a recent inversion of the interest yield curve favoring shorter terms, have started signaling a slowdown.

Euro area

Growth in the euro area picked up from 1.2% in Q4 of 2018 to 1.7% in Q1 of 2019 before slowing again to 0.8% in Q2 (Figure A1.5). Driving the regional performance in Q1 were private consumption, contributing 0.9 percentage points to GDP growth, and net exports contributing 1.2 points, while investment subtracted 0.6 points. Despite a strong rebound in

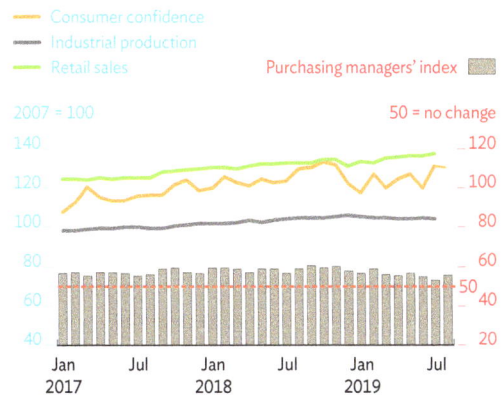

Figure A1.3 Business activity and consumer confidence indicators, United States

Note: A purchasing managers' index reading <50 signals deterioration, >50 improvement.
Source: Haver Analytics (accessed 15 September 2019).

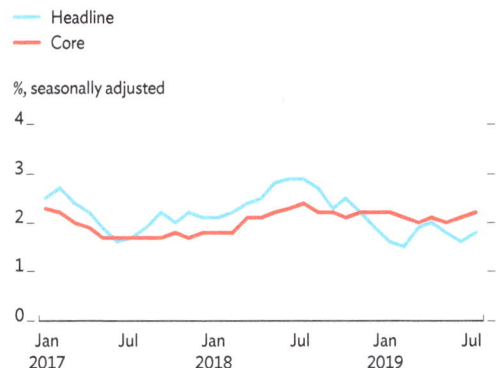

Figure A1.4 Inflation, United States

Source: Haver Analytics (accessed 15 September 2019).

fixed investment, growth in Q2 was held back by softening consumer spending and a downswing in global trade as net exports subtracted 0.4 points from growth. The slowdown in Q2 was felt across the major economies. Germany recorded the worst performance, with output declining by 0.3%. Elsewhere, growth slid to 0.1% in Italy and 1.9% in Spain, but slightly inched up to 1.3% in France.

Leading indicators at the beginning of Q3 broadly pointed to further economic weakening in the euro area but not recession. After recovering somewhat in May, industry returned to contraction in June with growth declining by 1.6% month on month. Growth in retail trade, having rebounded in June, also turned negative in July, by 0.6% month on month (Figure A1.6). Meanwhile, though still close to the threshold of 50 that separates growth from contraction, the PMI picked up slightly from 51.5 in July to 51.8 in August. In contrast with buoyant services and construction, the manufacturing PMI stayed in contraction territory at 47.0 in August. Economic sentiment dropped to 103.3 in June and further to 102.7 in July, the lowest in more than 3 years, before improving slightly to 103.1 in August (Figure A1.7).

The unemployment rate declined to 7.5% in July, the best rate since the global financial crisis of 2008–2009. Unemployment fell in Germany, Portugal, and Spain, remained broadly stable in France, but increased slightly in Italy. Having risen by 2.3% in Q4 of 2018, the labor cost index continued to climb in Q1 of 2019 by 2.4%. Wage growth accelerated in Germany and Spain but decelerated in Italy and France.

As labor markets improved and price pressure intensified in services, core inflation rose to 1.3% in June but then stabilized at 1.1% in July and August. Headline inflation also edged up to 1.3% in June before stabilizing at 1.0% in July and August. Consumer price inflation averaged 1.4% in the first half of the year, lower than the European Central Bank target of just below 2.0%. The central bank cut interest rates to record lows in early September, confirmed its forward-guidance pledge to keep rates very low at least through the first half of 2020, and approved additional monetary easing measures. Even so, in line with softening economic activity and subdued oil prices, inflation is forecast to remain moderate, averaging 1.4% in both 2019 and 2020.

In anticipation of prolonged weakness in the remainder of the year, the growth forecast for the euro area is revised down from 1.5% for both years in *ADO 2019* to 1.0%. Growth is expected to moderate as threats further materialize in the second half of 2019, when collateral damage from the US–PRC trade dispute and effects from the slowdown in Germany are likely to be compounded

Figure A1.5 Demand-side contributions to growth, euro area

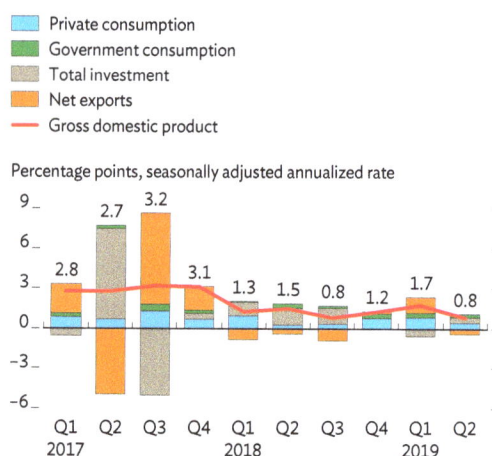

Q = quarter.
Source: Haver Analytics (accessed 9 September 2019).

Figure A1.6 Selected economic indicators, euro area

Source: Haver Analytics (accessed 9 September 2019).

Figure A1.7 Economic sentiment and purchasing managers' index, euro area

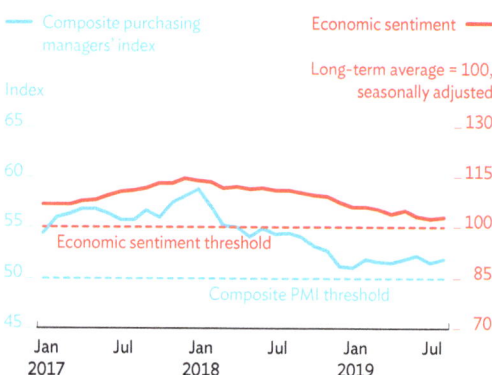

PMI = purchasing managers' index.
Sources: Bloomberg; Haver Analytics (both accessed 9 September 2019).

by a blow from Brexit. As weakness in manufacturing and deepening uncertainty dent exports and hinder investment, persistent economic softness is seen to carry over at least into the first half of 2020.

Downside risks to these projections are further escalation of trade tensions and rising protectionism, uncertainty surrounding a possible disorderly Brexit, lingering weakness in manufacturing, and market concern about debt sustainability in Italy. Moreover, although Eurosceptic parties did not do well in recent European parliamentary elections, the results revealed deepening divisions, suggesting little appetite for further integration and reform.

Japan

Confounding an earlier downbeat outlook for growth this year, expansion outperformed expectations in the first half of 2019 despite rising trade tensions and geopolitical uncertainties. The economy grew by a strong (upwardly revised) 2.8% in Q1 of 2019 and by 1.8% in Q2. In the first 3 months of the year, growth came mainly from imports falling much faster than exports, but in the second quarter domestic demand rebounded vigorously. Accordingly, private consumption added 1.4 percentage points to growth in Q2, with investment and government spending each contributing 0.7 points. Net exports subtracted 1.2 points as imports rose, partly reversing a sharp drop in Q1 (Figure A1.8). The outlook for the rest of 2019 is growth slowing as both domestic and external demand soften.

Manufacturing indicators remain weak, signaling a sector still constrained by trade policy uncertainty and weak global demand. After declining in Q1 by a monthly average of 2.5%, industrial production rose in Q2 but only by a negligible 0.6% (Figure A1.9). The PMI recovered from 49.3 in June to 49.6 in July but remains below the threshold of 50, which suggests that manufacturing is still contracting. The Bank of Japan quarterly business confidence index for large manufacturers, although positive, fell from 12.0 in Q1 to an 11-month low of 7.0 in Q2. While core machinery orders, a leading indicator of investment, spiked up in June, this may reflect a bulge in domestic spending ahead of a sales tax hike in October, with decline likely thereafter.

Anticipation of the tax hike will boost consumption in Q3. Although growth in retail sales was flat in June—and consumer confidence declined from 38.8 in June to 37.7 in July, the lowest value in 4.5 years—the Bank of Japan consumption activity index showed an uptick in Q2. As after previous tax increases, consumer spending will likely fall in Q4 and stay subdued in 2020 (Figure A1.10).

Figure A1.8 Demand-side contributions to growth, Japan

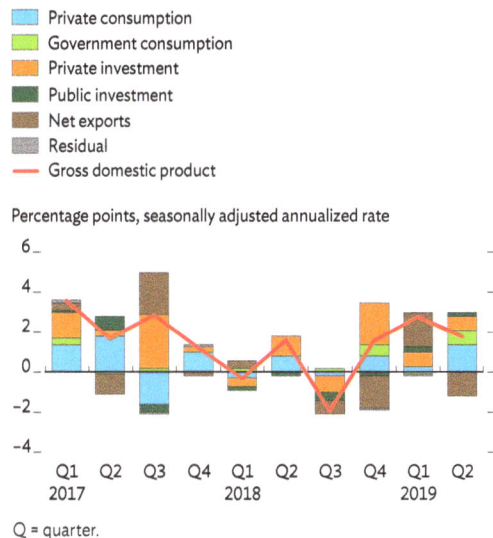

- Private consumption
- Government consumption
- Private investment
- Public investment
- Net exports
- Residual
- Gross domestic product

Percentage points, seasonally adjusted annualized rate

Q = quarter.
Source: Economics and Social Research Institute, Cabinet Office, Government of Japan, available: http://www.esri.cao.go.jp (accessed 9 August 2019).

Figure A1.9 Consumption and business indicators, Japan

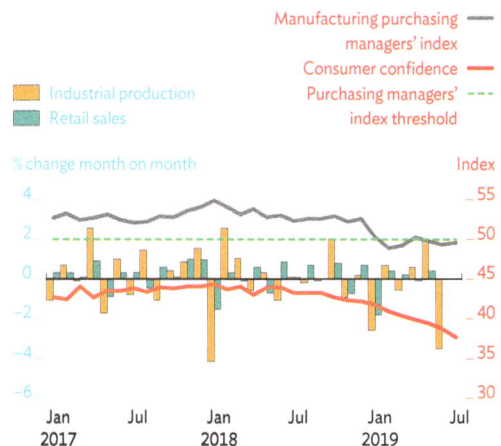

- Manufacturing purchasing managers' index
- Consumer confidence
- Purchasing managers' index threshold
- Industrial production
- Retail sales

% change month on month / Index

Notes: A purchasing managers' index reading <50 signals deterioration, >50 improvement. A consumer confidence reading >50 signals better conditions.
Sources: Haver Analytics; Bloomberg (both accessed 20 August 2019).

The unemployment rate improved to a 30-year low of 2.3% in June, yet wage pressure remain muted. Headline inflation was steady at 0.7% in both May and June, while core inflation, which excludes fresh food and fuel, fell from 0.4% in May to 0.3% in June. Amid subdued inflationary pressure and an uncertain global outlook, the Bank of Japan kept monetary policy unchanged, with the short-term policy rate at –0.1% and the 10-year Japanese government bond yield near zero.

Monthly external trade figures showed the declining trend in exports finally relenting. Merchandise exports picked up in July in US dollar terms for the first time in 9 months, growing by 1.3% year on year despite recent strengthening of the yen. Imports also picked up, by 1.7%, and are expected to strengthen further as consumers rush to buy ahead of the tax increase.

With 2.3% expansion in the first half of 2019 greatly exceeding expectations, this *Update* raises the growth outlook for Japan to 1.2% in 2019. It trims the outlook for 2020 to 0.5% because, if the government goes ahead with the sales tax hike in October 2019 and consumer demand temporarily picks up ahead of it, growth will likely weaken thereafter. On the upside, fiscal stimulus is expected to mitigate some of the adverse effects of the tax increase and thereby forestall a downturn similar to the one after the 2014 tax hike. In addition, accommodative financial conditions and spending on the 2020 Olympics will prop up growth in 2020. The main downside risk is a gloomy trade outlook in light of weak global growth, trade tensions, and a strong yen.

Recent developments and outlook in nearby economies

Australia

Economic expansion decelerated from 2.1% in Q1 of 2019 to 1.9% in Q2 as gross fixed capital formation subtracted 1.6 percentage points and change in inventories 2.2 points (Figure A1.11). Consumption was the largest growth driver, contributing 2.9 points and closely followed by net exports at 2.4 points.

Neither consumption nor investment seems likely to drive growth in Q3. Retail sales grew by 0.4% in June but contracted by 0.1% in July. Further, the consumer sentiment index dropped from 100.7 in June to 96.5 in July, its lowest reading since January 2018 and across the threshold of 100 signaling consumer pessimism. However, the business confidence index improved from 2.2 in June to 3.9 in July, indicating optimism, and the PMI rose from 49.4 in June

Figure A1.10 Private consumption growth in the 4 quarters before and after a tax hike, Japan

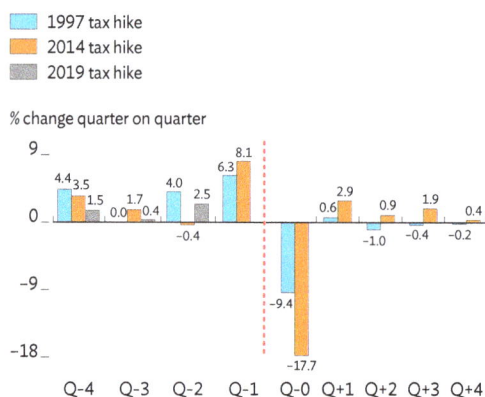

Q = quarter.
Source: Economics and Social Research Institute, Cabinet Office, Government of Japan, available http://www.esri.cao.go.jp (accessed 9 August 2019).

Figure A1.11 Demand-side contributions to growth, Australia

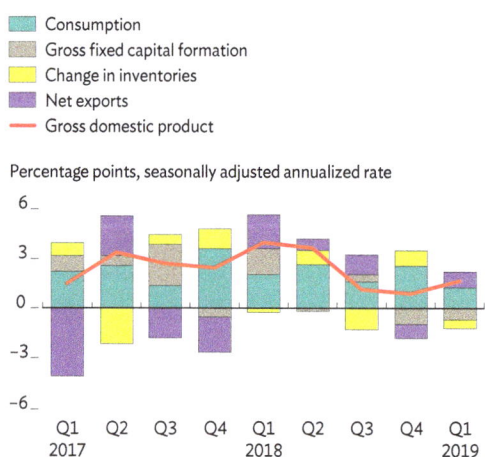

Q = quarter.
Source: CEIC Data Company (accessed 30 July 2019).

to 51.3 in July, crossing above the 50 threshold that indicates expansion likely to come. Another positive indicator was the unemployment rate, which improved from an average of 5.4% in the first 7 months of 2018 to 5.1% in the same period of this year.

Inflation accelerated from 1.3% in Q1 of 2019 to 1.6% in Q2, still below the target of 2.0%–3.0% set by the Reserve Bank of Australia, the central bank. In light of continued low inflation, a slowing economy, and heightened global trade tensions, the central bank decided at its 6 August 2019 monetary policy meeting to keep the cash rate unchanged at an all-time low of 1.00%.

Consumer spending will likely be held back in the remainder of 2019 by high household debt, slow wage growth, and falling home prices. Another major downside risk to the forecast is worsening global trade tension. On the upside, reduced taxes, lower interest rates, and relaxed standards for bank lending could stimulate growth, and higher revenue would foster increased infrastructure spending. On 20 August, the Consensus Forecast was for GDP growth at 1.9% in 2019 and 2.5% in 2020.

New Zealand

GDP growth accelerated from 2.3% in Q4 of 2018 to 3.4% in Q1 of 2019. Gross fixed capital formation was the largest contributor with 2.4 percentage points, followed by net exports with 2.3 points. Consumption also contributed positively, adding 1.8 points. Change in inventories was a significant drag, subtracting 3.3 points (Figure A1.12). Growth in retail sales decelerated from 3.8% in Q2 of 2018 to 3.4% a year later. The consumer confidence index slipped from 103.8 in Q1 of 2019 to 103.5 in Q2 of 2019 but remained above the optimism/pessimism threshold of 100. In contrast, the business confidence index, which has been negative since October 2017, fell from –38.1 in June to –44.3 in July, the lowest point so far in 2019. The manufacturing index sank from 51.1 in June to 48.2 in July, crossing below the threshold of 50 indicating future contraction.

Inflation rose from 1.5% in Q1 of 2019 to 1.7% in Q2, still below the target of 2.0% set by the Reserve Bank of New Zealand, the central bank. Unemployment improved from 4.2% in Q1 to 3.9% in Q2. In response to inflation and employment being close to target and growth slowing as headwinds strengthen—and recognizing the need for lower interest rates to support the economy—the central bank decided at its 7 August 2019 meeting to reduce the official cash rate to an all-time low of 1.0%.

In the remainder of 2019, growth is expected to moderate in light of a lack of spare capacity and low business confidence,

Figure A1.12 Demand-side contributions to growth, New Zealand

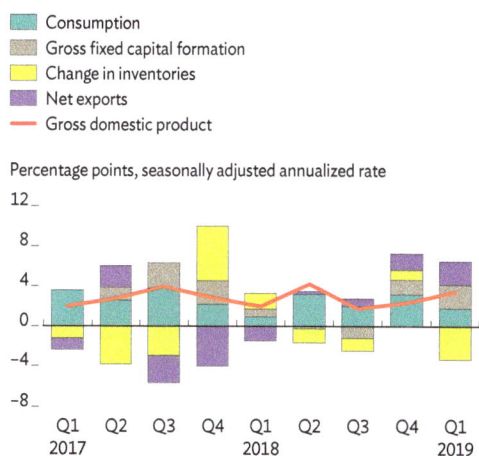

- Consumption
- Gross fixed capital formation
- Change in inventories
- Net exports
- Gross domestic product

Percentage points, seasonally adjusted annualized rate

Q = quarter.
Source: CEIC Data Company (accessed 30 July 2019).

which will affect investment. Other downside risks stem from weaker growth in Australia and the PRC. Upside risks are expansionary fiscal policies and the scrapping of the capital gains tax, which would improve the business climate. On 26 August, the Consensus Forecast was for GDP to grow by 2.4% in 2019 and 2.5% in 2020.

Russian Federation

Lackluster manufacturing and construction slowed GDP growth from 2.8% in Q4 of 2018 to 0.6% in Q1 of 2019 (Figure A1.13). Consumption contributed 1.1 percentage points to growth, and net exports 0.5 points. Gross capital formation subtracted 0.8 points.

Some economic indicators improved somewhat in Q2. Consumer confidence remained below the 0 threshold but improved slightly from –17 in Q1 of 2019 to –15. The industrial production index improved significantly from an average of 99 in Q1 to 105 in Q2. However, the Markit manufacturing PMI slipped from 51.8 in April to 49.8 in May, below the threshold of 50 indicating contraction, and further to 48.6 in June. Growth in retail trade turnover slipped from 7.5% in Q1 to 6.6% in Q2.

Average inflation more than doubled from 2.3% in the first half of 2018 to 5.1% in the same period of 2019, exceeding the 4.0% target set by the Central Bank of the Russian Federation. A value-added tax increase in January was one factor, and rising food prices another. Unemployment improved slightly from an average of 4.8% in the first 6 months of 2018 to 4.6% a year later. In response to moderating inflation and disappointing growth, the central bank cut its key policy rate to 7.25% on 29 July 2019.

Growth could suffer in the remainder of this year from weakening private consumption and an external slowdown, in particular lower oil exports. Growth is expected to improve subsequently in the short term on easier monetary policy. In the medium term, growth should further improve as a plan for national priority projects is implemented. On 27 August, the Consensus Forecast was for GDP to expand by 1.1% in 2019 and 1.9% in 2020.

Commodity prices

Oil price movements and prospects

Oil prices fluctuated significantly in the first 8 months of 2019. The price of Brent crude started quite low in January, at $52.82 per barrel, then jumped to $73.87 in late April before retreating to $59.20 at the end of August (Figure A1.14). The price decline largely reflected concerns about growth in global oil demand

Figure A1.13 Demand-side contributions to growth, Russian Federation

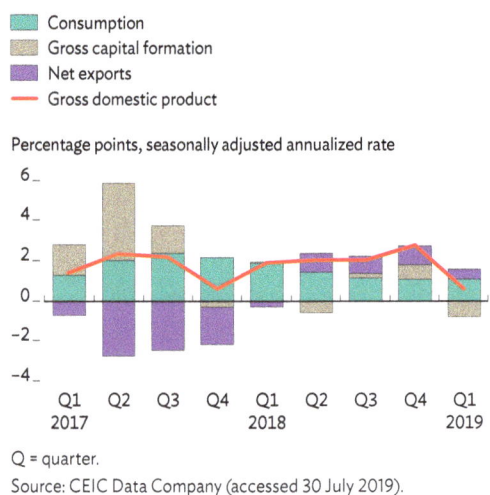

Q = quarter.
Source: CEIC Data Company (accessed 30 July 2019).

because of weakening global economic signals, such as the US manufacturing PMI, which in August hit its lowest since September 2009. Manufacturing PMI readings in the euro area, Japan, and the PRC were similarly low.

Oil demand remains weak, and healthy supply has held down prices. Global oil consumption in the first half of 2019 averaged 99.2 million barrels/day (mbd), while global oil supply averaged 100.1 mbd, generating a surplus of 0.9 mbd to add to already ample stocks built up in the second half of 2018. US crude oil production grew by 15.7% in the first 6 months of 2019 to average 12 mbd. Weak global demand and strong production in the US seem to have more than offset Saudi Arabian over-compliance with agreed volume cuts, as well as deep supply cuts in Azerbaijan, Mexico, and the Russian Federation.

The International Energy Agency forecasts that global oil demand should increase by 1.1 mbd in 2019 and 1.3 mbd in 2020. This forecast assumes that trade tensions will not worsen and further undermine global economic activity. On the supply side, the agency expects supply from outside the Organization of the Petroleum Exporting Countries (OPEC) to expand by 1.9 mbd in 2019 and 2.3 mbd in 2020, led by the US. The US Energy Information Agency forecasts US crude oil production to average 12.2 mbd in 2019 and 13.2 mbd in 2020. The supply outlook critically depends on OPEC and allied suppliers adhering to their agreement on 2 July 2019 to extend their existing supply curbs to the end of March 2020. Although compliance by OPEC members has been above 100% since March, non-OPEC compliance dropped from 169% in May to below 100% in June. Supply disruption remains a serious threat, as evidenced by a mid-September attack on Saudi Arabia's Abqaiq oil processing facility and its Khurais oil field. The attack interrupted an estimated 5.7 mbd of Saudi crude oil production, or more than 5% of global daily supply. The Brent crude spot price closed at $68.38/barrel 2 days later on 16 September, a $7.75 increase on the previous trading day and the largest 1-day change in more than a decade. Although prices have since retreated, the market now wrestles with additional uncertainty. Production is vulnerable as well in politically stressed countries like Libya, Nigeria, and Venezuela, and to oil shipments being cut off in the Strait of Hormuz.

Futures prices suggest that Brent crude will continue to trade at about $60/barrel for the next 2 years (Figure A1.15). This *Update* therefore revises the forecast for Brent crude to $65/barrel in 2019 and $63/barrel in 2020.

Figure A1.14 Price of Brent crude

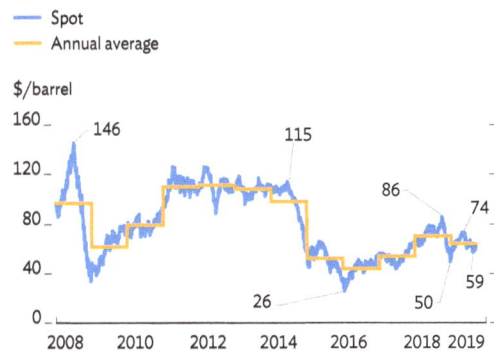

Sources: Bloomberg; World Bank. Commodity Price Data (Pink Sheet). http://www.worldbank.org (both accessed 2 September 2019).

Figure A1.15 Brent crude futures and spot prices

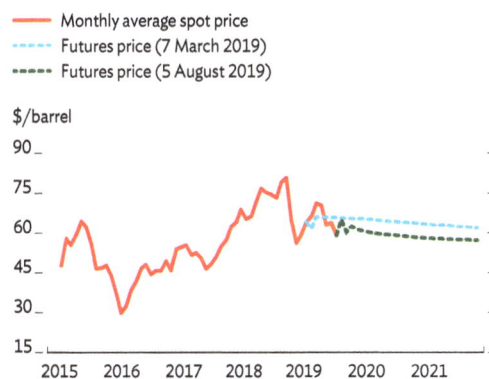

Sources: Bloomberg; World Bank. Commodity Price Data (Pink Sheet). http://www.worldbank.org (both accessed 6 August 2019).

Food price movements and prospects

Global food prices continued to weaken. The World Bank food price index averaged 84.74 in August 2019, 4.5% lower than in August 2018 (Figure A1.16). In the first 8 months of 2019, global food prices were 6.9% lower than in the same period of last year. All three World Bank price indexes fell.

Sluggish demand and abundant stocks weakened food prices. The price index for edible oil and meal fell by 13.9% from January–August 2018 to the same period in 2019 as higher prices for soybeans and soybean oil in June–August were not enough to offset earlier price drops for palm oil and soybean meal as sluggish demand left leading producers with bulging stocks. In the same period, the price index for "other food" fell by 4.2% year on year as a price recovery for sugar and beef in June and July reversed in August and was offset by a continued decline for poultry, which was in oversupply. Grain prices slid by 0.2%. Adverse weather pushed up maize prices in the first half of the year, but expectations of a maize harvest in the US much better than previously anticipated pushed them down sharply in August. While good supply prospects continue to push down wheat prices, rice prices edged up in August on concerns over drought in key producing areas in Thailand.

Improved weather forecasts look good for production in the near term. El Niño will wind down within the next couple of months, according to a US National Oceanic and Atmospheric Administration advisory in September. The US Department of Agriculture therefore projects in its September 2019 assessment a global grain production rise from an estimated 2,625.0 million tons in crop year 2018/2019 to 2,656.2 million tons in 2019/2020. Global supplies of wheat, maize, and rice are projected to increase by 1.1% in 2018/2019 and by an additional 0.5% in the next crop year. Similarly, the US Department of Agriculture forecasts global supplies of the 17 major edible oils to increase by 2.8% in 2018/2019 and then by 2.0%.

Although supply prospects for next year are promising, risks remain. According to the July 2019 Agricultural Market Information System Market Monitor of the Food and Agriculture Organization, the 2019/2020 season could be one of the most volatile in recent years. Factors highlighted by the report are trade disputes embroiling major market players, livestock disease outbreaks such as African swine fever, and uncertainty arising from extreme weather, such as recent heavy rains in some parts of the US that delayed maize and soybean planting. On balance, the food commodity price index is forecast to decline by 4.0% in 2019 before picking up by 1.5% in 2020.

Figure A1.16 Food commodity price indexes

— Food
— Edible oil
— Grain
— Other food

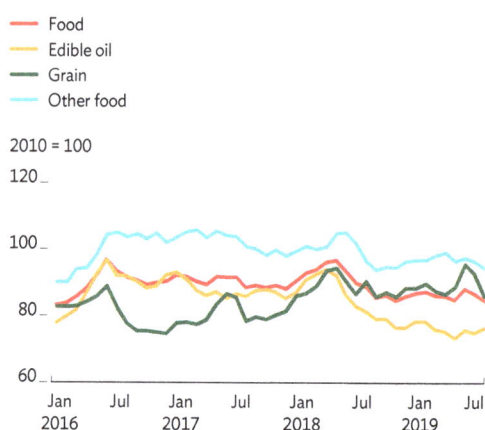

Source: World Bank. Commodity Price Data (Pink Sheet). http://www.worldbank.org (accessed 6 September 2019).

2

FOSTERING GROWTH AND INCLUSION IN ASIA'S CITIES

Fostering growth and inclusion in Asia's cities

Cities generate economic growth and good jobs. They are the locus of structural transformation and innovation, where more productive firms, better-paying jobs, and key institutions and amenities are located. They are where many goods and services can be produced most efficiently because, by concentrating workers and entrepreneurs, they enable gains in productivity through personal interaction and, thanks to economies of scale, they allow key infrastructure to be provided more economically.

Urbanization now under way in developing Asia thus portends well for regional economic prospects. Over the coming decades, the region's urban population is expected to grow from more than 1.8 billion people in 2017 to almost 3.0 billion in 2050, increasing the urban share of the population from 46% to 64%. Indeed, a number of Asian cities are distinguishing themselves as centers of innovation. More generally, the region's larger cities host many dynamic firms and generate better economic opportunities for workers, both skilled and less skilled.

The link between urbanization and economic dynamism is, however, not assured. Many of Asia's cities are sure to grow in size, but they may fail to fulfill their potential as engines of growth and job creation because of unsynchronized spatial and economic planning, a lack of affordable housing, significant air and water pollution, and deficits in key urban infrastructure, especially for transport and water supply and sanitation. Many cities are vulnerable to climate change and disaster risks such as flood surges stemming in part from rising sea levels (ADB 2018).

This chapter was written by Glenita Amoranto, Liming Chen, Eugenia Go, Rana Hasan, Matthias Helble, and Yi Jiang (lead) with research and technical support from Ann Jillian V. Adona, Ma. Adelle Gia Arbo, Patricia Thea Basilio, Renz Adrian Calub, Carlos Chua, Jed Francisco, Jade Laranjo, Marjorie Remolador, and Orlee Velarde. It draws on the background papers listed at the end of the chapter. Inputs from Stephane Bessadi, Kathleen Farrin, Emma Marsden, and Virinder Sharma are gratefully acknowledged. The chapter benefited from discussions with and advice from Gilles Duranton and Partha Mukhopadhyay. Other contributions are listed in the Acknowledgments section.

As populations concentrate in cities, they become natural platforms for efforts to ensure environmental sustainability and resilience. Moreover, access to high-quality education and health-care services has not kept pace with absolute growth in urban populations, undermining cities' ability to accumulate the human capital they need. Addressing these shortfalls requires integrated urban planning, as exemplified in the "livable cities" approach toward making cities inclusive, economically competitive, and environmentally sustainable in terms of their carbon footprint and resilience (AfDB et al., forthcoming; ADB 2019).

This chapter asks how Asia can ensure that its cities play their role as engines of growth and meet their promise as creators of productive employment. It examines this question through the lens of the city as a labor market. To be sure, cities are much more than places of work. However, they cannot thrive unless they function well for enterprises and workers. And, because cities are not isolated islands but rather connected to other localities, this chapter considers urbanization issues from a systems perspective.

The chapter first documents how developing Asia has been urbanizing, detailing the benefits and challenges that have accompanied urbanization from the perspective of cities as engines of growth and job creation. Charting the past is the first step in mapping the way forward.

To document how urbanization is evolving, the chapter uses both official statistics and a new database constructed at the city level using satellite imagery and gridded population data. The new database allows analysis of urbanization patterns using a common definition of urban spaces across countries and over time. It also allows urbanization to be defined in a way that captures the urbanization process beyond formal city limits. The resulting data highlight how cities expand without regard for administrative boundaries and how clusters of cities in close proximity form larger conurbations. Both of these features of current urbanization highlight the need for more metropolitan forms of urban planning and governance.

Analyzing data on enterprises and workers at the city level allows research to confirm, reassuringly, that many of Asia's larger cities do indeed act as engines of growth and centers of innovation. Moreover, larger cities are found to offer better employment outcomes, including for women and the less educated. However, the flip side is that medium-sized and smaller cities—home to 62% of the urban population—may need more attention. In particular, good infrastructure and other elements of a conducive business environment fall short in such cities, and this deficiency may well dampen the potential for reaping the benefits of agglomeration.

For developing Asia's cities to work for all, travel within them must be fast and cheap, firms and households must have the flexibility to relocate from one part of the city to another, and real estate must be affordable (Bertaud 2018). The chapter thus calls for urban public transport systems with significantly improved coverage, efficiency, and affordability; the provision of essential infrastructure such as planned road networks accompanying or even leading urban expansion; and land-use plans and regulations that ensure environmental sustainability yet are sufficiently flexible to respond to market signals. Measures to promote affordable housing are also proposed.

Policy concerns extend beyond the individual city. Cities are connected to one another and to their rural hinterlands through flows of goods, services, and people. This has several implications for policy, a key one being the need to better coordinate spatial and economic planning—not just at the city level, but also for city clusters and entire subnational regions. Further, robust and inclusive economic growth nationally depends not just on one or two large cities, or for that matter on just the urban sector. It requires vibrancy in all types of cities, including midsized ones and smaller market towns that specialize in marketing and distributing agricultural produce, as well as in rural areas.

While rural issues are outside the focus of this chapter, it is worth noting that cities cannot thrive without support from a dynamic rural economy. Productive and stable agriculture, the backbone of the rural economy, is crucial to ensuring food security in cities. It also generates business for cities, as rural incomes driven higher by rising agricultural productivity strengthen markets for the modern goods and services cities produce. Further, as agriculture modernizes in developing countries, rural areas release workers who can be employed in cities. And, as higher rural incomes raise the wage floor for workers in cities, they provide the basis for better living and working conditions for low-income workers in cities. Further, when cities suffer economic downturns, a vibrant rural sector is a safety net to which urban workers can temporarily return.

2.1 Urbanization in developing Asia

A good starting point for understanding patterns and trends in urbanization is the United Nation's World Urbanization Prospects dataset, which allows urbanization in over 200 countries and territories to be traced back 50 years and compared across regions and by development status. In addition, the dataset projects future urbanization to 2050.

2.1.1 Status and trends

According to World Urbanization Prospects data, the number of urban inhabitants in developing Asia has increased almost fivefold since 1970, from 375 million to 1.84 billion in 2017. The region led the global increase in urban population from 1970 to 2017, accounting for 53% of it. Two-thirds of the nearly 1.5 billion additional city dwellers in developing Asia live in the two most populous countries in the world: the People's Republic of China (PRC) and India (Figure 2.1.1).

Developing Asia outpaced the rest of world not only in terms of absolute growth in urban population but also by growth rate. Urban population in the region increased at an average of 3.4% per annum from 1970 to 2017, well above 2.6% in the rest of the developing world, mainly Africa and Latin America, and 1.0% in the developed economies. Within the region, East Asia had the highest annual growth rate, at 3.7%, followed by 3.6% in Southeast Asia and 3.3% in South Asia. The Pacific experienced 2.9% annual growth in urban population, and Central Asia 1.6% (Figure 2.1.2).

Figure 2.1.1 Urban population

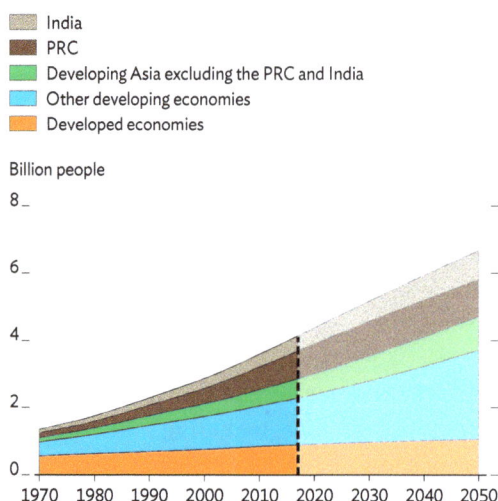

PRC = People's Republic of China.

Note: Developed economies include Australia, Austria, Belgium, Canada, Denmark, Finland, France, Germany, Greece, Iceland, Ireland, Italy, Japan, Liechtenstein, Luxembourg, the Netherlands, New Zealand, Norway, Portugal, Spain, Sweden, Switzerland, the United Kingdom, and the United States. Developing Asia includes the developing member economies of ADB. Other developing economies include economies other than the developed economies and developing Asia.

Source: ADB estimates using data from United Nations' 2018 Revision of World Urbanization Prospects (accessed 5 April 2019).

Figure 2.1.2 Average annual urban population growth rates, 1970–2017

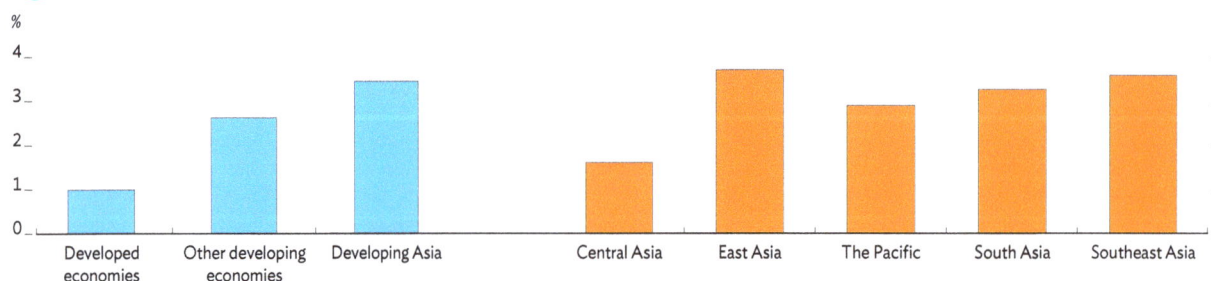

Note: Developed economies include Australia, Austria, Belgium, Canada, Denmark, Finland, France, Germany, Greece, Iceland, Ireland, Italy, Japan, Liechtenstein, Luxembourg, the Netherlands, New Zealand, Norway, Portugal, Spain, Sweden, Switzerland, the United Kingdom, and the United States. Developing Asia includes the developing member economies of ADB. Other developing economies include economies other than the developed economies and developing Asia.

Source: ADB estimates using data from United Nations' 2018 Revision of World Urbanization Prospects (accessed 5 April 2019).

Figure 2.1.3 Urbanization rates

- 1970
- 2017
- 2050

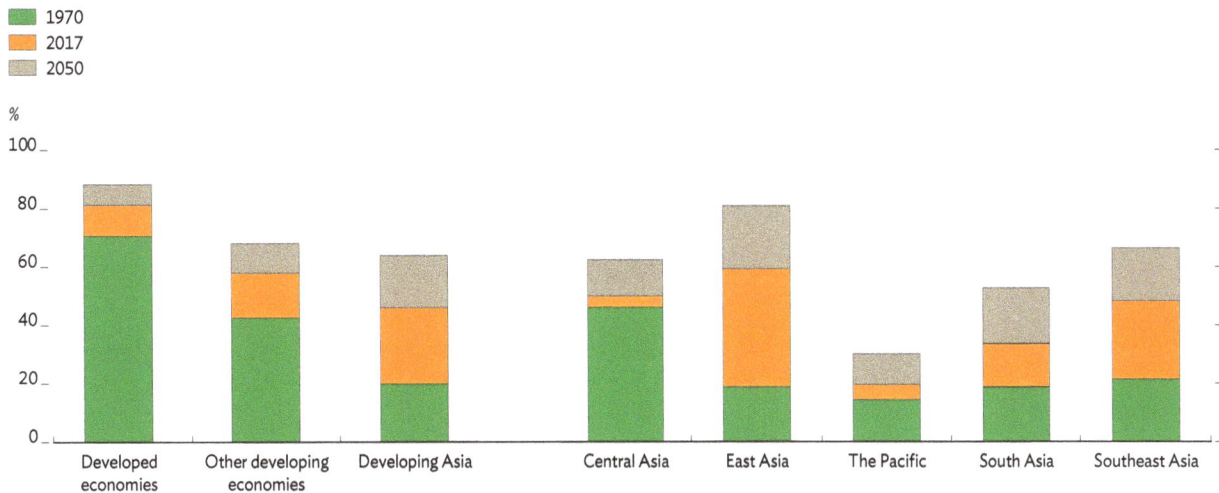

Note: Developed economies include Australia, Austria, Belgium, Canada, Denmark, Finland, France, Germany, Greece, Iceland, Ireland, Italy, Japan, Liechtenstein, Luxembourg, the Netherlands, New Zealand, Norway, Portugal, Spain, Sweden, Switzerland, the United Kingdom, and the United States. Developing Asia includes the developing member economies of ADB. Other developing economies include economies other than the developed economies and developing Asia.

Source: ADB estimates using data from United Nations' 2018 Revision of World Urbanization Prospects (accessed 5 April 2019).

Notwithstanding fast growth in urban population, developing Asia's urbanization rate still lagged at 46% in 2017. The United States achieved this rate in the early 1900s, and Japan in the early 1950s. Developing Asia's urbanization rate in 2017 was lower than the 58% average in other developing economies and the 81% average in the developed economies (Figure 2.1.3).

Asia and the Pacific show considerable heterogeneity in urbanization over the past 5 decades. East Asia had 59% of its population residing in urban areas in 2017, up from 19% in 1970. Southeast Asia has gone from 22% urban to 48%. Urbanization in South Asia has been more moderate, rising from 19% in 1970 to 34% in 2017. Urbanization has been more limited in the other two subregions. In the Pacific, the urban share rose from 14% in 1970 to only 20% in 2017. In Central Asia, urbanization was already high at 46% in 1970 and increased only marginally to reach 50% by 2017.

Relatively low urbanization rates across Asia and the Pacific as a whole suggest enormous potential for the region to further urbanize. As of 2017, there were 2.2 billion people living in rural areas in developing Asia. Regional urbanization will progress considerably if cities continue to attract large numbers of rural residents on top of natural growth in urban population. The United Nations thus projects that the urban population in developing Asia will increase by more than 1.1 billion to reach about 3.0 billion in 2050. By that time, the urbanization rate in the region will be 64%, or closer to the average of 68% expected in other developing economies worldwide.

Figure 2.1.4 GDP per capita versus urbanization rates

○ Rest of the world   ● Developing Asia
── World   ---- Developing Asia

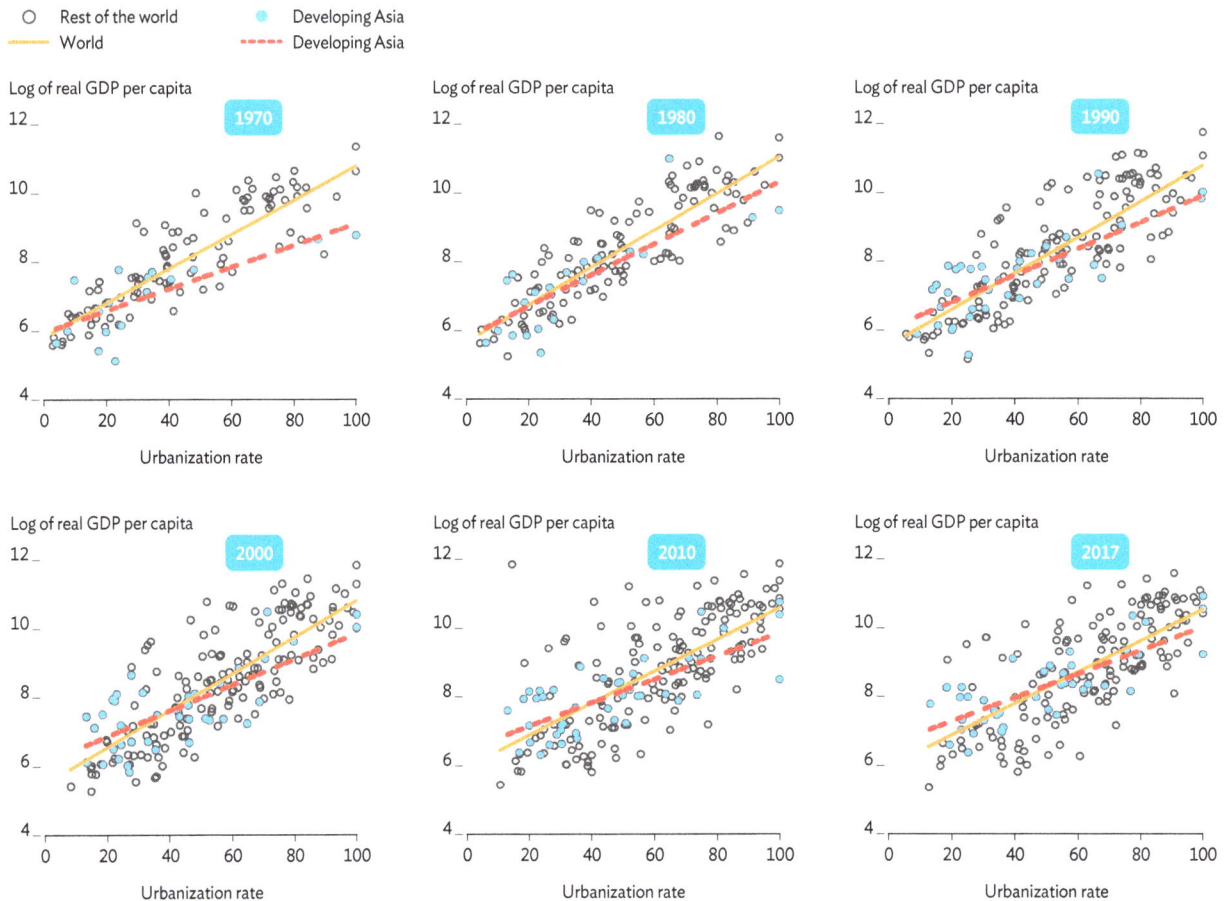

Source: ADB estimates using data from United Nations' 2018 Revision of World Urbanization Prospects (accessed 5 April 2019) and World Bank's World Development Indicators (accessed 27 May 2019).

Urbanization and economic growth

One of the most widely recognized facts in economic development is that urbanization strongly correlates with income. Whereas the developed economies of East Asia, Europe, and North America are all highly urban, low-income economies generally have a large share of their population residing in rural areas. Figure 2.1.4 shows this positive relationship between urbanization and real GDP per capita for the world as a whole and in developing Asia in particular at the turn of every decade since 1970. The estimated slopes of the fitted lines range from 4.6 to 5.4 for the world and from 3.1 to 4.5 for developing Asia, indicating that 1 percentage point increase in urbanization is associated with 3%–5% higher real GDP per capita.

It is commonly observed as well that countries undergoing robust economic growth experience rapid urbanization at the same time. Taking this more dynamic perspective, we examine the relationship between the growth rate of real GDP per capita and change in urbanization rate increase at 5-year intervals from 1970 and 2015 (Figure 2.1.5). Again, positive correlation appears between these variables across the world and specifically in developing Asia, the estimated coefficients being 1.0 and 3.2, respectively, both statistically significant at 1%.

While it is straightforward to show that economic growth and urbanization go hand-in-hand, it is more challenging to establish a causal link between them. Most likely, urbanization and growth are "mutually self-reinforcing processes" (Martin and Ottaviano 1999) with causality running both ways. Much of the theoretical literature has emphasized, on the one hand, that processes related to learning, or knowledge spillover, that occur within cities play critical roles in their becoming engines of growth (e.g., Jacobs 1969, Duranton and Puga 2004, Rossi-Hansberg and Wright 2007). On the other hand, the consequent accumulation of human capital among urban workers raises workers' net income, attracting more people to cities. However, Williamson (1965) and Bertinelli and Black (2004) suggested that agglomeration could be beneficial to economic growth mainly at early stages of development. That is because human capital accumulation is faster when occurring with urbanization, and gains that are larger at the initial stages of development outweigh the costs of congestion. Once an economy reaches a certain income level, the benefits of agglomeration decrease while the relative impact of congestion increases. The benefits urbanization confer on growth thus diminish.

While estimating the causal effects of urbanization on economic growth is beyond the scope of this chapter, it is noteworthy that a study by Brülhart and Sbergami (2009) obtained evidence that supported the Williamson (1965) hypothesis above. The study assembled a panel dataset of 105 countries from 1960 to 2000. Controlling for a rich set of variables cited in the literature as related to growth, and applying sophisticated econometric methods, it found that agglomeration, measured by urbanization rate or spatial concentration indexes, boosted GDP growth up to a certain stage of economic development. That stage was estimated at around $10,000 per capita in 2006 prices, suggesting that policies promoting urbanization would still be conducive to growth in most countries of developing Asia.

2.1.2 Natural cities based on nighttime lights

World Urbanization Prospects data are based on official statistics of urban areas of each country. However, there are many different ways of defining and distinguishing urban settlements from rural areas. For instance, India requires a human settlement to meet three criteria before it can be officially counted as city: a population of at least 5,000, a minimum density of 400 residents per square kilometer,

Figure 2.1.5 Five-year changes in GDP per capita versus change in urbanization, 1970–2017

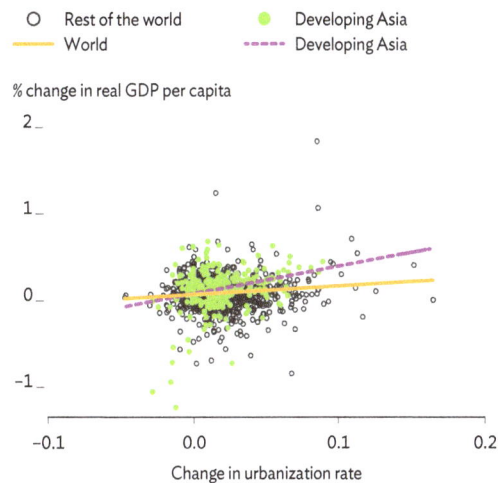

Source: ADB estimates using data from United Nations' 2018 Revision of World Urbanization Prospects (accessed 5 April 2019) and World Bank's World Development Indicators (accessed 27 May 2019).

and at least 75% of male full-time workers employed outside
of agriculture. Just across the Gulf of Mannar, Sri Lanka uses
a purely administrative definition, defining cities as areas
administered by municipal and urban councils.

More generally, four types of criteria typically define
urban areas: administrative boundaries, economic parameters,
population size and/or density, and other urban characteristics
(United Nations 2018a). With various combinations of these
criteria, at least 13 ways are known to define urban areas
among the 233 economies in the world. Administrative
designations are the sole criteria for defining a city in
59 economies, and another 62 combine an administrative
criterion with other criteria to distinguish between urban and
rural areas. Taking into account different numeric thresholds
used to apply these criteria, the number of city definitions
reaches much higher than 13.

A lack of consistency bedevils urban statistics, such as
between the population reported and the definition of
the urban area. Most governments count their urban
populations only for the city as defined by its administrative
boundaries, whatever criteria they use to define urban areas
(United Nations 2018a). Others count residents in the
contiguous suburban areas of a city proper, and still others
include people living far from the city center but connected
through transport networks. A comparable city dataset would
improve understanding of how urbanization has evolved across
developing Asia.

The desired dataset should have a common and consistent
definition of "city" across countries and measure urban
characteristics that coincide with the definition. For this study,
we developed such a dataset using nighttime light (NTL)
satellite imagery available since 1992. Satellite imagery that
has captured the NTL of human settlements was introduced
into economic research by Henderson, Storeygard, and
Weil (2012). Thereafter, the data has been creatively applied
to study important economic issues such as how national
institutions affect subnational development (Michalopoulos
and Papaioannou 2014) and the relationship between intercity
transport costs and cities' economic activity (Storeygard 2016).

We used the imagery to delineate the contours of urban
agglomerations, called "natural cities" to distinguish them
from administratively defined cities, with each contour
subsequently filled with grid population data from LandScan.
With this methodology, the geographic extent and population
size of the natural cities are consistently defined and estimated
across space and time. In the end, a geocoded panel dataset
thus created contains 1,459 natural cities in 42 economies
of developing Asia from 1992 to 2016, with population data
available from 2000. Box 2.1.1 provides more details on the
development of the dataset.

Box 2.1.1 Developing a natural city dataset with nighttime light and LandScan data

Developing the natural city dataset involved three main steps as outlined here. For more technical details, see Jiang (forthcoming). First, human settlements were delineated with nighttime light (NTL) satellite imagery, the raw NTL data for 1992–2016 obtained from the National Oceanic and Atmospheric Administration website. The data give until 2013 a luminosity measure for every latitude–longitude grid measuring approximately 0.86 square kilometers (km^2) at the Equator, and after 2013 the pixel resolution improved to about 0.22 km^2. Especially before 2013, "blooming" or "overglowing" issues were caused by relatively coarse spatial resolution, large overlap in the footprints of adjacent pixels, and/or the accumulation of geolocation errors in the compositing process (Small, Pozzi, and Elvidge 2005), making the boundaries of the illuminated areas appear blurry. See the left panel of the box figure for an illustration of the Metro Manila area in the Philippines in 1992.

We adopted the latest methodology developed in Abrahams, Oram, and Lozano-Garcia (2018) to deblur the imagery. After deblurring, we delineated polygons consisting of pixels with positive luminosity values as human settlements. We then aggregated the polygons with a 1-pixel gap between them into one polygon to allow for measurement errors as well as unlit areas such as wide roads within an integrated human settlement. The exercise yielded 88,000–187,000 geocoded polygons in developing Asia in various years. The middle panel in the box figure shows these polygons in the Metro Manila area.

Most of the polygons thus obtained were very small and discrete, likely representing rural settlements. The second step was to identify urban areas in the human settlements, for which we referred to a database generated by the Global Rural–Urban Mapping Project (GRUMP). This database contains the geocoded centers, names, and populations of over 70,000 human settlements around the world, as well as information about their upper administrative divisions. We focused on about 1,700 GRUMP units in developing Asia that had populations greater than 100,000 in 2000, and identified more than 1,300 NTL-based polygons that either covered these units or turned out to be the most relevant ones near the units, as revealed by visual checking. These polygons were treated as natural cities and named after their corresponding GRUMP units or else the unit with the largest population if a natural city contained multiple units.

To maximize country coverage and include large cities that were missing in the GRUMP database, we added to the data 115 polygons that were either related to major cities in small countries (mostly in the Pacific) or had an area greater than 100 km^2 in 2000 despite the associated GRUMP units having a small 2000 population. We reached a final set of 1,459 natural cities. As shown in the right panel of the box figure, there were nine natural cities in the Metro Manila area: Angeles, Batangas, Lipa, Lucena, Metro Manila, Olongapo, San Pablo, San Pedro, and Tarlac. The largest one, Metro Manila, contained 29 GRUMP units: Makati, Manila, Quezon, etc.

Natural cities extracted from nighttime lights of the Metro Manila area in the Philippines, 1992

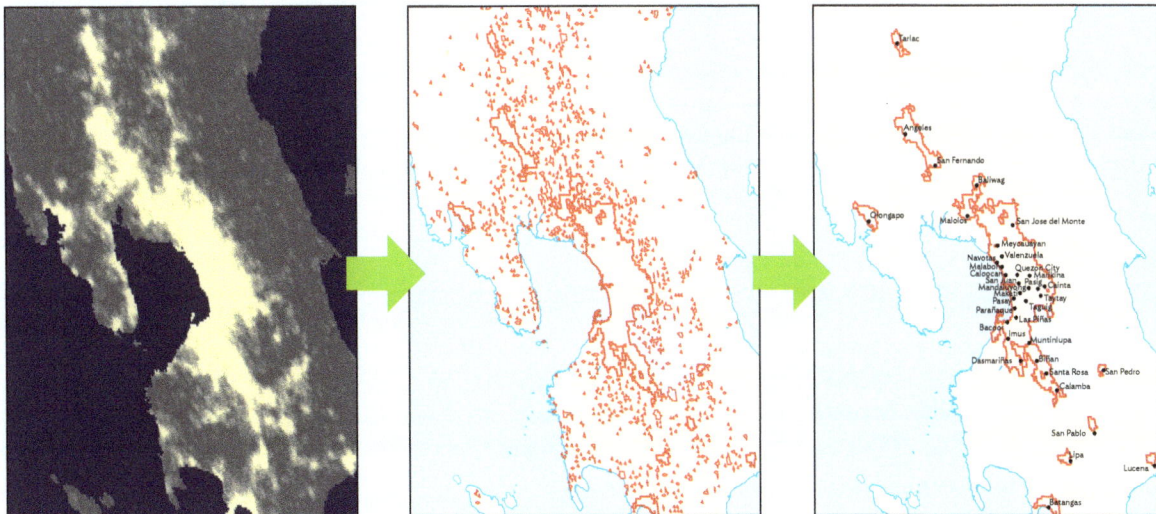

Raw nighttime lights image.

This map was produced by the cartography unit of the Asian Development Bank. The boundaries, colors, denominations, and any other information shown on this map do not imply, on the part of the Asian Development Bank, any judgment on the legal status of any territory, or any endorsement or acceptance of such boundaries, colors, denominations, or information.

Source: ADB estimates using nighttime lights images from the National Oceanic and Atmospheric Administration (accessed 1 April 2017 and 10 August 2018).

continued next page

Box 2.1.1 *Continued*

Some natural cities expanded and connected up over time. To maintain individual natural cities as primary units for analysis, we separated connected ones where luminosity was lowest to obtain the footprint of each. Though thus segregated, the connected natural cities were deemed to be city clusters and studied in detail (later in this section and section 2.3).

The third step was to estimate the populations of natural cities. We filled the delineated areas of the natural cities with grid population data from LandScan. LandScan provides global population counts at a spatial resolution of about 1 km^2, which are generated through spatial modeling and image analysis with inputs from census data, high-resolution imagery, land cover, and other spatial data such as various boundaries, coastlines, elevations, and slopes. We overlaid the natural city polygons with the grid population data. The population of a natural city is the sum of all cells falling within or interacting with the city contour. Note that a natural city's population could still be below 100,000, as the GRUMP population, often sourced from official statistics, might be for a very different urban scope.

References:

Abrahams, A., C. Oram, and N. Lozano-Gracia. 2018. Deblurring DMSP Nighttime Lights: A New Method Using Gaussian Filters and Frequencies of Illumination. *Remote Sensing of Environment* 210.

Jiang, Y. Forthcoming. Asian Cities: Spatial Dynamics and Driving Forces. *ADB Economics Working Paper Series*. Asian Development Bank.

Small, C., F. Pozzi, and C. D. Elvidge. 2005. Spatial Analysis of Global Urban Extent from DMSP-OLS Night Lights. *Remote Sensing of Environment* 96(3).

Figure 2.1.6 shows the distribution of the 1,459 natural cities across 42 economies in developing Asia. Those with large populations were home to more natural cities. The PRC had 680 natural cities, India 320, Indonesia 93, and Pakistan 63. Together, these four countries contained four-fifths of the natural cities in developing Asia.

The data suggest that the total area of the natural cities expanded more than threefold, from 170,000 kilometers (km^2) in 1992 to 560,000 km^2 in 2016, for an average annual growth rate of 5.1%. The number of natural city inhabitants increased from 0.82 billion in 2000 to 1.38 billion in 2016, for an average annual growth rate of 3.3%. In 2016, the total land area of the 42 economies studied was 24.8 million km^2 and the total population was 4.0 billion. Hence, natural cities hosted 34.7% of the population of developing Asia on only 2.3% of the land area.[1]

Evolution of city size

Most developing economies are in the middle of the urbanization process. Examining how cities of different size have evolved reveals the characteristics of ongoing urbanization and the direction toward which urbanization is heading in the region.

Figure 2.1.7 shows changes in the distribution of city size by area from 1992 to 2016 and by population from 2000 to 2016 in the 42 developing economies of Asia and the Pacific. Both distributions of city size, in terms of physical land area and population, shifted to the right considerably.

Figure 2.1.6 Number of natural cities by country

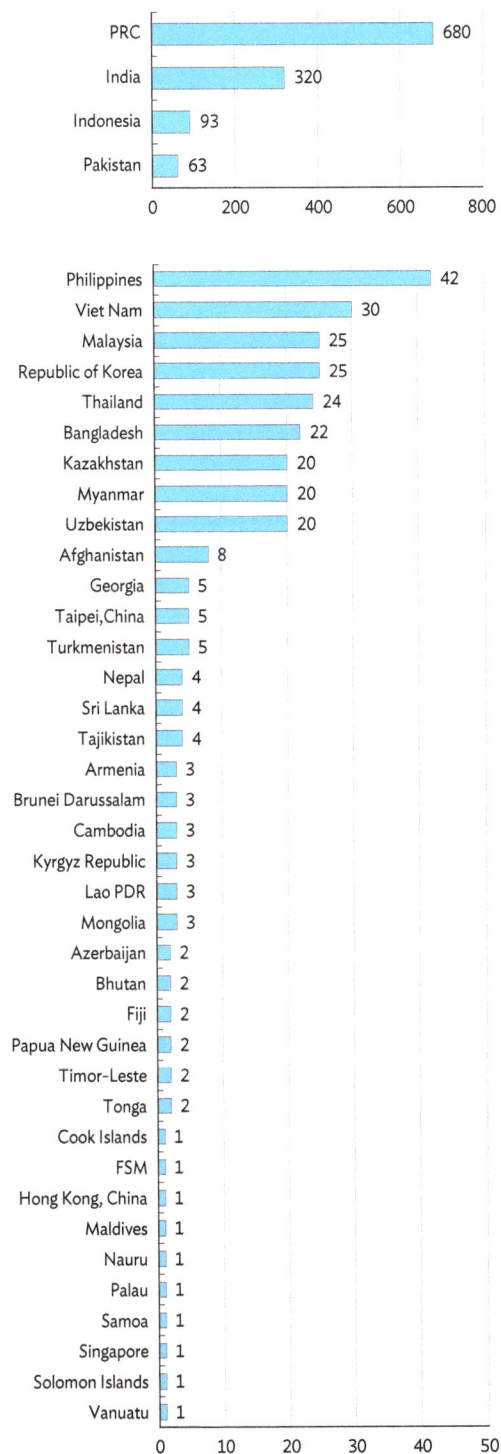

PRC	680
India	320
Indonesia	93
Pakistan	63

Philippines	42
Viet Nam	30
Malaysia	25
Republic of Korea	25
Thailand	24
Bangladesh	22
Kazakhstan	20
Myanmar	20
Uzbekistan	20
Afghanistan	8
Georgia	5
Taipei,China	5
Turkmenistan	5
Nepal	4
Sri Lanka	4
Tajikistan	4
Armenia	3
Brunei Darussalam	3
Cambodia	3
Kyrgyz Republic	3
Lao PDR	3
Mongolia	3
Azerbaijan	2
Bhutan	2
Fiji	2
Papua New Guinea	2
Timor-Leste	2
Tonga	2
Cook Islands	1
FSM	1
Hong Kong, China	1
Maldives	1
Nauru	1
Palau	1
Samoa	1
Singapore	1
Solomon Islands	1
Vanuatu	1

FSM = Federated States of Micronesia, Lao PDR = Lao People's Democratic Republic, PRC = People's Republic of China.

Source: ADB estimates using nighttime lights images from the National Oceanic and Atmospheric Administration (accessed 1 April 2017 and 10 August 2018) and grid population data from LandScan Datasets of the Oak Ridge National Laboratory (accessed 31 August 2017 and 31 August 2018).

Figure 2.1.7 Distribution of natural city size

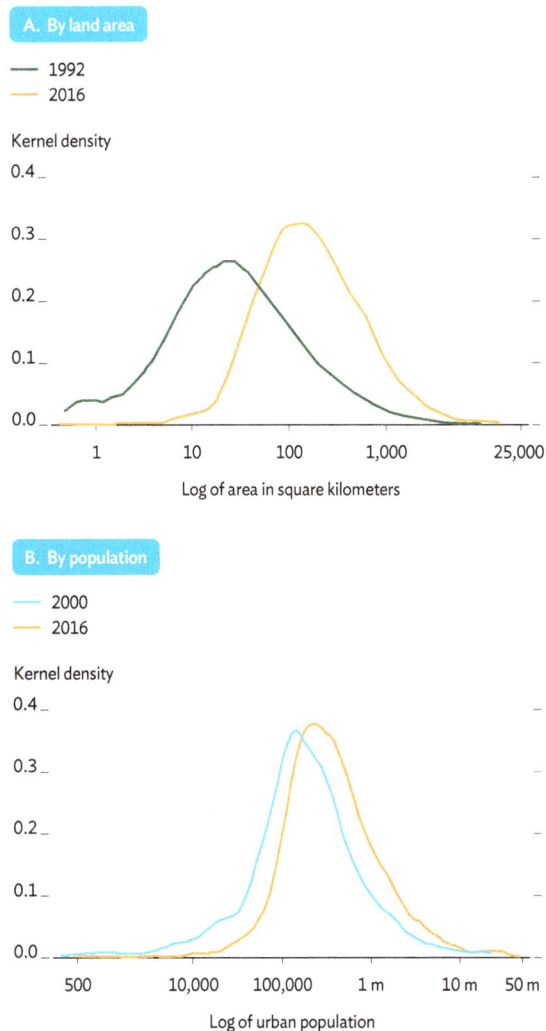

A. By land area

1992 / 2016
Kernel density; Log of area in square kilometers

B. By population

2000 / 2016
Kernel density; Log of urban population

m = million.

Source: ADB estimates using nighttime lights images from the National Oceanic and Atmospheric Administration (accessed 1 April 2017 and 10 August 2018) and grid population data from LandScan Datasets of the Oak Ridge National Laboratory (accessed 31 August 2017 and 31 August 2018).

The average area of a natural city increased from 116 km² in 1992 to 384 km² in 2016, for a 5.1% average increase per annum. Looking at the median, it increased from 26 km² in 1992 to 156 km² in 2016, for a 7.8% average increase per annum. The average population of a natural city rose from 562,000 to 944,000, or by 3.3% per year, and the median population rose from 178,000 to 327,000, or by 3.9% per year.

A question of interest is how cities of different initial size have grown. To answer the question, we divided the natural cities into six size categories based on their population in 2000 and examined population growth in each category (Figure 2.1.8). The data indicated that the growth rate decreased as city size grew except in the largest category. The population in the smallest city category grew by 121% from 2000 to 2016, substantially faster than the other categories. The largest category grew by 45%, slower than other categories except the next largest, which grew by 32%.

Nevertheless, the growth rates discussed above do not link directly with increase in the absolute size of different cities. Smaller cities have grown faster perhaps because they had a smaller population base. Figure 2.1.9 shows how the increase in urban population is distributed across different city sizes. Cities with populations in the range of 100,000–500,000 and of 1 million–5 million have each accommodated nearly 150 million additional urban inhabitants across the region since 2000. Next to them, megacities with populations above 10 million have attracted more than 110 million new inhabitants. This pattern of urban population increase across city size also holds for the subregions East Asia, South Asia, and Southeast Asia with their full spectrum of city sizes.

Figure 2.1.10 offers another perspective on the relative importance of cities of different size. In 2000, cities with populations above 1 million accounted for 64% of the total urban population in developing Asia. This share rose to 72% in 2016. This significant increase derives from both population growth in the bigger cities, as shown above, and from many cities moving up the city size ladder (a city that grew from 800,000 inhabitants in 2000 to 1,100,000 in 2016, for example, would have moved from the 0.5 million–1.0 million category to the 1.0 million– 5.0 million category). This climb up the ladder is exemplified by the increase in the number of larger cities from 2000 to 2016. The group with 1 million–5 million inhabitants grew from 124 to 230 across the region, while the one with 5 million–10 million grew from 12 to 22 and the one with more than 10 million grew from 12 to 17.

The enlarged share of the urban population residing in cities above 1 million is observed consistently across subregions. One notable difference between subregions is,

Figure 2.1.8 Urban population growth by size of natural city, 2000–2016

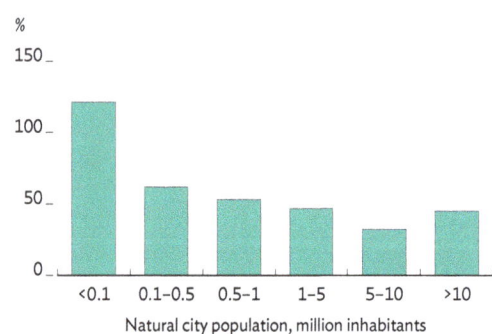

Source: ADB estimates using nighttime lights images from the National Oceanic and Atmospheric Administration (accessed 1 April 2017 and 10 August 2018) and grid population data from LandScan Datasets of the Oak Ridge National Laboratory (accessed 31 August 2017 and 31 August 2018).

Figure 2.1.9 Increase in urban population from 2000 to 2016 by size of natural city

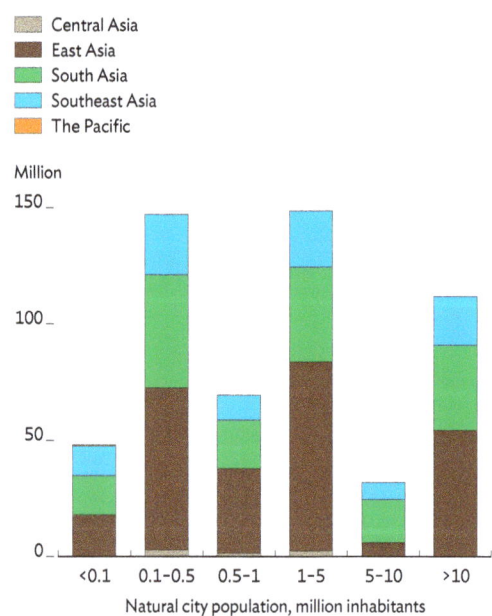

Source: ADB estimates using nighttime lights images from the National Oceanic and Atmospheric Administration (accessed 1 April 2017 and 10 August 2018) and grid population data from LandScan Datasets of the Oak Ridge National Laboratory (accessed 31 August 2017 and 31 August 2018).

Figure 2.1.10 Share of urban population by city sizes

Less than 0.1 m ▮ 0.1–0.5 m ▮ 0.5–1 m ▮ 1–5 m ▮ 5–10 m ▮ 10 m and above

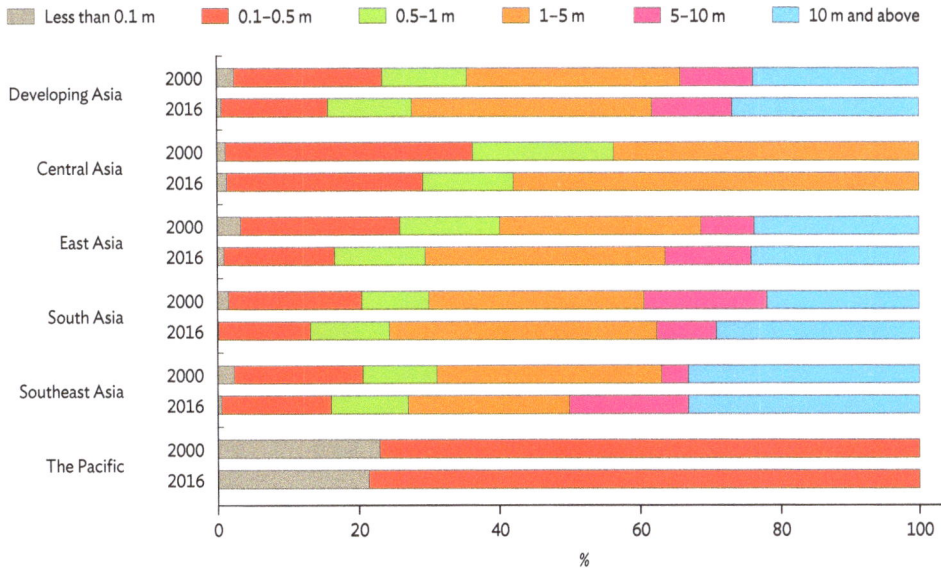

m = million.

Source: ADB estimates using nighttime lights images from the National Oceanic and Atmospheric Administration (accessed 1 April 2017 and 10 August 2018) and grid population data from LandScan Datasets of the Oak Ridge National Laboratory (accessed 31 August 2017 and 31 August 2018).

however, that in Southeast Asia the population share of cities with 5 million–10 million has increased substantially, from 4% to 17%, and the share of cities with 1 million–5 million has decreased from 32% to 23%, while in South Asia the share of the former has dropped from 17% to 8% as that of the latter increased from 30% to 38%.

Urban expansion beyond administrative boundaries

Natural cities according to NTL data often do not match the administrative divisions that demarcate and define cities and towns in different countries. For instance, prefectures and counties in the PRC are the main administrative units corresponding to cities. However, a prefecture can contain one or several urban areas as well as extensive rural areas. Most counties in the PRC also encompass an urban center and vast rural areas. In India, a natural city as identified through our NTL analysis can cover several adjacent administratively defined towns but also be much smaller than a district. Moreover, NTL-based actual cities appear to be more spatially dynamic than their corresponding administrative boundaries. With population increase, cities expand geographically every month, if not every day, while in most countries the boundaries of their administrative counterparts are fixed for many years.

Figure 2.1.11 illustrates how the footprint of each of the five selected natural cities has evolved since 1992. Table 2.1.1 provides their area, population, and administrative division and shows how these statistics align with administrative boundaries.

Figure 2.1.11 Spatial development of selected natural cities

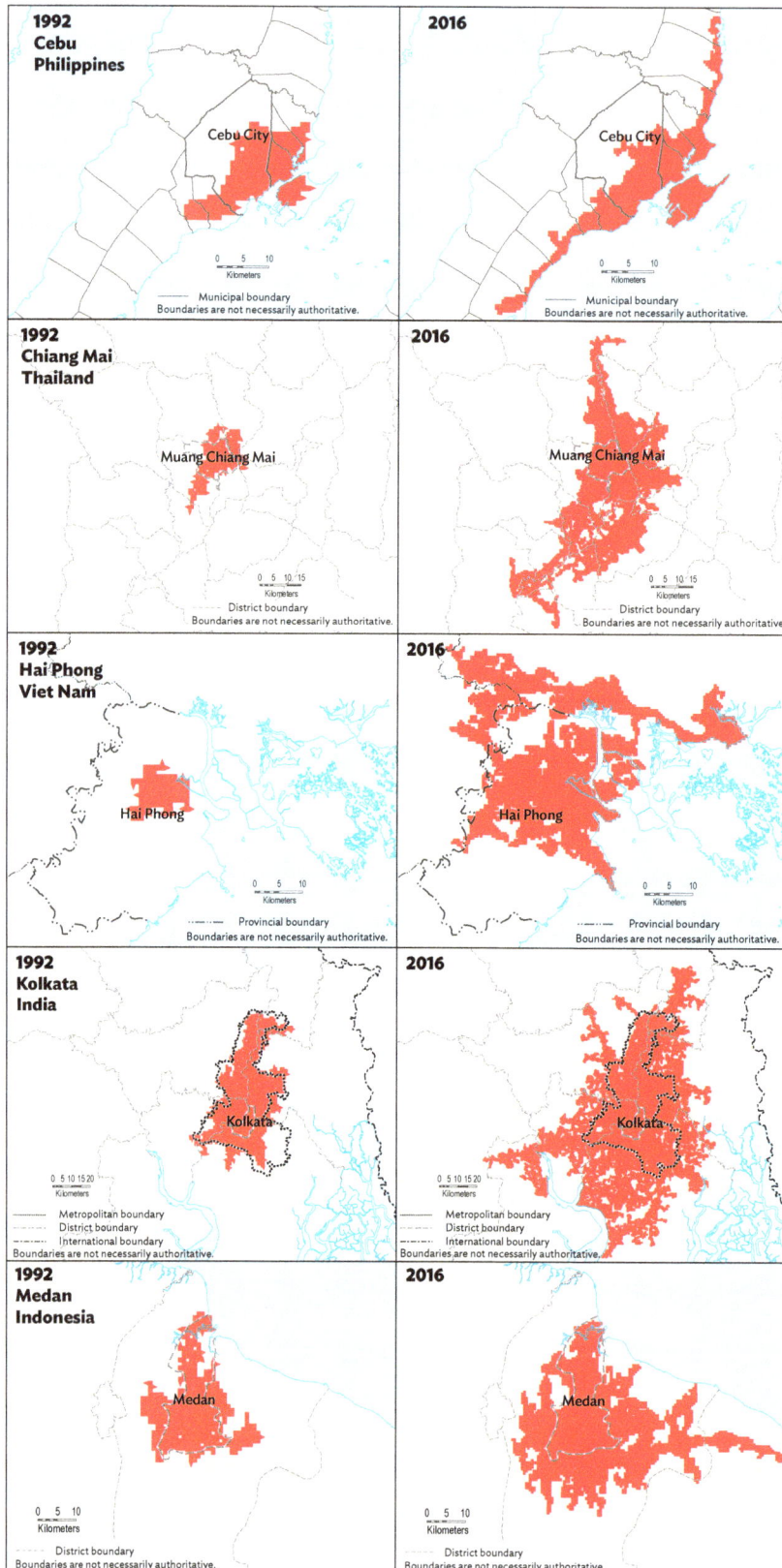

1992 Cebu Philippines — Cebu City; 0 5 10 Kilometers; Municipal boundary; Boundaries are not necessarily authoritative.	**2016** — Cebu City; 0 5 10 Kilometers; Municipal boundary; Boundaries are not necessarily authoritative.
1992 Chiang Mai Thailand — Muang Chiang Mai; 0 5 10 15 Kilometers; District boundary; Boundaries are not necessarily authoritative.	**2016** — Muang Chiang Mai; 0 5 10 15 Kilometers; District boundary; Boundaries are not necessarily authoritative.
1992 Hai Phong Viet Nam — Hai Phong; 0 5 10 Kilometers; Provincial boundary; Boundaries are not necessarily authoritative.	**2016** — Hai Phong; 0 5 10 Kilometers; Provincial boundary; Boundaries are not necessarily authoritative.
1992 Kolkata India — Kolkata; 0 5 10 15 20 Kilometers; Metropolitan boundary; District boundary; International boundary; Boundaries are not necessarily authoritative.	**2016** — Kolkata; 0 5 10 15 20 Kilometers; Metropolitan boundary; District boundary; International boundary; Boundaries are not necessarily authoritative.
1992 Medan Indonesia — Medan; 0 5 10 Kilometers; District boundary; Boundaries are not necessarily authoritative.	**2016** — Medan; 0 5 10 Kilometers; District boundary; Boundaries are not necessarily authoritative.

This map was produced by the cartography unit of the Asian Development Bank. The boundaries, colors, denominations, and any other information shown on this map do not imply, on the part of the Asian Development Bank, any judgment on the legal status of any territory, or any endorsement or acceptance of such boundaries, colors, denominations, or information.

Source: ADB estimates using nighttime lights images from the National Oceanic and Atmospheric Administration (accessed 1 April 2017 and 10 August 2018).

Table 2.1.1 Natural cities versus their administrative counterparts

Natural city	Cebu	Chiang Mai	Hai Phong	Kolkata	Medan
Country	Philippines	Thailand	Viet Nam	India	Indonesia
Area (km², 2016)	357	1412	918	4,581	882
Area growth (%, 1992–2016)	58.3	552.5	930.8	198.5	106.4
Population (million, 2016)	2.80	1.15	1.82	23.97	4.59
Number of same-level administrative divisions covered	14 (cities and municipalities)	17 (districts)	3 (provinces and city)	7 (districts)	4 (cities and regencies)
Number of top-level administrative divisions involved, 2016	1 (province)	2 (provinces)	3 (provinces)	1 (state)	1 (province)
Administrative counterpart	Cebu City	Muang Chiang Mai	Hai Phong City	Kolkata Metropolitan Area	Medan City
Administrative area (km²)	293	152	1407	1798	285
Administrative population (million)	0.92	0.23	1.98	14.11	2.23
Natural city area outside administrative boundary (%)	73.2	90.9	46.0	63.9	69.8

Notes: It is not always clear which administrative division each natural city corresponds to. Kolkata, for example, has the Kolkata Metropolitan Area, Kolkata Municipal Corporation, and Kolkata District, each of which has jurisdiction on varying administrative matters and different geographical coverage. Governance functions may be divided between local government and higher levels. For comparison, we chose the administrative units that most likely governed the largest portion of natural cities.

Source: General Statistics Office of Viet Nam, Government of India, Government of Thailand, Philippine Statistics Authority 2016, Statistics Indonesia.

First, all five natural cities grew considerably in area from 1992 and 2016: at one end of the range, Cebu growing by 58% and, at the other, Hai Phong growing by 930%. By 2016, the natural city areas were, except for Hai Phong, substantially larger than their administrative counterparts: 357 km² versus 293 km² for Cebu, for example, and 882 km² versus 285 km² for Medan.

The spatial expansion of the natural cities was by no means constrained by their administrative boundaries. In 2016, each of the five natural cities had a significant portion of its area lying outside of the corresponding administrative unit. Natural city sprawl reached beyond administrative borders by 73% for Cebu City, 91% for Muang Chiang Mai District, 46% for Hai Phong City, 70% for Medan City, and 64% for the Kolkata Metropolitan Area, contoured with dashed lines in Figure 2.1.11.

Finally, the extensive scope of each natural city inevitably involved multiple administrative units at the same level as the corresponding administrative city. In 2016, Cebu natural city spanned 14 cities and municipalities, Chiang Mai natural city 17 districts, Hai Phong natural city 1 city and 2 provinces, Kolkata natural city 7 districts, and Medan natural city 4 cities and regencies. Such spatial-administrative settings clearly call for cross-jurisdiction governance to effectively manage the natural cities. Moreover, Chiang Mai natural city ranges over two provinces, and Hai Phong, which is itself a province-level city, over three provinces—the province being the highest subnational division in both Thailand and Viet Nam.

This suggests that certain coordination mechanisms would be needed at the central government level to manage these large, important metropolises.

Emergence of city clusters

Over time, many natural cities have become spatially connected with one another through urban expansion and the development of intercity transport infrastructure. We refer to these urban agglomerations, each comprising two or more connected natural cities, as city clusters. Not only are the natural cities within a city cluster connected by roads and rail, but the former farmland along the transport arteries is developed, as well captured by NTL data.[2] City clusters host vast numbers of people and firms that are often hugely diverse, generating colossal flows of goods, services, and ideas that make them uniquely vibrant urban areas in the region.[3]

NTL-based data show that 476 of 1,459 natural cities that were spatially independent in 1992 had merged by 2016 into 124 city clusters, 71 of them consisting of 2 natural cities, 21 of them comprising 3 natural cities, and 32 of them encompassing 4 or more natural cities. Altogether, these city clusters have 892 million residents inhabiting a land area of 364,000 km², accounting for 64.7% of the population and 65.1% of the land area of all natural cities in developing Asia. If we consider average luminosity as a proxy for a city's economic activity, cities within clusters have a higher mean luminosity, at 5.97, than the mean of 5.71 for cities not in any cluster.

Figure 2.1.12 shows the largest 28 city clusters across the region, each home to more than 10 million people in 2016 and numbered to indicate ranking by population in 2016. Of the 28 city clusters, 8 are in the PRC, 7 in India, 3 in Indonesia, and 2 each in the Republic of Korea and Viet Nam. Economies with one city cluster are Bangladesh; Malaysia; Pakistan; the Philippines; Taipei,China; and Thailand. The largest cluster, both in terms of land area and population, centers on Shanghai in the PRC, connecting 53 natural cities in 4 province-level administrative divisions. This cluster, often referred to as the Yangtze River Delta Area, covers more than 45,000 km² and has 91.5 million inhabitants—making it more populous than all but 15 countries worldwide, after Viet Nam but ahead of Germany. Figure 2.1.13 illustrates the spatial transition of the Shanghai-centered cluster from 1992 to 2016. The smallest city cluster in terms of land area is the one centered on Dhaka in Bangladesh, which nevertheless has three times as many residents as Singapore.

Comparing these clusters' boundaries with administrative boundaries yields the number of top-level administrative divisions (province, state, etc.) involved in each cluster. While 9 city clusters are contained in a single state or province, the remaining 19 clusters span at least 2 top-level administrative divisions. This underscores again the importance of intergovernmental coordination mechanisms to enable large city clusters to develop in an efficient and concerted way.

Figure 2.1.12 Large city clusters with populations above 10 million in developing Asia, 2016

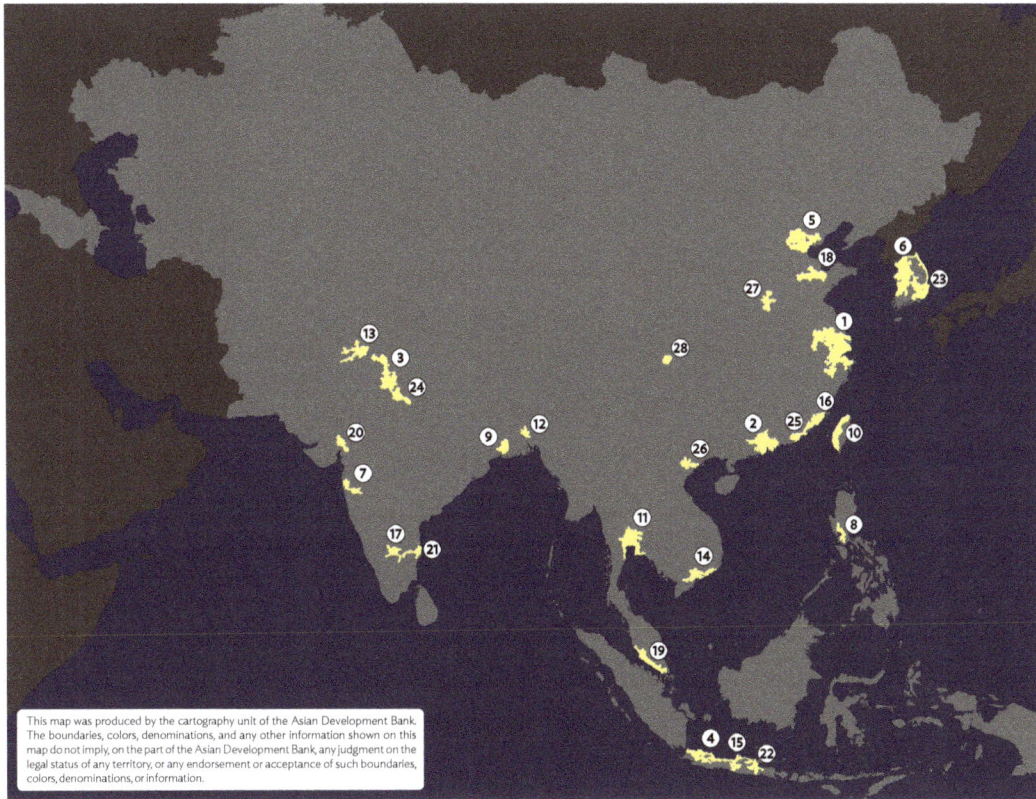

Note: Numbers indicate cluster ranking by population.
Source: ADB estimates using nighttime lights images from the National Oceanic and Atmospheric Administration (accessed 1 April 2017 and 10 August 2018) and grid population data from LandScan Datasets of the Oak Ridge National Laboratory (accessed 31 August 2017 and 31 August 2018).

Figure 2.1.13 Spatial transition of natural cities in the Yangtze River Delta Area

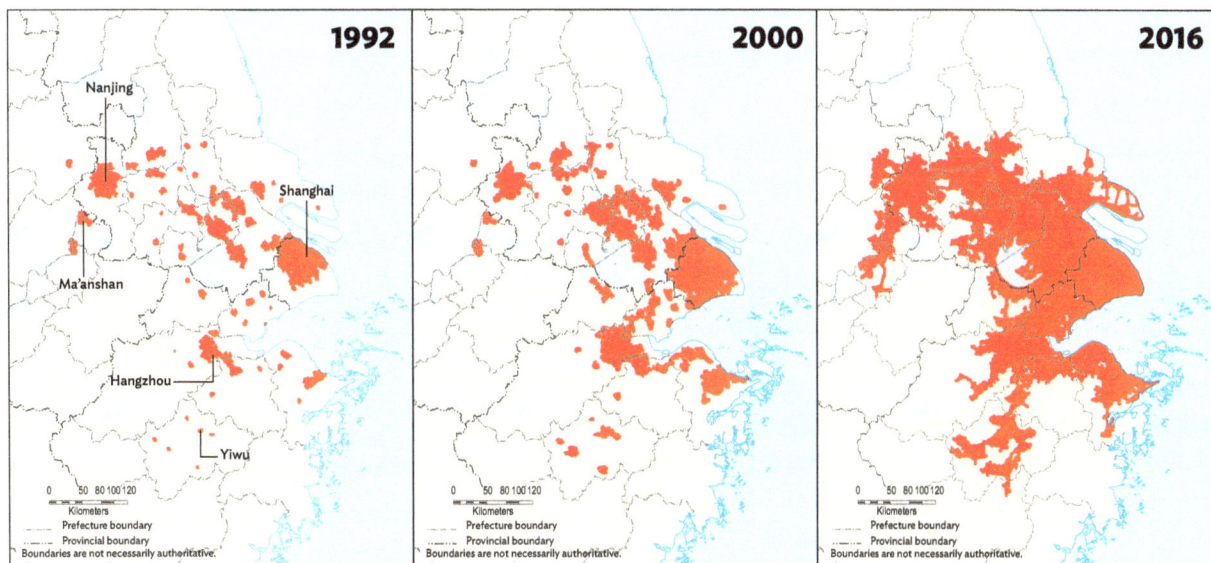

This map was produced by the cartography unit of the Asian Development Bank. The boundaries, colors, denominations, and any other information shown on this map do not imply, on the part of the Asian Development Bank, any judgment on the legal status of any territory, or any endorsement or acceptance of such boundaries, colors, denominations, or information.

Source: ADB estimates using nighttime lights images from the National Oceanic and Atmospheric Administration (accessed 1 April 2017 and 10 August 2018).

Figure 2.1.14 Distribution of natural city density

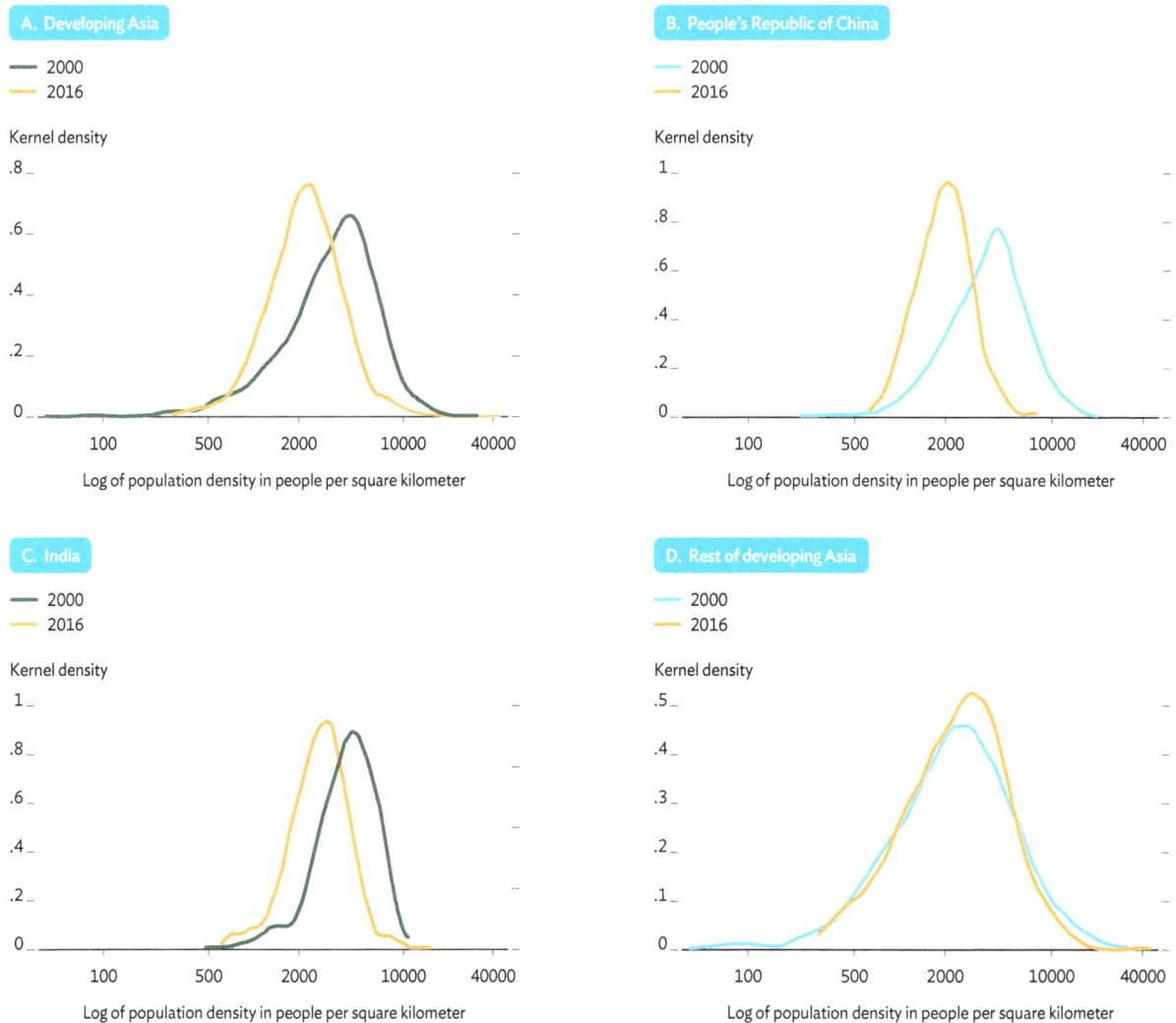

A. Developing Asia
— 2000
— 2016

Kernel density

Log of population density in people per square kilometer

B. People's Republic of China
— 2000
— 2016

Kernel density

Log of population density in people per square kilometer

C. India
— 2000
— 2016

Kernel density

Log of population density in people per square kilometer

D. Rest of developing Asia
— 2000
— 2016

Kernel density

Log of population density in people per square kilometer

Source: ADB estimates using nighttime lights images from the National Oceanic and Atmospheric Administration (accessed 1 April 2017 and 10 August 2018) and grid population data from LandScan Datasets of the Oak Ridge National Laboratory (accessed 31 August 2017 and 31 August 2018).

Urban densities

Urban density, as measured by population per unit of area, is related to many dimensions of city life such as the provision of amenities, sources and impacts of congestion, and agglomeration benefits. Figure 2.1.14 shows how density distributions of natural cities have shifted in India, the PRC, and the rest of developing Asia and the whole region. Overall, cities in developing Asia became less densely populated from 2000 to 2016. The average density of population within the natural cities decreased from 4,047 people per square kilometer in 2000 to 2,625 in 2016, as median density decreased from 3,619 to 2,237. Meanwhile, density variance also decreased as fewer natural cities had extremely low or high densities.

The significant drop in urban density in the region reflects mainly changes in India and the PRC, with other economies maintaining relatively stable density distributions over the period. This phenomenon in the PRC has been documented (e.g., Henderson, Quigley, and Lim 2009), and the trend does not appear to be reversing. It may be partly explained by urban land in the PRC becoming increasingly important as a source of fiscal revenue for local governments, who thus administratively convert rural land to urban land and lease it for urban development even as population inflows lag. In India's case, it is possible that strict land regulations, such as low floor area ratios in city cores, leave urban sprawl the answer to proscribed density. This raises concerns about foregone benefits of agglomeration.

Another pattern in the evolution of urban density is negative correlation between a city's initial density and change in its density over time (Figure 2.1.15). This relationship holds even after controlling for initial population size and indicates that cities that are already dense can become only slightly more dense; sparsely populated cities, on the other hand, have more potential to densify. Also, very dense cities may experience more pressure to expand spatially, thereby reducing their initial high density. Overall, density is found to be converging across cities in many individual economies in the region, notably India, Indonesia, and the PRC.

Figure 2.1.15 Correlation of initial urban density and density change, 2000 and 2016

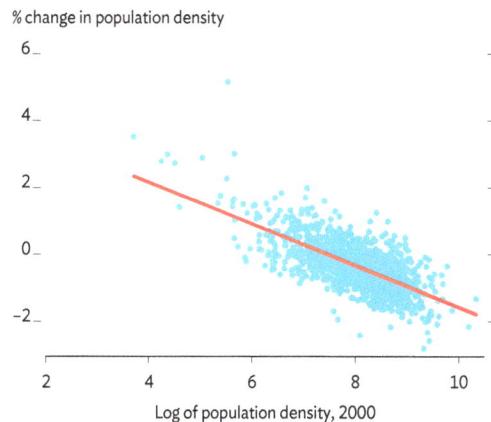

Source: ADB estimates using nighttime lights images from the National Oceanic and Atmospheric Administration (accessed 1 April 2017 and 10 August 2018) and grid population data from LandScan Datasets of the Oak Ridge National Laboratory (accessed 31 August 2017 and 31 August 2018).

2.1.3 Agglomeration effects

Historically, cities developed in places where large human settlements were enabled by locational fundamentals such as a mild climate, fertile farmland, and easy transport by road and waterway. The resulting physical concentration of households and firms facilitated close interactions, giving rise to economic gains or agglomeration economies. The mechanisms through which agglomeration economies operate are considered below, followed by an analysis of the experience in developing Asia.

Underlying mechanisms

Agglomeration economies are typically considered to work through three mechanisms: *matching, learning*, and *sharing* (Duranton 2015, Behrens and Robert-Nicoud 2015). Productivity tends to be higher in larger, denser cities as this facilitates the *matching* of input and output markets. Workers are more likely to find their most suitable jobs in larger cities, for example, and it is easier for firms in big cities to find suitable workers. These mechanisms are mutually complementary and reinforcing. Similarly, proximity to buyers and suppliers is often advantageous for firms and an important determinant of where they locate.

Learning happens through the spillover of ideas and knowledge as individuals and organizations engage in close interaction. The pool of knowledge thus generated is greater than the sum of the know-how of each worker and firm. This mechanism is intimately associated with the high degree of spatial concentration generally observed in research and development and innovation activities (Carlino and Kerr 2015, Galindo 2007). It applies as well in other contexts, such as when knowledge about relatively standard products and production processes spreads among urban entrepreneurs new and old in developing countries. Good examples are the development of a vibrant garment industry in Dhaka, Bangladesh (Mottaleb and Sonobe 2011), and the soccer ball industry in Sialkot, Pakistan (Atkin et al. 2016).

Finally, greater city size and density enables greater *sharing* of resources. For example, labor markets develop both deeper individual specialization and wider availability of diverse skills and expertise, thereby enhancing efficiency from the division of labor. Indeed, some scholars emphasize that the dynamism of cities stems from their facilitating the creation of a network of interdependent experts. Software companies in Bengaluru, India, for example, benefit from a high concentration of law firms specializing in intellectual property rights.

Similarly, economies of scale in the provision of physical and institutional infrastructure mean such amenities are shared more efficiently among city dwellers. It is estimated that the investment cost of infrastructure per capita in sub-Saharan Africa is 5 times higher in a low-density city than in a high-density one—and 10 times higher in rural areas (Foster and Briceño-Garmendia 2010). The network characteristics of most infrastructure generate savings when creating, operating, and maintaining it in denser places.

More generally, the productivity advantages in a thick factor market are important enough for firms to incur higher costs, rather than locate in cheaper areas that do not offer the scale and potential advantages of agglomeration. At the same time, firms have better market access in larger cities, which can allow them to source inputs at lower cost and sell their products for more (Combes and Gobillon 2015).

Nonetheless, city size and density do not automatically translate into agglomeration economies. Congestion and rigid land-use planning can limit how effectively factors of production respond to market forces. For example, India has seen slow growth in manufacturing employment, sometimes even shrinkage, in urban districts as firms move to the rural and peri-urban areas of large metropolitan areas (Ghani, Goswami, and Kerr 2012). This is typical as cities mature and become more functionally specialized. In the absence of appropriately sized industrial zones serviced by good infrastructure, accessible to workers, and located close to

urban areas with the full range of social amenities such as
health care and educational institutions, however, firms
may move away to diverse locations and lose the benefits of
agglomeration (Henderson 2014, Amirapu et al. 2019).

The activities that drive a city's economy may influence
the potential economic benefits of agglomeration. It may be
useful to compare Chongqing in the PRC and Lagos in Nigeria,
two cities with similar populations (United Nations 2018b).
Chongqing's economy is heavily based on tradeable activities
undertaken within the city and its immediate surroundings,
such as Jiangbei and Jiulongpo districts, where multinational
companies like Acer, Cisco Systems, Ford Motor Company,
Foxconn, Hewlett-Packard, Honeywell, and IBM manufacture
products. Lagos, on the other hand, is what Gollin, Jedwab,
and Vollrath (2016) would describe as a "consumption city"
that depends on economic activities located outside of it,
such as oil extraction, that generate incomes and profits that
are then consumed in the city. The city specializes in providing
non-tradable services to its residents. Most observers would
agree that Chongqing is in a better position to capitalize on
agglomeration economies and be a robust engine of growth.

Evidence on agglomeration economies

The literature commonly finds firms and workers in large
cities to be more productive. While this reflects to some extent
dynamic individuals moving to larger cities to seek their
fortune as either entrepreneurs or workers, the agglomeration
economies discussed above also play a role. It is a challenge
to disentangle causality and identify which of the various
channels drive agglomeration economies. However, several
studies, mainly of developed economies where longitudinal
data tracking firms or workers are available, have made
progress (Combes and Gobillon 2015).

Studies of agglomeration economies in developing
countries remain limited. While generally less conclusive
regarding the direction of causality, the results obtained in
Asian cities are remarkably consistent with those obtained in
the developed economies (Box 2.1.2). The empirical patterns
uncovered suggest that urbanization in developing countries
promotes economic growth (Duranton 2008, McKinsey Global
Institute 2011, Venables 2010, World Bank 2009).

Cities, firms, and jobs: Some new evidence

The following examines firm- and worker-level information
from selected Asian economies to shed additional light on
the relationship between city size and important economic
outcomes beyond the research literature discussed above.

Box 2.1.2 Agglomeration economies in Asian cities

Most studies suggest that patterns of productivity in Asian cities are generally consistent with agglomeration effects. The correlation between earnings and density is positive for cities in India and the PRC, and magnitudes are possibly larger than in US cities (Chauvin et al. 2017, Hasan, Jiang, and Rafols 2017). A study based on a panel of over 200 cities in the PRC in the 1990s demonstrated that workers experienced sharp rises in real incomes with greater city size, and that output per worker also increased with city employment (Au and Henderson 2006a, 2006b). Moreover, a study by the World Bank (2009) of 120 cities in the PRC showed doubling city size associated with firm productivity increases of 3%–8%. These effects seem to be larger in technology industries.

In the Republic of Korea, Henderson, Lee, and Lee (2001) found positive productivity effects from co-location with similar industries, or *localization economies*. Effects were especially strong in heavy industry and transportation. However, there was no evidence of *urbanization economies,* or cross-productivity spillover from the presence of different industries. This pattern is consistent with experience in developed countries, whereby big cities serve as nurseries for firms that then move to more specialized places once they become mature in their industry (Duranton 2015).

Studies of location choice for factories and small and medium-size firms in Indonesia similarly reported substantial localization economies but less pronounced urbanization economies (Henderson and Kuncoro 1996, Deichmann et al. 2005). Factories were more likely to choose locations with mature establishments in the same or related industries. In Thailand, spatial concentration of enterprises predicted subsequent growth around the area and growth convergence with neighboring contiguous areas (Felkner and Townsend 2011).

In India, productivity was found responsive to urban population size in most industries (Mitra and Gupta 2002). Moreover, factory-level studies identified urbanization economies as important channels for reducing cost per unit of output (Lall, Koo, and Chakravorty 2003, Lall, Shalizi, and Deichmann 2004).

Finally, agglomeration benefits were not limited to the formal sector. The informal sector benefitted from productivity spillover in cities in Cambodia (Tanaka and Hashiguchi 2019), as found in Colombia (García 2018, Duranton 2016).

References:

Au, C.-C. and J. V. Henderson. 2006a. Are Chinese Cities Too Small? *Review of Economic Studies* 73(3).

———. 2006b. How Migration Restrictions Limit Agglomeration and Productivity in China. *Journal of Development Economics* 80(2).

Chauvin, J. P., E. Glaeser, Y. Ma, and K. Tobio. 2017. What is Different About Urbanization in Rich and Poor Countries? Cities in Brazil, China, India and the United States. *Journal of Urban Economics* 98.

Deichmann, U., K. Kaiser, S. V. Lall, and Z. Shalizi. 2005. Agglomeration, Transport, and Regional Development in Indonesia. *Policy Research Working Paper* No. 3477. World Bank.

Duranton, G. 2015. Growing through Cities in Developing Countries. *World Bank Research Observer* 30(1).

———. 2016. Determinants of City Growth in Colombia. *Papers in Regional Science* 95(1).

Felkner, J. S. and R. M. Townsend. 2011. The Geographic Concentration of Enterprise in Developing Countries. *Quarterly Journal of Economics* 126(4).

García, G. A. 2018. Agglomeration Economies in the Presence of an Informal Sector the Colombian Case. *Working Papers* No. 18-01. Center for Research in Economics and Finance.

Hasan, R., Y. Jiang, and R. M. Rafols. 2017. Urban Agglomeration Effects in India: Evidence from Town-Level Data. *Asian Development Review* 34(2).

Henderson, J. and A. Kuncoro. 1996. Industrial Centralization in Indonesia. *World Bank Economic Review* 10(3).

Henderson, J., T. Lee, and Y. J. Lee. 2001. Scale Externalities in Korea. *Journal of Urban Economics* 49(3).

Lall, S., J. Koo, and S. Chakravorty. 2003. Diversity Matters: The Economic Geography of Industry Location in India. *Policy Research Working Paper* No. 3072. World Bank.

Lall, S. V., Z. Shalizi, and U. Deichmann. 2004. Agglomeration Economies and Productivity in Indian Industry. *Journal of Development Economics* 73(2).

Mitra, A. and I. Gupta. 2002. Rural Migrants and Labour Segmentation. *Economic and Political Weekly* 37(2).

Tanaka, K. and Y. Hashiguchi. 2019. Agglomeration Economies in the Formal and Informal Sectors: A Bayesian Spatial Approach. *Journal of Economic Geography.*

World Bank. 2009. *World Development Report 2009: Reshaping Economic Geography.*

To the extent possible, the concept of natural cities is used to capture firms and workers actually located in the cities' urban footprint.

Cities and jobs: Evidence from four Asian countries.
Following Amoranto et al. (forthcoming), labor force survey data from four Asian countries are used to examine various employment outcomes across locations. The data go beyond the usual rural–urban distinction and either identify the specific city in Indonesia or the Philippines where a worker resides or whether a worker in India or Pakistan resides in a city larger than roughly 1 million people or in a smaller city. This allows the analysis for Indonesia and the Philippines to be conducted in terms of natural cities.[4]

Several interesting patterns emerge from the data and are consistent with the presence of agglomeration economies, though the absence of longitudinal data prevents drawing any causal conclusions. First, manufacturing, a recognized driver of city dynamism (Venables 2017), accounts for a larger share of employment in large cities than in smaller cities and other urban areas (henceforth, smaller cities) in all four countries. It is also one of the largest employers in urban India, Indonesia, and Pakistan (Table 2.1.2).

Table 2.1.2 Distribution of employment across sectors by area type and city size

| | Employment Shares (%) | | | | | | | | | | | |
| | India (2012) | | | Indonesia (2015) | | | Pakistan (2014) | | | Philippines (2015) | | |
Industry	Rural	Smaller cities	Large cities[a]	Rural	Smaller cities	Large cities[a]	Rural	Smaller cities	Large cities[a]	Rural	Smaller cities	Large cities[a]
Agriculture	62.2	8.2	0.9	60.1	19.6	13.5	59.3	7.7	1.8	44.2	17.0	2.7
Mining	0.5	1.2	0.1	1.4	1.4	0.7	0.2	0.1	0.1	0.7	0.6	0.1
Manufacturing	7.9	20.1	26.6	7.8	12.1	20.0	9.6	23.1	27.3	5.7	9.6	11.9
Utilities	0.4	1.8	0.9	0.2	0.6	0.6	0.5	1.4	1.7	0.3	0.5	0.4
Construction	11.6	11.1	7.6	5.6	7.8	8.3	7.3	8.6	6.3	7.1	7.9	8.3
Trade services	7.0	24.7	23.2	13.3	29.8	29.2	9.9	29.9	31.2	17.9	27.2	29.9
TSIC	3.9	10.4	13.7	2.4	5.5	5.8	4.5	7.8	8.6	6.2	9.9	11.2
Business services	0.9	5.8	9.8	0.7	2.9	5.2	0.8	3.8	4.0	2.0	5.3	13.3
Public[b]	3.6	11.9	10.7	6.5	14.9	9.9	5.4	12.5	12.1	9.1	12.2	10.5
Personal services	1.9	4.7	6.5	2.0	5.5	7.0	2.4	5.1	6.9	6.9	9.8	11.8
Total	**100.0**	**100.0**	**100.0**	**100.0**	**100.0**	**100.0**	**100.0**	**100.0**	**100.0**	**100.0**	**100.0**	**100.0**

TSIC = transportation, storage, information, and communication.

[a] Cities with populations greater than 1 million. Cities are natural cities in Indonesia and the Philippines but administrative cities in India and Pakistan.

[b] Includes public administration and support service activities, education, and human health and social work.

Note: Estimates are for all types of workers: wage workers, the self-employed, and employers.

Source: ADB estimates using data from labor force surveys.

Table 2.1.3 Effects of city size on wages

Variables	Philippines 2015	Indonesia 2015	Pakistan 2014	India 2012
	Using natural city		Using administrative city	
	(1) logwage	(2) logwage	(3) logwage	(4) logwage
Area type (reference category: *smaller cities*)				
Large cities	0.1060***	0.1415***	0.0705***	0.1803***
	(0.0104)	(0.0079)	(0.0142)	(0.0178)
Rural areas	-0.0577***	0.0045	-0.0713***	-0.1570***
	(0.0063)	(0.0073)	(0.0105)	(0.0112)
Demographic controls	Yes	Yes	Yes	Yes
Region/province/state, sector, and occupation fixed effects	Yes	Yes	Yes	Yes
Constant	4.4689***	9.1957***	4.9846***	4.7843***
	(0.0456)	(0.0421)	(0.0504)	(0.0553)
Observations	39,324	123,061	28,373	46,259
R-squared	0.5323	0.2866	0.4043	0.5594

*** = $p<0.01$, ** = $p<0.05$, * = $p<0.1$, logwage = log of mean daily wage.

Notes: Ordinary least square estimates of the effects of city size on the log of the daily wage. Standard errors are in parentheses. Data excludes workers in public administration or defense, on social security, or working for extraterritorial organizations and bodies. Only wage workers are included. Demographic controls include age, age squared, education, sex, and marital status.

Source: ADB estimates using data from labor force surveys.

Table 2.1.4 Effects on wages of the proportion of college graduates in a locality

Variables	Philippines 2015	Indonesia 2015	Pakistan 2014	India 2012
	Using natural city		Using administrative city	
	(1) logwage	(2) logwage	(3) logwage	(4) logwage
Area type (reference category: *smaller cities*)				
Large cities	0.0963***	0.1072***	0.0321**	0.1153***
	(0.0105)	(0.0077)	(0.0147)	(0.0195)
Rural areas	-0.0447***	0.1233***	0.0334**	-0.0426***
	(0.0067)	(0.0102)	(0.0133)	(0.0148)
Proportion of college graduates in the locality	0.2181***	2.5485***	1.8315***	0.9971***
	(0.0377)	(0.1343)	(0.1468)	(0.0975)
Years of schooling	0.0474***	0.0762***	0.0256***	0.0342***
	(0.0009)	(0.0010)	(0.0009)	(0.0011)
Demographic controls	Yes	Yes	Yes	Yes
Region/province/state, sector, and occupation fixed effects	Yes	Yes	Yes	Yes
Constant	4.4354***	8.9783***	4.8655***	4.6463***
	(0.0459)	(0.0434)	(0.0513)	(0.0568)
Observations	39,324	123,061	28,373	46,259
R-squared	0.5327	0.2909	0.4090	0.5627

*** = $p<0.01$, ** = $p<0.05$, * = $p<0.1$, logwage = log of mean daily wage.

Notes: Ordinary least square estimates of the effects of the proportion of college graduates in a locality on the log of mean daily wage. Standard errors are in parentheses. Data excludes workers in public administration or defense, on social security, or working for extraterritorial organizations and bodies. Only wage workers are included. Demographic controls include age, age squared, sex, and marital status.

Source: ADB estimates using data from labor force surveys.

Second, workers with comparable demographic characteristics, educational attainment, sector of employment, and occupation receive higher wages in bigger cities (Table 2.1.3).[5] The results hold when population density is used as an alternative measure of city size.

Third, returns from an additional year of schooling in the form of higher wages are greater in larger cities than in smaller cities and rural areas (Figure 2.1.16). This suggests that large cities place a higher value on human capital. The difference is particularly large in Indonesia, where the average percentage increase in wage for an additional year of schooling of a worker in a big city is 2.2 percentage points more than the same worker in a small city.

Fourth, large cities have higher shares of college-educated workers, especially in India and the Philippines. Moreover, workers, including the less educated, benefit from the presence of a larger proportion of college degree holders in any given location (Table 2.1.4). This supports the idea that knowledge spillover is an important driver of agglomeration economies and is consistent with Bacolod, Blum, and Strange (2009) and Moretti (2004), which found that the presence of skilled labor had positive productivity spillover to other workers in US cities.

Fifth, most workers in cities and urban areas are wage workers, who normally have better jobs than those who are self-employed.[6] Wage workers' share in employment is biggest in large cities, ranging from 57.0% to 77.3%.

Sixth, large cities have a more diverse range of occupations than smaller cities, except in India. This is indicated by the average value of an occupational diversity index across cities and locations. Figure 2.1.17 presents the mean occupational diversity indexes.

Finally, large cities do not appear to be less inclusive. Quantile regressions confirm that the benefits of agglomeration extend to workers across the wage distribution. Moreover, the wage premium for being male is lower in large cities in three of the four countries, indicating less gender discrimination in large cities (Figure 2.1.18).

Cities and firms. The relationship between city characteristics and firm performance is examined, following Chen, Hasan, and Jiang (forthcoming), using a dataset that assigns 20,000 firms from the World Bank Enterprise Survey to 488 natural cities across 25 economies in developing Asia.[7] Several interesting patterns emerge.

First, innovation is heavily concentrated in a few urban areas in each country. Innovative firms are businesses that have introduced product innovations over the previous 3 years. Figure 2.1.19a plots the cumulative shares of natural city population and innovative firms in India, Indonesia, Malaysia, and the PRC.

Figure 2.1.16 Returns from an additional year of schooling, by city size

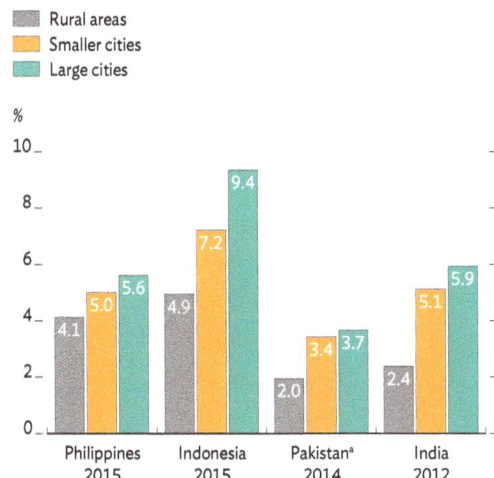

- Rural areas
- Smaller cities
- Large cities

%

	Philippines 2015	Indonesia 2015	Pakistan[a] 2014	India 2012
Rural areas	4.1	4.9	2.0	2.4
Smaller cities	5.0	7.2	3.4	5.1
Large cities	5.6	9.4	3.7	5.9

[a] Differences between large cities versus smaller cities are all statistically significant except in Pakistan.

Note: Estimates derived from the coefficients of ordinary least square estimates regressing log of mean daily wage with city size or area type and a host of controls for individual characteristics and location (e.g., region, province, or state).

Source: ADB estimates using data from labor force surveys.

Figure 2.1.17 Mean occupational diversity index by area type and city size

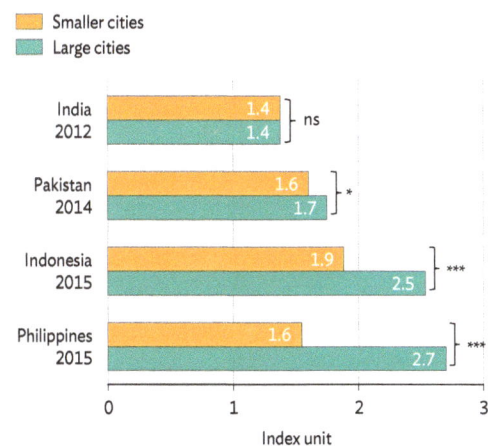

- Smaller cities
- Large cities

	Smaller cities	Large cities	
India 2012	1.4	1.4	ns
Pakistan 2014	1.6	1.7	*
Indonesia 2015	1.9	2.5	***
Philippines 2015	1.6	2.7	***

Index unit

* = difference significant at p<0.10, *** = difference significant at p<0.01, ns = difference is not significant.

Note: Excludes work in agriculture. The occupational diversity index (ODI) in each city or locality c is the inverse of the sum (across all occupation types) of the absolute value of the difference between each occupation type's share in city or locality employment and its share in national employment:

$$ODI_c = \frac{1}{\sum_c \left| O_{cj} - O_j \right|}$$

where O_{cj} is the share of occupation j in the total employment in city c, and O_j refers to the share of occupation j nationwide. The ODI increases the more the composition of occupation types in a city or locality mirrors the diversity of occupations nationally.

Source: ADB estimates using data from labor force surveys.

The curves can be interpreted similarly to Lorenz curves that measure inequality, with the degree skewed to the bottom right quadrant indicating greater concentration of innovation-related activities. In India, Indonesia, and the PRC, cities that host 50% of the national population have 80% of the firms that innovate, while the other half host only the remaining 20%. In Malaysia, the split is 90% versus 10%, with most innovation activities clustered in multinational firms in Seremban, Taiping, and Kuala Lumpur. Figure 2.1.19b zooms in on the most innovative cities in each country. It shows that three cities in the PRC—in descending order Guangzhou, Shanghai, and Zhengzhou—host 50% of innovative firms. In Indonesia, three cities—Bandung, Jakarta, and Semarang—host 70%. In Malaysia, Seremban alone hosts more than 50% of innovative firms.

Second, firms in bigger cities tend to be more productive and undertake some form of innovative activity, such as product or process innovation, or engaging in research and development (R&D). Table 2.1.5 shows the relationship between various measures of firm dynamism and city size as captured by population. City size is statistically significant and positively correlated with all firm performance measures: productivity, innovation, and R&D.

It would be premature to say that this positive relationship can be interpreted as causal. Better-performing firms may choose to locate in large cities for reasons that have little to do with agglomeration economies, such as easier market access or a better business environment. This question can be partly addressed by using lagged city size data in place of its contemporaneous value. Results remain significant after doing so.

Figure 2.1.18 Male wage premium by city size and area type

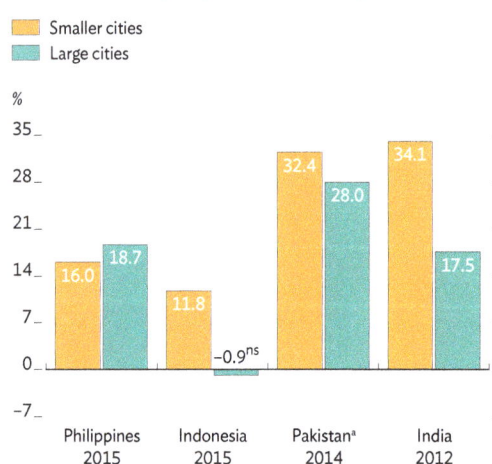

ns = not significant.

[a] Differences between large cities versus smaller cities are statistically significant except in Pakistan.

Notes: Values shown are derived from coefficients of ordinary least square estimates regressing log of mean daily wage with city size or area type and gender (male), their interaction, and controlling for individual characteristics, sector and type of occupation, location (e.g., region, province, or state), and female labor force participation rate in the city or locality.

Source: ADB estimates using data from labor force surveys.

Table 2.1.5 Firm performance and city size

Variables	(1) Log of labor productivity	(2) Process innovation	(3) Product innovation	(4) R&D
Log of population	0.0579*	0.2181***	0.2756***	0.1990***
	(0.0323)	(0.0568)	(0.0255)	(0.0321)
Observations	18,114	19,167	19,928	19,021
(pseudo) R-squared	0.3922	0.214	0.183	0.221
Sector, year, country fixed effect	Yes	Yes	Yes	Yes
Number of cities	488	488	488	488

* = $p<0.1$, ** = $p<0.05$, *** = $p<0.01$, R&D = research and development.

Notes: Heteroskedasticity-corrected standard errors clustered at the country level. Ordinary least square estimator used in column 1 and logit model used in columns 2, 3, and 4. Labor productivity is measured as total sales over the number employed. Process innovation means a firm has introduced a new or significantly improved process. Product innovation means a firm has introduced new products or services over last 3 fiscal years. R&D means a firm spent on R&D excluding market research in past fiscal year. Other controls include firm characteristics such as age, size, export status, and foreign direct investment share, as well as city business environment variables.

Source: ADB estimates using data from World Bank's Enterprise Surveys Data (accessed 11 August 2018) and nighttime lights images from the National Oceanic and Atmospheric Administration (accessed 1 April 2017 and 10 August 2018).

Figure 2.1.19 Innovative firms and cities

A. City population share and cumulative innovative firm share

Cumulative share of innovative firms (%)

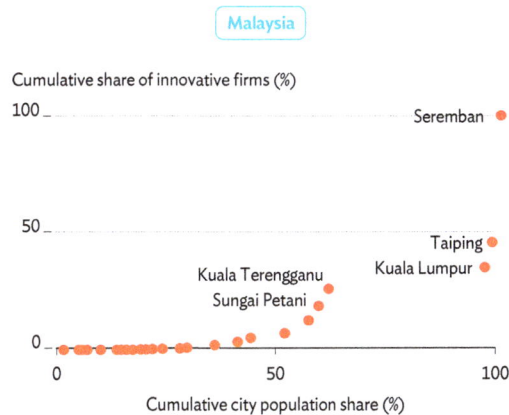

- India
- Indonesia
- Malaysia
- People's Republic of China

Cumulative city population share (%)

B. Top five innovative cities by country

India

Cumulative share of innovative firms (%)

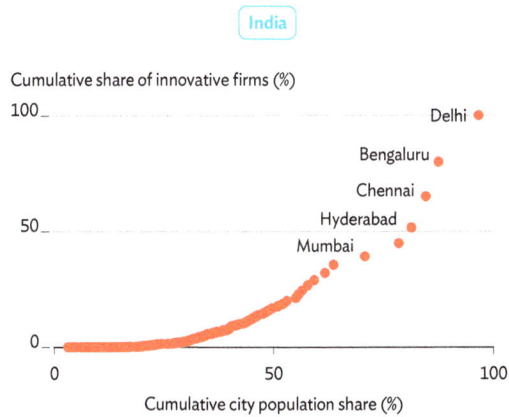

Delhi
Bengaluru
Chennai
Hyderabad
Mumbai

Cumulative city population share (%)

Indonesia

Cumulative share of innovative firms (%)

Bandung
Jakarta
Semarang
Surabaya
Medan

Cumulative city population share (%)

Malaysia

Cumulative share of innovative firms (%)

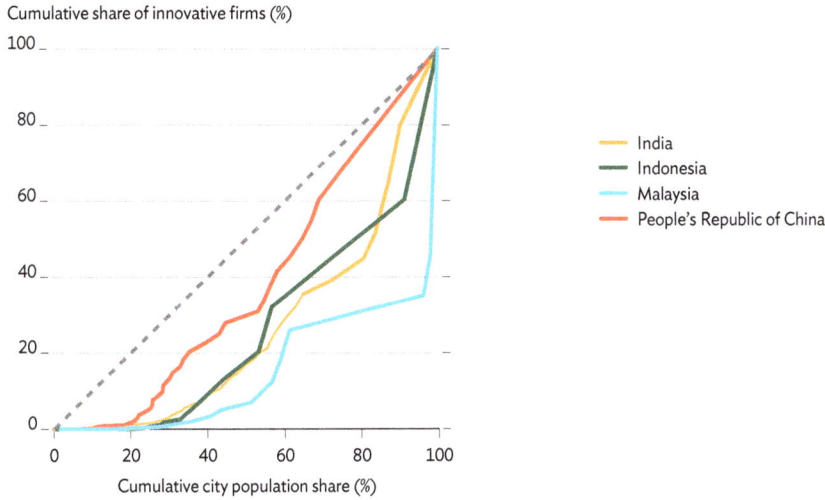

Seremban
Taiping
Kuala Terengganu
Kuala Lumpur
Sungai Petani

Cumulative city population share (%)

People's Republic of China

Cumulative share of innovative firms (%)

Guangzhou
Shanghai
Zhengzhou
Hangzhou
Nanjing

Cumulative city population share (%)

Notes: Population share is measured by the population in each natural city over the total population in all natural cities. The same method applies for innovative firm share. Cities are sorted by innovative firm share in ascending order.

Source: ADB estimates using data from World Bank's Enterprise Surveys Data (accessed 11 August 2018) and nighttime lights images from the National Oceanic and Atmospheric Administration (accessed 1 April 2017 and 10 August 2018).

Figure 2.1.20 Firm innovation near a top university

Without top university
With top university

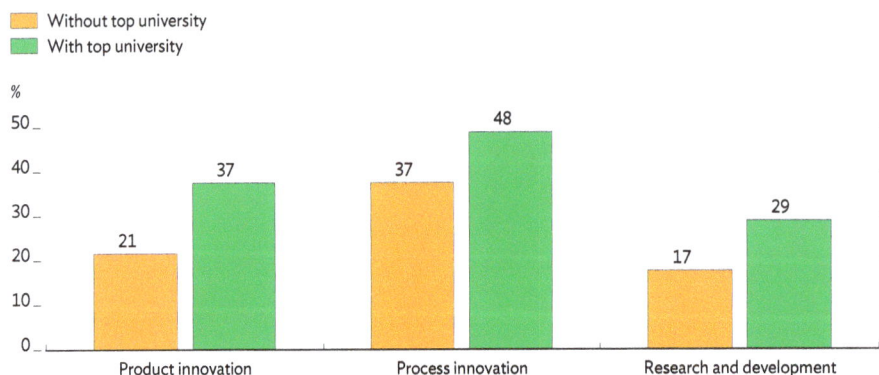

Note: Each bar indicates the average share of firms that conduct innovation activity in a city. "With top university" indicates that the natural city has at least one university ranked in the top 500 in Asia.

Source: ADB estimates using data from World Bank's Enterprise Surveys Data (accessed 11 August 2018), nighttime lights images from the National Oceanic and Atmospheric Administration (accessed 1 April 2017 and 10 August 2018), and QS World University Rankings 2019 (accessed 15 May 2019).

Finally, having high-quality educational institutions fosters innovation. Local universities and research institutes in developed countries are known to play critical roles in providing firms with a supply of well-trained experts (Bramwell and Wolfe 2008). Evidence in the sample is consistent with this. Firms located in cities with top-ranked universities are more likely to introduce new products and production processes and are more likely to conduct R&D (Figure 2.1.20). Firms that have nearby one or more top-ranking university in Asia are 16% more likely to innovate in new products, 11% more likely to innovate in new production processes, and 12% more likely to conduct R&D.[8] The positive effect of top universities on firm innovation is even more pronounced after controlling for country and sector fixed effects (Table 2.1.6). The odds that firms innovate are 67%–69% higher in cities with at least one top university than for firms in cities without any top universities.

Table 2.1.6 Firm performance near an educational institution

Item	Process innovation	Product innovation	R&D
Top university	1.68***	1.69***	1.67***
	(0.163)	(0.202)	(0.168)
Sector, year, country fixed effect	Yes	Yes	Yes
F-statistics	33.417	23.154	24.066
Observations	19,906	20,719	19,762
Number of cities	488	488	488

* = p<0.1, ** = p<0.05, *** = p<0.01, R&D = research and development.

Notes: Heteroskedasticity-corrected standard errors in parentheses clustered at the country level. Coefficients on top university are expressed as odds ratios.

Source: ADB estimates using data from World Bank's Enterprise Surveys Data (accessed 11 August 2018), nighttime lights images from the National Oceanic and Atmospheric Administration (accessed 1 April 2017 and 10 August 2018), and QS World University Rankings 2019 (accessed 15 May 2019).

Differences between larger and smaller cities

The findings above point to better employment- and firm-related outcomes in larger cities. Examining the ways in which large cities differ from smaller cities can shed some light on the factors that may influence the size of agglomeration economies.

The World Bank Enterprise Survey records firms' views on various obstacles to their operations and growth. The focus here is on two types of obstacles: The first covers regulatory issues that can vary at the local level such as the difficulty of access to land and business licenses or permits. The second group covers infrastructure provision and captures the sufficiency and reliability of local infrastructure for electricity and water supply, transportation, and telecommunications.

The exercise reveals that, compared with large cities with a population of over 1 million, smaller and medium-sized cities have more firms that deem the local business environment to be problematic. In smaller cities with fewer than 500,000 people, for example, 11% of the firms consider transportation to be a major or severe obstacle to business, compared with 7% in large cities (Figure 2.1.21). These obstacles to business are confirmed to be worse in cities with lower population and lower density in regressions that control for country and sector fixed effects, as well as for firm characteristics such as firm age and size (Chen, Hasan, and Jiang, forthcoming).

Figure 2.1.21 Obstacles to business by city size

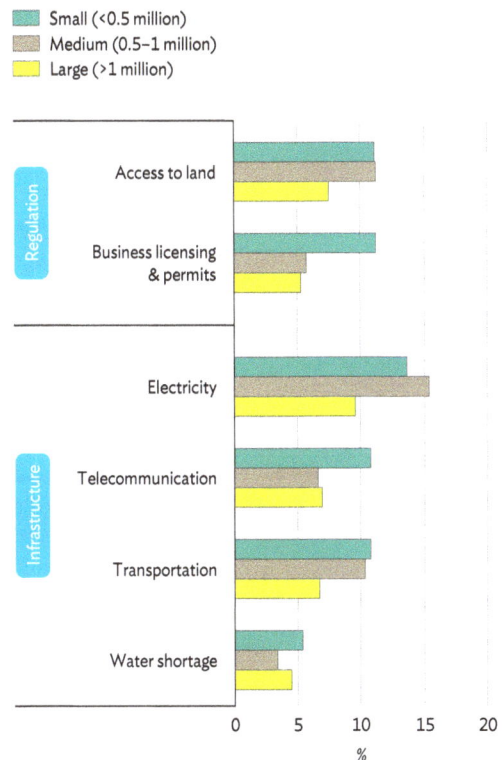

- Small (<0.5 million)
- Medium (0.5–1 million)
- Large (>1 million)

Note: Columns represent shares of firms that consider the business environment to be a major obstacle to operations.

Source: ADB estimates using data from World Bank's Enterprise Surveys Data (accessed 11 August 2018) and nighttime lights images from the National Oceanic and Atmospheric Administration (accessed 1 April 2017 and 10 August 2018).

2.2 The city as a labor market

Many agglomeration economies accrue from cities' ability to match workers with firms. Cities have diverse functions, but a critical one is their role as labor markets that connect households to jobs. Unless cities can function as integrated labor markets, their capacity to harness agglomeration economies and promote inclusion is greatly reduced. Ensuring that cities function well as labor markets is therefore an essential policy priority.

Duranton and Guerra (2016) argued convincingly that accessibility is the main consideration in urban development, as it links land use and transportation, both critical to the functioning of urban labor markets. Accessibility should be understood in two dimensions. First is mobility, which enables people to move easily and quickly between locations within an urban area. Second is locational choice, which allows a person or firm flexibility in where to locate.

Maintaining and improving accessibility requires an urban transport system that holds congestion to a level no worse than moderate and provides efficient and affordable public transportation. The urban poor, in particular, need affordable public transport to enable them to participate in a labor market broader than the distance that can be comfortably walked or cycled. This requires not only appropriate investment in different types of transport infrastructure but also that such investment be coordinated with land-use planning and regulation. Intelligent land use plays a key role in ensuring adequate land supply for housing, industry, commerce, and infrastructure. Housing policy also plays a significant role in making housing affordable to low-income residents. The following section turns to these features to provide an up-to-date assessment and to look at how policy can shape cities as successful labor markets.

2.2.1 Urban transport infrastructure

Congestion in cities

One way to gauge urban mobility is by the degree of congestion. Congestion arises when demand for travel exceeds the maximum capacity of the transportation network. Various ways exist to measure congestion. For example, congestion can be said to occur when average vehicle speed drops below a threshold over a certain period of time. Or it can be measured in terms of extra travel time required over the normal duration with free-flowing traffic. Some agencies measure congestion as the volume of traffic against the capacity of a transportation facility at a particular time.

Each measure has its advantages and disadvantages: speed is easy to measure, but appropriate thresholds may vary across regions and cities. The ratio of traffic volume to capacity reflects location-specific congestion more than regionwide congestion but is easy to understand (Rao and Rao 2012).

To measure the cost of congestion, researchers usually focus on travelers' time lost, vehicle operating costs, and air pollution. Research on the broader economic impact that congestion has on urban areas is still rare. However, a recent study provided compelling evidence that high congestion dampened subsequent employment growth in large US metropolitan areas (Hymel 2009). The finding suggested that improving urban mobility could spur local economies.

Lacking common datasets, studies examining congestion across cities in developing countries have been quite limited. Akbar et al. (2018) took a creative approach to measuring mobility in 154 Indian cities by using information about 22 million car trips collected from Google Maps. Following this methodology, we collected projected trip data from Google Maps for 278 natural cities in 28 regional economies with populations in 2016 greater than half a million.

In each natural city, we identified a number of hotspots in terms of luminosity, to capture employment, and population to determine where people lived. To collect representative data, random locations were sampled from these hotspots as origins and destinations (25 location pairs in cities with populations of 0.5 million–1.0 million, 100 for 1.0 million–5.0 million, and 400 for larger populations). Inquiries were made to Google Maps about driving in both directions between these origins and destinations at the off-peak hour of 3 a.m. and the peak hour of 8 a.m. or 6 p.m. on Monday, 3 June 2019. For each inquiry, Google Maps returned projected trip information including travel distance and duration. Figure 2.2.1 shows locations and the routes between them surveyed in Metro Manila, Philippines.

We calculated the ratio of driving duration during a peak hour to the off-peak hour between two locations in each direction and averaged across two opposite directions to obtain a congestion index for each location pair, which basically indicated the time needed to travel in peak-hour traffic relative to free-flowing traffic. Citywide congestion is measured as the average of congestion indexes across all location pairs in the city.

Across 278 cities studied, average citywide congestion was 1.24, which means on average 24% more time is needed to travel in peak hours than in off-peak hours. Congestion is more severe in larger cities. Average congestion reached 1.51 for 24 of the largest natural cities, with 2016 populations above 5 million. Figure 2.2.2 plots relative congestion in these cities (citywide congestion divided by the sample average, 1.24). Considerable variation is evident across cities, but large cities in middle-income countries tend to have more severe problems.[9]

Figure 2.2.1 Random locations and Google Maps trip routes
in Metro Manila natural city

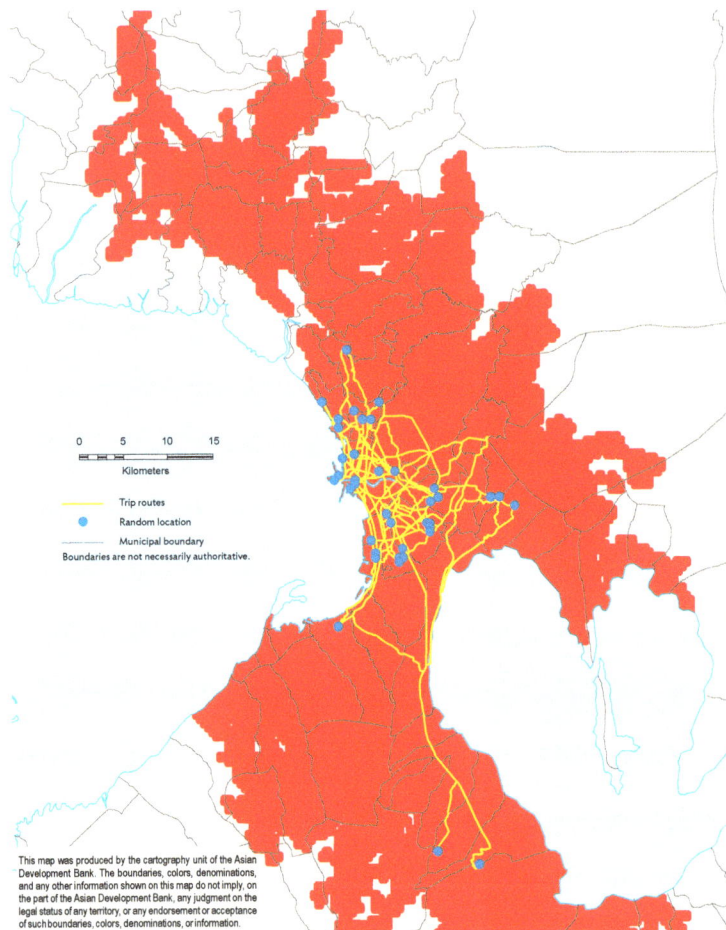

Source: ADB estimates using nighttime lights images from the National Oceanic and Atmospheric
Administration (accessed 1 April 2017 and 10 August 2018), grid population data from LandScan
Datasets of the Oak Ridge National Laboratory (accessed 31 August 2017 and 31 August 2018) and
trip routes from Google Maps (accessed 19 March 2019).

To further understand the causes of urban congestion,
we estimated regressions with citywide congestion as
the dependent variable, and city characteristics including
population, area, average NTL luminosity, and length of road
networks as explanatory variables (Table 2.2.1). Model 1 shows
that both the population and area of a natural city were
statistically significantly correlated with its congestion level.
The two variables jointly accounted for 64% of the variation
in congestion across 278 cities in the sample. This meant
that a city was more congested if it had more population in a
fixed area or had a smaller area holding population constant.
In other words, denser cities are more congested. Clearly,
population growth imposes pressure on mobility in a city, and
spatial expansion is necessary to some extent to mitigate the
pressure.

Table 2.2.1 City characteristics and traffic congestion

	Model 1	Model 2	Model 3	Model 4
Log population	0.162*** (0.016)	0.159*** (0.017)	0.134*** (0.018)	0.131*** (0.018)
Log area	–0.059*** (0.015)	–0.058*** (0.016)	–0.074*** (0.015)	–0.070*** (0.016)
Log mean luminosity		0.032 (0.045)		
Squared log mean luminosity		–0.007 (0.013)		
Log of total length of roads			0.039*** (0.010)	
Log of length of motorways				0.003 (0.008)
Log of length of primary roads				0.013*** (0.005)
Log of length of other roads				0.024*** (0.009)
Country fixed effects	Yes	Yes	Yes	Yes
Observations	278	278	277	265
R-squared	0.64	0.64	0.66	0.67

* = p<0.1, ** = p<0.05, *** = p<0.01.

Note: Values in parentheses are robust standard errors. We also applied the approach in Akbar et al. (2018) to regress the ratio of peak hour duration to the off-peak duration on the distance and direction of the trip. The city fixed effects were obtained as city-level congestion measure and regressed on city characteristics. The results were almost identical.

Source: ADB estimates using nighttime lights images from the National Oceanic and Atmospheric Administration (accessed 1 April 2017 and 10 August 2018), grid population data from LandScan Datasets of the Oak Ridge National Laboratory (accessed 31 August 2017 and 31 August 2018) and trip routes from Google Maps (accessed 19 March 2019).

In the absence of a citywide economic measure, we used average NTL luminosity as a proxy for city income level. Model 2 suggests that the economic proxy and its quadratic term have little correlation with congestion. Richer cities may have higher car ownership and more driving activity per car per day. On the other hand, higher-income cities generally have better transport infrastructure and capacity to manage traffic. The two factors may offset each other.

When road length variables are added to model 1, the total length of all types of roads (model 3), and in particular the length of primary roads and smaller roads (model 4), positively correlate with congestion. The results seem counterintuitive. However, it is well established that boosting road capacity does not ease urban congestion in the long run because it induces more driving (Duranton and Turner 2011). A positive correlation estimate between road length and congestion may result from the omission of some factors related to both road capacity and congestion. For example, cities experiencing more severe congestion may have invested more in road networks, but the networks remain far from sufficient to alleviate congestion.[10]

The analysis above may leave out a few important factors that have given rise to urban congestion in the region. One is rapid growth in car ownership and the demand for road capacity that it generates. According to data assembled by the International Organization of Motor Vehicle Manufacturers, which cover 139 economies

Figure 2.2.2 Relative congestion of natural cities with population greater than 5 million

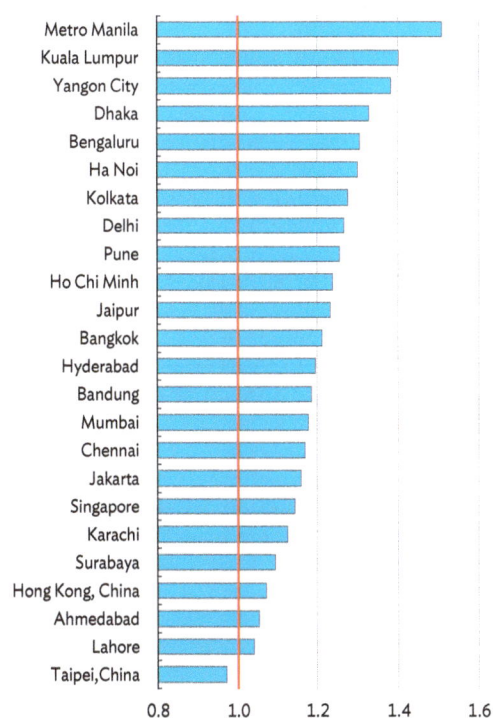

Note: Relative congestion equals the citywide congestion level divided by the sample average, 1.24. To the right of the red line means relative congestion of the city is higher than the sample average.

Source: ADB estimates using nighttime lights images from the National Oceanic and Atmospheric Administration (accessed 1 April 2017 and 10 August 2018), grid population data from LandScan Datasets of the Oak Ridge National Laboratory (accessed 31 August 2017 and 31 August 2018) and trip routes from Google Maps (accessed 19 March 2019).

around the world, the number of passenger cars increased by 293 million from 2005 to 2015. Twenty economies in developing Asia account for 56% of this increase, with the PRC alone contributing 39% (Figure 2.2.3). Besides the PRC, several economies in the region have maintained double-digit annual growth since 2005. Average annual growth rates in Brunei Darussalam, India, the Kyrgyz Republic, the PRC, and Viet Nam all exceeded 11%, more than twice the average growth rate in 70 developing economies outside of Asia (Figure 2.2.4).

Coverage, efficiency, and affordability of public transport

A lack of efficient and affordable public transportation is often considered a cause of urban congestion. Public transport becomes more attractive if it offers a cheap and speedy way for people to travel within cities, thus reducing urban congestion. Enhancing public transport is therefore considered necessary to tackle congestion and thus improve mobility within a city. However, it is possible that road capacity released when public transport is improved induces additional driving, thereby pushing congestion back to where it was before it was improved.

Evidence on the actual impacts of public transportation on congestion is mixed. Baum-Snow, Kahn, and Voith (2005) and Duranton and Turner (2011) found evidence that improving public transport does not reduce congestion in the US cities. On the other hand, Winston and Langer (2006) found that expanding rail mass transit reduced congestion, but expanding bus services did not. Anderson (2014) found that highway delays lengthened by an average of 47% during a mass transit strike in Los Angeles in 2003. Finally, Beaudoin and Lin Lawell (2018) showed that the effects of public transport supply on car travel were more prominent in the short run and in larger and more densely populated cities that had more extensive public transportation networks.

However, cities in developing Asia are generally more populous, denser, and focused on a single urban core, rather than distributed over several hubs in an urban area, as in the US. It is therefore difficult to tell whether the existing evidence, mainly from the US, also applies to developing Asia.

More importantly, car ownership in developing Asia, though growing rapidly, is still significantly lower than in the US. In many Asian cities, most urban residents rely on public transportation, including informal transport services, to commute and run daily errands. Therefore, efficient and affordable public transportation can improve urban mobility,

Figure 2.2.3 Share of passenger car increase, 2005–2015

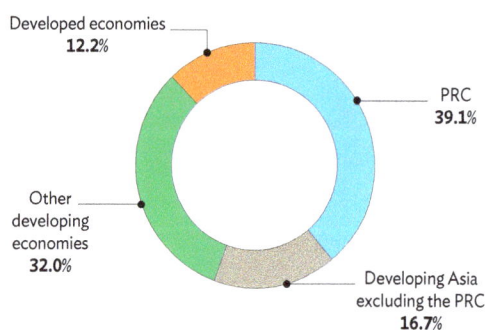

Developed economies **12.2%**

PRC **39.1%**

Other developing economies **32.0%**

Developing Asia excluding the PRC **16.7%**

PRC = People's Republic of China.
Source: ADB estimates using data from the International Organization of Motor Vehicle Manufacturers (accessed 3 July 2019).

Figure 2.2.4 Average annual passenger car growth rate in developing Asia and other economies, 2005–2015

Country growth rate
— Developing Asia
- - - Other developing economies
······ Developed economies

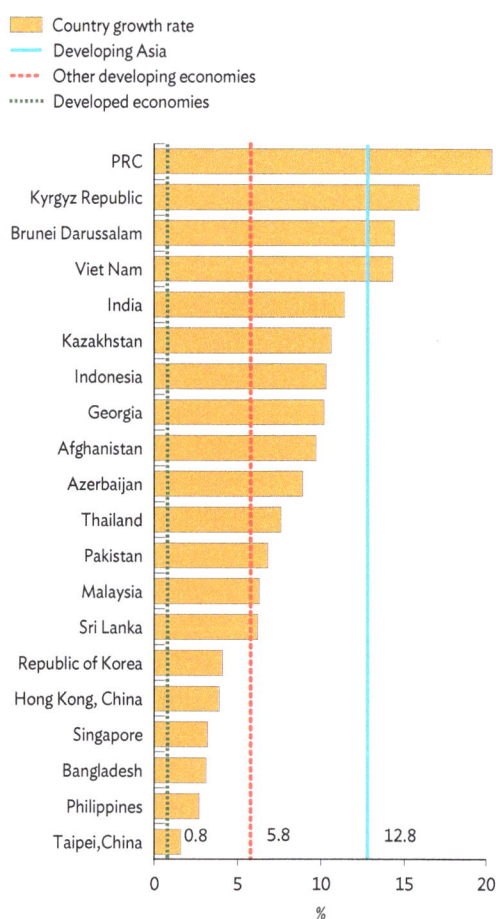

PRC
Kyrgyz Republic
Brunei Darussalam
Viet Nam
India
Kazakhstan
Indonesia
Georgia
Afghanistan
Azerbaijan
Thailand
Pakistan
Malaysia
Sri Lanka
Republic of Korea
Hong Kong, China
Singapore
Bangladesh
Philippines
Taipei,China

0.8   5.8   12.8

0   5   10   15   20
%

PRC = People's Republic of China.
Note: Passenger cars are defined as road motor vehicles other than motorcycles intended for carrying passengers and designed to seat no more than nine people. This covers taxis and hired passenger cars, provided that they have fewer than 10 seats, and may include pickups or microcars.
Source: ADB estimates using data from the International Organization of Motor Vehicle Manufacturers (accessed 3 July 2019).

especially for low-income residents, directly and greatly boosting their labor market participation. Public transport thus plays a key role in making Asian cities function as an effective labor markets.

Among the 278 natural cities for which Google Maps driving data was collected, information on travel by public transport, mainly bus and rail, was available for only 199, for which we collected public transport trip data using the same location pairs. Google Maps returned valid distance and duration results for 29,222 of 38,900 trips requested. This meant that the other 25% of the trips were not considered viable by public transport. Assuming that Google Maps has comprehensive information about public transport systems in these cities, the percentage of trips with valid results can be seen as approximating the coverage of public transport in the city. However, it is likely that Google Maps overlooks various forms of informal transport such as private hire motorcycles, tricycles, and jeepneys. These are common transport modes in many developing countries, in particular to cover the first and last mile where formal public transport systems commonly fall short. For trips in our sample with both driving and public transport information, we calculated the ratio of duration of taking public transport versus driving, considering the result an indicator of the time cost of public transport against driving as a benchmark.

A few patterns are revealed in Figure 2.2.5, which shows the share of trips with valid Google Maps transit results and the trip duration in cities of different size. Large cities with populations above 5 million showed valid results as often as 90%. This meant fairly good coverage by public transport networks in larger cities in the region despite their extensive sprawl. Medium-sized cities with populations of 1 million–5 million had the lowest percentage of viable trips by public transport, at less than two-thirds. Cities with populations of 0.5 million–1.0 million did a bit better, at 71%. This suggested considerable scope for small and medium-sized cities to improve the coverage of their formal public transport systems.

Regarding travel duration, trips by public transport are on average three times longer than driving a car. This is probably because public transport duration includes time spent walking to pickup points, waiting, stops, and walking from drop-off points. Although it is often faster to travel on less formal public transport in many cities in developing countries, and the Google Maps' likely focus on formal transport probably overstates the duration ratio, the result nevertheless signals how unattractive public transport options can be relative to driving, especially for someone sensitive to the time spent. The ratio is 2.5 in large cities but as high as 3.5 in small and medium-sized cities. Public transport is faster in large cities probably because of rail mass transit systems there. In small and medium-sized cities, where public transport largely shares roads and lanes with cars, it suffers from the same congestion delays as driving.

Figure 2.2.5 Share of trips viable by public transport and duration by city size

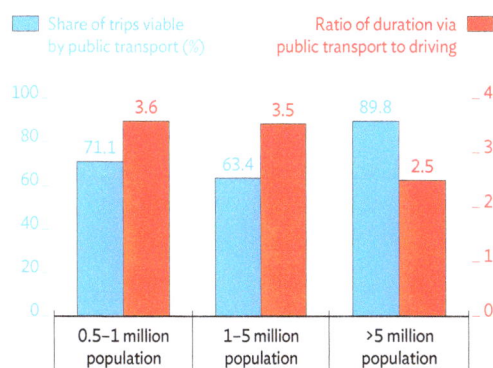

Source: ADB estimates using data from Google Maps (accessed 23 May 2019).

Figure 2.2.6 Share of income spent on 40 urban commuting trips per month in developing economies

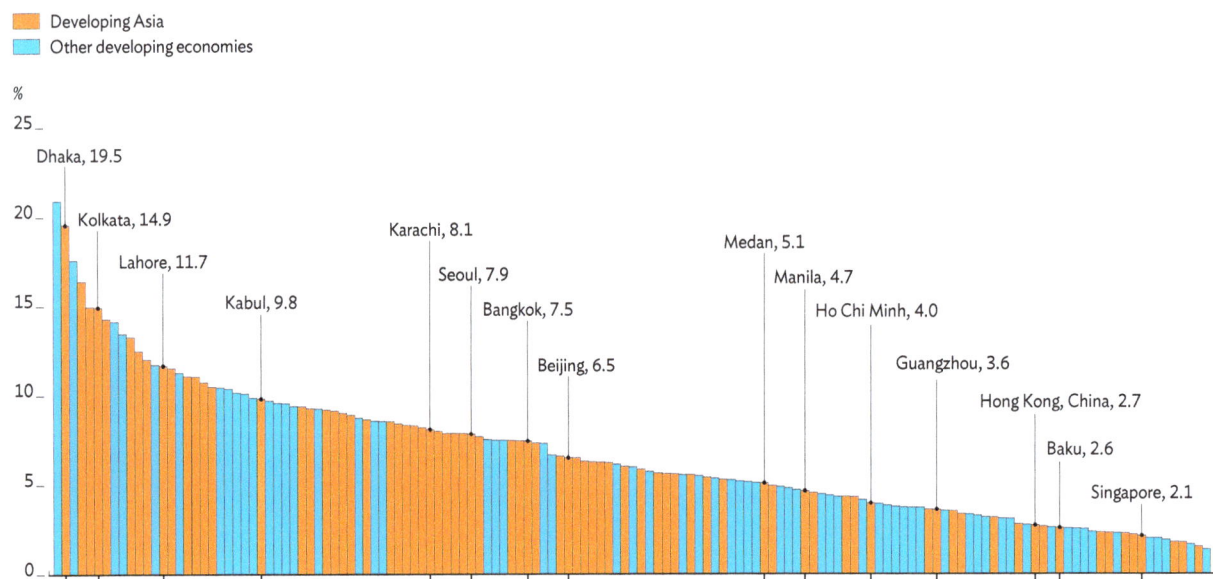

Note: Developing Asia is represented by 77 cities and developing economies in other regions by 65 cities.

Source: ADB estimates using data from the Land and Housing Survey in a Global Sample of 200 Cities of the New York University Urban Expansion Program 2016.

Aside from concern over the coverage and efficiency of existing public transport systems, affordability poses a significant challenge in the region. The Urban Expansion Program of New York University surveyed the average monetary cost of commuting on public transport in a global sample of 200 cities that included 77 cities in developing Asia and 65 cities in developing economies elsewhere. The data suggested that the average commuting cost for 40 trips per month was equal to 7.5% of monthly GDP per capita in developing Asia, well above the 6.3% average in other developing economies. Residents in a number of large cities, such as Dhaka, Kolkata, Lahore, and Kabul, spend on average 10% or more of their income on commuting (Figure 2.2.6). In these cities, public transport affordability is further compromised for low-income households because of their lower income and likely residence far from their workplace. The other options available for the urban poor are walking or riding a bicycle, but either option likely takes longer, is less convenient if not actually dangerous, and precludes job choices located far from their residence.

Other factors affecting urban mobility

Increased reliance on car travel and inadequate public transport services are not the only constraints on mobility in cities. Faulty land-use planning and sluggish policy response to urban growth can compound the problem. As shown in section 2.1, many cities in developing Asia have expanded rapidly, with residential areas probably decentralizing more rapidly than workplaces.

In the PRC, this trend can reflect the tendency of local governments to supply land for commercial use in the city core and for residential development in the suburbs, as businesses are major taxpayers. The motive of revenue maximization for local governments exacerbates the separation of jobs from residences, lengthening commutes (Jia et al. 2019).

The provision of public services typically lags the spatial development of expanding cities. Although populations increasingly move to peri-urban areas, high-quality schools and hospitals are still concentrated in city cores. Inadequate school bus services as homes move further from schools require large numbers of private vehicle trips to school during morning rush hours. Studying traffic data in Beijing, Lu, Sun, and Zheng (2017) found that trips in which parents drove children to school accounted for 15% of all car trips during rush hours. Congestion thus eased by 20% on workdays when schools were on holiday.

Urban transport directly reflects how a government manages a city, especially in metropolitan areas that sprawl over multiple jurisdictions. Weak institutional capacity and fragmented urban governance, both vertically and horizontally, are all too common in developing economies (Slack 2007). In the Philippines, for example, an estimated 31 national government agencies or more, and many more local bodies, are involved in delivering urban services (ADB 2014, Ang, Cruz, and Valle 2019). Overlapping mandates and duplicated functions are common, undermining interagency amity and coordination.

To a significant degree, in many cities across developing Asia, the dearth of effective transport planning and investment has left transport infrastructure overburdened, privately run public transport services poorly coordinated and unreliable, and private car numbers soaring.

Solutions to improve urban mobility

Urban mobility is key to realizing the economic potential of cities, keeping them dynamic, and making them more inclusive. Many cities in developing economies need to tackle the mobility problem urgently. While there is no one-size-fits-all solution, some common policy options bear consideration.

Governments should increase investment in public transport infrastructure to enlarge and improve the quantity of road and rail networks. Buses have an advantage in lower investment costs and less complex implementation and are an attractive option for small and medium-sized cities. Mass transit by rail has an advantage in larger carrying capacity and insulation from road traffic. Despite the high capital investment required, the economic benefits of rail mass transit can outweigh cost considerations in large, dense cities. As the opening of mass public transit services often drives up land value, the public capture of land appreciation is a promising option for funding urban infrastructure, as discussed in Box 2.2.1.

Box 2.2.1 Linking land value capture to sound planning maximizes funding for urban infrastructure

The rise of urbanization in developing Asia highlights significant infrastructure investment needs estimated at $26 trillion from 2016 to 2030 (ADB 2017). Given how populous and dense Asia's cities are, high-quality, well-functioning mass rapid transit networks are needed to ensure continued urban economic growth. However, mass rapid transit systems are much more expensive to build than roads, and many countries are not in a fiscal position to use debt and general budget funding to build mass rapid transit systems with the speed and scope necessary to support growing urban areas. And, because sustained investment over many years or even decades is required to produce extensive rail transit networks that can support large and dense cities, a self-sustaining approach to funding is needed.

One such funding approach is land value capture (LVC), which hinges on two assumptions. The first is that improved accessibility from transit investment adds value to property and creates other beneficiaries. The second is that all those who benefit from the value that mass transit adds should contribute their fair share to meet investment costs. If property owners are big beneficiaries from mass transit investment, it is only equitable that at least a portion of their windfall gains go to the mass transit investor, which can then use these proceeds to expand the rail network. This can generate a virtuous cycle of additional value uplift as the network expands, allowing more value retention and enabling continued investment. LVC can use a variety of mechanisms: real property taxes, special fees and levies, auctions of development rights, an urban renewal agency able to capture value, and direct property development by a rail agency (Abiad, Farrin, and Hale 2019). Cities that have successfully used LVC, including Singapore, Seoul, and Hong Kong, China, typically combine mechanisms rather than rely on just one.

The "design dividend" argues that LVC can be maximized if it is complemented by sound planning and transit-oriented development (TOD). TOD is broadly defined as mixed-use development near or oriented to mass rapid transit facilities that improves accessibility, amenities, and consequently the value of land near the station. TOD for LVC can be enacted through intelligent corridor planning and station location choices; initiatives that provide better access and connectivity to new or existing stations with the provision of feeder bus routes, bike paths, or improved pedestrian access; or initiatives to deliver better station facilities (Abiad, Farrin, and Hale 2019). Profitable public transportation is exceptionally hard to achieve but not impossible if innovative TOD and beneficiary funding mechanisms like LVC are incorporated into master transportation plans for urban areas.

Hong Kong, China has managed to ensure that more than half of all income to railway operators comes from property development in its "rail + property" model. With recent emphasis on pedestrian access in station development projects, a rail + property station with a TOD design averages 35,000 additional weekday passengers, and associated housing price premiums range from 5% to 30% (Cervero and Murakami 2009).

LVC is a promising approach, but operationalizing it in cities in developing Asia requires that a number of challenges be tackled.

Weak taxation systems can undermine the potential of LVC with typically outdated land and property assessments, underreporting of property sales values, poor tax enforcement and high tax avoidance, and inadequate regulatory provision for special levies to support transport projects. So can concentrated property development markets, which deprive governments of negotiating power as they attempt to recoup the costs of investment in public transit infrastructure. Megacities in developing Asia often have property markets dominated by few powerful developers who can influence land supply and price. One option that would generate more LVC revenue for governments is to open the property development market to more foreign competition, as more participants would make auctions of development rights more competitive.

Finally, some transit agencies are constrained in scope or have little experience in commercial development. In Bangkok, for example, transit agencies cannot engage in property development because a regulation forbids their acquiring land for uses other than transit development (Anantsuksomsri et al. 2018), severely limiting TOD opportunities from a rail agency as property developer. Charter or regulation changes would allow transit agencies in many Asian cities to plan and finance mass rapid transit from a more commercial perspective.

References:

Abiad, A., K. Farrin, and C. Hale. 2019. *Sustaining Transit Investment in Asia's Cities: A Beneficiary-Funding and Land Value Capture Perspective.* Asian Development Bank.

ADB. 2017. *Meeting Asia's Infrastructure Needs.* Asian Development Bank.

Anantsuksomsri, S., N. Tontisirin, S. Srisamran, S. T. Hansasooksin, E. Ayaragarnchanakul, and P. Chokesuwattanaskul. 2018. Assessing Impacts of Proximity to Mass Transit on Land Values in Thailand. *Background study prepared for the Asian Development Bank.*

Cervero, R. and J. Murakami. 2009. Rail and Property Development in Hong Kong: Experiences and Extensions. *Urban Studies* 46(10).

Multimodal transport systems can extend the coverage of public transport systems by improving connectivity in the first and last mile. Investment, policy, and comprehensive mobility planning and regulation may encourage complementary modes of travel using high-frequency and high-occupancy vehicles like minibuses and tricycles, which should be integrated seamlessly into existing public transport systems.

While privately run public transportation has a role to play in urban transport systems in many developing Asian cities, it should be regulated and coordinated under a government agency. Private operators should be asked to cover routes not only where passengers are abundant, but also where they are scarce, and the number of vehicles should be controlled and optimized. Whether operators are public or private, government subsidies should be offered as needed to make public transport affordable to low-income residents. The rise of ridesharing and bike-sharing modes fills gaps in urban transportation, but it poses new governance and regulatory challenges regarding induced traffic and customer safety.

It is desirable to unify urban transport governance functions under a few agencies responsible for planning and implementing transport development, supervising transportation operators, and managing traffic, even if the metropolitan area comprises multiple jurisdictions. While it is common to have separate agencies work on land-use planning and urban infrastructure development, the government should set up institutional mechanisms to foster coordination between them.

Mobility should be a priority of land-use planning. Not only should transport networks be adapted to the physical expansion of cities, land for public service facilities and commercial buildings should be allocated along with land for residences in newly developed urban areas. This can make a fair portion of driving trips shorter, undertaken outside core urban areas.

Demand-side management is needed to control the growth of car ownership and reduce automobile travel because supply-side interventions regularly lose out to induced demand. With worsening traffic problems, coding schemes adopted in some Asian cities seem inadequate. Though politically unpopular, pricing measures such as stiffer parking tariffs, gasoline taxes, and congestion fees merit more serious consideration as effective ways to tackle congestion and pollution. Quotas allocated by either auction or lottery are also recommended for issuing new license plates. Also worth considering is that reduced driving helps combat urban air pollution, another big challenge in Asian cities (Box 2.2.2).

Obviously, the institutional reforms and policy instruments enumerated above should be adapted and prioritized to fit local circumstances. It is unavoidable, though, that the government plays a pivotal role in designing, implementing, and enforcing them. Responsibility falls to the public sector to show the resolution and capacity necessary to ensure urban mobility.

Box 2.2.2 Tackling air pollution in Asian cities

The majority of Asia's densely populated and rapidly growing cities experience air pollution that poses a significant risk to health. An ADB study categorized the air in 61% of large cities and 52% of medium-sized cities in Asia as "poor to critical" in terms of air pollution and health implications (ADB 2018a). Research has linked air pollution to respiratory and cardiovascular disease, miscarriage, premature birth, neurological pathology in children, and dementia in the elderly (Schraufnagel et al. 2019). Indoor and outdoor air pollution prematurely kill 4 million people in urban and rural Asia each year, with children and the poor, infirm, and elderly particularly vulnerable (CCAC 2018).

Tackling urban air pollution is a highly complex task in light of its many sources, including energy and heat generation, transport, construction, and, in peri-urban areas, the open-air burning of solid waste or crop residues. Cities must adopt holistic, integrated, and multisector approaches involving diverse stakeholders, as well as sound urban planning and design and, finally, strong environmental governance to monitor air quality and enforce regulations.

Each city faces a unique combination of air pollution issues, but ADB (2018b) found several commonalities. Cities need to address the root causes of air pollution rather than its symptoms. Technical capacity to assess, monitor, and enforce compliance should be developed to ensure that air quality laws and regulations are upheld. Cities must move away from burning fossil fuels and building car-centric road networks in favor of cleaner and renewable energy—especially where households still rely on burning biomass, wood, coal, or kerosene to cook and to heat and light their homes—and in favor of integrated mass transit systems that combine trains, buses, bicycles, and footpaths. National governments need to introduce environmental regulations and economic instruments that support the rapid uptake of cleaner fuel, renewables, and technologies that are energy-efficient and control pollution. Where national governments have yet to adopt Euro 4, 5, or 6 vehicle emission and fuel standards, city streets continue to be plied by highly polluting vehicles.

Investment in air quality management requires a staged approach. First, cities should identify the extent and causes of air pollution across their jurisdiction through emission inventories, monitoring, and modelling studies, while evaluating their current practices for managing air quality. Next, a roadmap should be developed to prioritize and address air pollution issues through a clean air action plan, considering both policy and cost-effective technological solutions nationally and locally. The measures thus identified should be integrated into sector policies, plans and programs, and budgeting and financing mechanisms to support a phased program of air pollution management while, at the same time, raising awareness of the problem. This staged approach has successfully been adopted by ADB-supported programs in Ulaanbaatar (ADB 2018b, 2018c) and the Beijing–Hebei–Tianjin region (ADB 2013, 2018d). Beijing, for example, has shown that a city where air pollution is worsened by coal burning and motor vehicles can, with sufficient investment and political will, improve its air quality. From 2013 to 2017, the systematic introduction of measures to address air pollution reduced sulfur dioxide by 83%, nitrogen oxides by 43%, and fine particulate matter by 35% (United Nations Environment Programme 2019).

References:

Asian Development Bank (ADB). 2013. *Addressing Beijing Air Pollution.* ADB.

———. 2018a. *Mainstreaming Air Quality in Urban Development through South-South Twinning.* Consultant's report on TA 8751-Regional.

———. 2018b. ADB Loan to Help Improve Air Quality, Living Conditions in Ulaanbaatar. News release. 23 March.

———. 2018c. *Winning the Fight Against Air Pollution in Ulaanbaatar.* Asian Development Bank.

———. 2018d. ADB Loan to Pilot Clean Heating Systems, Cut Carbon Emissions in PRC. News release. 13 December.

CCAC. 2018. *New Report Outlines Air Pollution Measures That Can Save Millions of Lives and Slow Climate Change.* Climate and Clean Air Coalition.

Schraufnagel, D. E., J. R. Balmes, C. T. Cowl, S. D. Matteis, S.-H. Jung, K. Mortimer, R. Perez-Padilla, M. B. Rice, H. Riojas-Rodriguez, A. Sood, G. D. Thurston, T. To, A. Vanker, and D. J. Wuebbles. 2019. Air Pollution and Noncommunicable Diseases: A Review by the Forum of International Respiratory Societies' Environmental Committee, Part 1: The Damaging Effects of Air Pollution. *Chest* 155(2).

United Nations Environment Programme. 2019. Beijing Air Improvements Provide Model for Other Cities. News release. 9 March.

2.2.2 Land use management

Land-use management encompasses how land is developed and how its usage is defined and regulated. It affects urban mobility in profound ways and thus underlies a city's functioning as an efficient labor market. Land-use management starts with planning, in which governments ensure that land configuration, resources, facilities, and services advance the well-being of urban and rural communities. Time horizons for land-use planning vary from a short-term perspective of 1–3 years to longer-term plans looking ahead 10 or 20 years or more.

Urban land-use planning in developing Asia

While institutional arrangements for urban planning differ across countries, multiple government layers and agencies are usually involved. In India, for example, the Town and City Planning Organisation, a technical wing of the national Ministry of Housing and Urban Affairs, assists and advises central, state, and local governments in matters pertaining to urban and regional planning and development. In addition, perspective plans and regional plans are prepared by states, and development plans and local area plans by cities. While lower-level plans affect land use directly, upper-level plans can have at least indirect influence (Table 2.2.2).

Table 2.2.2 The planning framework in India

Broad plan	Scope and purpose	Time frame	Specific plans and documents	Government level and department
State Level				
Perspective plan	Develop vision and provide a policy framework for urban and regional development	20 years	Vision document, concept plan, and mission statement	State government's planning program, monitoring, and statistics department
Regional plan	Identify the region and regional resources for development within which a settlement or urban plan will be prepared and regulated by the district planning committee	20 years	Regional plan and subregional plan	State government's regional development authority, directorate of town planning, state town planning board, and regional development authority
City Level				
Development plan	Prepare comprehensive development plans for urban areas and peri-urban areas under the control of development authorities of the metropolitan planning committee	20–30 years	District development plan, comprehensive development plan, master plan, and revised development plan	Municipal corporation's development authority and metropolitan planning committee
Local area plan	Detail the sub-city land-use plan and integrate it with urban infrastructure, mobility plans, and services	5–20 years	Town planning scheme, zonal and sub-city plan, ward committee plan, coastal zone management plan and urban redevelopment plan, and city-level mobility plans	Municipal corporation's development authority, metropolitan planning committee, directorate of municipal administration, and urban development department

Source: Government of India 2014.

Across developing Asia, governments face common constraints on land-use planning. First, ministries and their subnational counterparts responsible for transport, housing, water supply and sanitation, and so on often take a sector approach to planning and operation. With distinct mandates and budgets, these agencies typically work in sectoral silos with little integrated infrastructure planning or service provision in cities. Instead of a sector approach to urban development, governments should consider the physical area as a whole. Land-use planning that integrates infrastructure planning and other public service planning can make the use of land and other resources more efficient and sustainable. In many countries, urban land use is managed under multiple government entities without much coordination.

Planning coordination can languish between local governments, creating friction and even contradiction as local governments pursue competing interests. The Bangkok Metropolitan Region, for instance, encompasses Bangkok and five adjacent provinces. However, as there is no single governing body, each province does its own land-use planning and management. Figure 2.2.7 illustrates conflict in the most current comprehensive land-use plans of Bangkok and Samut Prakan Province, announced in 2013. The Bangkok plan designated the green area within the dotted border as a rural and agricultural conservation zone to serve as a floodway running east from Bangkok to the Gulf of Thailand. Samut Prakan, however, placed Suvarnabhumi Airport in the blue area, blocking the floodway from Bangkok. A result of such crossed purposes is that residents face higher risk of natural hazards. Such lack of coordination between two province-level governments can require mediation by the national government. Recognizing this, the Department of Public Works and Town and Country Planning, under the Ministry of Interior, began in 2017 to collaborate with Bangkok Metropolitan Region province-level governments on a regional plan.

Local city governments should play a pivotal role in land-use planning in light of their local knowledge about demands and constraints. However, this is not always the case in developing Asia. In Pakistan, for example, cities are run mostly by federal civil service staff, with little or no participation by local governments. Civil servants occupy local government positions at the beginning of their career, graduate to the provincial government in midcareer, and end up holding senior positions in the national government. City governments thus tend to be too junior to strike an independent course, while most city supervisors have limited local buy-in and rarely stay long enough to belong (Haque 2015).

Figure 2.2.7 Conflicting Bangkok and Samut Prakan land-use plans in 2013

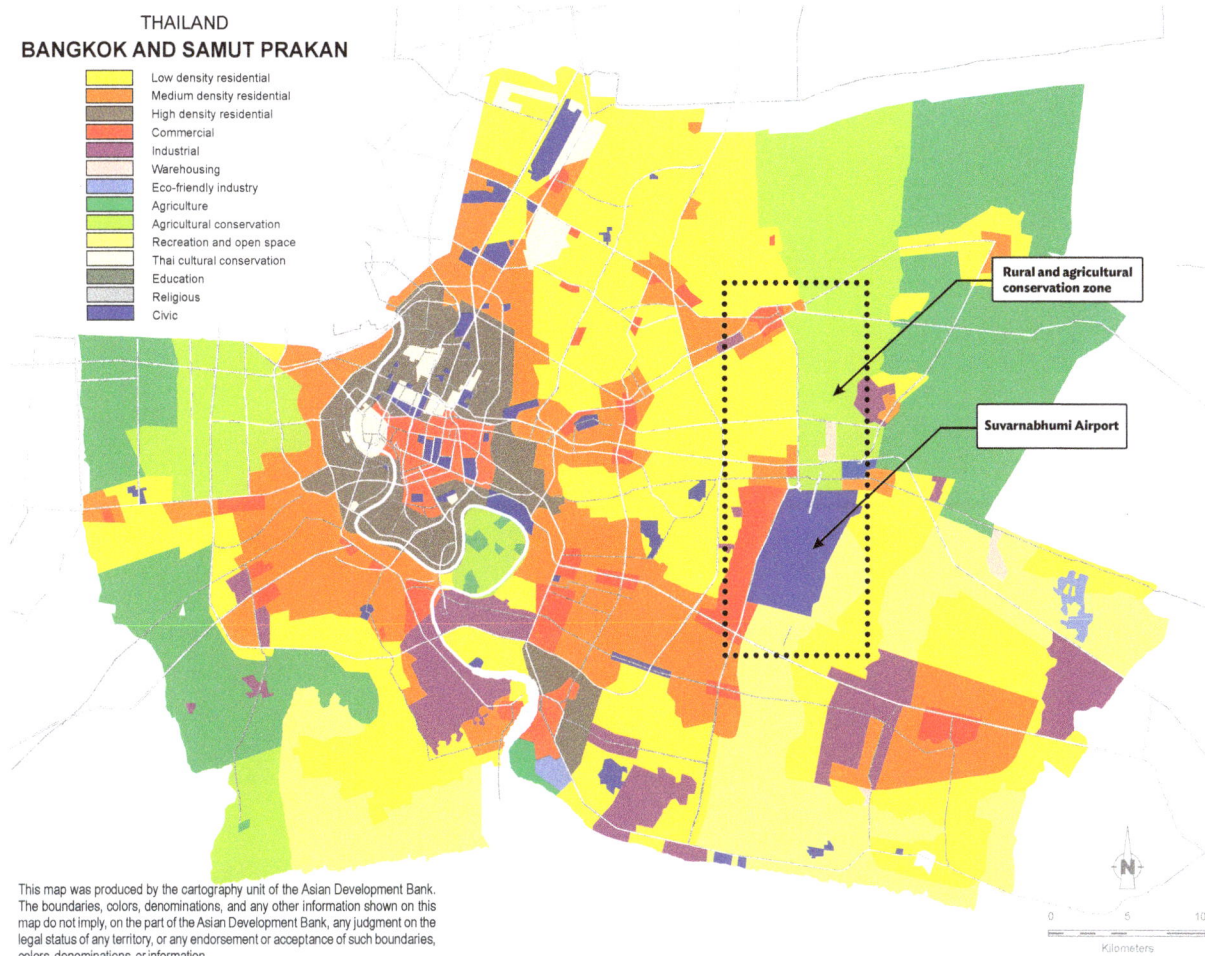

THAILAND
BANGKOK AND SAMUT PRAKAN

- Low density residential
- Medium density residential
- High density residential
- Commercial
- Industrial
- Warehousing
- Eco-friendly industry
- Agriculture
- Agricultural conservation
- Recreation and open space
- Thai cultural conservation
- Education
- Religious
- Civic

Rural and agricultural conservation zone

Suvarnabhumi Airport

This map was produced by the cartography unit of the Asian Development Bank. The boundaries, colors, denominations, and any other information shown on this map do not imply, on the part of the Asian Development Bank, any judgment on the legal status of any territory, or any endorsement or acceptance of such boundaries, colors, denominations, or information.

Source: Association of Siamese Architects.

Moreover, local governments depend heavily on upper-level governments for finance. In Thailand, municipal governments function as administrative arms of the central and provincial authorities despite officially being self-governing authorities. The country became more decentralized when the 1997 constitution was promulgated, but the responsibilities, functions, and budgets of local governments remain limited.

Lack of expertise and capacity hampers effective planning by local governments. Central and provincial or state governments often retain more competent planners even when planning power is delegated to local governments. In many cases, local planning officers have insufficient formal training, and the resulting lack of human capital contrasts sharply with the challenges posed by rapid urban growth. Moreover, local governments have only limited access to the disaggregated data and information necessary for detailed land-use planning.

Further, significant gaps often exist between land-use plans and their implementation. This partly reflects separate and uncoordinated planning and implementing bodies. Some countries' political economy condemns them to poor plan implementation, with land-use plans adjusted retroactively to accommodate unplanned developments even though they deviate from the public interest and optimal resource use.

Finally, land-use plans are unable to keep pace with rapid urban population increase and land development. Overly prescriptive land-use plans can go without updating for some time, are often limited to only part of the urban area, have no connection with other socioeconomic or investment plans, and are thus rendered unfeasible.

To overcome some of these issues, one approach now being used is to complement city master plans with integrated urban action plans. Action plans explicitly allow for mixed land use and emphasize multimodal transportation, low pollution, and high-quality public open spaces. They encourage participatory planning and investment-oriented decision-making, bringing together private businesses, government agencies, and civil society to address multisector institutional coordination issues. Whereas city master plans have a detailed spatial-planning perspective with a long time frame and list of projects, action plans comprise a matrix of investments over the short, medium, and long term. They bridge the gap between land-use plans and their implementation by linking them to appropriate financing mechanisms. Moving beyond the master plan, the action plan organizes a smaller number of projects into high-priority development initiatives with time-bound investment and implementation schedules (Sandhu et al. 2016).

Planning for urban expansion[11]

As shown in section 2.1, Asian cities have experienced considerable spatial expansion in the past few decades. The average area of a natural city increased from 116 km^2 in 1992 to 384 km^2 in 2016, with the median rising from 26 km^2 to 156 km^2. Evidence suggests that expansion, especially in developing countries, is largely unplanned and disorderly. This underscores the need for governments to lay out urban areas with foresight and obtain rights-of-way for later development before most of the land is occupied by other users.

As Jacobs (1992) recognized, street layout can significantly affect peoples' ability to obtain the benefits that come with sufficiently dense urban neighborhoods. O'Grady (2014) further noted how a grid layout, instituted from the initial demarcation of urban land to create uniform rectangular blocks, can prevent incompatible subdivisions. Connectivity between and within urban areas is thus facilitated, and the cost of basic urban infrastructure such as water supply and sewerage is held down. On the micro level, defining, measuring, and addressing property lots becomes easier. A grid layout makes urban spatial growth and functional development more predictable and therefore supportive of various actors' investment decisions.

Figure 2.2.8 Share of residential land not laid out at all or laid out only informally

Share of total residential land, %

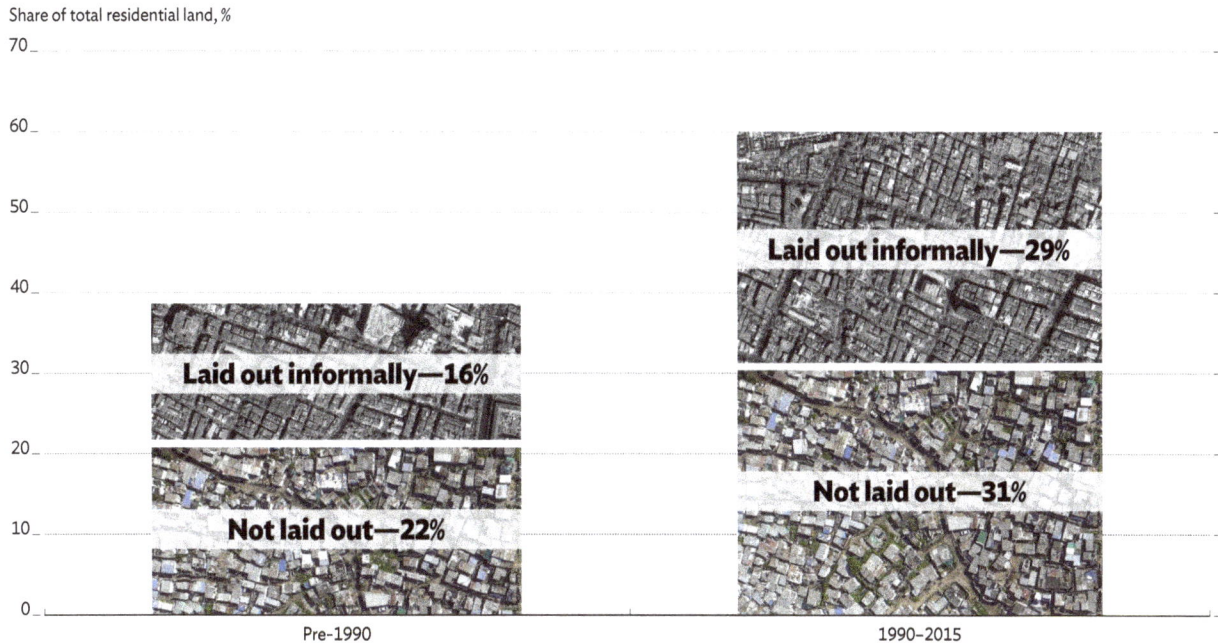

Source: Adapted from Angel et al. (2016).

It also facilitates the later redevelopment of rectangular properties, which can better accommodate changing use as demand evolves.

Despite the advantages of planned grid patterns, the share of gridded areas is in steady decline. The 200-city dataset from the Urban Expansion Program shows the share of residential land that is not laid out at all increasing from 22% before 1990 to 31% in urban areas developed from 1990 to 2015, and the share of land informally laid out almost doubling from 16% to 29%. This increases the share of residential land not planned by government from 38% to a staggering 60% within 25 years (Figure 2.2.8).

Figure 2.2.9 compares developing Asia with other developing regions. On average, the share of residential land laid out before development is lower in Asian cities than in other developing regions except sub-Saharan Africa. Within the region, cities of East Asia (mainly in the PRC) and Southeast Asia have witnessed since 1990 a significant drop in the share of residential land laid out before occupation.

Unplanned or informal layout compromises connectivity with the rest of the city and the provision of infrastructure. Indicatively, the Urban Expansion Program dataset shows that 60% of the new developments in cities in developing countries are not connected to a central water system, with many households depending on water from wells or a combination of wells, water trucks, and rainwater capture.

Figure 2.2.9 Share of residential land laid out before development by region

Pre–1990
1990–2015

Share of residential area, %

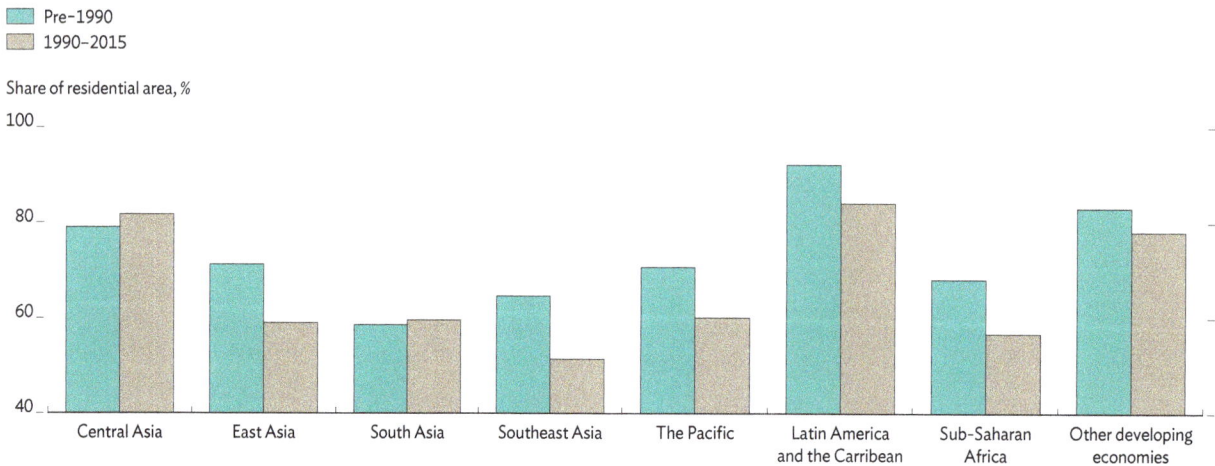

Source: ADB estimates using data from the Land and Housing Survey in a Global Sample of Cities of the New York University Urban Expansion Program 2016.

This lack of basic infrastructure poses numerous challenges, including higher service costs for low-income households, sustainability concerns about excessively discharging groundwater resources, and reduced productivity and income caused by health risks from unsafe water.

While a lack of gridded street layouts in expanded urban areas can be traced to a variety of causes in each city, at least two are worth noting. First, urban demarcation patterns are slow to change, and existing systems without grids can encourage disorderly street development. Because street pattern changes appear in "bursts of planning" (Ellickson 2013), implementing a grid system requires a great deal of coordinated effort. Second, land-use regulations are often too stringent, with outdated regulations that do not correspond to actual conditions or the incomes and characteristics of a significant number of households. This proliferates areas that are laid out informally at best before occupation. These considerations illustrate the importance of initial investments to create grid systems that can accommodate future urban growth and improve urban mobility.

Another important aspect of urban land use related to mobility is access to arterial roads and local streets. The spatial distribution of jobs evolves as cities become larger. To function as integrated labor markets over the long term, cities need to keep their residents mobile and as many jobs as possible within a reasonable commuting time. Expanding arterials roads and streets is essential to connect all residences to as many workplaces as possible in the city through a variety of transport modes.

Figure 2.2.10 Share of built-up area within walking distance (625 meters) of an arterial road, by region

Pre–1990
1990–2015

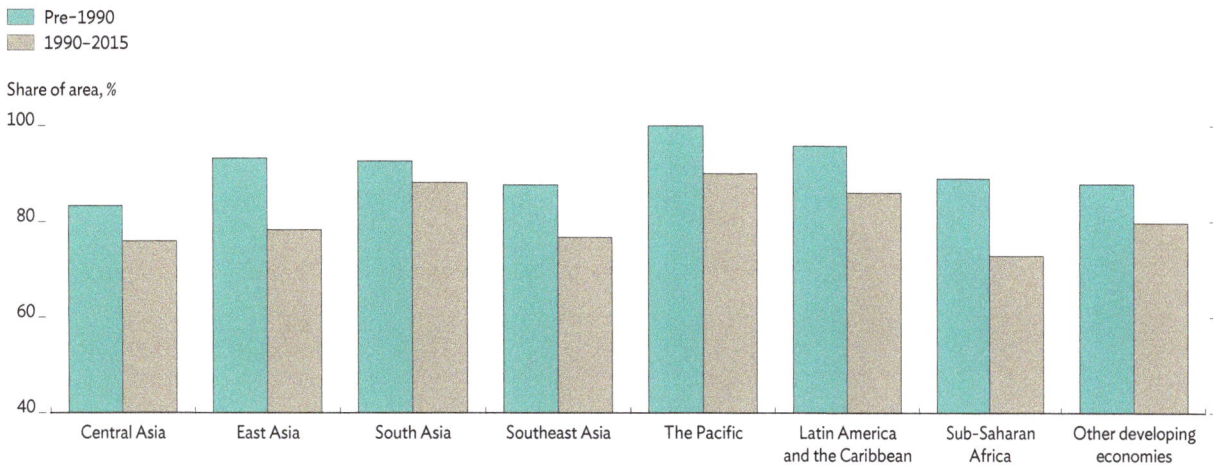

Source: ADB estimates using data from the Land and Housing Survey in a Global Sample of Cities of the New York University Urban Expansion Program 2016.

The Urban Expansion Program 200-city dataset shows that the share of built-up areas within walking distance (defined as 625 meters) from an arterial road has declined over time across developing countries (Figure 2.2.10). Cities in East Asia (mainly in the PRC), Southeast Asia, and sub-Saharan Africa have seen more dramatic decreases than the rest of the world. Reduced access to arterial roads in the expansion areas of cities constrains worker mobility and compromises cities' realization of the productivity gains associated with agglomeration economies. In an in-depth review of urbanization in sub-Saharan Africa—the region with the lowest share of built-up area within walking distance of arterial roads—Lall, Henderson, and Venables (2017) found that African cities were typically disconnected because they had developed as collections of small, fragmented neighborhoods lacking reliable transportation. This limited access to jobs and prevented firms from reaping the benefits of scale and agglomeration.

The data further reveal that, in the expansion areas of many cities, not enough land is allocated to local streets, which segregates neighborhoods, limits route options, and leaves severe bottlenecks going into and out of neighborhoods. Dhaka is particularly illustrative. In the city's expansion area, only 12% of the built-up area is allocated to streets, only half of the 24% allocated in Mumbai (Figure 2.2.11). Coupled with a deficient public transport system and a rising number of private cars, Dhaka has some of the worst traffic congestion in the world.

Given how long spatial patterns and road networks persist once they are built, and how profoundly they affect a city's economic outcomes, it is crucial for governments in developing Asia to plan ahead before urban expansion occurs. The government should identify areas for possible expansion and estimate the amount of land needed for the next 2 decades or longer.

Figure 2.2.11 Area devoted to streets in expansion areas of Dhaka (left) and Mumbai

Source: Adapted from Angel et al. (2016).

First it must obtain planning jurisdiction over the entire area. Good planning requires the government to lay out and acquire the land for an arterial grid with roads that are wide enough and properly spaced throughout the expansion area. The government should also acquire land rights for public open spaces to ensure that environmentally sensitive land is protected from new urban development.

These measures require minimal investment or changes to existing planning frameworks. Yet land acquisition can be time-consuming and legally challenging where local governments already strain to keep up with current urban management challenges—never mind planning far into the future. Given rapid urban expansion in developing Asia, governments need to plan ahead to ensure adequate breathing space for detailed urban planning later—developing plans based on efficiently laid-out grids.

Land-use regulations

Land-use regulation affects various aspects of urban development, including housing affordability, infrastructure provision, and even the ease of doing business. The many common land-use regulations fall into five categories: limits and geographic preferences on development density and intensity, design and performance standards for lots and buildings, monetary and time costs imposed on developers, the sequestering of land from development, and direct and indirect controls on the addition of buildings and population (Deakin 1989).

Table 2.2.3 Monetary and time costs imposed on developers by region, annual average, 2006–2019

	Developing Asia	Latin America and the Caribbean	Other developing economies	Developed economies
Dealing with construction permits				
Cost (% of warehouse value)	125.3	105.6	167.2	68.6
Time (days)	164.6	132.5	123.0	142.7
Procedure (steps)	15.7	13.1	12.9	13.4
Registering property				
Cost (% of property value)	4.5	5.9	8.2	4.2
Time (days)	79.4	67.2	63.5	35.7
Procedure (steps)	5.8	7.1	6.4	4.9
Number of cities	38	33	72	43

Source: ADB estimates using data from World Bank's Doing Business (accessed 15 May 2019).

Examples of land-use regulations are zoning laws, building height restrictions, and minimum lot sizes.

While directly comparing actual regulations and rules across cities is difficult, it is possible to gauge how stringent the regulatory environment is for urban land around the world using the World Bank's *Doing Business 2006–2019* survey (Monkkonen and Ronconi 2016). Interviews with business owners and professionals who deal with regulations, such as lawyers, are asked to estimate the monetary cost, time spent, and steps required to obtain a construction permit and register property in their locality. Using this information as a proxy for the stringency of land-use regulation, Table 2.2.3 shows averages of these values across cities from 2006 to 2019 in developing Asia, Latin American and the Caribbean (LAC), and other regions.

For construction permits, businesses in developing Asia spent 125% of warehouse value, as opposed to 106% in LAC and 69% in the developed economies. Not only is the financial cost higher, businesses bear longer waiting times: 165 days in developing Asia, 143 days in developed economies, 133 in LAC, and 123 days in other developing regions. They endure more administrative and bureaucratic steps: 16 steps in developing Asia versus 13 in other regions on average. When registering a property, businesses in developing Asia experience longer waiting times—79 days against 67 in LAC—but pay lower financial cost and traverse fewer procedural steps than in other developing regions.

This problem has hardly become less onerous over time. Figure 2.2.12 shows the trend of costs for developers from 2006 to 2019 by region. The monetary costs associated with acquiring a construction permit or registering a property remain relatively steady in each region, with some drops in the property registration cost in other developing economies.

Figure 2.2.12 Trends in monetary and time costs imposed on developers

- Developing Asia
- Latin America and the Carribean
- Other developing economies
- Developed economies

A. Construction permit cost

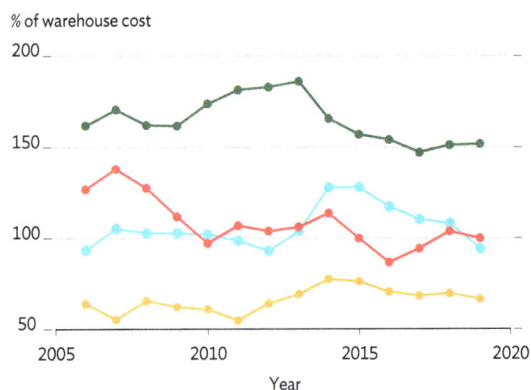

% of warehouse cost

B. Registering property cost

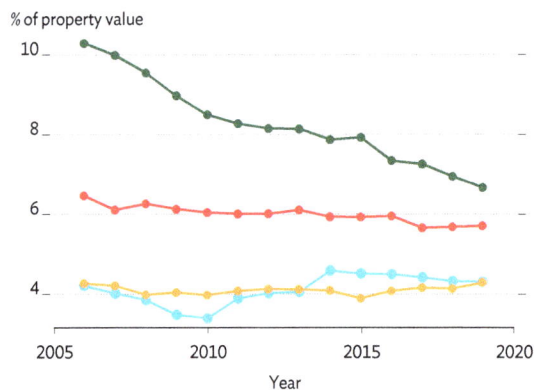

% of property value

C. Construction permit, number of procedures

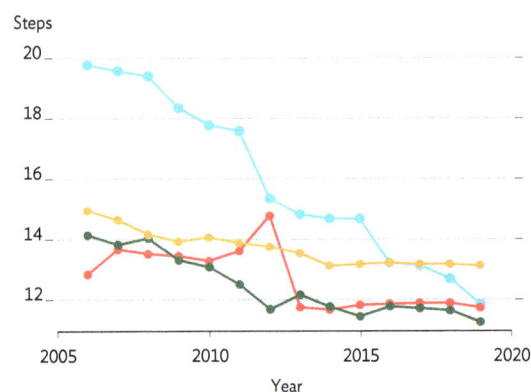

Steps

D. Registering property, number of procedures

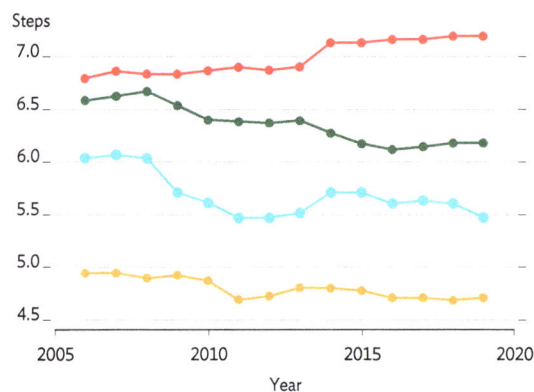

Steps

E. Construction permit, processing days

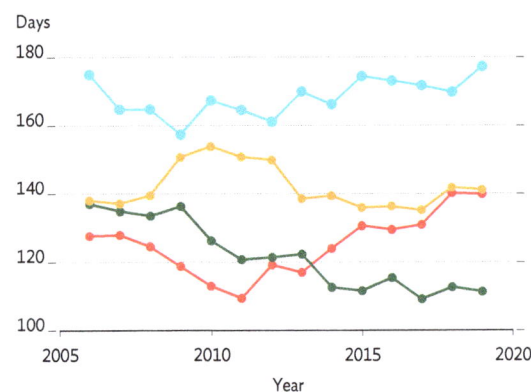

Days

F. Registering property, processing days

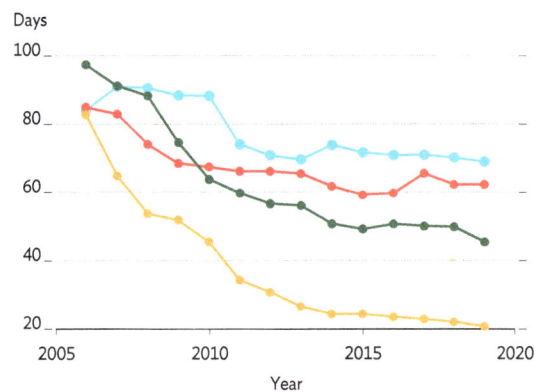

Days

Note: Each data point is a regional average across cities.

Source: ADB estimates using data from World Bank's *Doing Business* (accessed 15 May 2019).

The average number of steps required to acquire a construction permit in developing Asia, reduced from about 20 in 2006 to 12 in 2019, converges with other regions. However, the waiting time in the region for a construction permit did not drop—and even increased slightly in recent years. This implies that, despite efforts to relax construction permit regulations, the time spent acquiring a permit has not changed much. The number of days required to register a property has declined across regions, but with developing Asia remaining higher than others.

Evidence from individual Asian countries suggests that some other dimensions of land-use regulation such as floor area ratio (FAR) and building height limits are too restrictive. Vishwanath et al. (2013) showed that FARs in central areas of several cities in developing economies are much lower than for cities in developed economies (Figure 2.2.13). Sridhar (2010) summarized that, across Indian cities, the average residential FAR is just 2.4, with a minimum of 1.0 and a maximum of 4.0. Such restrictive land-use regulation can force households to locate far from their preferred neighborhood, shrinking a metropolitan area's effective labor market by expanding spatial area and commute time, and thus undermining productivity. Brueckner and Sridhar (2012) estimated that 1-unit relaxation in a typical Indian city's FAR could shrink its spatial area by 20%, reducing commuting times and costs correspondingly. If land-use regulations are not harmonized within metropolitan areas, a low FAR in the core area can encourage growth in and around adjacent cities that are less restrictive.

In sum, Asian cities have room to reduce urban development costs arising from restrictive land-use regulation. Limits on development density and intensity should be prescribed, with reference to international best practice, to enhance land-use efficiency and the quality of life. Still, sound land-use regulation should harmonize economic development with environmental sustainability.

2.2.3 Adequate affordable housing

Housing adequacy depends on affordability. As housing becomes unaffordable, households typically have no alternative but to occupy inadequate housing often remote from jobs and public amenities. For households to enjoy decent living conditions, the dwelling must be both affordable and adequate.

Housing affordability and adequacy

Ample anecdotal evidence exists that urban home prices in Asia and the Pacific have risen rapidly in recent years (ADB 2018).

Figure 2.2.13 City center floor area ratios in selected cities around the world

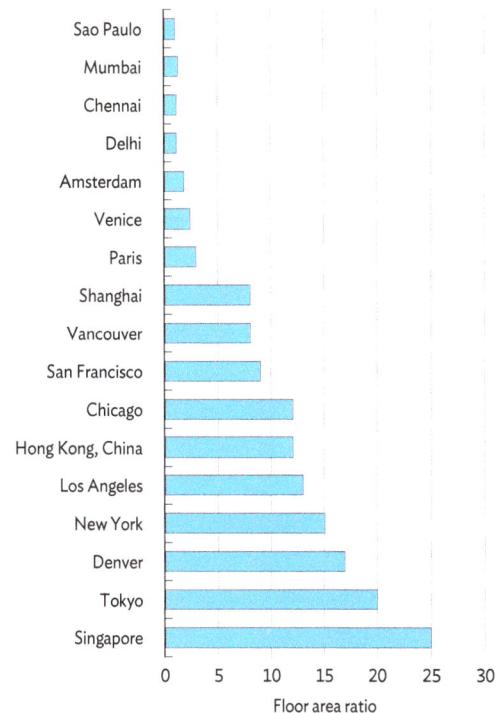

Source: Adapted from Vishwanath et al. (2013).

Rapid urbanization has combined with economic growth and higher incomes to substantially increase demand for urban housing. In addition, many cities have experienced natural growth as the number of individual households grows with lifestyle changes that, for example, mean fewer intergenerational households. Surging demand has met relatively inelastic supply, especially in cities with narrow administrative and geographic boundaries and strict land-use regulations. As housing demand outstrips supply, housing prices soar. However, the absence of comprehensive, consistent, and comparable data on housing prices across cities has impeded systematic analysis of housing affordability in the region. This section aims to close that gap.

We collected home price data at the city level from a variety of official and private sources to assemble estimates for 211 cities in 2018 in 27 ADB developing member countries: Armenia, Azerbaijan, Bangladesh, Bhutan, Fiji, Georgia, India, Indonesia, Kazakhstan, the Kyrgyz Republic, the Lao People's Democratic Republic, Malaysia, Maldives, Mongolia, Myanmar, Nepal, Pakistan, Papua New Guinea, the Philippines, the PRC, Solomon Islands, Sri Lanka, Tajikistan, Thailand, Timor-Leste, Vanuatu, and Viet Nam.[12]

To gauge housing affordability across cities, the price-to-income ratio (PIR) was computed as the median house price divided by the annual median household income.[13] Median household income data came from household income and expenditure surveys and from World Bank PovcalNet data on national average monthly household expenditure or income. Following the commonly used definition in Demographia (2019), housing is considered affordable if the PIR is not above 3.0, moderately unaffordable from 3.1 to 4.0, seriously unaffordable from 4.1 to 5.0, and severely unaffordable from 5.1.

Results show 98.6% of surveyed cities with unaffordable housing and more than 90% with severely unaffordable housing (Figure 2.2.14). The average PIR is 15.8, substantially worse than in the early 2000s when it was 11.3 (UN-Habitat 2001). This PIR is substantially higher than in developed countries, where the average is 3–6. Especially large cities might be expected to have high PIRs as they attract the largest absolute number of new residents. However, the PIR is similarly high in cities with populations just above 1 million, at 16.2, and below 1 million, at 15.3. Housing has thus become highly expensive in most cities across Asia and the Pacific, leaving hundreds of millions without affordable homes.

The PIR is an agreed measure of housing affordability, but no internationally agreed definition exists for housing adequacy. One reason is that perceptions of what constitutes adequate housing vary substantially across communities and countries. For this chapter, we argue that, the variety of perceptions notwithstanding, housing should satisfy four

Figure 2.2.14 Housing affordability in 211 cities in 27 economies in Asia and the Pacific

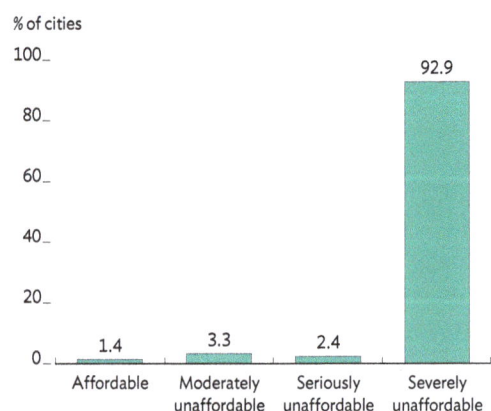

% of cities

Source: ADB estimates using data from Colliers International; Global Property Guide; household income and expenditure surveys, various countries; Knight Frank; Makaan; National Bureau of Statistics, People's Republic of China; Numbeo; World Bank's PovcalNet; Zameen.

basic criteria irrespective of local context: a finished roof that protects the household from weather, sufficient living area so that no more than three people need to share a bedroom, access in the dwelling or plot to spring water or improved piped water, and improved sanitation in the form of a flush toilet or ventilated pit latrine not shared by more than two households.

To evaluate housing conditions in the region along these four dimensions, we exploited recent data from the Demographic and Health Surveys program on 10 countries that together account for almost half of the regional population: Bangladesh, Cambodia, India, the Kyrgyz Republic, Myanmar, Nepal, Pakistan, the Philippines, Tajikistan, and Timor-Leste. The surveys are nationally representative samples and contain detailed information on housing conditions along the four dimensions described above. Finally, we used the locational data of household clusters and matched them with natural cities in the 10 countries.[14]

Results indicated that only 33.7% of the urban population in our sample had adequate housing. This reflected high housing unaffordability in regional cities and was consistent with earlier estimates in UN-Habitat (2011) that about one-third of urban residents in Asia lived in slums or informal settlements. Comparing rural and urban areas, we found urban areas offering significantly better housing. Dividing the sample into larger cities above 1 million and smaller cities below 1 million, larger cities offer better housing, with 36.2% in adequate housing, compared with 30.1% in smaller cities.

Figure 2.2.15 shows housing adequacy in terms of the four dimensions in rural areas, smaller cities, and larger cities. Larger cities are better in all four dimensions. The largest difference between urban and rural residents is access to clean water and improved sanitation. However, even though living in cities means better access to water and sanitation, the results reveal large gaps. Only 40.8% of households meet these two criteria in smaller cities and 49.2% in larger cities. While households can improve their homes in terms of structural quality and living area, they typically rely on other investors, private or public, to improve their access to safe water and sanitation. Meanwhile, lower-income neighborhoods are less attractive clients to service providers. Box 2.2.3 discusses how access to water and sanitation in cities can be improved and introduces an integrated approach ADB adopts to tackle the challenge.

Data from Demographic and Health Surveys allowed households to be ranked by wealth and thus analysis of how housing conditions differ by household wealth. The results suggested highly inequitable distribution of adequate housing in most countries (Aizawa, Helble, and Lee, forthcoming). While cities offer better housing than in rural areas, many low-income households cannot enjoy this benefit until cities become more inclusive.

Figure 2.2.15 Housing adequacy in four dimensions (%)

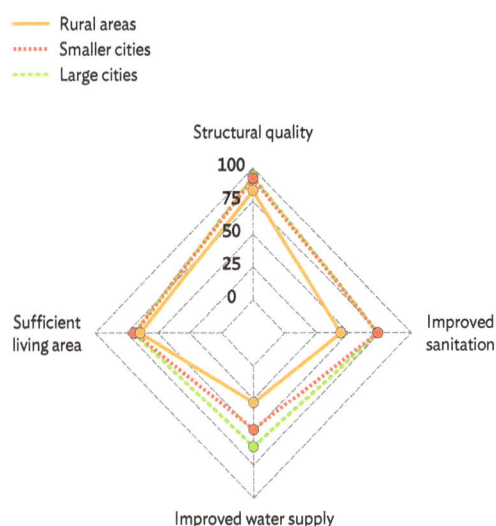

Source: ADB estimates using data from the Demographic and Health Surveys on 10 countries in Asia and the Pacific.

Box 2.2.3 Improving and managing water supply and sanitation in Asian cities

Recent cases of severe water shortage in Asian cities, such as in Chennai and Manila in 2019, offer stark reminders that water resources are being depleted in cities even as urban water demand increases. As water resources and distribution capacity are not easily expandable, careful attention needs to be paid to ensure water security. Water security in cities relies on three components: sufficient water resources and treatment, reliable water transmission and distribution systems, and adequate wastewater management.

Water resources and treatment. Cities typically have three main water sources: surface, underground, and desalination. Cities using surface water face ever stiffening competition from irrigation for agriculture. A study by Padowski and Gorelick (2014) of 70 cities worldwide that rely on surface water forecasted that, by 2040, 45% of them would be vulnerable to competition with demand from agriculture. When exploiting underground water, usage should respect aquifer capacity, but supplies are often overused for both domestic use and irrigation. Over-extraction can even cause cities to sink. Finally, desalination plants are needed where no other sources are available. ADB is currently preparing to cofinance the construction of a large desalination plant costing $60 million in South Tarawa, Kiribati.

Water transmission and distribution. This hinges crucially on there being capacity sufficient to satisfy growing authorized urban demand while minimizing unauthorized demand from physical and commercial water losses, so-called nonrevenue water. Such losses come from leakage and fraud made possible by low-quality infrastructure and inadequate water service management. These issues are aggravated by low water tariffs and inappropriate governance and regulation of water systems. While nonrevenue water is generally at 10%–20% in developed countries, it averages 50% in Asia and can reach 75% in very deteriorated systems.

Wastewater management. This is often poorly developed in Asian cities. Wastewater treatment plants are usually more complicated to operate than water treatment plants and involve more complex and sensitive chemicals and biological processes. Further, building wastewater collection networks is costly and difficult in dense cities. The need to charge a tariff is a complication. ADB recently supported a $150 million project in the PRC to implement integrated wastewater management concessions, including sludge treatment plants and sewage pipelines.

ADB has developed an integrated approach to improve water supply and sanitation services in cities, the various components of which support source protection, integrated water resource and drought management, safe water transmission and distribution, wastewater management, and water reuse. ADB catalyzes private development and public–private partnership in cities by helping to create enabling policies and institutional and regulatory frameworks to ensure efficient water service delivery for all, including slum dwellers. An important part of the ADB strategy is to improve utility performance through cost reduction, rationalized tariffs, enhanced staff capacity, more efficient billing and cost recovery, and better management of losses and assets.

Reference:

Padowski, J. C. and S. M. Gorelick. 2014. Global Analysis of Urban Surface Water Supply Vulnerability. *Environmental Research Letters* 9(10).

Finally, an important point is that affordable and adequate housing is not a feature just of the individual unit but also of its location and proximity to jobs, transportation networks, amenities such as parks, and social services providing, most importantly, health care and education. Definitions of what constitutes reasonable access vary. McKinsey Global Institute (2014) postulated that acceptable housing should not be more than an hour's commute to the place of employment. This contrasts starkly with reality in many larger Asian cities, in which hundreds of millions of commuters have significantly longer daily commutes, and it illustrates the urgent need for more investment in urban transportation infrastructure. Adequate and affordable housing also requires the development of social infrastructure within communities to create more complete neighborhoods that spare people the need to travel far to their doctor's office, their children's nursery, or a park. This links back to the earlier discussion of land-use planning for urban expansion.

Consequences of the housing affordability crisis

Unaffordable housing has an array of negative impacts. At the macroeconomic level, it undercuts cities' economic competitiveness through three main channels. First, it deters migration within and across cities, making the labor market less flexible and thus worsening the spatial misallocation of labor. Empirical studies in the US have shown that high home prices in highly productive cities impeded workforce mobility and substantially held down economic growth (Glaeser and Gyourko 2018, Hsieh and Moretti 2019). Research in the PRC found that worsening housing unaffordability in so-called superstar cities such as Beijing and Shanghai made them less attractive to certain population groups (Chen, Hu, and Lin 2019).

Second, housing price inflation can suppress aggregate productivity in cities through capital misallocation. It induces firms to invest capital in real estate speculation rather than in innovation and productivity enhancement. Additionally, as real estate inflation drives up the collateral value of firms that hold real estate, banks tend to offer more favorable loans to those firms, crowding out finance for other firms (Chaney, Sraer, and Thesmar 2012). Capital misallocation across and within firms has lowered productivity in India and the PRC vis-à-vis the US (Hsieh and Klenow 2009). Recent evidence from the PRC suggests that real estate inflation, particularly in the residential sector, significantly lowers productivity through speculation and crowding out (Chen et al. 2017).

Finally, unaffordable housing can slow urbanization, agglomeration-induced productivity, and aggregate welfare gains. As higher nominal wages are offset by higher home prices, household welfare improves less than it would with affordable housing and may even worsen (Glaeser and Gyourko 2018). In other words, housing price increases reflect higher housing demand, not better local amenities (Moretti 2013). At the same time, if higher nominal wages are paid primarily to meet higher home prices, rather than reward productivity growth, firms enjoy fewer benefits from being located in cities. This has happened in coastal cities in the PRC, which may become less competitive as their labor costs increase (Liang, Lu, and Zhang 2016).

The consequences of unaffordable housing can be substantial to individual households. If they overspend on housing, they must reduce other expenditure—including on education and health care, at the price of poorer health and worse school performance (Bentley, Baker, and Mason 2012, Newman and Holupka 2014, 2015, and 2016). Alternatively, households have to reside in substandard or distant housing to the detriment of their socioeconomic well-being. A strong relationship holds between defective or overcrowded housing and children's well-being (Dockery et al. 2013, Chambers et al. 2015). Living far from employment centers means longer commuting times and associated mental health problems, as Wang et al. (2019) recently showed in urban Latin America. Long commutes damage family life and interpersonal relationships as time spent commuting leaves less time for social and personal interaction.

Unaffordable housing may influence decisions on household formation, marriage, and childbearing, which have important demographic consequences. Evidence from developed countries suggests that it induces young adults to delay leaving the parental home to form their own households (Mulder and Billari 2010, Lee and Painter 2013, Chan, O'Regan, and You 2019). In Asian cities, anecdotal evidence shows young adults delaying marriage and deciding not to have children because of high housing costs, notably in Hong Kong, China; the Republic of Korea (ROK); and Taipei,China (Kim 2017). A survey done in advanced economies found unaffordable housing to be one of the strongest barriers to having more children (The Journal 2013). Such individual decisions can apply downward pressure on fertility rates and exacerbate demographic challenges as many Asian societies age.

Housing policies

To make housing more affordable, policies should enhance households' ability to pay for housing, reduce housing prices, or both. Policy options are to reduce housing prices by increasing housing supply, stabilize housing prices by reducing speculative housing demand, directly control housing prices, or boost household ability to pay for housing.

Most Asian countries have combined several policy options.[15] Table 2.2.4 summarizes the main policy interventions in selected economies in the region. Most Asian countries have directly provided housing to boost supply, with either government authorities or quasi-governmental corporations responsible for public housing provision and management. Some countries, such as Japan and the Philippines, have adopted idle land taxes to encourage housing construction. Governments have provided low-interest loans, land, subsidies, and tax credits to private developers, which is preferred in many developing countries over the direct provision of public housing because it costs less up front and taps private developers' resources and expertise in construction management. Examples include the Economic and Comfortable Housing Program in the PRC providing free land, the Philippine Board of Investments providing tax exemptions, and the State Bank of Pakistan subsidizing finance for the construction of new homes for low-income groups. Some countries have required specified shares of affordable housing units in newly developed private projects, notably in Malaysia's affordable housing scheme and Viet Nam's social housing for workers.

Table 2.2.4 Main policy options used in Asia toward affordable housing

Objective	Target	Measure	Examples
Reduce housing prices	Increase housing supply	Direct provision	Cambodia; Hong Kong, China; India; Indonesia; Japan; Kazakhstan; Malaysia; Myanmar; Philippines; PRC; Singapore; ROK; Taipei,China; Thailand; Viet Nam
		Subsidized production	Subsidies in Malaysia and Thailand; loans in Kazakhstan and the Philippines; tax credits in India, Indonesia, the Philippines, Thailand
		Mandated production	Indonesia, Malaysia, ROK, Viet Nam
		Land provided	Myanmar, Philippines, PRC, Singapore
		Tax on vacant land and unoccupied units	Indonesia, Japan, Malaysia, Philippines
	Contain housing demand	Anti-speculation through taxation or purchase restriction	Differential purchase and property tax in Singapore and Hong Kong, China; purchase restrictions in Malaysia and the PRC; seller stamp duties or capital gains taxes in Indonesia, Malaysia, the Philippines, the PRC, the ROK, Singapore, and Taipei,China
		Macroprudential (e.g., ratios of loan to income)	Indonesia, PRC, ROK, Singapore
	Directly price control	Price and rent controls	Rent control in India, Myanmar, the Philippines, and the PRC; price controls in the PRC and the ROK; price discounts in Malaysia
Increase ability to pay	Direct subsidy	Capital grant	Indonesia; Malaysia; Singapore; Taipei,China
		Allowance	Hong Kong, China; Japan; Malaysia; Singapore
	Tax incentives	Income tax deduction	India, Indonesia, Singapore
	Financing measures	Low-interest loan	Singapore; Hong Kong, China; India; Indonesia; Kazakhstan; Malaysia; ROK; Thailand; Viet Nam
		Guarantee and insurance	India; Indonesia; Kazakhstan; Hong Kong, China; Malaysia; Pakistan; Philippines; ROK; Viet Nam
		Savings scheme	Malaysia, Philippines, PRC, Singapore

PRC = People's Republic of China, ROK = Republic of Korea.
Source: ADB.

Asian governments have adopted tools to suppress speculation and housing demand that arises from it. Some have used such macroprudential measures as tightening the ratio of loan to value or of debt service to income. Taxing buyers, especially with differential purchase taxes, has emerged in many Asian real estate markets since 2010, primarily to stem rising foreign investment. Examples include higher taxes for nonresidents and for additional purchases by locals in Singapore and Hong Kong, China. Another measure is to restrict foreigners' housing purchases to condominiums, as in Singapore, and high-price homes, as in Malaysia. Thailand and Indonesia have land purchase restrictions for foreigners. Taxing sellers is another common measure, as in the ROK, which imposes punishing capital gains taxes on properties not occupied and resold quickly.

Finally, to enhance households' ability to pay, several countries have set up home finance agencies to provide low-interest loans either directly or through financial intermediaries. Income tax deductions or credit for mortgage interest have been used less widely in Asia than in the US or Europe, in favor of policy to lower household payments for housing. The ROK, for example, provides low-interest loans to lower-income first-time homebuyers and to renters under frontloaded *chonsei* leases. State-sponsored insurance or guarantees have been used extensively in Asia to manage primary or funding market risk, as in India, where the National Housing Bank recently set up a mortgage guarantee company. A few countries have offered state support for schemes to help people save for buying a home. Indonesia and the Philippines, for example, have compulsory savings schemes with monthly salary deductions to be used for certain housing purchases. Rent control has been used by some countries, notably the PRC and Myanmar. Finally, public rental housing with highly discounted rents have been offered to low-income groups in, for example, Indonesia; Hong Kong, China; and the Philippines.

Comparing housing policies and lessons learned

Asian governments have tried many policies to increase housing supply, often only to run up against a limited supply of developable land. Cities may consider relaxing land-use regulations, but opening up additional land for housing development alone is insufficient. Integrated neighborhood development is required to ensure the provision of public social services and incentivize the private sector and civil society to contribute to the other amenities that make for vibrant urban communities. An efficient and affordable transportation system is necessary to allow people to move around quickly in the city and thereby ease housing demand near employment centers.[16] Relocating slum dwellers to the outskirts of the city and far from their jobs typically fails. Upgrading slums where they are, as done under the Kampung Improvement Program in Indonesia, is often a better solution.

The crisis over unaffordable housing cannot be solved by the public sector alone. The active involvement of the private sector is essential. Unlike in developed countries, though, tax credits and inclusionary zoning that aim to subsidize and mandate private sector participation in the provision of affordable housing have not been popular in Asia. As low-cost housing poses, from the private sector's perspective, higher risk for lower returns, additional incentives are needed to attract more private sector investment. Financial incentives and simplified regulatory processes can expand private sector involvement.

Governments need to tailor housing policies for different income segments, taking into account the needs of each group. The ROK and Singapore, for example, provide public rental housing for very low-income households and financial assistance to first-time middle-income homebuyers. In Indonesia and the Philippines, community-based savings and housing microfinance organizations help low-income groups acquire land, upgrade homes, or build new ones. For more affluent people, the private sector plays an active role.

As the various housing segments interact, it is important to ensure that policies do not conflict. Effectively meshing different policies for different income groups is key to success.

Housing policies in the region emphasize homeownership. While homeownership offers advantages, such as asset appreciation, it carries risks such as overborrowing and limiting the labor mobility that is essential to agglomeration benefits. Compared with many developed countries, the rental market is small in most Asian cities, especially for low-income groups. Stocks of public rental housing are often insufficient and plagued with maintenance problems. Developing a thriving rental market that offers a healthy mix of public and private rental housing should be encouraged. Stocks of public rental housing need to be expanded and better managed and maintained. Housing society schemes, such as in Austria and Germany, could inform policy approaches here. Private sector participation can be encouraged by providing financial incentives such as tax exemptions or subsidies for building private rental housing. Rental housing regulations need to be improved and clarified to facilitate dispute settlement and gain private investors' confidence in rental housing. Figure 2.2.16 provides a summary of the housing policy options discussed.

Even the best policy design will not succeed if implemented poorly. In housing policy, the distribution of benefits and losses is particularly challenging to get right. Most affordable housing programs are not broad entitlements, and their benefits can be enjoyed only by a limited number of households. Long waiting lists for public housing often develop for lack of supply, and in the end some households in need are never served. Further, sometimes public housing benefits are misallocated.

Figure 2.2.16 Housing policy option tree

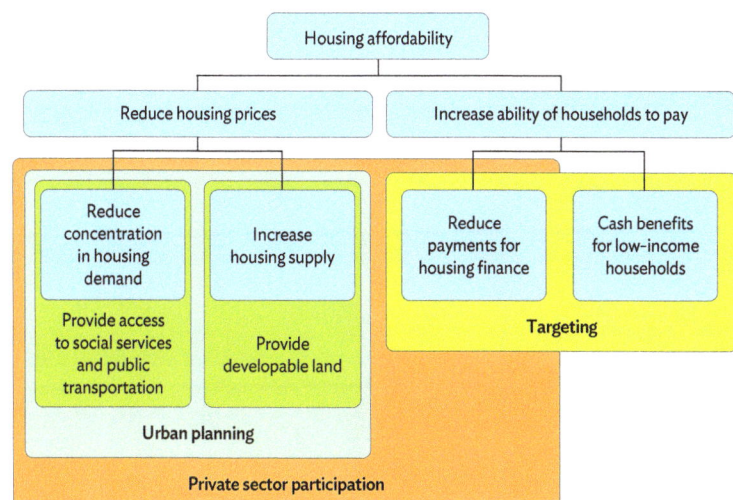

Source: ADB.

In many countries, income eligibility is assessed only when beneficiaries first enter public housing, though households improve their economic situation over time. Policies to lower speculative demand may fail if buyers declare lower property prices to tax assessor than they actually paid. To avoid such problems, policy makers should identify their target groups clearly, adopt stringent eligibility criteria, operate transparently, and ensure that staffers have the skills they need for implementation. Finally, in addition to targeting individual households, policy makers must ensure active community engagement.

This section highlighted that developing Asia faces a severe housing crisis. As long as the housing market is unable to deliver as much adequate and affordable housing as is needed, the benefits of urbanization will remain limited, and labor and capital will be misallocated, undermining agglomeration economies.

One prerequisite to tackling the housing crisis is to generate comprehensive and consistent data on housing markets. Several governments in the region, notably Malaysia and the Philippines, have recognized this need and introduced new programs to systematically collect more data. Further, rich new data sources are emerging in information technology, offering relatively inexpensive ways to improve understanding of housing markets.

Indeed, new technologies are transforming the housing market. Online platforms and apps provide efficient tools to match demand and supply for housing and are increasingly used throughout the region. In addition, innovations in finance technology permit new models for housing finance that are more inclusive. In the ROK, for example, proposed crowd financing schemes are expected to help home buyers.

Finally, cities need to redouble their efforts to create a level playing field in urban areas in terms of access to public infrastructure, which will encourage the scaling up of land and housing development. Addressing the housing crisis can create a more equal and accessible city, which forms the basis for thriving urban areas that enjoy all the economic benefits of agglomeration.

2.3 Managing the urban system

Cities are not isolated islands. They are connected to one another and to rural areas through flows of goods, services, and people, thereby constituting a system. The urban portion of the system consists of large, medium, and small cities; cities that produce many types of goods and services, as well as others specializing in a few products; and cities that serve as incubators of new products, as well as others that focus on the production of mature products (Duranton and Puga 2001). Figure 2.3.1 illustrates how cities of various size are distributed in Viet Nam and, despite the country's attenuated geography, well knit together by a road network to form an urban system.

The urban landscape needs to be seen as a "portfolio of places" (World Bank 2009). Urban economic growth and prosperity depend not just on the fortunes of one or two large cities. Well-functioning market towns that specialize in, for example, marketing and distributing agricultural produce are needed, as are other larger cities all the way to the metropolises that foster innovation. Indeed, a dynamic agriculture sector is also crucial for urban growth, as noted in the introduction of this chapter.

2.3.1 The urban system

An urban system is more vibrant than people normally perceive. As firms and jobs move across cities, the industrial composition of cities shifts with them. For instance, labor-intensive manufacturing used to be concentrated in the coastal cities of the People's Republic of China (PRC). In the past 10 years, though, it has moved to inland cities as the coastal cities embarked on more technology-intensive production and services. In India, Bengaluru started off as a hub for electrical engineering and business process outsourcing, coming to be known in the late 1990s as the undisputed Silicon Valley of India. By around 2010, however, Bengaluru's status was being challenged by Hyderabad, where information technology businesses had rapidly developed (Choe and Roberts 2011).

With changes in the extent and structure of economic activity, a city's size relative to others changes as well. Indeed, the size rankings of individual cities change continuously, though the distribution of city size tends to be stable over time (Duranton 2007). Table 2.3.1 tracks changes in quintile rankings by population and area from 2000 to 2016 for cities in six countries in developing Asia with more than 30 cities each. Regardless of population or area ranking, a high proportion of cities changed size quintiles.

Figure 2.3.1 Urban system with road networks in Viet Nam, 2016

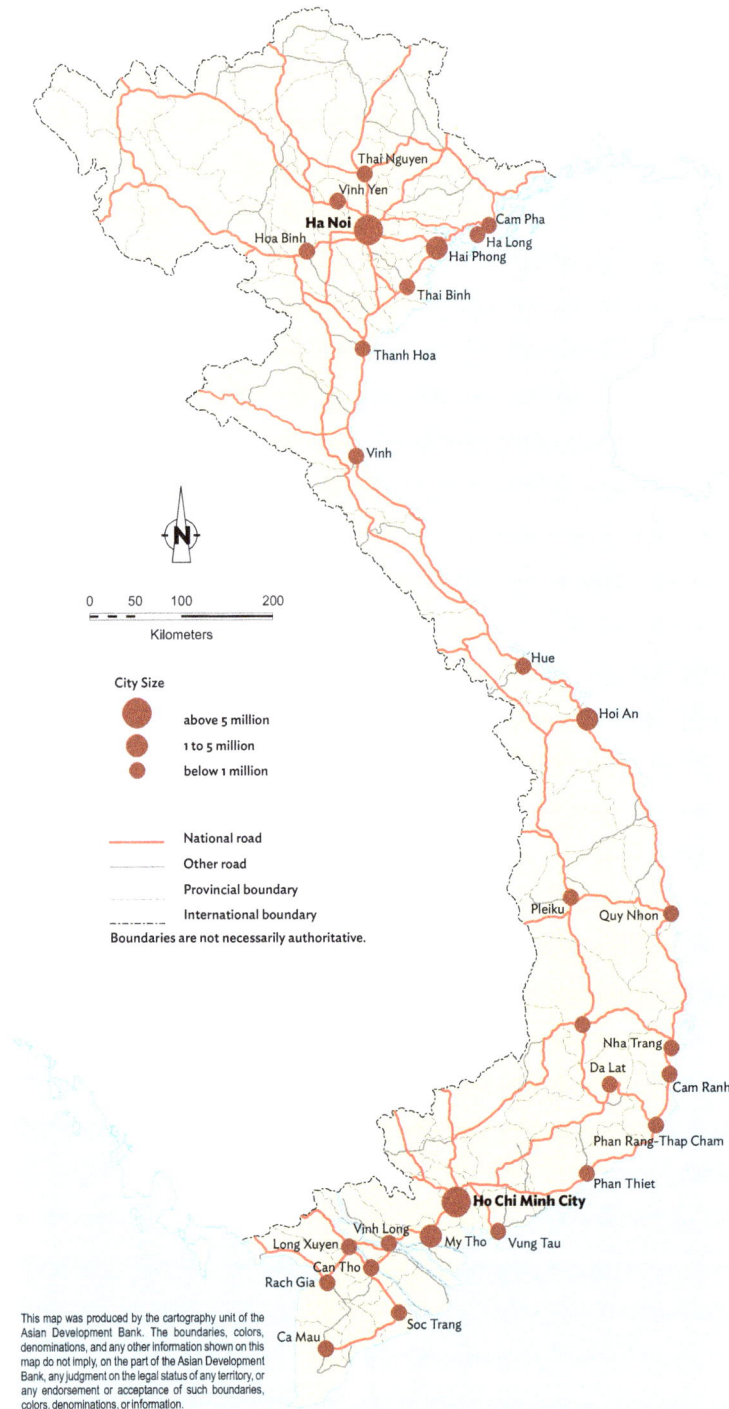

Thai Nguyen
Vinh Yen
Ha Noi
Hoa Binh
Cam Pha
Ha Long
Hai Phong
Thai Binh
Thanh Hoa
Vinh

0   50   100   200
Kilometers

City Size

- above 5 million
- 1 to 5 million
- below 1 million

National road
Other road
Provincial boundary
International boundary
Boundaries are not necessarily authoritative.

Hue
Hoi An

Pleiku
Quy Nhon

Nha Trang
Da Lat
Cam Ranh
Phan Rang-Thap Cham
Phan Thiet
Ho Chi Minh City
Vinh Long
Long Xuyen
My Tho
Vung Tau
Can Tho
Rach Gia
Ca Mau
Soc Trang

This map was produced by the cartography unit of the Asian Development Bank. The boundaries, colors, denominations, and any other information shown on this map do not imply, on the part of the Asian Development Bank, any judgment on the legal status of any territory, or any endorsement or acceptance of such boundaries, colors, denominations, or information.

Source: ADB estimates using nighttime lights images from the National Oceanic and Atmospheric Administration (accessed 1 April 2017 and 10 August 2018) and grid population data from LandScan Datasets of the Oak Ridge National Laboratory (accessed 31 August 2017 and 31 August 2018).

Table 2.3.1 Changes in natural city size quintile from 2000 to 2016

	PRC	India	Indonesia	Pakistan	Philippines	Viet Nam
Population quintile						
Down	142	82	21	10	6	8
Stay	410	175	49	44	30	13
Up	128	63	23	9	6	9
Cities changing, %	40	45	47	30	29	57
Area quintile						
Down	164	80	20	15	8	8
Stay	356	169	51	32	26	12
Up	160	71	22	16	8	10
Cities changing, %	48	47	45	49	38	60
Total number of cities	**680**	**320**	**93**	**63**	**42**	**30**

PRC = People's Republic of China.

Source: ADB estimates using nighttime lights images from the National Oceanic and Atmospheric Administration (accessed 1 April 2017 and 10 August 2018) and grid population data from LandScan Datasets of the Oak Ridge National Laboratory (accessed 31 August 2017 and 31 August 2018).

Underlying these figures is the movement of large numbers of people and, presumably, industries across cities. Exactly what drives all these changes is uncertain, but several forces can be seen to significantly affect an urban system. Some are factors specific to individual cities that affect their prospects for growth and thus their place in the urban system. Box 2.3.1 reviews some key results from the literature on city growth.

Also important are changes in macroeconomic policy and the broader economic environment. The opening of the PRC to international trade in the late 1970s, for example, considerably boosted the economic fortunes of coastal cities.

Meanwhile, investment in transport infrastructure linking cities plays a crucial role in determining the spatial distribution of economic activities across locations. Better connectivity between cities makes the urban system more efficient, often mitigating the degree of primacy—or share of the urban population in the largest city in an economy—and bringing tangible economic benefits to connected localities in the hinterland. For example, Ghani, Goswami, and Kerr (2016) studied India's national highway development program in its early phases and found substantially higher manufacturing growth in districts located 10 km away from the highway than in otherwise similar districts 10 km–50 km away. Similarly, a recent study examining the effects of high-speed rail in the PRC showed that scholars in secondary cities connected by high-speed rail to major cities hosting the nation's best universities were enabled to collaborate more effectively with counterparts in major cities (Dong, Zheng, and Kahn 2018).

Box 2.3.1 Drivers of city growth

The literature has identified several factors that affect urban growth. Cities that offer higher wages and incomes attract more people. This is enabled partly by agglomeration economies but also by the human capital available in a city. Studies have routinely found that cities with more university graduates grow more quickly (Glaeser et al. 2004, Shapiro 2006). As discussed in section 2.2, cities with lower commuting and living costs tend to grow more quickly.[a] Similarly, spatial characteristics often associated with better land-use planning, such as compact cities without excessive urban sprawl, had both larger city populations (Harari 2017) and more economic dynamism (Tewari and Godfrey 2016). Urban amenities also matter. In developed countries, mild weather, low crime rates, and public facilities like museums and libraries attracted migrants (Glaeser, Kolko, and Saiz 2001, Rappaport 2009, Cheshire and Magrini 2006). Indeed, cities deemed to be charming and beautiful were found to grow more quickly (Carlino and Saiz 2019). This suggests that government-led efforts to improve the ambience of cities, especially where tourism is a major attraction, are worthwhile. Better connectivity to major markets can also help speed a city's growth (Hasan, Jiang, and Kundu 2018).

A more complex question is how the type of economic activity undertaken in a city affects growth. Some studies found a relatively large share of manufacturing employment associated with faster city growth and better employment outcomes (Duranton 2016). More generally, cities with a lot of small, young establishments under 5 years old were found to grow faster (Faberman 2011, Glaeser, Kerr, and Kerr 2014, Hasan, Jiang, and Kundu 2018), perhaps because small establishments had more robust

consumer–supplier linkages and because the presence of young firms suggested high growth expectations and an enabling environment for entrepreneurship.

Such results explain why some cities make special efforts to attract new businesses and even particular firms. When the technology and e-commerce company Amazon announced in 2017 plans to build a second headquarters, for example, more than 200 cities in the US, Canada, and Mexico placed bids. There is no simple answer to the question of whether such endeavors pay off.[b] However, some efforts, especially those aligned with a city's comparative advantage, seem to be worthwhile.

[a] A simple monocentric urban model found that reduced commuting costs expanded a city geographically and attracted immigrants to live and work there. However, restrictions on housing supply—usually limits on the supply of developable land—could dampen city growth. Indeed, Glaeser, Gyourko, and Saks (2005) found that cities with more stringent land-use regulations had lower population growth from 1980 to 2000 than otherwise predicted.

[b] Greenstone and Moretti (2003) examined attempts by US cities to attract major car manufacturers, comparing counties that successfully bid for large industrial plants with those that narrowly lost out to the competition. It found that a plant opening pushed up salaries by 1.5% in the industry of the new plant and property values by 1.1%. Follow-up research found that existing plants that shared similar labor and technology pools with the new plants benefited through positive spillover and sharply increased productivity (Greenstone, Hornbeck, and Moretti 2010). It concluded that subsidies to attract large industrial plants brought significant gains to the economy and local residents' welfare. Other studies found only limited benefits relative to the cost of attracting business, however, and questioned claims that cities' economic development came from large firms locating in them, and that incentives really attracted firms (Kenyon, Langley, and Paquin 2012).

continued next page

Connectivity boosted the quantity and quality of their research. However, adverse effects can also emerge for some locations. Faber (2014) studied the national expressway program of the PRC from the early 1990s to 2007 and found that, as expressways reduced trade costs between large metropolitan areas and their peripheral counties, some industries chose to relocate to the core cities, presumably to benefit from their greater agglomeration economies. As a result, these counties suffered slower growth in industry and in government revenue than did counties not similarly connected.

Governments may implement policies that implicitly or explicitly favor certain cities and regions. A tendency is to concentrate considerable resources on particular cities,

Box 2.3.1 *Continued*

References:

Carlino, G. A. and A. Saiz. 2019. Beautiful City: Leisure Amenities and Urban Growth. *Working Papers* No. 19-16. Federal Reserve Bank of Philadelphia.

Cheshire, P. C. and S. Magrini. 2006. Population Growth in European Cities: Weather Matters—but Only Nationally. *Regional Studies* 40(1).

Duranton, G. 2016. Determinants of City Growth in Colombia. *Papers in Regional Science* 95(1).

Faberman, R. J. 2011. The Relationship between the Establishment Age Distribution and Urban Growth. *Journal of Regional Science* 51(3).

Glaeser, E. L., J. Gyourko, and R. E. Saks. 2005. Urban Growth and Housing Supply. *Journal of Economic Geography* 6(1).

Glaeser, E. L., S. P. Kerr, and W. R. Kerr. 2014. Entrepreneurship and Urban Growth: An Empirical Assessment with Historical Mines. *Review of Economics and Statistics* 97(2).

Glaeser, E. L., J. Kolko, and A. Saiz. 2001. Consumer City. *Journal of Economic Geography* 1(1).

Glaeser, E. L., A. Saiz, G. Burtless, and W. C. Strange. 2004. The Rise of the Skilled City [with Comments]. *Brookings-Wharton Papers on Urban Affairs*.

Greenstone, M., R. Hornbeck, and E. Moretti. 2010. Identifying Agglomeration Spillovers: Evidence from Winners and Losers of Large Plant Openings. *Journal of Political Economy* 118(3).

Greenstone, M. and E. Moretti. 2003. Bidding for Industrial Plants: Does Winning a "Million Dollar Plant" Increase Welfare? *NBER Working Paper Series* No. 9844. National Bureau of Economic Research.

Harari, M. 2017. *Cities in Bad Shape: Urban Geometry in India*. University of Pennsylvania.

Hasan, R., Y. Jiang, and D. Kundu. 2018. Growth of Indian Cities and "Good" Jobs: Evidence from the 2000s. In S. Shah, B. Bosworth and K. Muralidharan, eds. *India Policy Forum 2017-18*. SAGE Publications India.

Kenyon, D. A., A. H. Langley, and B. P. Paquin. 2012. *Rethinking Property Tax Incentives for Business*. Lincoln Institute of Land Policy.

Rappaport, J. 2009. Moving to Nice Weather. In T. L. Cherry and D. Rickman, eds. *Environmental Amenities and Regional Economic Development*. Routledge.

Shapiro, J. M. 2006. Smart Cities: Quality of Life, Productivity, and the Growth Effects of Human Capital. *Review of Economics and Statistics* 88(2).

Tewari, M. and N. Godfrey. 2016. *Better Cities, Better Growth: India's Urban Opportunity*. New Climate Economy, World Resources Institute, and Indian Council for Research on International Economic Relations.

especially national capitals. To some extent, this can be efficient, as when the introduction of a metro system allows agglomeration economies to triumph over congestion. Given finite resources for public investment, though, this can mean underinvestment in other cities and localities. Very high population gaps can result between the largest city and the second largest, as in Thailand (Table 2.3.2).

Governments may concentrate on developing smaller cities and relatively backward regions partly as a conscious effort to counter big city bias. In India, for example, concerns that emerged decades ago about growing congestion in large cities spawned industry licensing policies that encouraged the dispersal of industrial investment to smaller cities and rural areas. Even after this policy was abandoned in the early 1990s, various programs were instituted to promote industrialization in backward regions. One program initiated in 1994 offered tax exemptions and infrastructure investment to selected backward areas. More recently, a number of important academic and research institutes, such as the Indian Institutes of Technology and the Indian Institutes of Management, have set up branches in smaller cities and towns.

Table 2.3.2 The two largest natural cities and their share of total urban population, 2016

Country	Largest city		Second-largest city	
	Name	Percent	Name	Percent
Bangladesh	Dhaka	0.49	Chittagong	0.12
People's Republic of China	Guangzhou	0.09	Shanghai	0.05
India	Delhi	0.09	Kolkata	0.07
Indonesia	Jakarta	0.26	Bandung	0.07
Kazakhstan	Almaty	0.25	Shymkent	0.10
Malaysia	Kuala Lumpur	0.35	Johor Bahru	0.09
Myanmar	Yangon City	0.52	Mandalay	0.18
Pakistan	Karachi	0.33	Lahore	0.14
Philippines	Manila	0.62	Cebu	0.07
Republic of Korea	Seoul	0.55	Busan	0.14
Thailand	Bangkok	0.65	Nakhon Pathom	0.05
Uzbekistan	Tashkent	0.25	Andijan	0.16
Viet Nam	Ho Chi Minh	0.37	Ha Noi	0.24

Note: Countries with 20 or more natural cities are shown.

Source: ADB estimates using nighttime lights images from the National Oceanic and Atmospheric Administration (accessed 1 April 2017 and 10 August 2018) and grid population data from LandScan Datasets of the Oak Ridge National Laboratory (accessed 31 August 2017 and 31 August 2018).

In between these two extremes are policies that affect the urban system by, for example, creating special economic zones (SEZs), which are formally delimited areas where relatively liberal investment, trade, and operating rules apply (Baissac 2011). SEZs are usually administered by a dedicated governance structure and supported by superior physical infrastructure (ADB 2015). When sufficiently large and located in or close to an urban area, they can catalyze urban development. The most successful SEZs in terms of seeding urban development are in the PRC and the ROK. One of the largest cities today in the PRC, known globally for its dynamic high-technology industries, is Shenzhen, which was only a village before it became a SEZ with city status in 1979.

2.3.2 City clusters

City clusters are natural cities that have connected spatially through urban expansion and the development of intercity transport infrastructure. They display remarkable concentration of economic activity and are often the most vibrant regions in a country. An example is the Pearl River Delta city cluster, described in Box 2.3.2.

Box 2.3.2 Pearl River Delta city cluster: Growth and expansion through reform and integration

The Pearl River Delta (PRD), in southeastern Guangdong Province, is one of the largest and most dynamic city clusters in the world. This polycentric urban cluster comprises 12 natural cities in Guangdong Province plus Hong Kong, China and Macau, China. It has experienced one of the most rapid urban expansions in human history, enlarging its built-up area from 11,000 square kilometers in 1992 to 20,000 square kilometers in 2016, and its population from 26 million in 2000 to 60 million in 2016 (box figure).

The PRD is one of the world's most productive economic subregions, growing at 12% annually over the last decade and boasting a GDP estimated in 2017 at more than $1.2 trillion. Although the subregion occupies less than 1% of the People's Republic of China (PRC) land area (including Hong Kong, China and Macau, China) and has just 5% of its population, it attracts more than 20% of foreign direct investment into the PRC and generates more than 12% of its GDP and 25% of its exports (Groff and Rau 2019, Jha, Raghuram, and Awasthi 2019).

The story of the PRD subregion is one of manufacturing-led growth using a planned approach to regional integration and entailing a series of reforms. Early in 1979, the Government of the PRC allowed Shenzhen, Zhuhai, and Shantou to set up special economic zones in Guangdong Province to attract foreign investment. They were granted greater autonomy and played a major role in triggering rapid investment and PRD cluster expansion.

In 1988, Guangdong Province was designated a comprehensive economic reform area, with powers to set its own economic direction. One result was the Shenzhen Stock Exchange and another an attractive land-lease system. In 2008, the PRC announced plans to weave nine PRD cities into one single megacity. Large infrastructure projects have since begun to merge transport, energy, water, and telecom networks across them. A rail transport network featuring three circular and eight outbound routes will be completed in 2020 to allow an intercity circuit to be traveled within an hour. In 2017, the Guangdong–Hong Kong–Macau Greater Bay Area (GBA) Development Agreement aimed to integrate the two special administrative regions with the rest of the PDR cluster. A 55-kilometer bridge and tunnel link opened in 2018 to connect Zhuhai; Macau, China; and Hong Kong, China. In February 2019, the PRC issued a more detailed development plan for the GBA until 2035.

References:

Groff, S. P. and S. Rau. 2019. China's City Clusters: Pioneering Future Mega-Urban Governance. *American Affairs* 3(2).

Jha, S., S. Raghuram, and S. Awasthi. 2019. *Exploring Strategies for Planned Urban Cluster Development in South Asia*. Asian Development Bank.

The evolution of Pearl River Delta city cluster

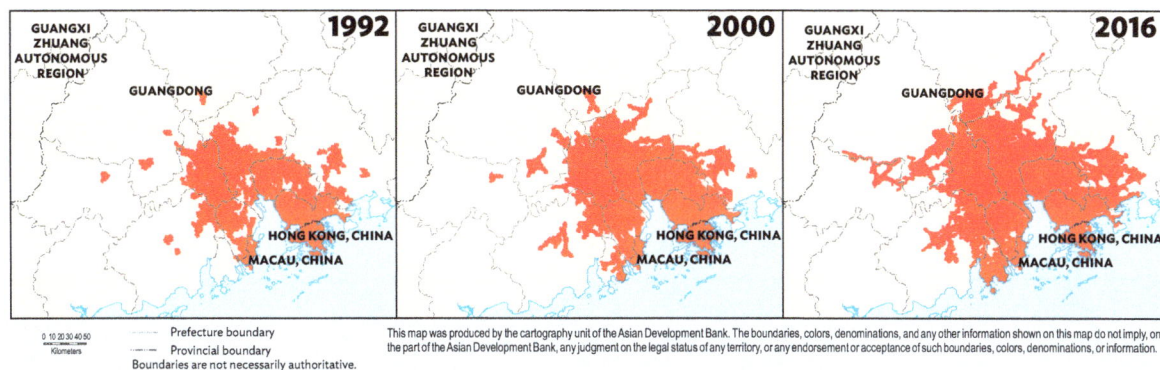

Source: ADB estimates using nighttime lights images from the National Oceanic and Atmospheric Administration (accessed 1 April 2017 and 10 August 2018).

City clusters offer opportunities for firms and workers to benefit from enhanced agglomeration effects. This can happen through several channels that spread over a larger population the fixed costs of urban infrastructure such as metro rail networks and wastewater treatment plants, generate a thicker labor market for workers, and create opportunities for firms to exploit more efficient input–output linkages in the city cluster with a wider variety of industries, both upstream and downstream. City clusters also offer opportunities to invest in better environmental protection. Especially as local governments of individual cities compete for investment, they may neglect the environment by either relaxing entry for polluting industries or failing to regulate the indiscriminate use of natural resources. A regionwide approach toward planning can help urban clusters develop in an environmentally sensitive and sustainable manner.

Being part of a cluster means that a small or medium-sized city is able to borrow agglomeration economies from the large cities in the cluster. This concept is referred to as "borrowed size" (Alonso 1973). In this way, secondary cities are able to undertake activities normally associated with larger cities. However, the effects of borrowed size can be attenuated by "agglomeration shadows," under which smaller cities find it difficult to compete with giant neighbors (Fujita, Krugman, and Venables 1999, Dobkins and Ioannides 2001, Partridge et al. 2009).

In fact, both borrowed size and agglomeration shadows can occur within a single cluster. Depending on which effect dominates, the smaller city may be better off economically or worse off. Empirical evidence to date from developed countries shows the effect as generally positive (Meijers and Burger 2015, Meijers, Burger, and Hoogerbrugge 2016, Partridge et al. 2009).

Realizing the full benefits of city clusters quite clearly requires good transport connectivity between their constituent cities and peri-urban areas. It also requires an appropriate governance framework. All too often, clusters suffer fragmented governance, with multiple administrations coexisting within a cluster, each with independent authority over tax and budget systems, land-use planning, transport infrastructure, industrial park development, environmental protection, and even labor markets, such that any amalgamation of authority and responsibility is unrealizable (Groff and Rau 2018).

This can have dire consequences. As Tables 2.3.3 and 2.3.4 show, firms located in city clusters are more likely to report obstacles to business from regulatory and infrastructure factors, among them difficulty in access to land and licenses and connecting to electricity and telecommunication services, as well as transportation woes. Problems are exacerbated if the city cluster crosses a provincial or state boundary, which appears in the table as a positive and significant coefficient on the variable capturing clusters that span one or more top-level administrative divisions (Chen, Hasan, and Jiang, forthcoming).

Table 2.3.3 City cluster governance and regulation

Variables	Access to land obstacles		Licensing and permits obstacles	
City cluster	0.0164***	0.0122**	0.0134***	0.0077*
	(0.0047)	(0.0042)	(0.0034)	(0.0036)
Level 1 admin (cluster)		0.0094**		0.013***
		(0.0031)		(0.003)
Observations	20,606	20,606	20,606	20,606
R-squared	0.338	0.342	0.176	0.186
Other controls	Yes	Yes	Yes	Yes
Country/year/sector fixed effects	Yes	Yes	Yes	Yes

* = $p<0.1$, ** = $p<0.05$, *** = $p<0.01$.

Notes: Regulatory variables are from World Bank Enterprise Survey. "City cluster" is a dummy variable that equals 1 if the firm resides in a natural city that belongs to a city cluster. "Level 1 admin (cluster)" is a dummy variable that equals 1 if the firm's city cluster is governed by one or more top-level administrative bodies. Robust standard errors clustered by country in parentheses. Other controls include firm age, size, export status, and share of foreign direct investment, as well as other city characteristic variables.

Source: ADB estimates using data from World Bank's Enterprise Surveys Data (accessed 11 August 2018) and nighttime lights images from the National Oceanic and Atmospheric Administration (accessed 1 April 2017 and 10 August 2018).

Table 2.3.4 City cluster infrastructure provision

Variables	Electricity obstacles		Telecom obstacles		Transportation obstacles	
City cluster	0.0246***	0.0144*	0.0241***	0.0215***	0.0341***	0.0253***
	(0.0063)	(0.0056)	(0.0056)	(0.0046)	(0.0058)	(0.0045)
Level 1 admin (cluster)		0.0242***		0.0057		0.0208***
		(0.0052)		(0.0044)		(0.0048)
Observations	20,606	20,606	20,606	20,606	20,606	20,606
R-squared	0.336	0.340	0.235	0.238	0.159	0.166
Other controls	Yes	Yes	Yes	Yes	Yes	Yes
Country/year/sector fixed effects	Yes	Yes	Yes	Yes	Yes	Yes

* = $p<0.1$, ** = $p<0.05$, *** = $p<0.01$.

Notes: Infrastructure variables are from World Bank Enterprise Survey. "City cluster" is a dummy variable that equals 1 if the firm resides in a natural city that belongs to a city cluster. "Level 1 admin (cluster)" is a dummy variable that equals 1 if the firm's city cluster is governed by one or more top-level administrative bodies. Robust standard errors clustered by country in parentheses. Other controls include firm age, size, export status, and share of foreign direct investment, as well as other city characteristic variables.

Source: ADB estimates using data from World Bank's Enterprise Surveys Data (accessed 11 August 2018) and nighttime lights images from the National Oceanic and Atmospheric Administration (accessed 1 April 2017 and 10 August 2018).

2.3.3 Policy imperatives

The foregoing discussion raises two sets of issues for policy makers. One set addresses the need to coordinate spatial and economic planning. The other concerns efforts to improve spatial efficiency in an urban system while protecting the welfare of residents in lagging localities.

Better coordination of spatial and economic planning

An especially challenging imperative at all geographic scales, from the individual city to subnational regions and beyond, is to better coordinate spatial and economic planning.

This is perhaps best understood by considering city clusters, especially those where daily commuting is possible. In them, some form of metropolitan governance is needed toward realizing synergies and other benefits of connectivity. Metropolitan governance allows governments at all levels— constituent cities and peri-urban areas, as well as state and provincial governments—to work with such nongovernment actors as civil society, business associations, and unions toward comprehensive development planning, policy formulation, and delivery of public services. Decisions on land use at a regional level require effective metropolitan governance to decide where to locate industrial parks, water treatment and solid waste facilities, and transport hubs, as well as how to coordinate transport services across administrative boundaries.

Metropolitan governance is not easy to achieve. Significant international experience in it is found mostly in developed economies. Properly functioning arrangements are rarely found in developing Asia (other than in the PRC and the ROK) or in other emerging markets, where they could shore up often weak local institutions and help cope with rapid urbanization. Introducing effective forms of metropolitan governance requires legitimacy acquired through appropriate national and state legislation and mechanisms for involving other key stakeholders. They require clearly defined and effective assignment of responsibility for revenue and expenditure, geographic boundaries that accurately define the economic region, and fiscal autonomy. Finally, capacity must be adequate in terms of trained staff and of revenue that matches expenditure (Bird and Slack 2014). Yet experience shows that no governance arrangement is effective or sustainable unless local governments actively support it. The bottom line is that coordination among local governments is essential for enacting ordinances, zoning codes, tax regulations, and land-use regulations in a way that can ensure a uniform and positive business environment across the cluster.

A greater role for local governments in local economic development

In many parts of developing Asia, the role of local government in promoting local economic development is quite limited. Government efforts to promote new economic activities or nurture existing ones are typically undertaken by national and state or provincial agencies. In effect, governance systems end up treating urbanization and economic development as separate processes entailing distinct management systems. Thus, while local governments are responsible for providing infrastructure such as roads and water supply and sanitation systems, local economic development is not a core function.

Further, local governments are rarely equipped to attract investment directly. In India, Pakistan, and Thailand, for example, the power to offer fiscal incentives to businesses lies with the state or national government. Local governments in Indonesia and the Philippines have greater fiscal autonomy. However, some exceptions aside, local governments have rarely used it to attract businesses. One reason is that local government revenue is often insufficient to cope with expanded responsibilities. Ideally, local financing systems should map expenditure responsibilities with revenue, and revenue with political accountability. Autonomy may be meaningless in practical terms if local governments are unable to influence revenue amounts and composition (Bird and Slack 2014).

In sharp contrast is the PRC, where local governments have strong incentives and authority to formulate and implement plans for economic development and to attract private investment. Local economic performance is a key criterion used by higher levels of government to assess local officials and their promotion prospects (Edin 2003, Li and Zhou 2005). With tax-sharing reform implemented in 1994, local governments in the PRC have exclusive rights to business tax receipts and share collections of value-added tax. To maximize fiscal revenue, local governments seek to attract investment into businesses that constitute their main tax base. Local officials have considerable freedom to attract investment. They can negotiate with the central government to exempt businesses from regulations, for example, or improve local infrastructure or provide land and sometimes credit at prices below the market. At the same time, competition among local governments instills discipline on officials because firms can relocate away from incompetent or abusive local governments (Bai, Hsieh, and Song 2019).

The deep involvement of local governments in directing local economic development is viewed as a key driver of spectacular economic growth in the PRC since the 1980s, as is intense competition among localities (Xu 2011). The model has drawbacks, however, such as when competition leads local governments to adopt an overly short-term focus on investment and growth, with inadequate consideration for longer-term sustainability or environmental safeguards, or when the discretion to intervene presents a channel for rent seeking. However, a major strength of the model is its recognition that production ultimately takes place locally and that local conditions—such as availability of land, infrastructure, and a skilled workforce, as well as how promptly government offices respond on permits—are key determinants of the investment climate. Incentives for local officials to attract investment, and empowering them to coordinate the many inputs required for modern production, bring local knowledge to bear.

The PRC approach of incentivizing and empowering local governments is probably not directly transferable to other economies in developing Asia because of variance in the institutional frameworks that determine the responsibilities of different branches of government. Nevertheless, initiatives in other economies are worth examining further and perhaps adopting more widely. One notable example is an approach in the Indian state of Gujarat to governing urban agglomerations that emphasizes economic development. Gujarat's Special Investment Region Act, 2009 identifies where industrial and urban development can take place. Pursued by the state's industry department with the objective to attract investment and new businesses, the legislation incorporates key provisions of town planning and urban development. One provision is an innovative land-pooling model used to assemble land for industrial parks and infrastructure efficiently and equitably. The model allows town planning, land-use regulation, and the delivery of urban infrastructure to follow standards that are closely attuned to the needs of both urban and industrial development.

Spatial efficiency and lagging areas

Some improvements in the spatial efficiency of urban system may have adverse effects on particular localities, as mentioned in several contexts above. While many smaller cities may benefit from the formation of city clusters through borrowed agglomeration, for example, in other instances businesses in smaller cities may be unable to compete under new spatial arrangements that create for it agglomeration shadows. Similarly, government efforts to improve intercity transport are very likely to improve overall spatial efficiency but often at the cost of adversely affecting some localities. An example emerged in Japan with the completion of the Tōhoku and Jōetsu lines of the Shinkansen high-speed rail in 1982. Li and Xu (2016) found that cities within 100 km of Tokyo grew but more distant cities shrank. On the other hand, big city bias and government efforts to promote lagging regions may detract from spatial efficiency in an urban system—though the latter impulse is at least intended to improve the welfare of low-income groups.

What is an appropriate response for public policy? When dealing with spatial inequality, spatially neutral policies should be the first response. Progressive tax rates and transfers that foster human capital development through affordable education and health care are prime examples, as is the provision of basic infrastructure to lagging regions to supply electricity, safe water, and sanitation. This approach proved in the past to be a potent force for equitable development in most countries that are now considered fully developed (World Bank 2009).

A big city bias in the allocation of public funding must be avoided. Studies have found that favoring a particular area, even if because it is the most productive city, can displace economic activity from other places (Duranton and Venables 2018). Especially because the return on investment in big cities is likely to be higher on account of agglomeration economies, governments must seek ways to attract private investment in big cities through, for example, land value capture, as discussed in section 2.2. At the same time, where possible, the spatial allocation of public resources should follow the flow of people and resources across locations. As shown in section 2.1, many medium-sized cities with populations of 1 million–5 million in the region, and some smaller cities with populations 0.1 million–0.5 million, continue to grow rapidly despite considerable shortcomings in infrastructure and governance capacity. Investment in these cities may help overcome these shortcomings and allow them to benefit from agglomeration economies. These areas deserve policy attention and public support. In sum, any framework for the spatial allocation of public resources must be kept flexible and informed by assessments of how the urban system is evolving.

As for lagging areas, government support for them should follow certain principles. The first step is to identify why a city or locality is lagging. If agglomeration forces in core regions have put it in an agglomeration shadow, it is important to ask who is left behind. If, for example, outmigration by the young is causing demographic imbalance, better elderly care should ease concerns. In general, a detailed demographic profile of the worst affected populations should provide insights on the correct policy to adopt.

If, on the other hand, a locality lags for multiple reasons that reinforce one another—bad infrastructure, a lack of skilled workers, insufficient local input suppliers, and long distances to major markets, for example—it is unlikely that a simple incentive package of, say, tax breaks to attract private companies will have the intended effect. Moreover, even if some firms do relocate, they may do so only temporarily, just for as long as the tax breaks apply, or the benefits to one locality may come at the cost of others (Hasan, Jiang, and Rafols 2017). More effective alternatives may be to invest in transport infrastructure that connects the lagging area to major markets and to support the development of industries such as agro-processing and labor-intensive manufacturing (World Bank 2009).

When deciding where to place an SEZ, a location's potential should be carefully considered. All too often, even successful SEZs fail to do much good for neighboring areas (Frick, Rodríguez-Pose, and Wong 2019). Yet, designed appropriately, an SEZ may be able to catalyze urban development in its neighborhood. Agglomeration effects are more likely to kick in if SEZs are placed near cities with economic density and skills that can feed them than if relegated to places where they can become only isolated enclaves (Akinci et al. 2008). The Bataan Export Processing Zone, for example, was placed 170 kilometers from Manila in 1969. Despite expensive investment to get the SEZ up and running, it featured the same number of enterprises in 2011 as in 1989 (Manasan 2013).

Beyond having potential as a prime location, the neighborhood of a successful SEZ must have people ready to exploit the opportunities it brings. This harks back to the desirability of local governments playing bigger roles in economic planning and development than they currently do in many parts of the region. A proactive strategy is required to attract local and foreign investment; plan long-term infrastructure needs in terms of land, transport, basic services, and housing; and understand how economic hubs and SEZs can best interact with other urban and peri-urban areas in a region.

2.4 The promise of cities

Cities in Asia are thriving, but they are also beset by problems that hamper their roles as engines of economic growth and generators of productive, well-paid jobs. Looking at the city as a labor market—where workers and firms engage and interact—this chapter has focused mostly on three issues: transport, land use, and housing.

These issues are closely interlinked. If traffic congestion in Asian cities is left unchecked, it can overwhelm the economic benefits that arise from the agglomeration of firms and households in a chosen location. Tackling congestion requires, among other things, developing a multimodal urban transport system that integrates investments in public transport with appropriately regulated privately run transport and ride-sharing services. Meanwhile, these investments must be better integrated with decisions on land use. Cities that fail to coordinate building height restrictions, for example, with investments in the transport network, such as in metro rail and bus rapid transit systems, undercut how effective their transport investments can be.

Similarly, a lack of affordable housing—a common problem across much of Asia—deters people from moving within and between cities and makes it harder to match workers with firms. Tackling this problem requires policies that address both housing supply and housing demand. Thus, while favorable housing finance schemes targeting low-income groups are part of the solution, land-use policies that restrict the supply of developable land and excessively raise real estate values make achieving any solution much harder. Conversely, a plentiful supply of land not served by public transport leaves a city's labor market spatially fragmented.

Arguably, the need to improve land-use planning and regulations is perhaps the most urgent requirement, if only because it has been neglected by economists and policy makers alike. One issue that is especially deserving of more attention is the outward expansion of cities, as this key feature of urbanization often progresses in an unplanned and disorderly fashion. It is essential that economic and urban planners identify likely expansion areas, obtain planning jurisdiction over them, earmark arterial road grids, and acquire land rights for public facilities and open space.

This chapter has considered the role of cities as engines of growth also from the perspective of the urban system—that is, cities connected to one another through flows of goods, services, and people. A key implication is that the links between urbanization and economic growth depend not just on how well one or two large cities function. Instead, growth depends on a portfolio of places that features vibrant market towns and up-and-coming midsized cities as well as the larger agglomerations and city clusters.

A particularly important phenomenon is the rise of city clusters, which encompasses cities large and small and peri-urban areas, all spatially connected through the development of intercity transport infrastructure. City clusters achieve remarkable concentrations of economic activity and are typically among the most vibrant regions in a country. Making the most of these clusters requires, however, improvements in the coordination of spatial and economic planning. Implementing effective forms of metropolitan governance in city clusters must be part of making the most of urban potential.

Simultaneously, the role that local governments play in fostering local economic development needs to be considered carefully. One of the features underlying a stellar growth record in the PRC in recent decades is that local city officials have enjoyed both the incentive and the authority to attract investments and jobs to their cities. In many other parts of the region, by contrast, local governments have little to do with economic planning or development, armed with neither the mandate nor the resources. As noted above, the PRC approach may not be directly transferable to other economies, considering countries' distinct institutional frameworks. Nevertheless, the basic principle of better coordination of spatial and economic planning across agencies and levels of government is key. Policy makers must assess ways to make this happen for cities to fulfill their promise as engines of growth and inclusion.

Endnotes

1   The urban population estimated for natural cities comes to 76% of the urban population in developing Asia as reported in United Nations (2018b). Multiple factors may contribute to the gap. In general, the two estimates are based on distinct urban definitions and accounting methods, so they are not directly comparable. Specifically, most natural cities were required to cover human settlements listed in the GRUMP with populations of 100,000 or more in 2000. Note, however, that a natural city could still have population below 100,000 as the GRUMP population, often sourced from official statistics, might be for a very different urban scope, but the natural city definition could still leave out many small cities.

2   Some natural cities such as Seoul, Guangzhou, and Metro Manila were de facto city clusters, containing multiple administrative cities, way back in 1992. However, the number of such cases is limited in developing Asia.

3   We do not distinguish here between metropolitan areas and city clusters because the two share important commonalities, such as both crossing municipal boundaries to involve multiple administrations.

4   This alleviates potential confounding effects coming from workers who reside beyond the administrative boundaries of a large and dynamic city, either in a small city or even a rural area, but work in the big city. The concept of natural cities treats workers who reside in settlements that are contiguous with a large administrative city (the kernel of the natural city) as part of the natural city. The labor force survey data for India and Pakistan, by contrast, allow us to distinguish between large administrative cities and other urban areas only within a district, which is a lower administrative unit than the state in India and the province in Pakistan.

5   The analysis uses nominal wages, as is common in the literature on testing the presence of agglomeration economies. This is because nominal wages better capture the productive advantages of cities than real wages. The former reflect how much more firms are willing to pay in bigger cities to comparable workers (De La Roca and Puga 2016). Using real wages is appropriate when analyzing the welfare implications of different types of employment and studies of location choice. Nonetheless, wages adjusted for differences in the cost of living were used for India, Indonesia, and the Philippines, where some information is available. The results were found to be qualitatively similar to those reported in Table 2.1.3.

6   Most studies in the literature use employment status as a proxy for job quality in the absence of information on non-pecuniary benefits and job security. Included under "self-employed" are own-account workers, contributing family workers, and members of producers' cooperatives.

7 Countries covered in the Enterprise Survey dataset are Afghanistan, Armenia, Azerbaijan, Bangladesh, Bhutan, Cambodia, the People's Republic of China, Georgia, India, Indonesia, Kazakhstan, the Kyrgyz Republic, the Lao People's Democratic Republic, Malaysia, Mongolia, Myanmar, Nepal, Pakistan, Papua New Guinea, the Philippines, Tajikistan, Thailand, Timor-Leste, Uzbekistan, and Viet Nam. One caveat is that the sample firms are not necessarily representative at the natural city level, as natural cities in this chapter are constructed using nighttime light, which is not part of the sampling stratification for the Enterprise Survey.

8 Universities are ranked according to QS World University Rankings (2019), available at https://www.topuniversities .com/university-rankings/asian-university-rankings/2019. Rankings in 2019 were adopted because they offered the top 500 universities, while rankings in previous years showed only the top 100 or fewer. Most universities in the sample were established well before the firm survey time frame of 2012–2016.

9 The results should be taken as suggestive as time and budget constraints meant the analysis was based on a limited sample of trips collected in one day.

10 An alternative explanation is that congestion becomes worse if cities focus their investments on roads and neglect public transport. We added to model 4 public transport variables from Google Maps. The estimated coefficients of road length remained positive and significant, and public transport variables were not significant. In short, more research on the relationship between congestion, road capacity, and public transport system is needed, especially in developing countries.

11 This subsection draws on Kallergis and Simet (2019).

12 A detailed description of the data sources and methodology is available in Helble, Lee, and Arbo (forthcoming).

13 There may be an upward bias in price-income ratio due to the use of household expenditure data in countries without household income surveys. For an in-depth discussion on concepts and measures of housing affordability, see Galster and Lee (forthcoming).

14 The exact definition of each dimension and methodology is available in Aizawa, Helble, and Lee (forthcoming).

15 For a detailed analysis of housing policies, their merits, and their pitfalls in several Asian countries, see Yoshino and Helble (2016).

16 Recent research in the US showed that improved transport infrastructure lowered housing prices in city centers by 1.3% (Baum-Snow 2019).

Background Papers

Aizawa, T., M. Helble, and K. O. Lee. Forthcoming. Housing Adequacy and Inequality in Cities in Developing Asia. *ADB Economics Working Paper Series*. Asian Development Bank.

Amoranto, G., E. Go, R. Hasan, and Y. Jiang. Forthcoming. Cities and Jobs: Evidence from Labor Force Surveys from Four Asian Economies. *ADB Economics Working Paper Series*. Asian Development Bank.

Anantsuksomsri, S. and N. Tontisirin. 2019. Cities and Economic Dynamism: Challenges and Opportunities in Thailand. *Background study prepared for the Asian Development Bank*.

Ang, A. C., J. P. Cruz, and J. J. Valle. 2019. The State of Philippine Urbanization in 2019: Growth and Governance in the New Urban Economy. *Background study prepared for the Asian Development Bank*.

Chen, L., R. Hasan, and Y. Jiang. Forthcoming. City Characteristics and Firm Performance: Evidence from Asia. *ADB Economics Working Paper Series*. Asian Development Bank.

Hasan, S. M., M. Javaid, and H. Majid. 2019. A Review of Urbanization in Pakistan: Practices, Policies and Challenges. *Background study prepared for the Asian Development Bank*.

Helble, M., K. O. Lee, and M. A. G. Arbo. Forthcoming. The Housing Affordability Crisis in Cities in Developing Asia. *ADB Economics Working Paper Series*. Asian Development Bank.

Jia, N., P. Li, Y. Liu, and M. Lu. 2019. Cities and Economic Dynamism: The PRC Case. *Background study prepared for the Asian Development Bank*.

Jiang, Y. Forthcoming. Asian Cities: Spatial Dynamics and Driving Forces. *ADB Economics Working Paper Series*. Asian Development Bank.

Kallergis, A. and L. Simet. 2019. Urbanization in Asian Cities: Fostering Growth and Inclusion. *Background study prepared for the Asian Development Bank*.

Santoso, J. and L. Winayanti. 2019. Cities and Economic Dynamism in Indonesia. *Background study prepared for the Asian Development Bank*.

Sridhar, K. 2019. Cities and Economic Dynamism: Challenges and Opportunities. *Background study prepared for the Asian Development Bank*.

Tewari, M., D. Rodriguez, W. Freer, C. MacManus, L. Tafur, and E. Yarnall. 2019. Lessons on Transit Oriented Development from Global Experience. *Background study prepared for the Asian Development Bank*.

References

ADB. 2014. *Republic of the Philippines National Urban Assessment*. Asian Development Bank.

———. 2015. *Asian Economic Integration Report 2015: How Can Special Economic Zones Catalyze Economic Development?* Asian Development Bank.

———. 2018. *Asian Development Outlook 2018 Update: Maintaining Stability Amid Heightened Uncertainty*. Asian Development Bank.

———. 2019. Operational Priority 4: Making Cities More Livable, 2019–2024. Asian Development Bank. Draft report.

AfDB, ADB, EBRD, and IDB. Forthcoming. *Creating Livable Cities–Regional Approaches*. African Development Bank, Asian Development Bank, European Bank for Reconstruction and Development, and Inter-American Development Bank.

Akbar, P. A., V. Couture, G. Duranton, and A. Storeygard. 2018. Mobility and Congestion in Urban India. *NBER Working Paper Series* No. 25218. National Bureau of Economic Research.

Akinci, G., J. Crittle, G. Akinci, and J. Crittle. 2008. Special Economic Zone: Performance, Lessons Learned, and Implication for Zone Development. *Foreign Investment Advisory Service Occasional Paper*. World Bank.

Alonso, W. 1973. Urban Zero Population Growth. *Daedalus* 102(4).

Amirapu, A., R. Hasan, Y. Jiang, and A. Klein. 2019. Geographic Concentration in Indian Manufacturing and Service Industries: Evidence from 1998 to 2013. *Asian Economic Policy Review* 14(1).

Anderson, M. L. 2014. Subways, Strikes, and Slowdowns: The Impacts of Public Transit on Traffic Congestion. *American Economic Review* 104(9).

Angel, S., P. Lamson-Hall, M. Madrid, A. M. Blei, and J. Parent. 2016. *Atlas of Urban Expansion*. Vol. 2: Blocks and Roads, *The 2016 Edition*. NYU Urban Expansion Program at New York University, UN-Habitat, and Lincoln Institute of Land Policy.

Association of Siamese Architects. Ministerial Regulations for Comprehensive Town Planning. https://asa.or.th/mr-cp/#/pl.

Atkin, D., A. Chaudhry, S. Chaudry, A. K. Khandelwal, T. Raza, and E. Verhoogen. 2016. On the Origins and Development of Pakistan's Soccer-Ball Cluster. *World Bank Economic Review* 30(Supplement 1).

Bacolod, M., B. S. Blum, and W. C. Strange. 2009. Skills in the City. *Journal of Urban Economics* 65(2).

Bai, C.-E., C. T. Hsieh, and Z. M. Song. 2019. Special Deals with Chinese Characteristics. *NBER Working Paper Series* No. 25839. National Bureau of Economic Research.

Baissac, C. 2011. Brief History of SEZs and Overview of Policy Debates. In *Special Economic Zones in Africa*. World Bank.

Baum-Snow, N. 2019. Urban Transport Expansions and Changes in the Spatial Structure of US Cities: Implications for Productivity and Welfare. *The Review of Economics and Statistics.*

Baum-Snow, N., M. E. Kahn, and R. Voith. 2005. Effects of Urban Rail Transit Expansions: Evidence from Sixteen Cities, 1970–2000 [with Comment]. *Brookings-Wharton Papers on Urban Affairs.*

Beaudoin, J. and C. Y. C. Lin Lawell. 2018. The Effects of Public Transit Supply on the Demand for Automobile Travel. *Journal of Environmental Economics and Management* 88.

Behrens, K. and F. Robert-Nicoud. 2015. Agglomeration Theory with Heterogeneous Agents. In G. Duranton, J. V. Henderson, and W. C. Strange, eds. *Handbook of Regional and Urban Economics*. Elsevier.

Bentley, R., E. Baker, and K. Mason. 2012. Cumulative Exposure to Poor Housing Affordability and Its Association with Mental Health in Men and Women. *Journal of Epidemiol Community Health* 66(9).

Bentley, R., E. Baker, K. Mason, S. V. Subramanian, and A. M. Kavanagh. 2011. Association between Housing Affordability and Mental Health: A Longitudinal Analysis of a Nationally Representative Household Survey in Australia. *American Journal of Epidemiology* 174(7).

Bertaud, A. 2018. *Order without Design: How Markets Shape Cities.* MIT Press.

Bertinelli, L. and D. Black. 2004. Urbanization and Growth. *Journal of Urban Economics* 56(1).

Bird, R. M. and E. Slack. 2014. Local Taxes and Local Expenditures in Developing Countries: Strengthening the Wicksellian Connection. *Public Administration and Development* 34(5).

Bramwell, A. and D. A. Wolfe. 2008. Universities and Regional Economic Development: The Entrepreneurial University of Waterloo. *Research Policy* 37(8).

Brueckner, J. K. and K. S. Sridhar. 2012. Measuring Welfare Gains from Relaxation of Land-Use Restrictions: The Case of India's Building-Height Limits. *Regional Science and Urban Economics* 42(6).

Brülhart, M. and F. Sbergami. 2009. Agglomeration and Growth: Cross-Country Evidence. *Journal of Urban Economics* 65(1).

Carlino, G. A. and W. R. Kerr. 2015. Agglomeration and Innovation. In G. Duranton, J. V. Henderson, and W. C. Strange, eds. *Handbook of Regional and Urban Economics*. Elsevier.

Chambers, E., D. Fuster, S. Suglia, and E. Rosenbaum. 2015. Depressive Symptomology and Hostile Affect among Latinos Using Housing Rental Assistance: The AHOME Study. *Journal of Urban Health* 92(4).

Chan, S., K. O'Regan, and W. You. 2019. Geographic Mobility and Parental Co-Residence among Young Adults. *Working paper.* Peter G. Peterson Foundation.

Chaney, T., D. Sraer, and D. Thesmar. 2012. The Collateral Channel: How Real Estate Shocks Affect Corporate Investment. *American Economic Review* 102(6).

Chauvin, J. P., E. Glaeser, Y. Ma, and K. Tobio. 2017. What is Different About Urbanization in Rich and Poor Countries? Cities in Brazil, China, India and the United States. *Journal of Urban Economics* 98.

Chen, J., M. Hu, and Z. Lin. 2019. Does Housing Unaffordability Crowd out Elites in Chinese Superstar Cities? *Journal of Housing Economics* 45.

Chen, T., L. X. Liu, W. Xiong, and L. A. Zhou. 2017. Real Estate Boom and Misallocation of Capital in China. Preliminary draft.

Choe, K. A. and B. H. Roberts. 2011. *Competitive Cities in the 21st Century: Cluster-Based Local Economic Development.* Asian Development Bank.

Combes, P.-P. and L. Gobillon. 2015. The Empirics of Agglomeration Economies. In G. Duranton, J. V. Henderson, and W. C. Strange, eds. *Handbook of Regional and Urban Economics.* Elsevier.

De La Roca, J. and D. Puga. 2016. Learning by Working in Big Cities. *The Review of Economic Studies* 84(1).

Deakin, A. 1989. Growth Controls and Growth Management: A Summary and Review of Empirical Research. In D. J. Brower, D. R. Godschalk, and D. R. Porter, eds. *Understanding Growth Management: Critical Issues and a Research Agenda.* Urban Land Institute.

Demographia. 2019. 15th Annual Demographia International Housing Affordability Survey. *Rating Middle-Income Housing Affordability.*

Dobkins, L. H. and Y. M. Ioannides. 2001. Spatial Interactions among U.S. Cities: 1900–1990. *Regional Science and Urban Economics* 31(6).

Dockery, M., R. Ong, S. Colquhoun, J. Li, and G. Kendall. 2013. Housing and Children's Development and Wellbeing: Evidence from Australian Data. *AHURI Final Report No. 201.* Australian Housing and Urban Research Institute.

Dong, X., S. Zheng, and M. E. Kahn. 2018. The Role of Transportation Speed in Facilitating High Skilled Teamwork. *NBER Working Paper Series* No. 24539. National Bureau of Economic Research.

Duranton, G. 2007. Urban Evolutions: The Fast, the Slow, and the Still. *American Economic Review* 97(1).

——. 2008. Viewpoint: From Cities to Productivity and Growth in Developing Countries. *Canadian Journal of Economics/ Revue canadienne d'économique* 41(3).

———. 2015. Growing through Cities in Developing Countries. *World Bank Research Observer* 30(1).

Duranton, G. and E. Guerra. 2016. *Developing a Common Narrative on Urban Accessibility: An Urban Planning Perspective*. Brookings Institution.

Duranton, G. and D. Puga. 2001. Nursery Cities: Urban Diversity, Process Innovation, and the Life Cycle of Products. *American Economic Review* 91(5).

———. 2004. Micro-Foundations of Urban Agglomeration Economies. In J. V. Henderson and J. F. Thisse, eds. *Handbook of Regional and Urban Economics*. Elsevier.

Duranton, G. and M. A. Turner. 2011. The Fundamental Law of Road Congestion: Evidence from US Cities. *American Economic Review* 101(6).

Duranton, G. and A. J. Venables. 2018. Place-Based Policies for Development. *Policy Research Working Paper* No. 8410. World Bank.

Edin, M. 2003. State Capacity and Local Agent Control in China: CCP Cadre Management from a Township Perspective. *The China Quarterly* 173.

Ellickson, R. C. 2013. The Law and Economics of Street Layouts: How a Grid Pattern Benefits a Downtown. *Faculty Scholarship Series* No. 4807. Yale Law School.

Faber, B. 2014. Trade Integration, Market Size, and Industrialization: Evidence from China's National Trunk Highway System. *Review of Economic Studies* 81(3).

Foster, V. and C. Briceño-Garmendia, eds. 2010. *Africa's Infrastructure: A Time for Transformation*. The World Bank.

Frick, S. A., A. Rodríguez-Pose, and M. D. Wong. 2019. Toward Economically Dynamic Special Economic Zones in Emerging Countries. *Economic Geography* 95(1).

Fujita, M., P. Krugman, and A. J. Venables. 1999. *The Spatial Economy: Cities, Regions, and International Trade*. MIT Press.

Galindo, V. M. N. 2007. La Aglomeración Como Una Causa De La Innovación En Colombia. *Planeación & desarrollo* 38(1).

Galster, G. and K. O. Lee. Forthcoming. Housing Affordability: A Framing, Synthesis of Research and Policy, and Future Directions. *International Journal of Urban Sciences*.

General Statistics Office of Viet Nam. Statistical Data: Population and Employment. https://www.gso.gov.vn/default_en.aspx?tabid=774.

Ghani, E., A. G. Goswami, and W. R. Kerr. 2012. Is India's Manufacturing Sector Moving Away from Cities? *NBER Working Paper Series* No. 17992. National Bureau of Economic Research.

———. 2016. Highway to Success: The Impact of the Golden Quadrilateral Project for the Location and Performance of Indian Manufacturing. *Economic Journal* 126(591).

Glaeser, E. and J. Gyourko. 2018. The Economic Implications of Housing Supply. *Journal of Economic Perspectives* 32(1).

Gollin, D., R. Jedwab, and D. Vollrath. 2016. Urbanization with and without Industrialization. *Journal of Economic Growth* 21(1).

Government of India, Office of the Registrar General & Census Commissioner. *2011 Census Data*. http://www.censusindia .gov.in/.

——, Ministry of Urban Development. 2014. *Urban and Regional Development Plans Formulation and Implementation (URDPFI) Guidelines*. New Delhi.

Government of Thailand, Department of Provincial Administration. 2014. *Annual Population and House Statistics Report*. http://stat.dopa.go.th/stat/statnew/ statMenu/newStat/home.php.

Groff, S. and S. Rau. 2018. No Reason for City Clusters Not to Succeed. *Op-Eds and Opinion*. Asian Development Bank.

Haque, N. U. 2015. Flawed Urban Development Policies in Pakistan. *PIDE-Working Papers* No. 119. Pakistan Institute of Development Economics.

Hasan, A., N. Ahmed, M. Raza, A. Sadiq, S. D. Ahmed, and M. B. Sarwar. 2013. Land Ownership, Control and Contestation in Karachi and Implications for Low-Income Housing. *Urbanization and Emerging Population Issues* 10. International Institute for Environment and Development.

Hasan, R., Y. Jiang, and R. M. Rafols. 2017. Place-Based Preferential Tax Policy and Its Spatial Effects: Evidence from India's Program on Industrially Backward Districts. *ADB Economics Working Papers* No. 524. Asian Development Bank.

Henderson, J. V. 2014. Urbanization and the Geography of Development. *Policy Research Working Paper* No. 6877. World Bank.

Henderson, J., J. Quigley, and E. Lim. 2009. Urbanization in China: Policy Issues and Options. *Working paper*. Brown University.

Henderson, J., A. Storeygard, and D. N. Weil. 2012. Measuring Economic Growth from Outer Space. *American Economic Review* 102(2).

Hsieh, C.-T. and P. J. Klenow. 2009. Misallocation and Manufacturing TFP in China and India. *Quarterly Journal of Economics* 124(4).

Hsieh, C.-T. and E. Moretti. 2019. Housing Constraints and Spatial Misallocation. *American Economic Journal: Macroeconomics* 11(2).

Hymel, K. 2009. Does Traffic Congestion Reduce Employment Growth? *Journal of Urban Economics* 65(2).

Jacobs, J. 1969. *The Economy of Cities*. Penguin Books.

——. 1992. *The Death and Life of Great American Cities*. Vintage Books.

Kim, S. 2017. Experts Discuss Low Fertility Rate. *Korea JoongAng Daily*. 14 July.

Lall, S. V., J. V. Henderson, and A. J. Venables. 2017. *Africa's Cities: Opening Doors to the World*. World Bank.

Lee, K. O. and G. Painter. 2013. What Happens to Household Formation in a Recession? *Journal of Urban Economics* 76.

Li, H. and L. A. Zhou. 2005. Political Turnover and Economic Performance: The Incentive Role of Personnel Control in China. *Journal of Public Economics* 89(9).

Li, Z. and H. Xu. 2016. High-Speed Railroad and Economic Geography: Evidence from Japan. *ADB Economics Working Papers* No. 485. Asian Development Bank.

Liang, W., M. Lu, and H. Zhang. 2016. Housing Prices Raise Wages: Estimating the Unexpected Effects of Land Supply Regulation in China. *Journal of Housing Economics* 33.

Lu, M., C. Sun, and S. Zheng. 2017. Congestion and Pollution Consequences of Driving-to-School Trips: A Case Study in Beijing. *Transportation Research Part D: Transport and Environment* 50.

Manasan, R. G. 2013. Export Processing Zones, Special Economic Zones: Do We Really Need to Have More of Them? *Policy Notes* No. 2013-15. Philippine Institute for Development Studies.

Martin, P. and G. I. P. Ottaviano. 1999. Growing Locations: Industry Location in a Model of Endogenous Growth. *European Economic Review* 43(2).

McKinsey Global Institute. 2011. *Urban World: Mapping the Economic Power of Cities*. McKinsey & Company.

———. 2014. *A Blueprint for Addressing the Global Affordable Housing Challenge*. McKinsey & Company.

Meijers, E. J. and M. J. Burger. 2015. Stretching the Concept of 'Borrowed Size'. *Urban Studies* 54(1).

Meijers, E. J., M. J. Burger, and M. M. Hoogerbrugge. 2016. Borrowing Size in Networks of Cities: City Size, Network Connectivity and Metropolitan Functions in Europe. *Papers in Regional Science* 95(1).

Michalopoulos, S. and E. Papaioannou. 2014. National Institutions and Subnational Development in Africa. *Quarterly Journal of Economics* 129(1).

Monkkonen, P. and L. Ronconi. 2016. Comparative Evidence on Urban Land-Use Regulation Bureaucracy in Developing Countries. In E. L. Birch, S. Chattaraj, and S. M. Wachter, eds. *Slums: How Informal Real Estate Markets Work*. University of Pennsylvania Press.

Moretti, E. 2004. Workers' Education, Spillovers, and Productivity: Evidence from Plant-Level Production Functions. *American Economic Review* 94(3).

———. 2013. Real Wage Inequality. *American Economic Journal: Applied Economics* 5(1).

Mottaleb, K. A. and T. Sonobe. 2011. An Inquiry into the Rapid Growth of the Garment Industry in Bangladesh. *Economic Development and Cultural Change* 60(1).

Mulder, C. H. and F. C. Billari. 2010. Homeownership Regimes and Low Fertility. *Housing Studies* 25(4).

Newman, S. J. and C. S. Holupka. 2014. Housing Affordability and Investments in Children. *Journal of Housing Economics* 24.

———. 2015. Housing Affordability and Child Well-Being. *Housing Policy Debate* 25(1).

———. 2016. Housing Affordability and Children's Cognitive Achievement. *Health Affairs* 35(11).

O'Grady, T. 2014. Spatial Institutions in Urban Economies: How City Grids Affect Density and Development. Harvard University.

Partridge, M. D., D. S. Rickman, K. Ali, and M. R. Olfert. 2009. Do New Economic Geography Agglomeration Shadows Underlie Current Population Dynamics across the Urban Hierarchy? *Papers in Regional Science* 88(2).

Philippine Statistics Authority. 2016. Population of Region VII— Central Visayas (based on the 2015 Census of Population). https://psa.gov.ph/content/population-region-vii-central-visayas-based-2015-census-population.

Rao, A. M. and K. R. Rao. 2012. Measuring Urban Traffic Congestion—a Review. *International Journal for Traffic and Transport Engineering* 2(4).

Rossi-Hansberg, E. and M. Wright. 2007. Urban Structure and Growth. *Review of Economic Studies* 74(2).

Sandhu, S. C., R. N. Singru, J. Bachmann, V. Sankaran, and P. Arnoux. 2016. *GrEEEn Solutions for Livable Cities*. Asian Development Bank.

Slack, E. 2007. Managing the Coordination of Service Delivery in Metropolitan Cities : The Role of Metropolitan Governance. *Policy Research Working Paper* No. 4317. World Bank.

Sridhar, K. S. 2010. Impact of Land Use Regulations: Evidence from India's Cities. *Urban Studies* 47(7).

Statistics Indonesia. Statistics of Sumatera Utara Province. https://sumut.bps.go.id/.

Storeygard, A. 2016. Farther on Down the Road: Transport Costs, Trade and Urban Growth in Sub-Saharan Africa. *Review of Economic Studies* 83(3).

The Journal. 2013. Financial Pressures and Lack of Affordable Housing Linked to Low Fertility Rates.

UN-Habitat. 2001. *The State of the World's Cities Report 2001*. UN-Habitat.

———. 2011. *Affordable Land and Housing in Asia*. UN-Habitat.

United Nations. 2018a. *World Urbanization Prospects: The 2018 Revision, Methodology*. United Nations.

———. 2018b. World Urbanization Prospects: The 2018 Revision. https://population.un.org/wup/.

Venables, A. J. 2010. Economic Geography and African Development. *Papers in Regional Science* 89(3).

——. 2017. Breaking into Tradables: Urban Form and Urban Function in a Developing City. *Journal of Urban Economics* 98.

Vishwanath, T., S. V. Lall, D. Dowall, N. Lozano-Gracia, S. Sharma, and H. G. Wang. 2013. *Urbanization Beyond Municipal Boundaries: Nurturing Metropolitan Economies and Connecting Peri-Urban Areas in India*. World Bank.

Wang, X., D. A. Rodríguez, O. L. Sarmiento, and O. Guaje. 2019. Commute Patterns and Depression: Evidence from Eleven Latin American Cities. *Journal of Transport & Health* 14.

Williamson, J. G. 1965. Regional Inequality and the Process of National Development: A Description of the Patterns. *Economic Development and Cultural Change* 13(4).

Winston, C. and A. Langer. 2006. The Effect of Government Highway Spending on Road Users' Congestion Costs. *Journal of Urban Economics* 60(3).

World Bank. 2009. *World Development Report 2009: Reshaping Economic Geography*.

Xu, C. 2011. The Fundamental Institutions of China's Reforms and Development. *Journal of Economic Literature* 49(4).

Yoshino, N. and M. Helble, eds. 2016. *The Housing Challenge in Emerging Asia: Options and Solutions*. Asian Development Bank Institute.

These are the labor force surveys from government statistical agencies used in this study.

Government of India. National Sample Survey Office. *National Sample Survey—Employment and Unemployment Survey (NSS-EUS) 2011-2012*.

Government of Indonesia. Badan Pusat Statistik—Statistics Indonesia. *National Labor Force Survey (SAKERNAS) 2015*.

Government of Pakistan. Bureau of Statistics. *Labor Force Survey 2013–2014*.

Government of the Philippines, Philippine Statistics Authority. *Labor Force Survey 2015*.

3

ECONOMIC TRENDS AND PROSPECTS IN DEVELOPING ASIA

Central Asia

Subregional growth prospects for Central Asia in 2019 and 2020 have improved with faster growth forecast in several economies, including Kazakhstan, the region's largest. Projected inflation is revised up, reflecting forecasts for Georgia, Tajikistan, and Turkmenistan. The combined current account deficit is now projected narrower in both 2019 and 2020, with a larger surplus for Azerbaijan.

Subregional assessment and prospects

Growth accelerated in the first half of 2019 in Azerbaijan, the Kyrgyz Republic, Tajikistan, and Uzbekistan from the same period in 2018. With projected growth higher for Armenia, Azerbaijan, Kazakhstan, and Uzbekistan, this *Update* raises the subregional growth forecast for 2019 from 4.2% in *ADO 2019* to 4.4%, partly reflecting expansion in the first half of the year. The forecast for 2020 is raised from 4.2% to 4.3%, with higher projections for Kazakhstan, Tajikistan, and Uzbekistan (Figure 3.1.1).

Growth in Kazakhstan in the first 6 months of 2019 decelerated slightly from 4.2% in the same period of 2018 to 4.1%. Adherence to internationally agreed supply restrictions and maintenance at the Kashagan oil field trimmed oil production, but growth in the rest of the economy was largely sustained. With government spending for social programs greater than earlier expected, this *Update* raises growth projections from 3.5% to 3.7% for 2019 and from 3.3% to 3.4% for 2020. The growth forecast for Azerbaijan is raised from 2.5% to 2.6% for 2019 on account of record high gas production at the Shah Deniz field, but the projection for 2020 is trimmed from 2.7% to 2.4% in line with expected stabilization of gas production. With Turkmenistan reportedly growing at 6.2% in the first half of 2019, its growth outlook remains at 6.0% for 2019 and 5.8% for 2020. With investment-led growth in Uzbekistan rising to 5.8% in the first half of 2019, the growth projection for 2019 is raised from 5.2% to 5.8% and for 2020 from 5.5% to 6.0%.

Figure 3.1.1 GDP growth, Central Asia

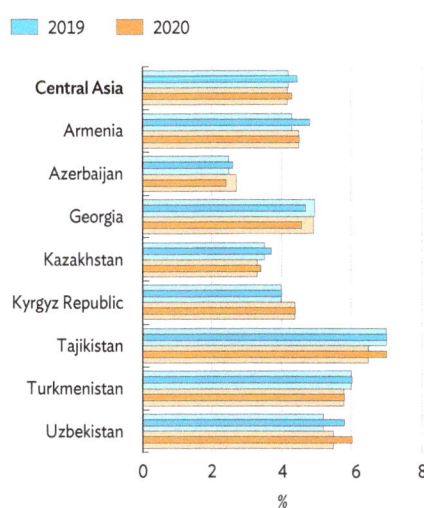

Note: Lighter colored bars are *ADO 2019* forecasts.
Source: *Asian Development Outlook* database.

The subregional assessment and prospects were written by Kenji Takamiya. Kazakhstan was written by Genadiy Rau, and the other economies by Muhammadi Boboev, Grigor Gyurjyan, Jennet Hojanazarova, George Luarsabishvili, Gulkayr Tentieva, Nail Valiyev, and Begzod Djalilov. All authors are in the Central and West Asia Department of ADB.

As Armenia grew robustly on private consumption in the first quarter of 2019, its growth projection for the whole year is raised from 4.3% to 4.8%, while the earlier forecast of 4.5% growth in 2020 is retained. For Georgia, investment contraction in the first quarter of 2019 and a weak outlook for private investment prompt reductions to forecast growth from 5.0% to 4.7% for 2019 and from 4.9% to 4.6% for 2020. Buoyant gold production drove growth in the Kyrgyz Republic from 0.3% in the first half of 2018 to 6.4% a year later, but earlier growth projections of 4.0% for 2019 and 4.4% for 2020 are retained because gold production is expected to slow again. The growth projection for Tajikistan is raised from 6.5% to 7.0% for 2020 with public investment expected higher.

Average annual inflation in the first half of 2019 slowed in most subregional economies with data available: Armenia, Azerbaijan, Kazakhstan, the Kyrgyz Republic, and Uzbekistan. However, the inflation projection for the subregion as a whole in 2019 is raised from 7.8% to 8.0%, reflecting higher forecasts for Georgia and Tajikistan and double-digit inflation in Turkmenistan. The same factors prompt a higher subregional forecast for 2020, from 7.2% to 7.4%, despite downward revisions for Azerbaijan, Kazakhstan, and Uzbekistan (Figure 3.1.2). Kazakhstan's inflation projection is trimmed from 6.0% to 5.8% for 2019 and from 5.5% to 5.2% for 2020 with price controls on food, other goods, and utilities likely to be continued. The largest forecast adjustment is for Turkmenistan, up from 9.0% to 13.4% in 2019 and from 8.2% to 13.0% in 2020, in view of subsidy reform, expansionary credit policy, and rising import prices attributable to foreign exchange shortages.

The projection for the combined subregional current account deficit is lowered from the equivalent of 1.7% of GDP to 1.3% in 2019 and from 1.8% to 1.7% in 2020 (Figure 3.1.3) even though a number of economies in the subregion run sizable deficits. For both years, deficit projections are widened for Armenia, Kazakhstan, and Tajikistan but narrowed for Georgia and Turkmenistan. Only Azerbaijan is projected to run a current account surplus, revised up from 13.6% of GDP to 13.9% for 2019, and from 10.8% to 11.6% for 2020, in light of the higher oil price outlook and expected growth in tourism with the introduction of a simplified visa processing system.

Figure 3.1.2 Inflation, Central Asia

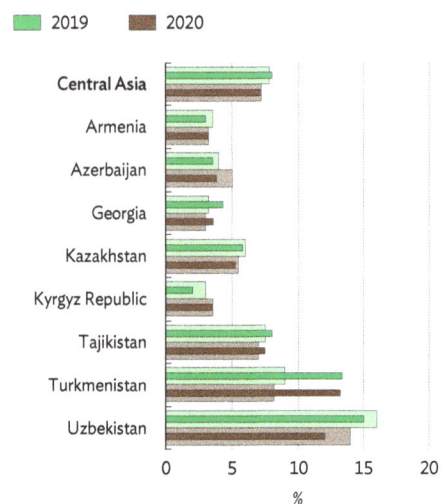

Note: Lighter colored bars are *ADO 2019* forecasts.
Source: *Asian Development Outlook* database.

Figure 3.1.3 Current account balance, Central Asia

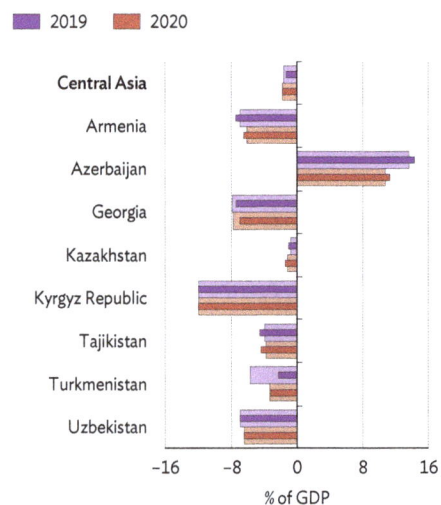

Note: Lighter colored bars are *ADO 2019* forecasts.
Source: *Asian Development Outlook* database.

Kazakhstan

Broad gains outside of the important petroleum industry largely sustained GDP growth in the first half of 2019. With government social programs contributing to private consumption and investment more than anticipated in *ADO 2019*, growth forecasts are raised slightly for both 2019 and 2020. Meanwhile, slowing inflation in the first half and price controls introduced by the government prompt lower projections for inflation in both years. With curbs on oil production trimming the forecast trade surplus, the current account balance is now projected to move deeper into deficit in 2019 and widen further in 2020.

Updated assessment

The economy grew at an annual rate of 4.1% in the first half of 2019, slowing slightly from 4.2% in the same period of 2018 (Figure 3.1.4). Industry expanded by 2.6% as state industrialization programs supported manufacturing growth at 3.4%. Mining expanded by 2.1% despite a 1.9% decline in oil production as maintenance at the Kashagan oilfield restrained output, as did Kazakhstan's adherence to production cuts agreed by a coalition led by the Organization of the Petroleum Exporting Countries (OPEC). Agriculture expanded by 3.8% on increases of 6.7% in crop production and 3.7% in livestock. Growth in construction accelerated from 3.8% in the first half of 2018 to 11.1%, strongly supported by state housing and infrastructure programs. Support came as well from record 30.5% mortgage credit growth year on year in June 2019, expanding the segment to 11.6% of total credit. Services grew by 4.2% as higher income from increases in the minimum wage and social programs boosted trade by 7.5%, while transportation expanded by 5.3% and education by 3.7%.

Demand-side data, available for only the first quarter of 2019, show consumption up by 4.7%, reflecting increases of 5.0% in private consumption and 3.4% public (Figure 3.1.5). Lower spending on machinery and equipment limited the gain in investment to 0.2%, despite a 3.4% rise in fixed investment largely from oil and gas modernization projects and residential construction. The GDP share of net exports of goods and services expanded by 1.7%, while those of consumption and investment contracted.

Average annual inflation slowed from 6.3% in the first 7 months of 2018 to 5.1% a year later as price increases for services decelerated to 1.5%, and despite increases of 7.3% for food and 6.1% for other goods (Figure 3.1.6). Government-ordered declines in utility charges since January 2019 cut average utility prices by 2.8% relative to the same period in 2018. In addition, gasoline prices fell by 6.1% with self-sufficiency in gasoline production and tight controls on exports.

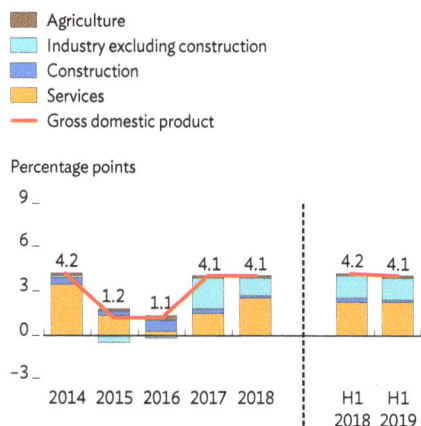

Figure 3.1.4 Supply-side contributions to growth

- Agriculture
- Industry excluding construction
- Construction
- Services
- Gross domestic product

Percentage points

H = half.
Source: Republic of Kazakhstan. Ministry of National Economy. Committee on Statistics.

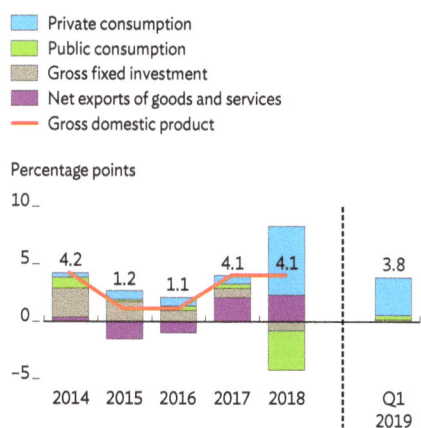

Figure 3.1.5 Demand-side contributions to growth

- Private consumption
- Public consumption
- Gross fixed investment
- Net exports of goods and services
- Gross domestic product

Percentage points

Q = quarter.
Source: Republic of Kazakhstan. Ministry of National Economy. Committee on Statistics.

Inflation targeting within 4%–6% in 2019 remains the primary objective of monetary policy.

In the first 6 months of 2019, budget revenue rose by 18.1% to equal 22.4% of estimated GDP as tax revenue increased by 15.3% under better administration. Transfers from the National Fund of the Republic of Kazakhstan (NFRK) grew by 26.9% to $4.8 billion. Expenditure rose by 16.8% to equal 21.6% of estimated GDP, with increases of 28.2% for debt service, 24.0% for social programs, and 14.2% for education, leaving a budget deficit equal to 0.4% of GDP. Three revisions of the central government budget raised expenditure for 2019 by 10.1%, with increases of 8.7% for social assistance, 8.0% for education, and 7.0% for health care. Net receipts into the NFRK rose by 14.1% with increases of 13.4% in tax revenue from oil companies and 33.0% in revenue from product-sharing agreements, the latter providing 28.2% of total NFRK inflows. Outward transfers were up by 43.3%.

In April 2019, the National Bank of Kazakhstan, the central bank, lowered its policy rate to 9.0% (Figure 3.1.7). Broad money reversed growth of 2.3% in the first half of 2018 to shrink by 6.1% a year later as total credit fell by 1.4% and deposits by 2.3%. Lending to firms contracted by 9.2%, but consumer credit expanded by 10.1%. Foreign currency deposits fell by 9.4% to account for 43.4% of all deposits, while deposits in tenge, the national currency, rose by 3.8% (Figure 3.1.8). Official figures released by the central bank show nonperforming loans worsening from 7.4% at the end of 2018 to 9.4% in June 2019. In a much-awaited move, the central bank announced plans for a sweeping asset quality review covering half of the country's 28 commercial banks and 87% of bank assets. In the first half of 2019, the average tenge value against the US dollar was 16.1% below the average in the same period in 2018. The central bank reported no net interventions in the foreign exchange market in the period.

Preliminary estimates indicate a current account deficit of $2.0 billion, equal to 2.7% of GDP, in the first half of 2019 as the trade surplus in goods shrank by 10.3% and the deficit in services widened by 13.9% (Figure 3.1.9). Merchandise imports expanded by a sharp 10.2% on increases of 36.6% for textiles, clothing, and footwear and of 23.9% for machinery and equipment. Merchandise exports expanded slightly, by 1.1%. Foreign direct investment fell by 24.1% to $3.2 billion. Gross foreign exchange reserves declined by 6.2% to an estimated $28.2 billion as government and state-owned enterprises repaid $4.3 billion in external debt. In June 2019, international reserves covered 7.2 months of imports of goods and services, while NFRK assets reached $59.9 billion (Figure 3.1.10). External debt at the end of the first quarter of 2019 was $157.7 billion, equal to 90.7% of estimated GDP.

Figure 3.1.6 Monthly inflation

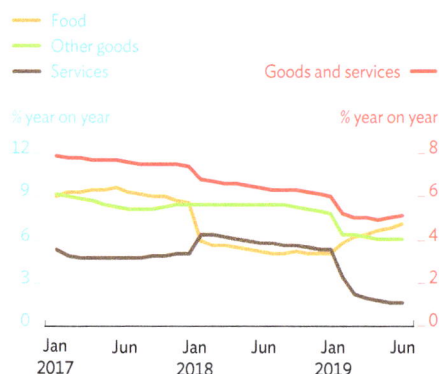

Source: Haver Analytics (accessed 4 September 2019).

Figure 3.1.7 Interest rate and broad money

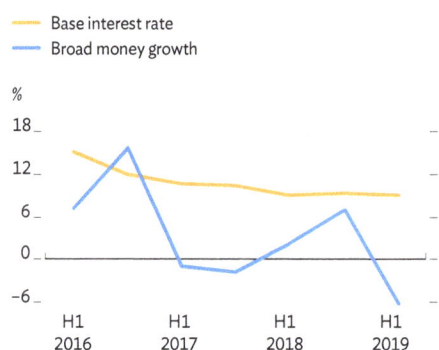

H = half.
Note: Broad money growth refers to percent change from December of the previous year.
Source: National Bank of the Republic of Kazakhstan.

Figure 3.1.8 Dollarization in the banking system

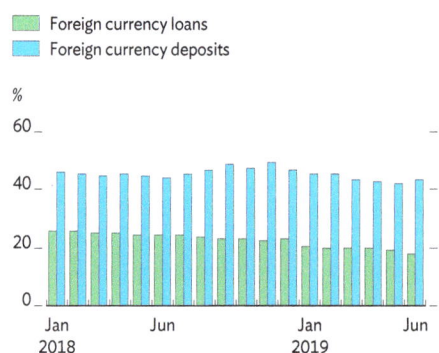

Source: National Bank of the Republic of Kazakhstan.

Intercompany debt, primarily for oil and gas projects, declined to $100.8 billion, or 63.9% of GDP, of which $18.5 billion was due in 2019. Public and publicly guaranteed external debt decreased to $14.0 billion, equal to 8.1% of GDP, of which $1.3 billion was due in 2019.

The official unemployment rate has stood at 4.8% since July 2018. Self-employed workers remained at about 23% of the labor force, despite efforts to reduce self-employment through a modest tax on it.

Prospects

On the demand side, consumption is now projected to grow by 3.7% in 2019, revised up from 1.3% in *ADO 2019*, and by 3.0% in 2020. This trend reflects a 3.8% rise in real household income during the first half of 2019 from its level during the same period in 2018, mainly from government measures that have tripled the number of social assistance recipients, as well as from a program announced in June to help households in economic hardship by writing off $800 in bad loans per member. Benefiting from increased state support for housing construction and infrastructure, total investment is now projected to grow faster than earlier forecast.

On the supply side, services have become a main driver of expansion with trade, transport, and communications now forecast to grow somewhat faster in 2019 and 2020 than earlier projected. Meanwhile, growth prospects for mining are limited by an extension of the OPEC-led agreement and maintenance plans for the Tengiz and Karachaganak oilfields in the second half of 2019. Other projections are unchanged. In view of acceleration in consumption and services, this *Update* raises the growth projection for 2019 to 3.7% and for 2020 to 3.4%.

With recently announced government price controls for staple foods and continued restraint on utility and petroleum prices, this *Update* projects somewhat lower inflation than forecast in *ADO 2019*, now 5.8% in 2019 and at 5.2% in 2020, notwithstanding faster growth in real incomes, currency depreciation, and government fiscal stimulus. The central bank is expected to moderate inflationary pressure by raising the policy rate and absorbing excess liquidity with a view to keeping inflation within the band of 4%–6% throughout 2020–2021. Food price inflation is now projected at 6.8% in 2019 and 6.2% in 2020, with forecast inflation for other goods trimmed to 6.6% in 2019 and 5.8% in 2020.

With the three amendments of the 2019 state budget, expenditure is now projected at 21.6% of GDP, revised up from 18.5% in *ADO 2019*. The revenue forecast is also raised, from 17.0% of GDP to 19.4%, reflecting a decision to increase transfers from the NFRK by more than 18%, not reduce them as earlier envisioned. Accordingly, the budget deficit is now projected higher by half, from the equivalent of 1.5% of GDP

Figure 3.1.9 Current account balance

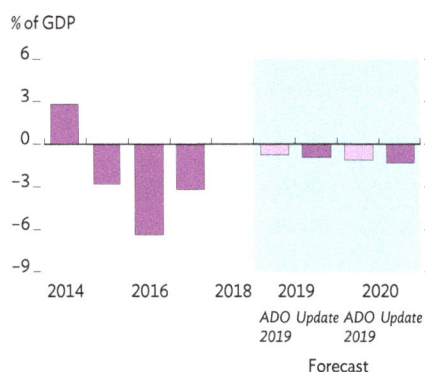

Source: *Asian Development Outlook* database.

Figure 3.1.10 Reserves and assets

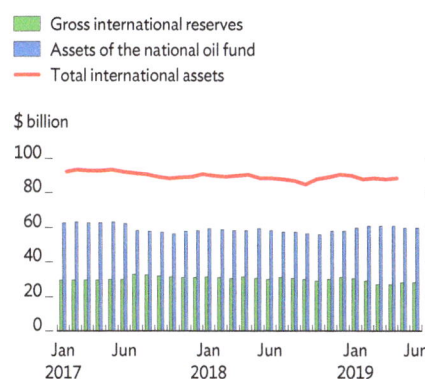

Source: Haver Analytics (accessed 4 September 2019).

to 2.2%, with the projected non-oil deficit revised up from 7.0% of GDP to 7.6%. The projected non-oil deficit in 2020 is raised from 6.5% of GDP to 7.0% to cover the government's continuing social support and stimulus programs. Public debt is now forecast to equal 27.2% of GDP at the end of 2019 and 25.0% at the end of 2020.

With crude oil output projected lower and average prices now forecast somewhat higher, at $65 per barrel in 2019 and $63 in 2020, merchandise exports will likely grow little from 2018. Rising consumer spending on imports, supported by higher income and credit, will narrow the surplus in merchandise trade to $23.8 billion in 2019 before it rises again to $24.5 billion in 2020. With deficits in services and primary income expected to persist, this *Update* raises forecasts for the current account deficit to 1.0% of GDP in 2019 and 1.4% in 2020. Higher transfers to the budget are projected to trim NFRK assets to $58.5 billion at the end of 2019, below the previous forecast of $59.5 billion, rising to $59.0 billion at the end of 2020, revised down from $60.7 billion. Projections for international reserves are also reduced, from $31.0 billion to $30.0 billion at the end of 2019, or cover for 7.5 months of imports, and from $32.4 billion to $31.5 billion at the end of 2020. External debt including intercompany debt is now forecast to fall to the equivalent of 93.0% of GDP at the end of 2019, revised down from 98.0%, and to 90.0% at the end of 2020, revised down from 95.0%, as oil and gas subsidiaries continue repaying debts owed to their parent companies.

The recently elected President has reaffirmed the government's key role in promoting economic growth. The government has provided additional funding and extended to 2025 three key initiatives: the Nurly Zher program for housing construction, Nurly Zhol program for connective infrastructure, and Business Road Map to promote entrepreneurship. Further, an industrialization program that was to end this year will be renewed. However, a privatization program and the development of the Astana International Financial Center, announced earlier, will likely play smaller roles than earlier expected.

Solid fundamentals and accumulated international reserves should allow the government to stimulate the economy and raise real household income through social spending, but these efforts could be undermined by external shocks stemming from geopolitical tensions and commodity price fluctuations.

Table 3.1.1 Selected economic indicators, Kazakhstan (%)

	2019		2020	
	ADO 2019	Update	ADO 2019	Update
GDP growth	3.5	3.7	3.3	3.4
Inflation	6.0	5.8	5.5	5.2
Current acct. bal. (share of GDP)	–0.8	–1.0	–1.2	–1.4

Source: ADB estimates.

Other economies

Armenia

Growth moderated from 8.7% year on year in the first half of 2018 to 6.8% in the same period of this year—still robust, reflecting buoyant domestic demand. Industry excluding construction performed strongly, expanding by 5.2% as growth in manufacturing and mining outweighed lower electricity production. Construction grew by 3.5%, largely from higher household construction. Services rose by 9.8% on strong gains in information technology, finance, insurance, and recreation. Unfavorable weather constrained agriculture, which, having contracted by 8.5% in the whole of 2018, contracted further by 6.9% in the first half of 2019.

On the demand side, private consumption expanded by 14.0% in the half year, encouraged by moderate inflation, positive consumer sentiment, and low interest rates that boosted consumer borrowing. Fiscal consolidation cut public consumption by 5.9%. With sluggish public investment, total investment fell by 20.1%. Net exports continued to constrain growth as imports outgrew exports. In light of strong rises in services and private consumption, this *Update* raises the growth projection for 2019 while keeping the 2020 forecast unchanged.

The Central Bank of Armenia maintained its accommodative monetary stance to support growth while the government continued to pursue fiscal tightening. With low inflation and a stable exchange rate against the US dollar, the central bank lowered its policy interest rate by 25 basis points to 5.75% in January 2019. Average annual inflation slowed from 2.4% in the first half of 2018 to 2.0% in the same period in 2019, with price increases of 3.6% for food, 1.2% for consumer goods, and 0.2% for services. Inflation was 2.5% year on year in June 2019, at the lower bound of the central bank target of 2.5%–5.5%. This *Update* thus trims the inflation forecast for 2019 but keeps a higher forecast for 2020 in light of cuts in income tax rates to reduce the tax burden on low- and middle-income earners, planned salary increases for certain public employee categories from September and October 2019, pension increases from January 2020, and higher customs duties planned for imports from outside the Eurasian Economic Union.

The current account deficit widened from the equivalent of 10.4% of GDP in the first quarter of 2018 to 10.9% a year later as the terms of trade worsened, the Armenian dram appreciated against the currencies of major trade partners, including the euro and the ruble, and investment income, employee earnings from abroad, and remittances declined. Exports fell at an annual rate of 7.8%, and imports by 2.8%, widening the merchandise trade deficit from the equivalent of 14.2% of GDP in the first quarter of 2018 to 14.4% a year later. In view of developments in the first quarter of 2019, this *Update* raises projections for current account deficits in 2019 and 2020.

Table 3.1.2 Selected economic indicators, Armenia (%)

	2019		2020	
	ADO 2019	Update	ADO 2019	Update
GDP growth	4.3	4.8	4.5	4.5
Inflation	3.5	3.0	3.2	3.2
Current acct. bal. (share of GDP)	-6.9	-7.5	-6.1	-6.5

Source: ADB estimates.

Azerbaijan

Growth accelerated from 1.3% in the first half of 2018 to 2.4% in the first half of this year on higher domestic demand. Industry expanded by 1.8% on gains of 1.6% in mining and 13.5% in refineries, though oil production fell by 3.0% as the largest oil platform shut for regular maintenance. Gas output rose by a record 35.0% as full production began at the Shah Deniz gas field. Construction fell by 11.2% because of slowing investment. Services grew by 3.0% with transportation up by 2.5%, retail by 2.8%, and tourism and recreation by 3.3%. Good weather favored crop production and boosted agriculture by 13.1%.

On the demand side, with data available for only the first quarter, private consumption grew by 2.4% year on year as higher credit, minimum wages, and pensions boosted household income. Public consumption rose as the government raised outlays by 15.0%, primarily for social programs. Investment declined as the large South Gas Corridor project reached completion. With a 20.3% rise in gas exports boosting net exports, and with rising domestic demand, this *Update* raises the *ADO 2019* growth forecast for 2019 but revises down the forecast for 2020, when gas production is assumed to return to more stable growth.

Inflation slowed in the first half of 2019 from 3.0% a year earlier to 2.5% as continued exchange rate stability curbed imported inflation. Prices rose by 2.7% for food, 1.3% for other goods, and 3.2% for services. With inflation slowing in the first half of the year, the central bank gradually reduced its policy rate from 9.75% in February 2019 to 8.25% in July 2019. The prospective impact of a projected decline in global food prices is seen as largely offsetting those of wage increases and rising demand in 2019, prompting this *Update* to trim the forecast inflation in 2019. Although food prices are expected to recover in 2020, the forecast for inflation acceleration in 2020 is trimmed as well because growth in aggregate demand is expected to slow.

The merchandise trade surplus fell from $5.0 billion in the first half of 2018 to $2.4 billion in the same period of this year as oil exports declined by 3.7% and despite the rise in gas output. Exports grew marginally by 0.1%, while imports jumped by 51.3%, led by food, machinery, and equipment. International oil prices higher than earlier projected are now forecast to offset in the full year a decline in oil export volume. The service deficit will likely narrow as the visa processing period is shortened partly through the introduction of online visa application. With oil prices above earlier projections and tourism growth outpacing expectations, this *Update* raises its projections for current account surpluses in 2019 and 2020.

Table 3.1.3 Selected economic indicators, Azerbaijan (%)

	2019		2020	
	ADO 2019	*Update*	*ADO 2019*	*Update*
GDP growth	2.5	2.6	2.7	2.4
Inflation	4.0	3.7	5.0	3.8
Current acct. bal. (share of GDP)	13.6	13.9	10.8	11.6

Source: ADB estimates.

Georgia

Growth is estimated at 4.9% in the first half of this year, down from 5.4% in the same period of 2018 but outperforming last year as a whole. In services, 8.1% expansion reflected gains in tourism, trade, transport, health, and education. Meanwhile, despite upticks in cottage industries and in utilities, industry contracted by 2.7%, with construction down by 9.6% and mining and quarrying by 3.8%. Agriculture shrank by 0.3%.

Supporting growth on the demand side were increased public investment at the end of 2018, large refunds of value-added tax advances, faster credit growth, and an 8.0% rise in remittances that encouraged private consumption. However, total investment including from private sources contracted by 3.1% in the first quarter of 2019, a significant decline from growth of 11.2% in the same period of 2018. Given the modest outlook for growth in private investment, this *Update* reduces its growth forecasts for both 2019 and 2020. Potential risks to economic prospects include regional geopolitical tension.

Average inflation accelerated to 3.6% in the first half of 2019—above the 3.0% target set by the National Bank of Georgia, the central bank—reflecting higher prices for food, energy, and imported intermediate goods such as petroleum, along with higher excise taxes on tobacco. Prices rose by 5.2% for food, 2.9% for other goods, and 1.9% for services. Average inflation in the 12 months to June reached 3.0%. The central bank, having reduced the refinancing rate by half a percentage point to 6.5% in March 2019, raised it back to 7.0% in early September to moderate inflationary pressure. With the Georgian lari depreciating and triggering further price increases, this *Update* significantly raises the inflation forecasts for 2019 and 2020.

The current account deficit narrowed to the equivalent of 6.2% of GDP in the first quarter of 2019, as higher reexports drove merchandize export growth by 12.8%, and as imports fell by 4.7% with the winding down of energy investment projects. A surplus in service trade equaled 10.1% of GDP in the first quarter of the year. With merchandise exports expected to remain robust, this *Update* projects narrower current account deficits than those published in *ADO 2019*.

Table 3.1.4 Selected economic indicators, Georgia (%)

	2019		2020	
	ADO 2019	*Update 2019*	ADO 2019	*Update 2019*
GDP growth	5.0	4.7	4.9	4.6
Inflation	3.2	4.3	3.0	3.5
Current acct. bal. (share of GDP)	−7.9	−7.3	−7.8	−7.1

Source: ADB estimates.

Kyrgyz Republic

Growth accelerated from 0.3% in the first half of last year to 6.4% in the same period of 2019. Industry expanded by 19.7%, reversing 4.6% decline in the first half of 2018, thanks to gains of 24.2% in manufacturing, 5.9% in construction, and especially 31.0% in mining, notably higher gold output. Agriculture grew by 1.7% as livestock production rose by 2.0%, and services expanded by 1.4% on gains of 4.3% for trade and 2.2% for transport. GDP growth outside the large gold industry was 2.1%, with private consumption estimated to have grown by 1.9%.

Table 3.1.5 Selected economic indicators, Kyrgyz Republic (%)

	2019		2020	
	ADO 2019	*Update 2019*	ADO 2019	*Update 2019*
GDP growth	4.0	4.0	4.4	4.4
Inflation	3.0	2.0	3.5	3.5
Current acct. bal. (share of GDP)	−12.0	−12.0	−12.0	−12.0

Source: ADB estimates.

Slower growth is expected in the second half of the year, in particular in the last quarter, as gold production slows at Kumtor, the country's largest gold mine. In sum, this *Update* maintains the *ADO 2019* growth projection for 2019 and—with growth in the Russian Federation, a key trade partner, expected to accelerate—for 2020.

Average inflation fell from 2.3% in the first half of 2018 to 0.1% deflation a year later as substantial food imports from Uzbekistan cut food prices by 1.6% and the Kyrgyz som appreciated slightly against the US dollar. Prices rose by 2.0% for other goods and 0.4% for services. The annual inflation rate in June was 0.9%. Enabled by low inflation, the National Bank of the Kyrgyz Republic, the central bank, lowered the policy rate from 4.50% to 4.25% in May 2019. In view of these developments, this *Update* cuts the inflation forecast for 2019 but not for 2020.

Exchange rate policy remained cautious, with the central bank limiting its currency interventions to smoothing excess exchange rate volatility. The fiscal deficit is projected to widen to equal 3.3% of GDP in 2019 and stabilize at 3.0% or so in 2020, in line with a draft fiscal rule currently under consideration in Parliament that would cap government debt at 70% of GDP and the budget deficit at 3%.

In the first quarter of 2019, the current account deficit equaled 7.8% of GDP, with the trade deficit narrowing by 18.1% from a year earlier. Exports grew by 14.6%, mainly on gains for gold, cement, cotton, tobacco, meat, and vegetables. Imports shrank by 6.9% in tandem with declines for machinery and equipment, apparel, sugar, and tobacco. Remittances were 6.4% higher than in the same period of 2018 but declined in the second quarter. This *Update* retains *ADO 2019* projections for a higher current account deficit in 2019 that persists into 2020.

Tajikistan

Growth accelerated marginally from 7.2% in the first 6 months of 2018 to 7.5% in the same period of 2019, buoyed mainly by externally financed investment, both public and private. Expansion in industry slowed from a high of 16.7% to 12.5% as growth in mining slipped to 9.0% and in manufacturing to 12.4%, although the first phase of the Rogun hydropower project boosted growth in electricity generation from 4.0% to 10.4%. Expansion in agriculture accelerated from 8.5% to 10.8% on favorable weather and greater cultivated area. With remittances falling by 5.1% in the first quarter of 2019, growth in services slowed sharply from 7.9% in the first half of last year to 0.9% in the first half of this year, despite retail trade expanding by 9.6%.

On the demand side, fixed investment fell by 8.6%, and net exports improved by 0.7%. With declining remittances expected to constrain private consumption later this year and

Table 3.1.6 Selected economic indicators, Tajikistan (%)

	2019		2020	
	ADO 2019	Update	ADO 2019	Update
GDP growth	7.0	7.0	6.5	7.0
Inflation	7.5	8.0	7.0	7.5
Current acct. bal. (share of GDP)	−4.0	−4.5	−3.8	−4.3

Source: ADB estimates.

the Rogun project proceeding more slowly than expected, this *Update* retains the *ADO 2019* forecast for slower growth in 2019 than in 2018 but no longer sees further slowing in 2020, when growth will likely be sustained by high public investment to accelerate industrialization and expand production to replace imports.

Average inflation more than doubled from 3.2% in the first half of 2018 to 7.6% in the same period of this year, reflecting external inflationary pressures, supply shocks in agriculture, faster credit growth, and higher household income. Prices rose by 13.5% for food, 4.7% for other goods, and 1.3% for services. The National Bank of Tajikistan, the central bank, reduced its policy rate by 150 basis points to 13.25% in June. The Tajik somoni remained stable against the US dollar. With credit expanding by 34.6% in the first half of the year and electricity tariffs projected to rise by 17.0% in September, this *Update* revises up inflation forecasts for both years.

The trade deficit narrowed by 0.7% to $995.7 million in the first half of 2019 as higher electricity sales abroad boosted exports by 8.0%, albeit down from 15.3% growth a year earlier. Imports rose by only 2.3% as Rogun project construction progressed at the low end of the expectations. This *Update* nevertheless projects wider current account deficits in 2019 and 2020 in light of expected growth in domestic demand and weak remittances.

Turkmenistan

The government reported GDP growth at 6.2% year on year in the first half of 2019, driven by both services and industry, the latter benefiting from higher hydrocarbon output and improving energy prices. Industry reportedly expanded by 4.0% in the first half of the year and services by an estimated 9.7%, with growth in wholesale and retail trade soaring by 11.9%. Agriculture was estimated to expand by 3.5% as it attained the government's production target for wheat and improved on its growth rate in 2018 despite adverse weather. With the coming cotton harvest, this important crop appears set to meet targets as well.

On the demand side, public investment continued to support growth, though efforts to address external imbalances have brought it down sharply since 2017, when it represented 40.8% of GDP. The International Monetary Fund projects gross investment, most of it public, rising from 28.2% of GDP in 2018 to 29.2% this year and 31.2% in 2020. This *Update* maintains *ADO 2019* growth projections for 2019 and 2020.

The state budget will likely stay broadly balanced under budget consolidation that curtails investment and cuts social spending. However, off-budget spending on ad hoc construction projects is expected to be large, requiring fiscal reform to strengthen public spending efficiency and prioritization.

Table 3.1.7 Selected economic indicators, Turkmenistan (%)

	2019		2020	
	ADO 2019	Update	ADO 2019	Update
GDP growth	6.0	6.0	5.8	5.8
Inflation	9.0	13.4	8.2	13.0
Current acct. bal. (share of GDP)	−5.7	−2.3	−3.4	−3.2

Source: ADB estimates.

Inflation is projected to remain elevated because of subsidy reform, rising import prices, shortages of foreign exchange, and expansionary credit policy, which boosted credit to the private sector by 26.1% in the first half of 2019 and total credit by 9.9%. High inflation and social subsidy cuts have considerably affected household real income and purchasing power. The official exchange rate appears to overvalue the Turkmen manat considerably compared with the parallel market rate, and the Central Bank of Turkmenistan continues to ration foreign exchange and promote noncash payments. Reflecting these developments, this *Update* significantly raises inflation projections for 2019 and 2020.

Higher gas exports to the People's Republic of China and the recent resumption of gas exports to the Russian Federation are now expected to boost export revenue substantially in 2019 and, to a lesser extent, in 2020. Accordingly, this *Update* cuts its forecasts for current account deficits for both years. External public debt is projected to rise to the equivalent of 27.3% of GDP in 2019 and 27.7% in 2020.

Uzbekistan

The government reported growth rising from 5.1% in the first half of 2018 to 5.8% in the same period of 2019. Industry accelerated from 6.1% to 6.9%, with manufacturing higher by 7.8% and mining and quarrying by 4.7%. Growth in services picked up from 4.4% to 5.1% with gains of 3.8% in trade and 4.3% in transport and storage. A boom in housing and commercial buildings boosted reported growth in construction to 20.0%. Expansion in agriculture slowed from 2.7% to 2.1%, with growth in livestock sharply down from 5.4% to 1.7% a year earlier but crop production up from 1.1% to 3.2% with better rainfall.

On the demand side, investment was the key driver, offsetting lower net exports. Growth in gross capital formation soared from 13.4% in the first half of 2018 to 58.9% a year later on rapid credit expansion, primarily for industrial modernization and infrastructure development, and as foreign investment and loans rose from $2.2 billion in the year-earlier period to $3.8 billion, mainly for energy, mining, and manufacturing. With these developments, this *Update* substantially raises its growth projections for both 2019 and 2020.

Inflation slowed to 13.5% in July 2019 from 16.3% a year earlier. Average inflation fell more steeply, from 19.0% in the first 7 months of 2018 to 13.7% in the same period of this year. Tariff increases for electric and gas utilities were postponed from June 2019 to the third quarter. While food prices rose by 15.8%, inflation for other goods decelerated, as did inflation for services. In anticipation of tighter monetary policy later in this year to contain pressure generated by a 23.4% rise in credit in the first half, this *Update* trims the *ADO 2019* projection

Table 3.1.8 Selected economic indicators, Uzbekistan (%)

	2019		2020	
	ADO 2019	Update	ADO 2019	Update
GDP growth	5.2	5.8	5.5	6.0
Inflation	16.0	15.0	14.0	13.0
Current acct. bal. (share of GDP)	−7.0	−7.0	−6.5	−6.5

Source: ADB estimates.

for inflation in 2019. Inflation is expected to slow further in 2020 thanks to the expected government restraint in fiscal spending and lending to the economy, as well as ongoing structural reform.

The current account deficit more than doubled, from 2.6% of GDP in the first quarter of 2018 to 6.7% in the first quarter of this year, as the trade deficit jumped by 74.7%. In the same period, import growth, mostly for industry and construction, slowed from 41.9% year on year to 27.3%. Export growth plunged from 71.1% to 15.0% with slower growth in hydrocarbons and gold exports. The service deficit narrowed by 7.1% after a 66.2% widening a year earlier as 29.3% contraction in tourism offset a 20.4% rise in transport. Growth in remittances dropped from 19.9% to 6.1%. The current account deficit is expected to stop widening by the end of 2019, though, with an anticipated slowdown in capital goods imports. On balance, this *Update* retains earlier current account projections for 2019 and 2020.

East Asia

Growth moderated in East Asia in the first half of 2019 as demand faltered at home and abroad. Inflation edged up on rising food prices, and the subregional current account surplus strengthened as imports declined. The growth forecast is lowered for 2019 and 2020 as trade tensions take their toll. Inflation will be higher than earlier projected in both 2019 and 2020, as will the current account surplus as imports continue to fall.

Subregional assessment and prospects

Economic expansion in East Asia slowed in the 6 months to June 2019 below *ADO 2019* projections in April. In the People's Republic of China (PRC), GDP growth decelerated to 6.3% with cooling in all sectors. Consumption rose more slowly than expected, and investment growth weakened as growth in infrastructure spending and manufacturing outlays moderated, though real estate investment accelerated. Growth also moderated in the other economies in the subregion except Mongolia, where robust credit-driven private consumption and investment pushed up the growth rate.

Subregional inflation remained tame despite rising in the first half of 2019 mainly on higher food prices. Inflation accelerated to 2.2% in the PRC on sharply rising food prices and rose as well in Mongolia, on stronger domestic demand, and in Hong Kong, China. But it moderated in the Republic of Korea (ROK) and Taipei,China on lower domestic demand and oil prices.

East Asia's current account surplus widened in the first half of 2019 because imports fell while exports increased marginally. In the PRC, the current account surplus equaled 1.6% of GDP. In Mongolia, the deficit narrowed on rising exports. Surpluses were narrower elsewhere in the subregion as exports and net receipts from services moderated.

The subregional GDP growth rate will fall from 6.0% in 2018 to 5.5% in 2019 and 5.4% in 2020, both forecasts lower than in April as the US–PRC trade conflict takes its toll on exports and investment (Figure 3.2.1).

Figure 3.2.1 GDP growth, East Asia

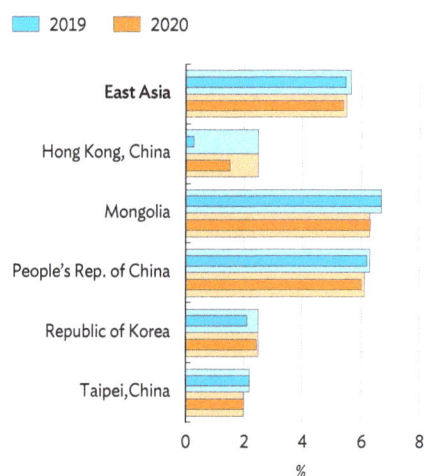

Note: Lighter colored bars are *ADO 2019* forecasts.
Source: *Asian Development Outlook* database.

The section on the PRC was written by Dominik Peschel and Jian Zhuang, and the part on other economies by Cindy Castillejos-Petalcorin, Matteo Lanzafame, Declan Magee, Nedelyn Magtibay-Ramos, Donghyun Park, Irfan Qureshi, and Michael Timbang, consultant. Authors are in the East Asia and Economic Research and Regional Cooperation departments of ADB. Subregional assessment and prospects were written by Reza Vaez-Zadeh, consultant, Economic Research and Regional Cooperation Department.

Growth in the PRC, following a similar pattern, will slip from 6.6% in 2018 to 6.2% in 2019 and 6.0% in 2020—below previous projections but only marginally so as increased government spending and a robust housing market temper the impact of the trade dispute and sluggish manufacturing investment.

Recent political tensions in Hong Kong, China will weaken inbound tourism and, combined with global uncertainties, slow growth in 2019 and 2020 substantially beyond *ADO 2019* projections. The growth forecast for the ROK is also downgraded for 2019, and less so for 2020, in light of a weak performance in the first half and persistently strong external headwinds, tempered by accommodative monetary and fiscal policies. In Taipei,China, government infrastructure spending and export recovery will keep a growth slowdown from exceeding the forecast in *ADO 2019* despite waning business confidence. The growth forecast for Mongolia remains unchanged for 2019 in light of results in the first half and continuing dynamism in mining but is lowered for 2020 as mining exports moderate.

Inflation in East Asia is forecast at 2.3% in 2019 and 2.1% in 2020, both projections higher than in April (Figure 3.2.2). The PRC will see prices climb by 2.6% in 2019 and 2.2% in 2020, above previous forecasts, as food prices rise substantially in 2019 but less so in 2020. Forecasts remain unchanged from earlier projections for the rest of East Asia except the ROK, where the forecast is lowered markedly for 2019 because of sluggish domestic demand but remains unchanged for 2020 with demand expected to recover.

Moderating imports into the PRC will push the subregional current account surplus from the equivalent of 1.3% of subregional GDP in 2018 to 1.6% in 2019, subsiding to 1.1% in 2020, both forecasts substantially higher than in April (Figure 3.2.3). With a surplus in the first half of 2019 and exports to Southeast Asia expected to grow, compensating for a drop in exports to the US, the current account surplus of the PRC will increase from the equivalent of 0.4% of GDP in 2018 to 1.0% in 2019 before falling back again to 0.4% in 2020, both forecasts higher than in *ADO 2019*. Surpluses will shrink in the ROK and Hong Kong, China, however, beyond earlier forecasts because of slumping exports, while they will rise in Taipei,China with expected export recovery. Mongolia's deficits will be markedly wider than forecast in both 2019 and 2020 as imports rise to supply mining investment.

Downside risks to the growth outlook outweigh upside risks. They are notably intensified global trade tensions and rising tariffs, which, if realized, could further depress consumer and investor confidence, disrupt supply chains, and impede foreign direct investment. Heightened volatility in food prices and deeper commodity price swings are other downside risks to the outlook.

Figure 3.2.2 Inflation, East Asia

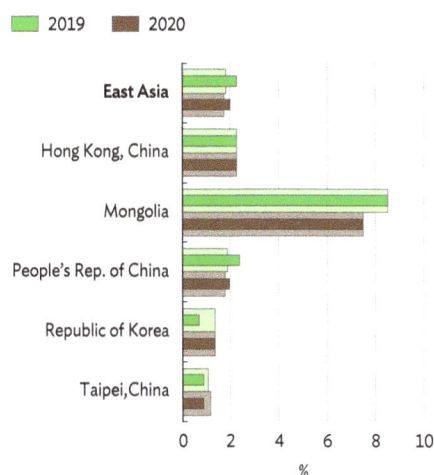

Note: Lighter colored bars are *ADO 2019* forecasts.
Source: *Asian Development Outlook* database.

Figure 3.2.3 Current account balance, East Asia

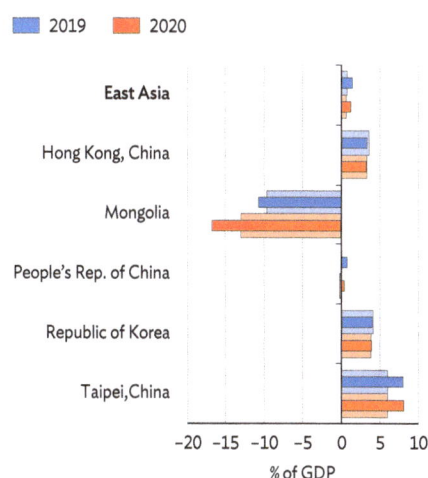

Note: Lighter colored bars are *ADO 2019* forecasts.
Source: *Asian Development Outlook* database.

People's Republic of China

Economic growth continues to decelerate as trade tensions hit the country's exports and weigh on domestic investor and consumer confidence. However, as fiscal and monetary policies will support GDP growth, *ADO 2019* forecasts are revised down only slightly for 2019 and 2020. Reflecting sizeable food price increases, inflation is projected higher in both years. The current account will stay in surplus, outperforming earlier forecasts. Improved resource allocation in favor of local governments would help sustain growth as demand moderates.

Updated assessment

GDP growth decelerated from 6.8% year on year in the first half of 2018 to 6.3% in the same period of 2019. Within the first half, it slowed further to 6.2% in the second quarter as uncertainty stemming from the trade conflict continued to weigh on consumer and investor confidence (Figure 3.2.4).

On the supply side, services remained the main driver of growth, though sector expansion eased from 7.6% in the first half of 2018 to 7.0% a year later. Transport, banking, and information technology services maintained high growth, while expansion in domestic trade and real estate services decelerated. Secondary industries—notably manufacturing, mining, construction, and utility production and supply— saw growth slow slightly to 5.8%. Government-supported high-tech manufacturing grew rapidly, but garment and shoe output suffered as export growth stagnated, as did expansion in general equipment and automobiles as domestic demand weakened. Growth in agriculture slowed from 3.3% to 3.0%, mainly because investment fell in the sector.

The contribution of industry to GDP growth edged down to 2.3 percentage points, and that of services declined to 3.8 points, while agriculture maintained its contribution of 0.2 points (Figure 3.2.5).

Supported by cuts in the value-added tax (VAT) on 1 April 2019 and reductions in employers' pension contributions from 1 May 2019, the labor market remained healthy on the whole in the first 8 months of 2019. The surveyed unemployment rate was broadly stable at 5.0%–5.3%, slightly higher than a year earlier.

On the demand side, consumption continued to be the key driver of growth in the first half of 2019, but its contribution fell from 5.4 percentage points in the first half of 2018 to 3.8 percentage points in the same period of this year, reflecting weaker household consumption and slower growth in retail sales (Figure 3.2.6). While real growth in household income declined by only 0.1 percentage points to 6.5%, real growth in household consumption slowed more sharply, from 6.7% to 5.2%. Growth in retail sales also sagged, to 6.4% in real terms in the first 8 months of 2019, or 0.9 percentage points lower than a year earlier.

Figure 3.2.4 Economic growth

- Gross domestic product
- Real growth in industrial value added
- Real growth in retail sales

Q = quarter.
Sources: National Bureau of Statistics; ADB estimates.

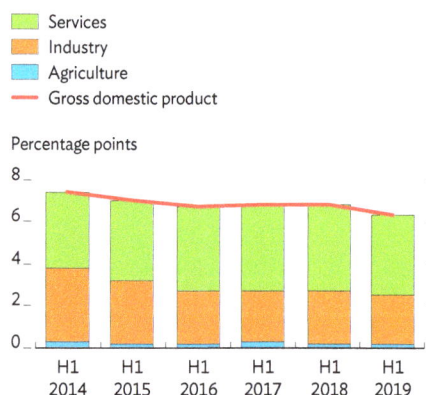

Figure 3.2.5 Supply-side contributions to growth

- Services
- Industry
- Agriculture
- Gross domestic product

H1 = first half.
Source: National Bureau of Statistics.

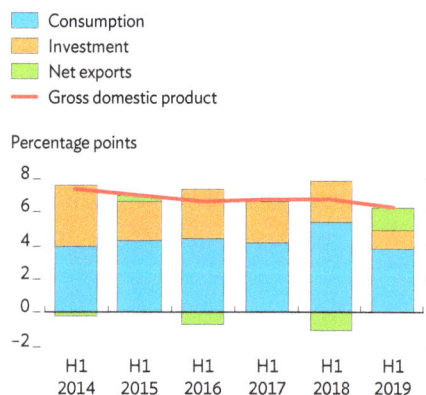

Figure 3.2.6 Demand-side contributions to growth

- Consumption
- Investment
- Net exports
- Gross domestic product

H1 = first half.
Source: National Bureau of Statistics.

In the first half of 2019, investment contributed 1.2 percentage points to growth, down by half from a year earlier. In the first 8 months, fixed asset investment grew by 5.5% in nominal terms, up slightly from 5.3% reported in the year-earlier period (Figure 3.2.7). Adversely affected by a decline in corporate profits and slower growth in exports, growth in manufacturing investment plunged from 7.5% in the first 8 months of 2018 to 2.6% in the same period of this year, despite VAT cuts. Having gradually recovered from its low in September 2018, growth in infrastructure investment reached 4.2% in the first 8 months of 2019, the same as a year earlier. Real estate investment surpassed 10.1% expansion a year earlier to reach 10.5%, driven by vigorous growth in housing construction despite a significant drop in land sales.

Despite virtually flat export growth in the face of external headwinds, net exports contributed 1.3 percentage points to growth in the first half of 2019 as weaker domestic demand drove down merchandise imports. This contribution reversed net exports' subtraction of 1.1 points from growth in the first half of 2018.

A spike in food prices drove up headline consumer price inflation year on year to 2.4% on average in the first 8 months of 2019, though other inflation remained subdued (Figure 3.2.8). Tight pork supply caused by African swine fever ended 25 consecutive months of declining pork prices to March 2019, followed by an average monthly increase of 25.5% year on year in April–August. Fruit and vegetable prices also rose rapidly owing to bad weather. However, nonfood price inflation softened from an average of 2.3% in the first 8 months of 2018 to 1.5% as domestic demand weakened. Producer price inflation remained marginal at 0.1%. Driven by high demand for housing, prices for newly constructed homes in the top 70 cities averaged 10.7% higher than in the first 8 months of 2018, with the steepest increases in second- and third-tier cities (Figure 3.2.9).

Monetary policy has remained largely accommodative in 2019 to date, with interest rates in the interbank market slightly softening (Figure 3.2.10). The People's Bank of China, the central bank, reduced the reserve requirement ratio for some small and medium-sized banks in May, having already reduced it for all banks by 100 basis points in two steps in January 2019. In early September 2019, the central bank announced another broad-based cut in the ratio by 50 basis points effective on 16 September, and a targeted cut of an additional 100 basis points for some city commercial banks to become effective in two tranches later this year.

The central bank and the banking and insurance regulator announced in late May 2019 that they would take control of Baoshang Bank to address serious credit risks. Despite the central bank fully guaranteeing all retail deposits in the midsized bank, it was announced that corporate deposits

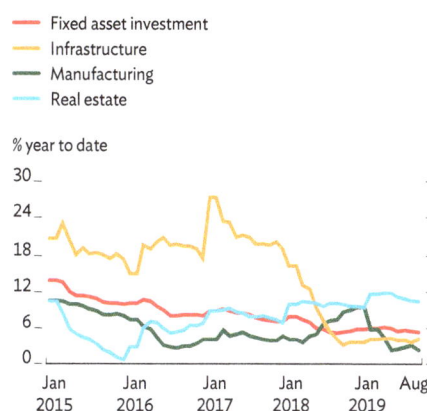

Figure 3.2.7 Growth in fixed asset investment

- Fixed asset investment
- Infrastructure
- Manufacturing
- Real estate

% year to date

Source: National Bureau of Statistics.

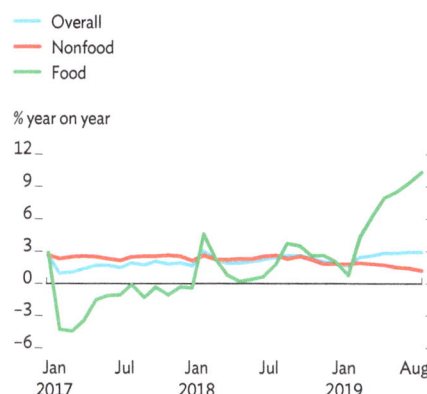

Figure 3.2.8 Monthly consumer price inflation

- Overall
- Nonfood
- Food

% year on year

Source: National Bureau of Statistics.

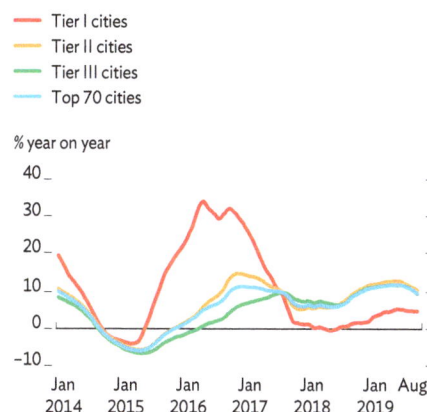

Figure 3.2.9 Increase in prices for newly constructed residences

- Tier I cities
- Tier II cities
- Tier III cities
- Top 70 cities

% year on year

Note: Tier 1 cities are Beijing, Guangzhou, Shanghai, and Shenzhen; tier 2 has 31 provincial capitals and larger municipalities; and tier 3 has 35 other cities.
Sources: National Bureau of Statistics; ADB estimates.

and interbank liabilities exceeding CNY50 million would be dealt with case by case. The announcement surprised market participants and raised concern about potential losses from additional small and medium-sized bank failures and consequent spillover in the market.

While big commercial banks have vast nationwide retail branch networks through which they collect deposits and channel them into the interbank market, small and medium-sized banks depend heavily on wholesale funding. Following the regulators' taking control of Baoshang Bank, lower-rated banks and nonbank financial institutions struggled to place negotiable certificates of deposits—a resalable financial instrument issued by banks and qualified nonbank financial institutions in the interbank market—as potential buyers feared possible losses like those suffered by some Baoshang creditors. The central bank injected sizable liquidity into the interbank market, which drove the rate on short-term collateralized interbank lending down (Figure 3.2.10). However, interest rates on negotiable certificates of deposits rose for all banks except the highest-rated ones, which market participants were confident would not default (Figure 3.2.11).

Total social financing—a broad credit aggregate that includes shadow banking and, from September 2018, special bonds issued by local governments—was up by 10.6% at the end of August 2019 from a year earlier, as bank loans outstanding increased by 12.2% despite an 8.5% decline in shadow bank finance outstanding (Figure 3.2.12). Net special bond issues from local governments picked up rapidly, as did net corporate bond issues, but new equity financing shrank to negligible. Broad money (M2) was 8.2% higher at the end of August 2019 than a year earlier.

Fiscal policy was expansionary in the first half of 2019 as general government fiscal expenditure grew by 10.7%, or three times a 3.4% increase in revenue, thereby doubling the consolidated government budget deficit from the equivalent of 1.7% of GDP recorded a year earlier to 3.5% (Figure 3.2.13). Higher fiscal expenditure reflected accelerated spending on environmental protection, transportation and communication, and agriculture, while the slowdown in revenue growth reflected both the VAT cuts in April 2019 and earlier reform to personal income taxes, which became effective in two phases, in October 2018 and January 2019.

Merchandise export growth in US dollar terms decelerated from 12.0% in the first 8 months of 2018 to a scant 0.4% in the same period of 2019 (Figure 3.2.14). This reflected a softening global economy, which saw growth in exports to the European Union and Southeast Asia moderate, but more importantly trade conflict with the US, which intensified after the US announced in early May 2019 a tariff hike from 10% to 25% on $200 billion worth of imports from the PRC.

Figure 3.2.10 Policy and interbank market interest rates

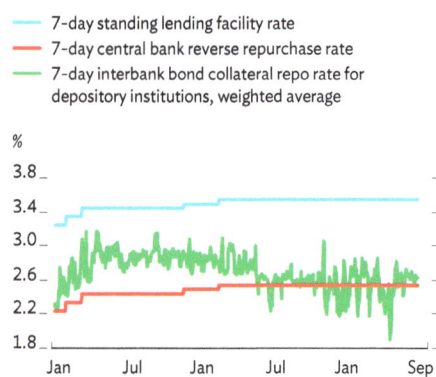

- 7-day standing lending facility rate
- 7-day central bank reverse repurchase rate
- 7-day interbank bond collateral repo rate for depository institutions, weighted average

Sources: People's Bank of China; National Interbank Funding Center.

Figure 3.2.11 Interest rates on negotiable certificates of deposits by issuer credit rating

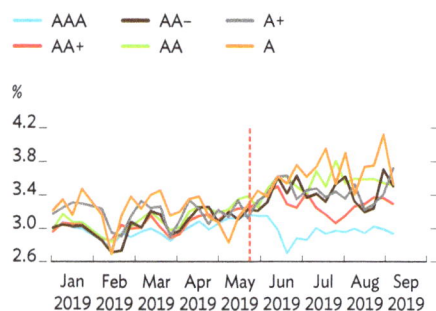

- AAA
- AA+
- AA−
- AA
- A+
- A

Note: Red dotted line = 27 May 2019, the first day of trading after the Baoshang Bank announcement.
Source: Wind database based on the National Interbank Funding Center.

Figure 3.2.12 Growth of broad money, total social financing, bank loans, and shadow banking

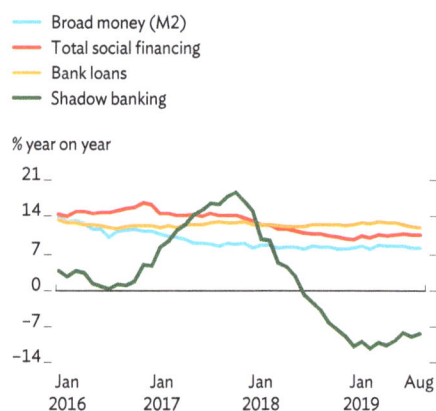

- Broad money (M2)
- Total social financing
- Bank loans
- Shadow banking

Note: Shadow banking comprises entrusted loans, trust loans, and bankers' acceptance bills.
Sources: People's Bank of China; ADB estimates.

In the first 8 months of 2019, exports to the US fell by 9.3%, reversing expansion by 12.3% a year earlier. Global imports also declined, by 4.6%, after having risen by 21.0% in the same period of 2018, with notably lower machinery imports reflecting deceleration in domestic manufacturing investment.

The merchandise trade surplus soared from $155 billion in the first half of 2018 to $223 billion a year later. With a slightly narrower service account deficit, this raised the current account surplus to $106 billion, equal to 1.6% of GDP. However, net inflow of foreign direct investment fell by more than half in the first 6 months of 2019 from a year earlier as inbound investment declined sharply in response to escalating trade tensions while outflow stayed virtually constant (Figure 3.2.15). Official reserves increased by $53.5 billion to stand at $3.2 trillion at the end of August 2019.

At the end of July 2019, the renminbi was virtually unchanged from the end of 2018 in nominal effective terms, against a trade-weighted basket of currencies, and up by 0.1% in real effective terms, taking inflation into account. In nominal terms, it depreciated by 3.3% against the US dollar in the first 8 months of the year (Figure 3.2.16).

Prospects

GDP growth is expected to remain above 6.0% in the second half of the year, supported by further gradual loosening of monetary policy, increased government spending including infrastructure investment, and resilient growth in the housing market—all of which should help to keep the labor market generally in good health. These factors will partly offset continued downward pressure on growth from the trade conflict with the US, softening external trade, and sluggish manufacturing investment. The *ADO 2019* growth forecast is thus revised down slightly to 6.2% for 2019 and 6.0% for 2020 (Figure 3.2.17).

On the supply side, services are expected to outgrow industry in 2019 and 2020. Value added in financial services should continue to grow solidly, driven by rising bank profits from increased lending. While construction and some upstream industries, especially steel and cement, will benefit from resilient housing demand and rising government infrastructure investment, manufacturing as a whole will remain hampered by lackluster growth in domestic demand. Government support will spur high-tech manufacturing and innovative industries, but manufacturing for export will continue to face external headwinds.

On the demand side, consumption will remain the main driver of growth in 2019 and 2020 despite having taken a hit from the trade conflict. Consumer staples should stay largely resilient, and consumer discretionary spending may benefit from recent government policies, announced in late August, to support logistics services and private consumption.

Figure 3.2.13 General government fiscal revenue and expenditure

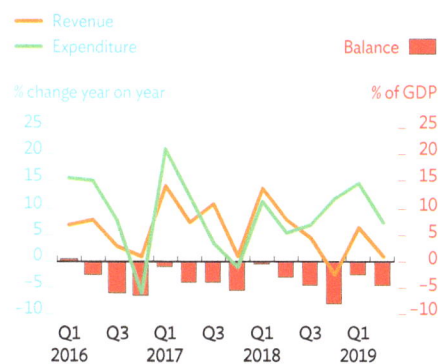

Q = quarter.
Sources: Ministry of Finance; ADB estimates.

Figure 3.2.14 Merchandise trade growth by region or country

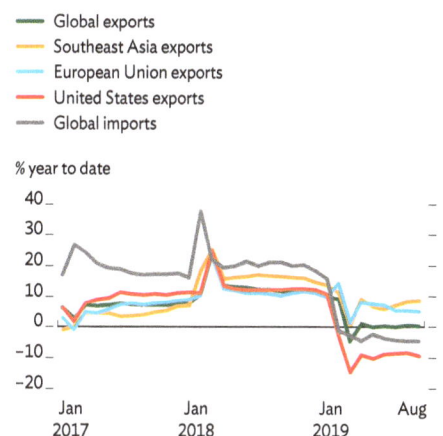

Sources: General Administration of Customs; ADB estimates.

Figure 3.2.15 Balance of payments

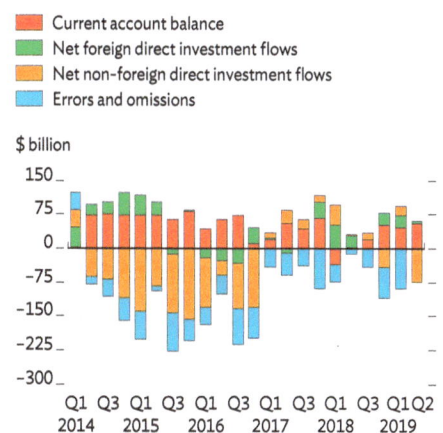

Q = quarter.
Sources: State Administration of Foreign Exchange; ADB estimates.

At the same time, car sales are expected to remain weak in the second half of 2019, in the wake of car dealers clearing stocks in June 2019 in anticipation of stricter emission rules.

Investment growth is expected to accelerate slightly in the balance of 2019 and should stay solid in 2020. Despite a decline in land sales in the first half of 2019 and some regulatory tightening in local housing markets in the second quarter of 2019, construction growth is expected to remain strong this year as many developers still need to complete residential units already sold. Moreover, government infrastructure investment is expected to accelerate notably in the second half of 2019, following a pickup in local government special bond issues in June 2019 and rule changes that now allow certain projects to use proceeds from special bonds as project capital (Figure 3.2.18).

In early September 2019, the State Council announced an acceleration of new special bond issues from local governments. The full annual quota of CNY2.15 trillion for 2019 must be reached by the end of September 2019. The State Council further announced that part of the special bonds quota for 2020, which is not yet known, will be allocated in 2019. Local governments will therefore be permitted to issue additional special bonds after September, exceeding the annual quota for 2019.

The recent high contribution to growth from net exports is forecast to moderate in the remainder of 2019 but remain positive through 2020, as the unexpectedly steep plunge in merchandise imports in the first half of 2019 is unlikely to persist. Indeed, the falling trend in merchandise imports is seen to moderate in the second half of 2019 as domestic demand stabilizes and imports of materials for further processing likely pick up again to replenish stocks. Merchandise exports to the US will continue to shrink, hampered by a hike in existing US tariffs on $250 billion worth of imports from the PRC, to become effective on 15 October 2019, and additional 15% tariffs on another $300 billion worth of imports, some having become effective on 1 September 2019 and the remainder to follow in mid-December 2019. Meanwhile, decelerating growth in Europe clouds the outlook for exports to that market. On the other hand, exports to Southeast Asia are expected to continue growing moderately.

Consumer price inflation is now forecast to accelerate to an average of 2.6% in 2019. Revised inflation forecasts for this year and next are higher than forecast in *ADO 2019* to accommodate surprisingly stiff food price hikes in the first 8 months of 2019 and likely further increases for pork (Figure 3.2.19). Low inflation for other goods and services is expected to prevail in the remainder of 2019 as growth in domestic demand remains moderate and pass-through from a weaker renminbi stays only marginal. In 2020, consumer

Figure 3.2.16 Renminbi exchange rates

Sources: Bank for International Settlements; People's Bank of China; ADB estimates.

Figure 3.2.17 GDP growth

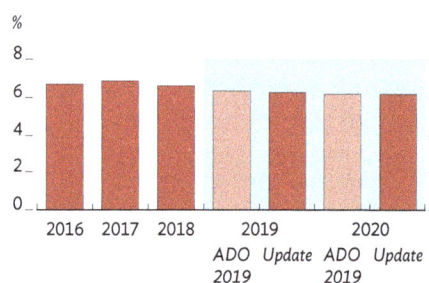

ADO = Asian Development Outlook.
Source: *Asian Development Outlook* database.

Table 3.2.1 Selected economic indicators, People's Republic of China (%)

	2019		2020	
	ADO 2019	Update	ADO 2019	Update
GDP growth	6.3	6.2	6.1	6.0
Inflation	1.9	2.6	1.8	2.2
Current acct. bal. (share of GDP)	0.0	1.0	−0.1	0.4

Source: ADB estimates.

Figure 3.2.18 Local government special bond issues

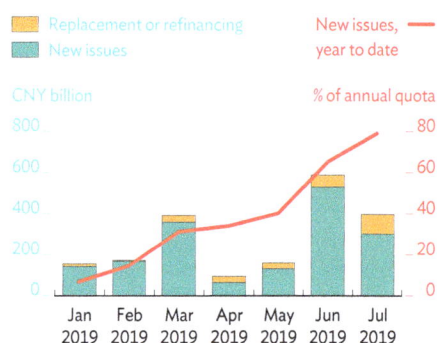

Sources: Ministry of Finance; ADB estimates.

price inflation is expected to retreat gradually to average 2.2% as fruit and vegetable prices normalize. Meanwhile, producer prices are projected to soften in the remainder of 2019, though demand for construction materials will rise alongside higher infrastructure investment; in 2020, they could decline further as growth in domestic demand weakens.

With fiscal expenditure likely to remain high in the second half of 2019, following marked deficit expansion in the first half, the consolidated budget deficit looks set to exceed the government target equal to 2.6% of GDP. In addition, infrastructure financing through special bond issues is expected to continue in the remainder of 2019 and remain high in 2020. Consolidated government debt, which climbed by 3.3 percentage points to equal 49.8% of GDP in 2018, is expected to rise further (Figure 3.2.20).

Containing accumulated debt will become more challenging over time owing to structural imbalance in local government budgets caused by high spending needs overburdening a weak fiscal revenue base. Local government fiscal revenue will likely erode further, especially following the recent VAT cuts (Figure 3.2.21). This is because local governments receive half of VAT revenue, which accounted for nearly one-third of their fiscal revenue in 2018.

Monetary policy is expected to remain largely accommodative. The central bank will probably keep interbank rates low by providing ample liquidity to banks both this year and next. Further cuts to the reserve requirement ratio remain likely, freeing up more funds for banks to lend. Aiming to lower interest cost for the real economy, the State Council approved in mid-August 2019 a new mechanism for pricing bank loans (Box 3.2.1).

A continuing clampdown on shadow bank financing has prompted credit re-intermediation through the banking system, thereby transferring more potential risk to banks. That said, additional credit risks from the economic slowdown, and sharply decelerating growth in corporate sales revenue in 2019 to date, have not yet translated into a broad increase in declared nonperforming loans (Figure 3.2.22). However, default risk is likely to worsen in 2020 with economic growth expected to moderate further and nonperforming loans to rise after a customary lag. A broadly looser monetary policy that encourages more lending to weaker borrowers would exacerbate risk accumulation in banks.

External trade will remain lackluster, but with the goods surplus in the first half of 2019, and assuming no major change in service trade, the current account surplus is now forecast to increase from the equivalent of 0.4% of GDP in 2018 to 1.0% in 2019, before falling back to 0.4% in 2020— both projections significantly higher than in *ADO 2019*.

Figure 3.2.19 Inflation

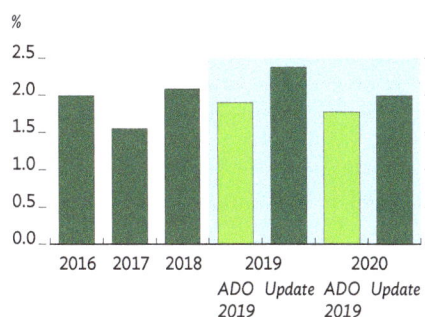

ADO = Asian Development Outlook.
Source: *Asian Development Outlook* database.

Figure 3.2.20 Debt structure

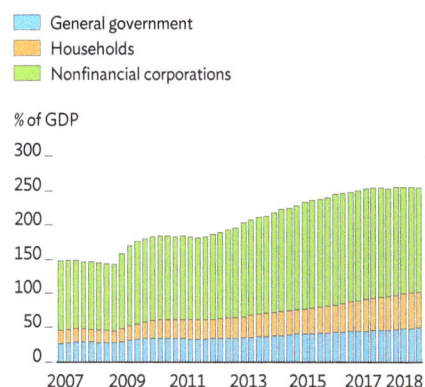

Source: Bank for International Settlements.

Figure 3.2.21 Government fiscal revenue and value-added tax

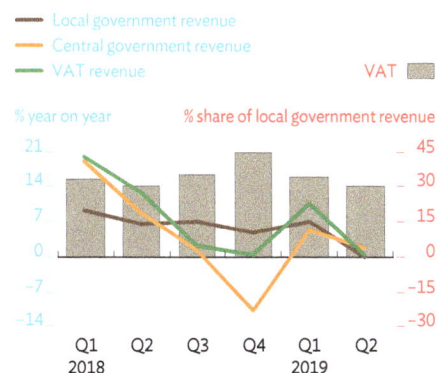

Q = quarter, VAT = value-added tax.
Sources: Ministry of Finance; ADB estimates.

Box 3.2.1 A new mechanism for pricing bank loans

Aiming to reduce financing costs for the real economy and improve the transmission of monetary policy, the State Council approved in mid-August 2019 changes to how banks should price their loans. Banks are now required to price new loans with tenors of 1 year or above 5 years based on the respective loan prime rate (LPR). The revised 1-year LPR is chiefly linked to the medium-term lending facility (MLF) rate, set by the central bank, plus a premium. The central bank will monitor in its quarterly macroprudential assessment banks' progress toward pricing new loans under the new mechanism. Linking the 1-year LPR to the MLF rate gives the central bank a direct transmission mechanism, with the MLF rate now serving as a policy instrument to affect bank lending rates. These changes, part of the central bank's ongoing efforts to move toward a single-track mechanism, aim to unify the dual-track interest rate system, under which regulated benchmark deposit and lending rates coexist with market-determined rates in the money and bond markets. However, existing loans will not be repriced, benchmark lending rates will continue to be reference rates for existing loans, and the changes do not affect benchmark deposit rates.

Prior to the change to the loan pricing mechanism, banks were required to price their loans against benchmark lending rates, which could not be changed without State Council approval. While banks were rarely willing to price loans below 0.9 times the benchmark rate, which constituted an effective floor on lending rates, they would often charge lending rates higher than the benchmark, which provided them with higher interest income but increased the cost of financing for the real economy (box figure). To reduce bank lending rates, the central bank and the banking regulator sometimes resorted to window guidance, as happened in the last quarter of 2018 and was discussed in *ADO 2019*.

Since August 2019, the revised 1-year LPR is published on the 20th day of each month, and adjustments to it are made in increments of 5 basis points. The LPR is now calculated as the average of quotations from 18 banks after excluding the highest and lowest quote. These banks derive their individual quotes by adding a bank-specific premium to a rate mostly determined by the MLF rate.

This contrasts with the LPR originally calculated on each trading day using quotes from 10 reporting banks, which frequently based their quotes on the 1-year benchmark lending rate (box figure). In addition, a new LPR for terms longer than 5 years was added as a reference for new long-term loans such as mortgages.

On 20 August 2019, the revised 1-year LPR was, at 4.25%, lower by 6 basis points than before the change and 10 basis points below the 1-year benchmark lending rate. The central bank is expected to lower the MLF rate, with the 1-year LPR following it. However, as the reform does not affect deposit rates, room for reducing borrowing costs for the real economy will remain limited as long as banks' funding costs either stay unchanged or decline by a smaller margin. Absent any changes in benchmark deposit rates, lower lending rates will squeeze banks' net interest margins as the interest they receive declines. Acknowledging that the new loan pricing mechanism will reduce the banks' net interest margins, the central bank will have to walk a tightrope to help the real economy without overly compressing margins and thereby making banks less profitable and thus more vulnerable, especially to an increase in nonperforming loans.

Bank lending, refinancing, and interbank market rates

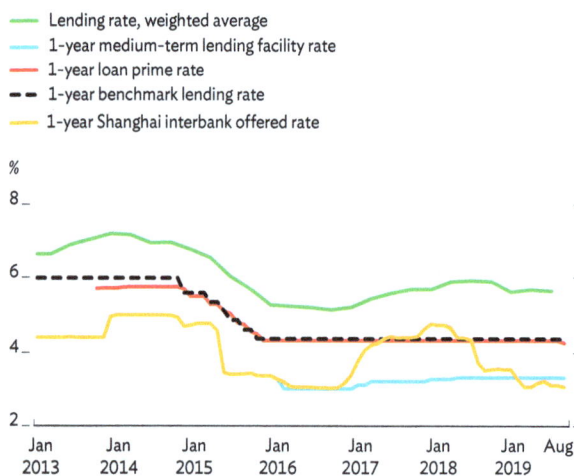

Sources: People's Bank of China; Shanghai Interbank Offered Rate; National Interbank Funding Center; ADB estimates.

The current account surplus now forecast for 2020 reflects both reduced demand for imports as the domestic economy slows further and weaker demand for exports as the global economy cools.

Uncertainty stemming from the trade conflict and persistently slowing growth momentum continue to weigh on the renminbi vis-à-vis the US dollar, despite recent renminbi depreciation starting in August 2019 (Figure 3.2.16). However, ongoing depreciation pressure is mitigated by the previously unforeseen current account surplus; capital inflows arising from higher weighting for the PRC in global bond and equity indexes, which raises demand for PRC bonds and equity; and a widened spread in government bond yield over the US (Figure 3.2.23).

External circumstances have worsened since the publication of *ADO 2019* in April, with possible further intensification of the trade conflict with the US, including through higher tariffs, continuing to pose the main downside risk to the outlook. Domestic risks include pressure on budget revenue that poses medium-term challenges. While the central government still has fiscal latitude, local governments, which meet the vast majority of health care and education costs, are challenged to expand expenditure in line with rising need. Aside from public debt management in general, sustaining growth depends on a better balance in resource allocation in favor of local governments. This requires accelerated reform to fiscal relations between the central and local governments.

Figure 3.2.22 Problematic bank loans by category

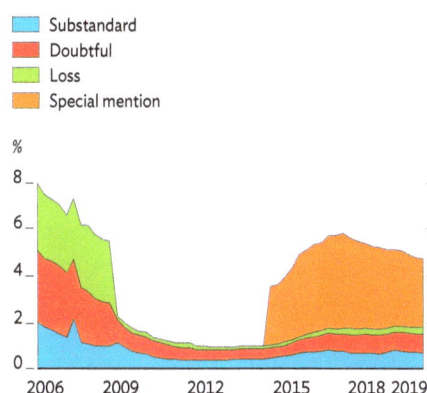

Note: "Special mention" loan data started in 2014.
Source: China Banking and Insurance Regulatory Commission.

Figure 3.2.23 Differences in government bond yields

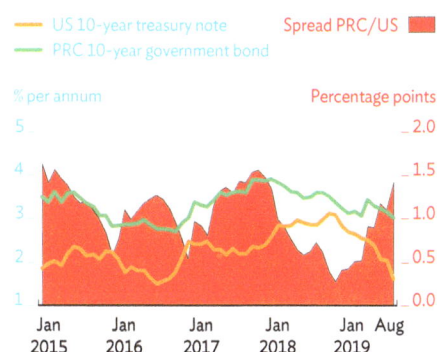

PRC = People's Republic of China, US = United States.
Sources: PRC National Interbank Funding Center; US Federal Reserve Board; ADB estimates.

Other economies

Hong Kong, China

A lackluster global economy and sluggish domestic demand dragged down growth in Hong Kong, China in the first half of 2019, as output expansion slowed sharply from 4.1% year on year in the first half of 2018 to 0.5%. Private consumption grew by only 0.8% in real terms amid cautious consumer sentiment despite a favorable labor market, while government spending remained broadly stable at 4.3%. Meanwhile, gross fixed capital formation plummeted by 9.4% as building and construction remained contractionary and business sentiment continued to slide. A downswing in global investment and trade weighed heavily on goods exports in the first half of 2019, which dropped by 4.7%, reversing 4.9% growth in the first half of 2018. Growth in service exports likewise decelerated in the same period, from 6.7% to 0.3%, despite continued support from inbound tourism. Imports of goods also dropped, by 5.6% from 6.6% growth in the first half of 2018, while growth in imports of services stagnated. As a result, net exports remained negative.

On the supply side, manufacturing growth accelerated from 1.2% in the last quarter of 2018 to 1.4% in the first quarter of 2019, but the challenging external environment was reflected in slower growth in most sectors. Notably, construction contracted by 2.6%, and wholesale and retail trade by 2.9%.

A consistently tight labor market provides some support to the economy in the rest of the year, but deepening economic uncertainty globally and, in particular, the trade conflict between the People's Republic of China (PRC) and the US continue to weigh on exports and growth. Meanwhile, recent political tensions at home have started to weaken inbound tourism and worsen already prudent local economic sentiment as evidenced by a continued fall in retail sales. Growth forecasts for 2019 and 2020 are thus downgraded significantly from projections in *ADO 2019*.

Headline consumer price inflation averaged 2.6% in the first half of 2019, driven up by higher prices for tourism services and a surge in meat prices owing mainly to an African swine fever outbreak in the PRC. Netting out the effects of all one-off relief measures from the government, the underlying inflation rate rose to 2.8%. Inflationary pressures in the rest of this year and next year are expected to remain moderate in view of likely easing of rental costs, modest global inflation, and the expected growth slowdown, though food prices will remain elevated. On balance, the *ADO 2019* inflation forecast is maintained for both years.

The current account surplus fell to equal 4.9% of GDP in the first quarter of 2019 and is now expected to be narrower than forecast in April, both this year and next, in light of recent external economic developments. Worsening global trade conditions and domestic tensions are the main risks to the outlook.

Table 3.2.2 Selected economic indicators, Hong Kong, China (%)

	2019		2020	
	ADO 2019	Update	ADO 2019	Update
GDP growth	2.5	0.3	2.5	1.5
Inflation	2.3	2.3	2.3	2.3
Current acct. bal. (share of GDP)	3.5	3.3	3.3	3.1

Source: ADB estimates.

Mongolia

Economic growth remained strong at 7.3% in the first half of 2019, buoyed by vigorous domestic demand. Consumption contributed 4.6 percentage points as government expenditure grew by 11.2% and private consumption by 4.7%. Investment contributed 9.8 points thanks to high domestic private investment, rising credit to corporations, and a 60.9% increase in public investment. Net exports meanwhile subtracted 7.1 points from growth as imports linked to new investment outgrew exports. On the supply side, mining and construction grew rapidly, propelling industrial expansion by 9.3% year on year in the first half. Growth in services remained strong at 7.4%, with trade services boosted by mining expansion. Agriculture continued to recover, growing by 4.7%.

The budget recorded a surplus equal to 4.7% of GDP in the first half of 2019 as revenue grew by 21.9% on rising corporate income tax receipts and social security contributions, outstripping expenditure growth by 14.1%. Broad money supply increased by 16.6% year on year in first half, mainly reflecting a surplus in the balance of payments, and real interest rates tumbled as inflation accelerated and loan and deposit rates declined. However, macroprudential measures introduced in January successfully contained growth in newly issued loans to 5.1% in the first 6 months. Nonperforming loans climbed to 10.6% of all loans. Bank recapitalization, initiated in 2018 by the Bank of Mongolia, the central bank, continued into this year.

While economic expansion was strong in the first half of 2019, and domestic demand is expected to grow rapidly in the second half, net exports are likely to deteriorate further as demand for mining exports declines in tandem with slower growth in the PRC and as imports rise to meet higher domestic demand. On balance, the growth forecast is unchanged for 2019 and downgraded slightly for 2020 owing to the anticipated impact of the PRC slowdown on Mongolia's exports.

Inflation is similarly on track to meet *ADO 2019* forecasts for 2019 and 2020. Despite some appreciation of the Mongolian togrog, consumer prices rose by 8.1% year on year in June as food prices climbed and domestic demand strengthened, and the trend is expected to continue. The current account deficit narrowed to equal 10.2% of GDP in the first half of 2019, driven by a rapid increase in merchandise exports. However, strong import demand will likely keep the current account deficit from narrowing in 2019 as much as forecast in April and widen it in 2020 more than projected.

Risks to the outlook include possible disruption to the implementation of a financial program with the International Monetary Fund or to bank recapitalization, major changes to foreign direct investment, a sharper slowdown in the PRC, and fluctuation in commodity prices.

Table 3.2.3 Selected economic indicators, Mongolia (%)

	2019		2020	
	ADO 2019	Update 2019	ADO 2019	Update 2019
GDP growth	6.7	6.7	6.3	6.1
Inflation	8.5	8.5	7.5	7.5
Current acct. bal. (share of GDP)	-9.6	-10.7	-13.0	-16.1

Source: ADB estimates.

Republic of Korea

Buffeted by faltering investment and exports, GDP growth weakened from 2.8% year on year in the first half of 2018 to 1.9% in the same period of this year. Slumping global demand and prices for semiconductors, a mainstay of the economy, weakened profits, which dented business confidence and shrank investment by 4.3%. Government consumption expanded by 6.4%, providing the main support for growth, while weak consumer confidence dampened private consumption growth to 2.0%. Net exports increased as real growth weakened for both exports and imports.

On the supply side, growth in all sectors slowed in the first half of 2019, to 2.4% in services; 1.0% in industry, largely reflecting the weak export performance; and 0.9% in agriculture, coming off last year's bumper harvest.

Falling world oil prices and the absence of demand pressure muted consumer price inflation in the first 7 months of 2019 to 0.6%, below the revised target of 0.7% for the year set by the Bank of Korea, the central bank. In July, citing concerns over weakening growth, the central bank cut its policy interest rate by 25 basis points to 1.50%, its first adjustment since November 2017. The fiscal deficit rose to W36.5 trillion in the first half of 2019, the highest since 2011, as the government frontloaded expenditure despite a slowdown in tax collection.

Merchandise exports contracted by 9.8% in the first 6 months of the year, and merchandise imports shrank by 5.7%, both affected by prolonged trade tensions. The current account surplus fell to 2.7% of GDP, its decline tempered by a narrower deficit in services, better net travel receipts, and a surplus in the primary income account. The ROK won fell by 8.2% against the dollar in the first half of the year, the largest depreciation in that period in Asia and the Pacific.

The growth forecast is downgraded from *ADO 2019* for 2019, and less so for 2020, in light of the weak performance in the first half and persistently strong external headwinds—and despite monetary and fiscal policies expected to remain broadly accommodative, including the adoption this year, as in 2018, of a supplementary budget. Assuming tame price pressures in the rest of the year, inflation is projected to decelerate in 2019, now expected at only half of the *ADO 2019* forecast, and then reaccelerate in 2020 on somewhat stronger growth, matching the earlier forecast. The current account surplus will continue to narrow, doing so more than projected in *ADO 2019* because of the slump in exports. Downside risks to growth, outweighing upside risks, include intensified global trade tensions and Japan tightening restrictions on exports of chemicals vital for making memory chips, which may disrupt the semiconductor industry.

Table 3.2.4 Selected economic indicators, Republic of Korea (%)

	2019		2020	
	ADO 2019	Update	ADO 2019	Update
GDP growth	2.5	2.1	2.5	2.4
Inflation	1.4	0.7	1.4	1.4
Current acct. bal. (share of GDP)	4.1	3.9	3.9	3.8

Source: ADB estimates.

Taipei,China

GDP growth slowed from 3.2% year on year in the first half of 2018 to 2.1% in the same period of this year. Gross capital formation was the largest contributor to growth, adding 1.5 percentage points as it grew by 6.7% on the strength of the government's infrastructure development program. Next came private consumption, which slowed from 2.4% growth in the first half of 2018 to 1.5%, nevertheless adding 0.8 points. Government consumption declined by 3.0%, reversing 6.2% growth a year earlier and subtracting 0.4 points from GDP growth. Net exports expanded by 3.6%, contributing 0.3 points to GDP growth as exports rebounded in the second quarter.

On the supply side, services were the main driver of growth, adding 1.5 points as trade and real estate services, rental, and leasing expanded. Agriculture and industry both contracted, with industry deducting 0.2 points from growth. The Nikkei manufacturing purchasing managers' index improved from 45.5 in June, its lowest in 10 months, to 48.1 in July. Nevertheless, on balance, *ADO 2019* forecasts in April for GDP growth in 2019 and 2020 are unchanged in expectation of continued growth in government expenditure on infrastructure, low unemployment continuing to shore up consumption, and exports performing better than earlier expected.

Slow recovery from a price plunge in December 2018 dragged the average inflation rate in the first 7 months of 2019 down by more than two-thirds, from 1.7% a year earlier to 0.5%, despite food inflation accelerating from 1.2% to 1.7%. Core inflation, excluding food and energy, similarly slowed from an average of 1.2% to a scant 0.2%. Considering the weak core inflation outturn, prices will likely remain subdued in the remainder of the year. The forecast for inflation is therefore revised down from April projections for both 2019 and 2020.

The current account surplus narrowed from the equivalent of 13.5% of GDP in the first half of 2018 to 12.1% in the same period of 2019 as trade surpluses in both goods and services fell. Nevertheless, the forecast for the current account surplus is revised upward for both 2019 and 2020 because the trade surplus outperformed expectations in the second quarter of 2019, indicating that the dismal export performance in the first quarter was bottoming out and that exports are now recovering, outpacing import growth.

The main risks to the outlook continue to be external. While the threat of tighter global financial conditions seems to have subsided, the outlook remains vulnerable to escalating trade tensions.

Table 3.2.5 Selected economic indicators, Taipei,China (%)

	2019		2020	
	ADO 2019	Update 2019	ADO 2019	Update 2019
GDP growth	2.2	2.2	2.0	2.0
Inflation	1.1	0.9	1.2	0.9
Current acct. bal. (share of GDP)	6.0	8.0	6.0	8.0

Source: ADB estimates.

South Asia

Subregional growth is expected to slow in 2019 before picking up in 2020. Projections for India are downgraded after growth fell to a 6-year low in the April–June quarter of 2019. The inflation projection is reduced for 2019 but retained for 2020. The current account deficit is forecast to narrow more than projected in April as domestic demand slows. Heavy dependence on energy imports leaves forecasts for South Asia vulnerable to oil price swings.

Subregional assessment and prospects

Growth in South Asia is projected to be 6.2% in 2019 and 6.7% in 2020, sharply lower than forecast in *ADO 2019* mainly because India has slowed much more than expected (Figure 3.3.1). India's GDP grew by only 5.0% in the first quarter of fiscal year 2019 (FY2019, ending 31 March 2020), with consumption, investment, and production lackluster. Industry growth slowed in the quarter to 2.7% year on year as manufacturing grew by a disappointing 0.6%. Expansion in services slipped to 6.9%, the lowest rate in 7 quarters. The government, re-elected in May 2019, announced various measures to boost investor and consumer confidence and acted to strengthen the ability of the financial sector to revive credit flows. The Reserve Bank of India has cut its policy rate by a total of 110 basis points since February 2019, with more cuts expected in the coming months. As monetary stimulus and government measures to support growth gain traction, growth in India is expected to recover to 6.5% in the whole of FY2019, still well below 7.2% forecast in *ADO 2019*. Growth in FY2020 is expected to strengthen to 7.2%, still marginally lower than projected in April.

This *Update* revises 2019 growth forecasts for every South Asian economy except Maldives. With stronger recovery in agriculture, growth projections for Afghanistan are revised

Figure 3.3.1 GDP growth, South Asia

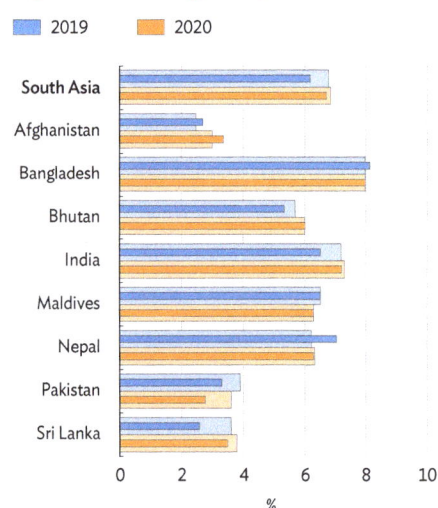

Note: Lighter colored bars are *ADO 2019* forecasts.
Source: *Asian Development Outlook* database.

The subregional assessment and prospects were written by Lei Lei Song. The section on Bangladesh was written by Jyotsana Varma, Soon Chan Hong, and Barun K. Dey; India by Abhijit Sen Gupta, Lei Lei Song, and Shalini Mittal, consultant; Pakistan by Farzana Noshab and Ali Khadija; and other economies by Eshini Ekanayake, Abdul Hares Halimi, Manbar Singh Khadka, Kanokpan Lao-Araya, Tshering Lhamo, and Masato Nakane, as well as consultants Abdulla Ali, Macrina Mallari, and Danileen Parrel. Authors are in the Central and West Asia and South Asia departments of ADB.

slightly upward for 2019 and 2020. In FY2019, Bangladesh (ended 30 June 2019) and Nepal (ended 16 July 2019) outperformed *ADO 2019* projections, with Bangladesh accelerating to 8.1% on robust private consumption and exports, and Nepal expanding by 7.1% with production exceeding expectations in all sectors, most notably agriculture. As growth in these two economies will likely remain strong, forecasts for FY2020 are retained. Growth in Bhutan is estimated to have slowed to 5.3% in FY2019 (ended 30 June 2019), below the April forecast as hydroelectric generation declined from a year earlier. With more hydropower units commissioned, the 6.0% growth projection for FY2020 is retained.

Provisional estimates show growth in Pakistan in FY2019 (ended 30 June 2019) falling to 3.3%, reflecting lower investment amid persistent macroeconomic imbalances. Pakistan's growth projection is lowered to 2.8% for FY2020, but a 3-year program of stabilization and structural reform with the International Monetary Fund since July 2019 promises to help address large macroeconomic imbalances. After Sri Lanka suffered terror attacks in April, this *Update* lowers its growth projections for 2019 and 2020. Growth forecasts for Maldives in 2019 and 2020 are retained as the mainstay of this island economy continues to perform strongly, with tourist arrivals expanding by 18.7% in the first half of 2019.

Inflation in South Asia remains benign, largely thanks to low food prices and moderate global oil prices, as well as watchful monetary policy making (Figure 3.3.2). The subregional inflation projection for 2019 is revised down to 4.0%, mainly reflecting a lower forecast for India with only modest food inflation, and then rise to 4.9% in 2020, as forecast in *ADO 2019*, in large part to reflect a steep rise expected in Pakistan. Inflation this year has been at least no higher than expected in Afghanistan, Bangladesh, Bhutan, India, Maldives, Pakistan, and Sri Lanka and only slightly higher than forecast in Nepal. This *Update* raises the 2020 inflation projection only for Nepal, revised up to 5.5% on a pickup in government expenditure, and Pakistan, markedly higher at 12.0% in anticipation of planned tariff hikes for domestic utilities, higher taxes, and especially the lagged impact of currency depreciation.

South Asia's combined current account deficit is forecast to equal 2.5% of subregional GDP in both 2019 and 2020, or slightly smaller than in *ADO 2019* (Figure 3.3.3). Individual forecasts for every economy except Bhutan are for smaller current account deficits in 2019 than were projected in *ADO 2019*, with Afghanistan now expected to post a small surplus. Both Bhutan and Maldives have large deficits reflecting externally financed investments.

Figure 3.3.2 Inflation, South Asia

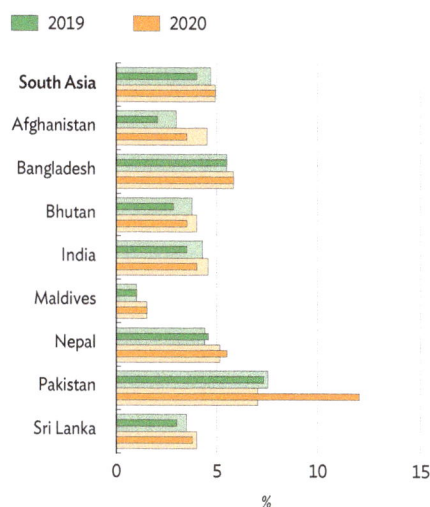

Note: Lighter colored bars are *ADO 2019* forecasts.
Source: *Asian Development Outlook* database.

Figure 3.3.3 Current account balance, South Asia

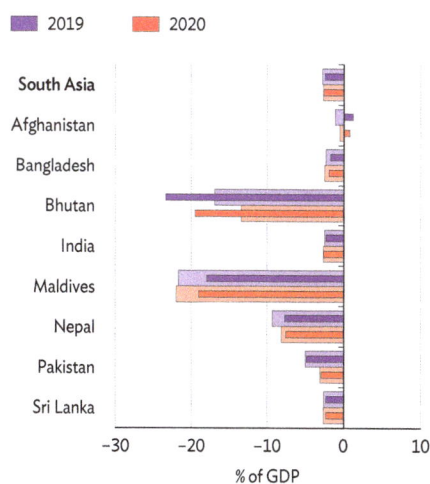

Note: Lighter colored bars are *ADO 2019* forecasts.
Source: *Asian Development Outlook* database.

Bangladesh

The economy grew robustly in fiscal year 2019 (FY2019, ended 30 June 2019) on strong expansion in industry. Inflation moderated with a good harvest. The current account deficit was narrower than forecast in *ADO 2019* as import growth slowed and exports accelerated beyond expectations, and as remittances rose to a new record. For FY2020, this *Update* anticipates sustained high GDP growth despite some deterioration in global growth and trade conditions, slightly higher inflation, and a continued moderate current account deficit.

Updated assessment

GDP growth was 8.1% in FY2019, according to preliminary official estimates, slightly higher than projected in *ADO 2019* as growth in industry accelerated from 12.1% in FY2018 to 13.0%, exceeding expectations thanks to robust growth in manufacturing and electricity, water, and gas utilities (Figure 3.3.4). Output from large and medium-sized industrial enterprises grew briskly by 15.6% as exports picked up, especially to the US and some newly penetrated markets. Small manufacturers also excelled. Service growth rose slightly from 6.4% to 6.5%, mainly on better performance in wholesale and retail trade and transport services. Growth in agriculture moderated from a high base of 4.2% in FY2018 to 3.5%.

On the demand side, growth was lifted by a 1.3 percentage point contribution by net exports as exports outpaced imports. Record remittances at $16.4 billion underpinned 5.4% expansion in private consumption, which allowed total consumption to contribute 4.0 percentage points to growth. Although investment growth eased from a year earlier, gross domestic investment rose from the equivalent of 31.2% of GDP to 31.6% as public investment expanded from 8.0% to 8.2% and private investment edged up from 23.3% to 23.4%. Total investment contributed 2.8 percentage points to growth.

Inflation slowed from an average of 5.8% in FY2018 to 5.5% thanks to a good crop harvest and lower global food prices. Food inflation slowed to 5.5% year on year in June 2019 from 7.1% a year earlier, while nonfood inflation picked up from 3.7% to 5.4%, largely in line with rising domestic gas prices and currency depreciation (Figure 3.3.5).

Broad money growth accelerated in FY2019 from 9.2% a year earlier to 9.9% but ended up short of the FY2019 monetary program target of 12.0% (Figure 3.3.6). Private credit growth slowed from 16.9% a year earlier to 11.3%, also falling short of its 16.5% program target. Net credit to the public sector increased by 19.1% as the government borrowed more from banks for its domestic financing of the FY2019 budget deficit, thereby easing its reliance on nonbank financing, mainly through high-interest national savings certificates, from 85%

Figure 3.3.4 Supply-side contributions to growth

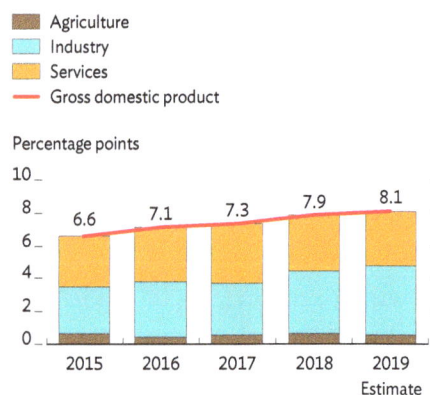

Note: Years are fiscal years ending on 30 June of that year.
Sources: Bangladesh Bureau of Statistics. http://www.bbs.gov.bd; ADB estimates.

Figure 3.3.5 Monthly inflation

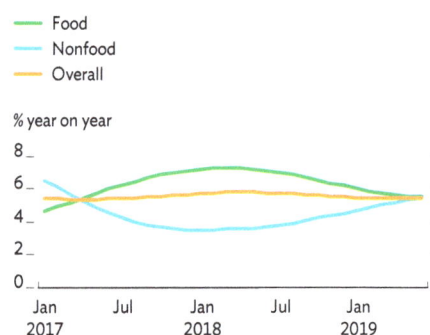

Source: Bangladesh Bank. 2019. *Monthly Economic Trends.* July. https://www.bb.org.bd.

Figure 3.3.6 Contributions to broad money growth

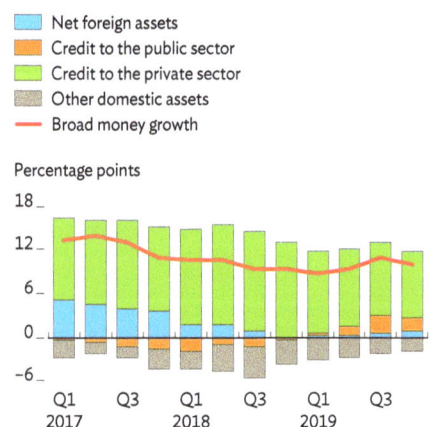

Q = quarter.
Note: Years are fiscal years ending on 30 June of that year.
Sources: Bangladesh Bank. 2019. *Major Economic Indicators, Monthly Update.* June. https://www.bb.org.bd; ADB estimates.

in FY2018 to about 60%. With a decline in reserve liabilities, growth in net foreign assets continued to improve. Bangladesh Bank, the central bank, kept its policy interest rates unchanged as liquidity pressures moderated (Figure 3.3.7).

The official revised budget for FY2019 raised the revenue collection target from the equivalent of 9.6% of GDP in FY2018 to 12.5%. However, more recent data from the National Board of Revenue indicates that revenue underperformed the revised target by about 20% with shortfalls in the collection of income and value-added taxes. Total revised spending was targeted to jump from 14.3% of GDP in FY2018 to 17.4% on augmented annual development program spending and on higher current spending mostly for subsidies and pay and allowances. When budget accounts are next revised, the revenue shortfall is expected to be offset by lower spending than under the current revised budget to hold the budget deficit under a ceiling equal to 5.0% of GDP, which should keep the ratio of public debt to GDP broadly stable. Domestic sources financed 63% of the deficit.

Export growth accelerated from 6.7% in FY2018 to 10.1% (Figure 3.3.8). Growth in garment exports rose from 8.8% to 11.5%, reflecting strong demand from the US and newer markets for Bangladesh like Australia, Canada, India, Japan, the People's Republic of China (PRC), and the Republic of Korea. Garments accounted for 84.2% of exports. Other exports increased by 5.8% on higher demand for agricultural, petroleum, and chemical products.

Imports grew modestly by 1.8% in FY2019 from a high base set in the previous year. Petroleum products, raw materials for garments, and construction materials rose markedly, reflecting strong growth in industry. Imports of capital goods rose little as investment fell short of expectations, while bountiful crop production drove down food imports substantially.

The trade deficit narrowed from $18.2 billion to $15.5 billion. Remittances grew strongly by 9.6% to reach a record $16.4 billion (Figure 3.3.9). This occurred as the Bangladesh taka depreciated and measures were taken to enhance money transfers through official channels. With the markedly improved trade deficit and larger remittances, the current account deficit narrowed sharply to $5.3 billion, equal to 1.7% of GDP. This was only half of the FY2018 deficit of $9.6 billion, or 3.5% of GDP, and much less than the *ADO 2019* forecast in April (Figure 3.3.10).

The surplus in the combined capital and financial account, adjusted for errors and omissions, shrank from $8.7 billion in FY2018 to $5.3 billion mainly because of larger repayments of trade credit and less use of commercial bank credit and short-term loans. Notably, net foreign direct investment increased by over 40% to $2.5 billion. With net financing about equal to the current account deficit, the overall balance of payments

Figure 3.3.7 Interest rates

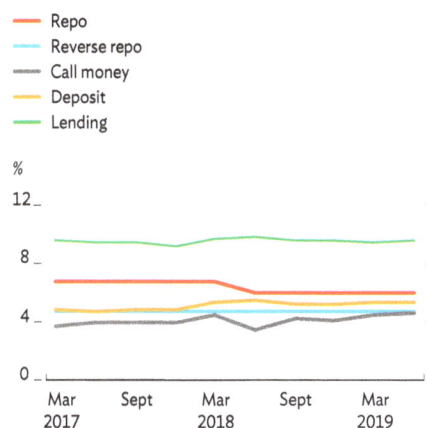

Source: Bangladesh Bank. 2019. *Major Economic Indicators, Monthly Update*. July. https://www.bb.org.bd.

Figure 3.3.8 Exports

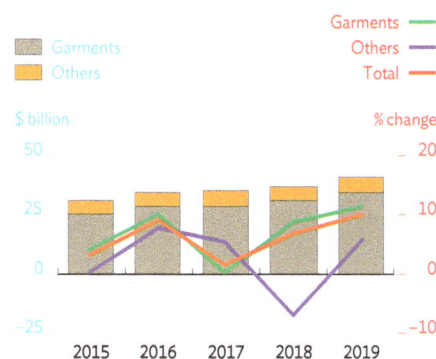

Note: Years are fiscal years ending on 30 June of that year.
Sources: Export Promotion Bureau; ADB estimates.

Figure 3.3.9 Remittances

Note: Years are fiscal years ending on 30 June of that year.
Source: Bangladesh Bank. https://www.bb.org.bd.

improved from a deficit of $857.0 million to a small surplus of $12.0 million in FY2019. Gross foreign exchange reserves in the central bank, including valuation adjustments, fell marginally to $32.8 billion, or cover for 6.0 months of imports (Figure 3.3.11).

The taka depreciated by 0.9% against the US dollar in FY2019 as Bangladesh Bank, the central bank, sold $2.3 billion to commercial banks to meet demand for foreign exchange and to tamp down excessive market volatility (Figure 3.3.12). Taking into account inflation differentials, the taka appreciated by 5.1% in real effective terms, indicating eroded competitiveness.

Prospects

GDP growth is expected at a strong 8.0% in FY2020 (Figure 3.3.13), as projected in *ADO 2019*, on continued buoyant exports underpinned by trade redirection in response to tensions between the US and the PRC, robust private consumption expenditure with higher remittances, accommodative policy on private sector credit, ongoing reform to improve the cost of doing business including the establishment of a one-stop service for private investment, and stepped up budget spending, especially to develop infrastructure.

Agriculture is expected to edge up to 3.8% growth in FY2020 as government policy improves farm prices. Industry growth is expected to stay high at 12.5% with domestic demand continuing to be powered by remittances and the central bank promoting investment in productive pursuits. Services are expected to grow by 6.4%, supported by sustained growth in agriculture and industry.

Inflation is forecast to accelerate to 5.8% in FY2020, as forecast in *ADO 2019*, on upward adjustments to domestic natural gas rates, higher prices for goods and services as value-added tax (VAT) coverage expands, and taka depreciation as demand rises for foreign exchange.

Central bank monetary policy will continue to be accommodative in FY2020 to support the government's target for growth but without breaching the 5.5% cap on inflation. The central bank will adjust its sector-specific financing support policies and programs as needed. With money and foreign exchange markets poised to improve liquidity conditions, and with the economy running at full steam, the central bank made no changes in its monetary policy statement for FY2020 to its main policy interest rates, cash reserve requirement, or statutory liquidity ratio. It will handle liquidity stress at weak banks case by case. To make monetary policy transmission more efficient, the central bank is continuing preparations for adopting a monetary policy regime based on a policy interest rate.

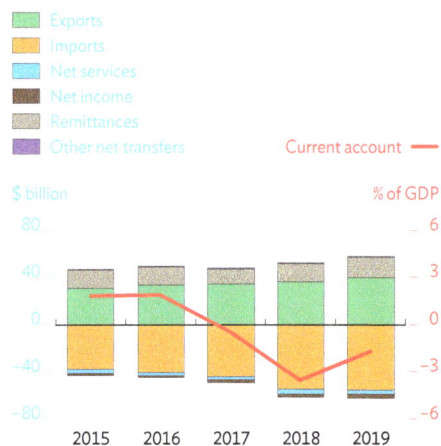

Figure 3.3.10 Current account components

Note: Years are fiscal years ending on 30 June of that year.
Sources: Bangladesh Bank. https://www.bb.org.bd; ADB estimates.

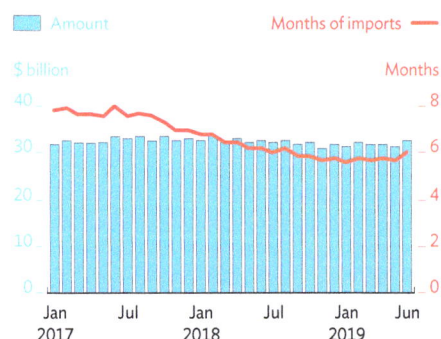

Figure 3.3.11 Foreign exchange reserves

Source: Bangladesh Bank. 2019. *Monthly Economic Trends*. August. https://www.bb.org.bd.

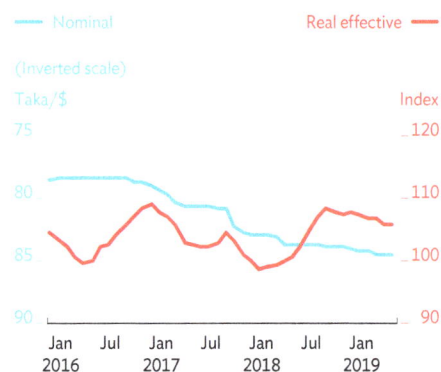

Figure 3.3.12 Exchange rates

Source: Bangladesh Bank. 2019. *Monthly Economic Trends*. July. https://www.bb.org.bd.

The FY2020 budget sustains an expansionary approach. To finance a bigger annual development program, the government aims to raise revenue collection to the equivalent of 13.1% of GDP and increase spending to 18.1% (Figure 3.3.14). Current spending is expected to grow by 12.2%, mostly for higher pay and allowances, interest payments, and subsidies. Development expenditure is envisaged to grow by 22.0% to expedite the implementation of high-priority projects to enhance growth. The budget deficit is targeted equal to 5.0% of GDP, with 53.0% financed domestically. To further reduce reliance on national saving certificates as begun in FY2019, 61% of domestic financing is anticipated from banks and only 39% from certificates.

The Value-Added Tax and Supplementary Duty Act, 2012 came into effect on 1 July 2019 with provision for four rates: 5.0%, 7.5%, 10.0%, and 15.0%. The new VAT law is expected to generate additional revenue with more comprehensive coverage, better auditing, and market price accounting. Online services are provided for VAT registration, submitting returns, making payments, and requesting refunds. Other revenue-enhancing measures are expected to help improve revenue mobilization, but various VAT exemptions and tax holidays will likely offset some of these efforts.

Despite global economic slowing, export growth is expected to be strong at 10.0% in FY2020 as Bangladesh benefits from trade redirection caused by US–PRC trade tensions. Exports to newly penetrated markets are expected to rise further. Exports should benefit as well from government efforts to improve the investment climate by reducing the cost of doing business.

Imports are expected to grow by 9.0% in FY2020, though less than forecasted in *ADO 2019* as expansion in public investment moderates more than expected in April 2019. Still, import growth will be substantially higher than in FY2019 as the implementation of large infrastructure projects picks up and boosts imports of capital equipment and raw materials. Liquified natural gas will become a sizeable new import with the installation of two floating storage and regasification units. Food imports will continue to be subdued, assuming a good crop harvest and with the revival of an import duty on rice.

Growth in remittance inflows is likely to slow to 9.0% in FY2020 as fewer people take jobs overseas. While import growth picks up, continued strong expansion in exports will broadly stabilize the trade deficit. As remittances will still be sizable, the current account deficit is projected to edge up slightly in FY2020 to equal 1.8% of GDP. With import payments exceeding export receipts, some pressure on foreign exchange reserves will continue, causing them to fall moderately.

Table 3.3.1 Selected economic indicators, Bangladesh (%)

	2019		2020	
	ADO 2019	Update 2019	ADO 2019	Update 2019
GDP growth	8.0	8.1	8.0	8.0
Inflation	5.5	5.5	5.8	5.8
Current acct. bal. (share of GDP)	-2.3	-1.7	-2.5	-1.8

Note: Years are fiscal years ending on 30 June of that year.

Sources: Bangladesh Bureau of Statistics. http://www.bbs.gov.bd; ADB estimates.

Figure 3.3.13 GDP growth

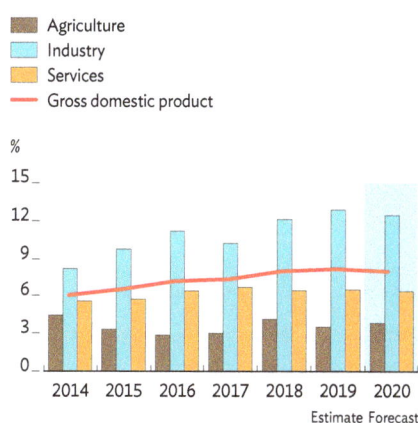

Note: Years are fiscal years ending on 30 June of that year.
Sources: Bangladesh Bureau of Statistics. http://www.bbs.gov.bd; ADB estimates.

Figure 3.3.14 Fiscal indicators

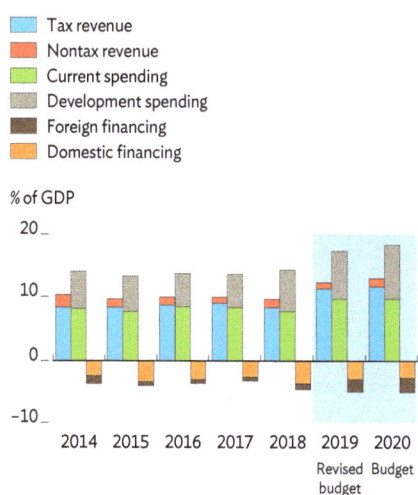

Note: Years are fiscal years ending on 30 June of that year.
Sources: Ministry of Finance. *Annual Budget 2018–19, Budget in Brief.* https://www.mof.gov.bd; ADB estimates.

India

With GDP growth weakening considerably in the first quarter (Q1) of fiscal year 2019 (FY2019, ending 31 March 2020), slower growth at 6.5% is now forecast for this year. Proactive policy interventions should foster recovery into FY2020, with growth expected to rise to 7.2%, only marginally lower than forecast in *ADO 2019*. A slowing economy, benign food inflation, and declining oil prices motivate reductions to inflation forecasts, even as monetary policy loosens. The current account forecast is revised for a narrower deficit in FY2019 than projected in April, reflecting weaker aggregate demand and lower oil prices, but, with GDP growth expected to revive, the forecast is retained for a wider deficit in FY2020.

Updated assessment

GDP growth declined from 5.8% year on year in Q4 of FY2018 to 5.0% in Q1 of FY2019, the lowest in 6 years (Figure 3.3.15). Moderation in growth was widespread as consumption, investment, manufacturing, and services suffered slowdowns. Although agriculture grew by 2.0% in Q1 of FY2019, reversing contraction in the previous quarter, it remained below the sector's 5-year average growth of 2.9%.

Industry growth declined from 4.2% year on year in Q4 of FY2018 to 2.7% in Q1 of FY2019, as manufacturing grew by a disappointing 0.6%. Weakness in manufacturing is corroborated by a growth slowdown indicated in the volume-based index of industrial production from 5.1% in Q1 of FY2018 to 3.0% a year later. While capital goods and consumer durables contracted, intermediate goods and consumer nondurables grew at a healthy pace. The automobile industry, which makes up a large share of manufacturing, suffered in Q1 of FY2019 a 10.5% sales slump year on year. This was its worst such downturn since December 2008—until August 2019, which recorded a decline of 19.7% caused by reduced lending, consumer confusion over a coming transition to new emission standards, and deferred purchases. Construction also slowed, to 5.7%, as indicated by weak sales of cement and steel, while mining and quarrying grew by 2.7%.

Growth in services decelerated to 6.9%, the sector's slowest rate in 7 quarters. The slowdown reflected weak 5.9% expansion in financial, real estate, and professional services. It was indicative of disruption caused by the foundering and rescue of a major nonbanking financial company (NBFC) and how this situation had substantially reduced the availability of funds for NBFCs to lend in FY2018 and Q1 of FY2019. Trade, hotels, and transport and communication services grew by 7.1%, and public administration, defense and others expanded by 8.5%, as they were less affected by weakness in industry.

Private consumption, which has been a strong driver of growth in recent years, grew by only 3.1% in Q1 of FY2019,

Figure 3.3.15 Supply-side contributions to growth

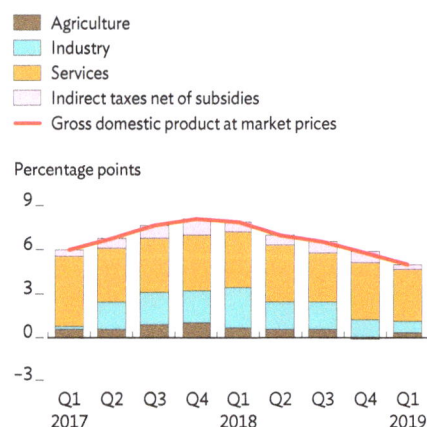

- Agriculture
- Industry
- Services
- Indirect taxes net of subsidies
- Gross domestic product at market prices

Percentage points

Q = quarter.
Notes: Years are fiscal years ending on 31 March of the next year. Sectoral output valued at basic prices.
Sources: Ministry of Statistics and Programme Implementation. http://www.mospi.nic.in; CEIC Data Company (accessed 2 September 2019).

Figure 3.3.16 Demand-side contributions to growth

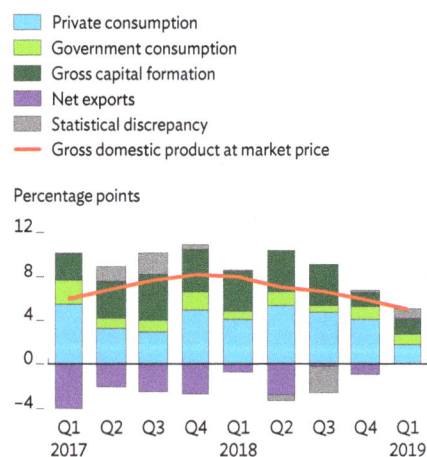

- Private consumption
- Government consumption
- Gross capital formation
- Net exports
- Statistical discrepancy
- Gross domestic product at market price

Percentage points

Q = quarter.
Note: Years are fiscal years ending on 31 March of the next year.
Sources: Ministry of Statistics and Programme Implementation. http://www.mospi.nic.in; CEIC Data Company (accessed 2 September 2019).

its lowest rate in more than 4 years (Figure 3.3.16). Urban consumption was likely affected by subdued wage growth and a credit crunch, while continued rural stress constrained rural consumption. Government consumption remained healthy, however, growing by 8.8%.

Gross fixed capital formation grew by 4.0% in Q1 of FY2019, marginally up from 3.6% in the previous quarter but well below 13.3% in the same quarter of FY2018. With general elections held during the quarter, muted private investment was deepened by the usual postponement of investment until after elections. Moreover, capital expenditure by the central government contracted, which further slowed growth. Even as export growth deteriorated because of the fragile global environment, previous drag on growth from net exports fell to nil in the quarter as weak domestic demand markedly pulled down import growth.

After remaining below 3% in the second half of FY2018, inflation inched up a little in the first 5 months of FY2019 to average 3.1%, as food prices previously depressed by a supply glut, especially for vegetables and pulses, started rising in FY2019. Core inflation remained at 4.3% (Figure 3.3.17).

With headline inflation staying below 4.0%, which is the midpoint of the target range, the Reserve Bank of India, the central bank, has cut policy rates by a cumulative 110 basis points since February 2019 and, in its most recent policy statements, indicated further scope for monetary easing (Figure 3.3.18). Recapitalization by the government and loan-resolution procedures helped ease stress on banks as the share of nonperforming loans declined from 11.5% in March 2018 to 9.3% a year later (Figure 3.3.19). This decline was broadly based, with the ratio declining for all major industries, including infrastructure, metals and metal products, textiles and food processing.

Growth in bank credit excluding lending by banks to Food Corporation of India for procuring food slowed somewhat from an average of 12.1% year on year in FY2018 to 11.0% in the first 5 months of FY2019. (Figure 3.3.20). Growth in credit for infrastructure, engineering goods, cement, and chemical products experienced an uptick, but growth in credit for textiles, metals and metal products, and food processing moderated from the previous year. Within the service sector, credit growth to software services declined significantly to become negative, while credit growth increased markedly for real estate, tourism, and hotels and restaurants.

In contrast, NBFCs experienced worsening stress from rising nonperforming loans, slower profit growth, and declining capital adequacy. Net flow of financial resources from systematically important NBFCs to commercial borrowers reversed from $42.6 billion in FY2017 to contraction by $5.6 billion in FY2018, reflecting severe stress in the sector.

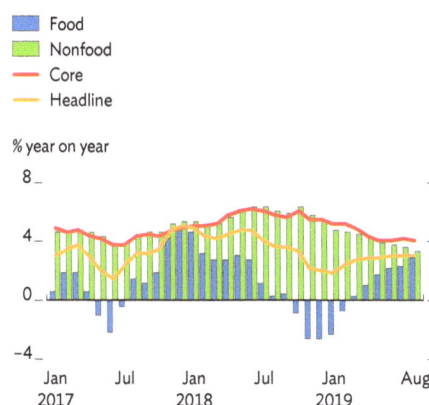

Figure 3.3.17 Monthly inflation

Food
Nonfood
Core
Headline

% year on year

Sources: CEIC data company (accessed 16 September 2019); ADB estimates.

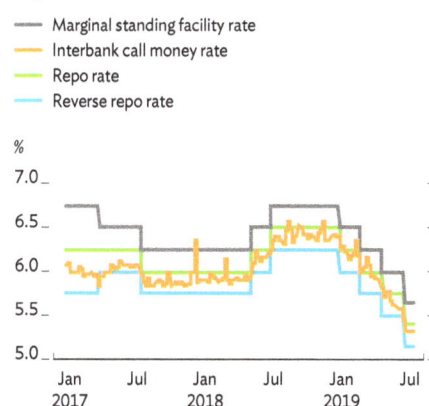

Figure 3.3.18 Policy interest rates

Marginal standing facility rate
Interbank call money rate
Repo rate
Reverse repo rate

%

Sources: Bloomberg; CEIC Data Company (accessed 2 September 2019).

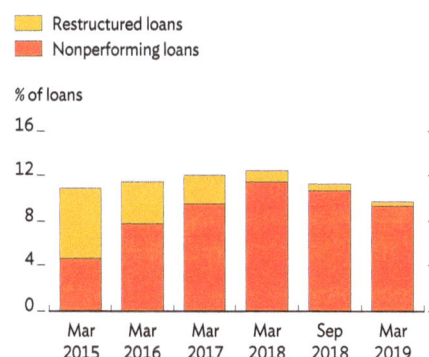

Figure 3.3.19 Stressed loan ratio

Restructured loans
Nonperforming loans

% of loans

Source: Reserve Bank of India. http://www.rbi.org.in (accessed 3 September 2019).

The central government fiscal deficit for FY2019 is budgeted at the equivalent of 3.3% of GDP, but in the fiscal year to July this target was already 77.8% met. Tax revenue collection in the first 4 months of FY2019 remained subdued, growing by only 6.6%, about two-thirds of annual targeted growth of 9.5%. Despite measures to improve compliance, growth in income tax collection was slow. Sluggish corporate tax collection likely reflected lower tax rates set in the budget for most domestic corporations and subdued economic growth. Collection of goods and services tax (GST) increased by only 6.4% in the first 5 months of FY2019, implying continued implementation issues. Nontax revenue received a boost as the central bank transferred to the government a record $25 billion, equal to 0.9% of GDP and well above the budgeted 0.7% of GDP. In addition to a dividend that is transferred every year, the central bank transferred part of its excess capital, in line with a recommendation from an expert committee.

Expenditure grew at a similarly muted rate, rising by 6.5% in the first 4 months of FY2019. Current expenditure increased by 7.9% in the period, mainly on higher outlays for fertilizer and fuel subsidies. Capital expenditure contracted by 3.4%, possibly because general elections curbed public investment.

After recording double-digit growth in most of FY2018, imports fell by 5.6% in the first 5 months of FY2019 from the year earlier (Figure 3.3.21). Muted oil prices meant oil imports shrank by 6.1% in US dollar terms despite an increase in volume. Imports aside from oil and gold contracted by 5.7%, highlighting weak growth in aggregate demand. Rising gold prices and monetary stress may explain a 3.4% decline in gold imports.

Exports also contracted in the first 5 months of FY2019, by 1.4%, reflecting worsening global trade tensions, rising protectionism, and a growth slowdown in the advanced economies. Exports to major destinations grew in April–July 2019—to the US by 4.5% and to the People's Republic of China (PRC) by 8.5%—but other export markets contracted, notably Germany; Hong Kong, China; the United Arab Emirates; and the United Kingdom. Lower oil prices caused petroleum exports to fall by 6.4%.

Net foreign direct investment (FDI) inflows grew by a strong 61% to $18.3 billion in the first 4 months of FY2019, a result of continued liberalization of guidelines and improvement in the ease of investment (Figure 3.3.22). Portfolio investment by foreign institutional investors provided net inflow during April–August 2019 (Figure 3.3.23). While debt inflows have been strong, outflow in the equity segment in July–August added to domestic pressures on the stock market, which saw prices fall by 4.0% in the first 5 months of FY2019 (Figure 3.3.24). This primarily reflects rising trade tensions, which typically induce capital flight to safe havens. Consequently, the Indian

Figure 3.3.20 Bank credit

Source: Bloomberg (accessed 12 September 2019).

Figure 3.3.21 Trade indicators

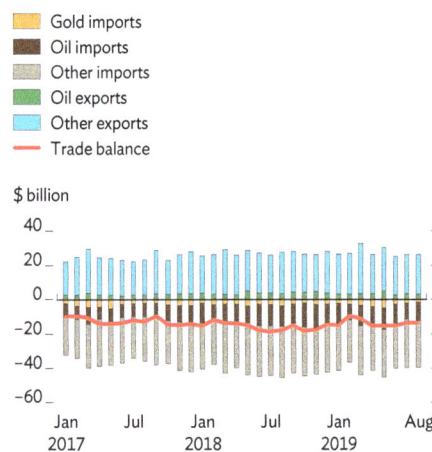

Sources: CEIC Data Company; Centre for Monitoring India Economy (accessed 16 September 2019); ADB estimates.

Figure 3.3.22 Foreign direct investment

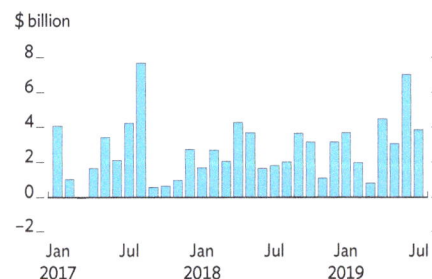

Source: CEIC Data Company (accessed 16 September 2019).

rupee depreciated by 3.2% against the US dollar from the beginning of FY2019 to the end of August 2019 (Figure 3.3.25). In the first 5 months of FY2019, strong FDI inflows and a lower trade deficit helped international reserves climb by $17 billion to $429 billion (Figure 3.3.26).

Prospects

Following weak growth in Q1, expansion in the remaining quarters of FY2019 will depend on how much domestic demand grows, but the result will certainly be less than forecast in *ADO 2019*. Government initiatives—including those in a revised budget for FY2019 and measures announced in August and September—promise to boost confidence and foster a rapid recovery. Direct income support for smallholder and marginal farmers is expected to boost rural consumption and compensate to some degree for losses from an uneven monsoon. Urban consumption is expected to improve as cuts in monetary policy rates lower the cost of borrowing and as disposal income improves following tax relief included in the budget for low-income taxpayers.

The latest corporate tax cuts, announced on 20 September, are a large fiscal stimulus equal to 0.7% of GDP. The average effective corporate tax rate including all surcharges will fall from 30% to 25% and, for new manufacturing companies, to 17%. This will place India among the emerging economies with the lowest corporate tax rates, promising to boost investment and growth and make India more competitive internationally.

The recapitalization of state-owned banks and mergers of 10 public banks into 4 will improve the health of the banking sector, as will governance reform announced in August. This action, recent policy rate cuts, and likely further easing will reduce the cost of borrowing and improve the flow of credit to industry and infrastructure projects, while supporting higher business investment as the growth outlook improves. The government's decision to provide additional liquidity to housing finance companies and partial credit guarantees for purchasing the pooled assets of NBFCs will help NBFCs to repair their balance sheets and restore lending.

The automobile industry, which has seen sharply declining sales, is expected to revive on account of steps taken to improve bank and NBFC credit flows, as well as on such demand-boosting measures as deferring a hike in registration fees, clearing up uncertainty over emission standards, and renewing the government automotive fleet. Policy action to ensure the fast-tracking of GST refunds should provide an important boost to small and medium-sized firms that have been constrained by a crunch on working capital. The Nikkei purchasing managers' index for manufacturing had shown strength in recent months before declining a bit in August, as did the index for services (Figure 3.3.27).

Figure 3.3.23 Portfolio capital flows

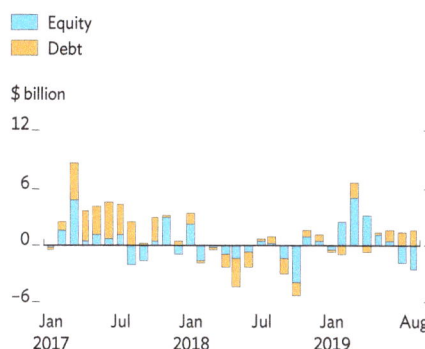

Source: Security and Exchange Board of India.

Figure 3.3.24 Bombay stock prices

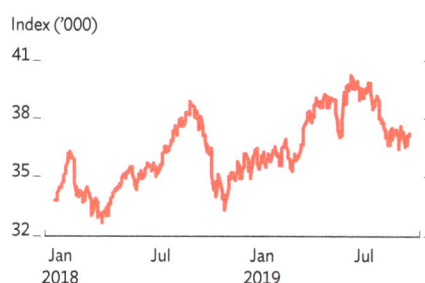

Source: Bloomberg (accessed 12 September 2019).

Figure 3.3.25 Exchange rate

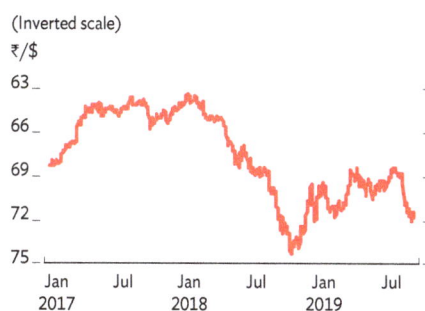

Source: Bloomberg (accessed 2 September 2019).

On balance, growth is expected to slow to 6.5% in FY2019, not accelerate to 7.2% as forecast in *ADO 2019*. Recovery from a 6-year low of 5.0% growth in Q1 of FY2019 depends on there being proactive policy interventions. Such measures should continue to aid recovery in FY2020, with the growth rate in the first half benefiting as well from a low base set in early FY2019. Growth is expected to reaccelerate to 7.2% in FY2020, albeit marginally less than 7.3% forecast in *ADO 2019*.

Risks to the growth outlook tilt primarily to the downside as the lag between growth-enhancing policy measures and impact on aggregate demand may extend longer than anticipated. A revenue shortfall because of weak economic activity would constrain government spending and further dampen aggregate demand.

Food inflation is expected to accelerate in FY2019 as an uneven monsoon spells a somewhat weaker harvest and as higher procurement prices are instituted to better compensate farmers. Moderation in global oil prices is expected to apply downward pressure on retail prices for petroleum products, albeit less than expected in *ADO 2019* and partly offset by surcharges on petroleum products announced in the budget. However, as this *Update* went to press, a recent drone attack on Saudi Arabia's oil-producing infrastructure could reverse the trend of global oil prices. Domestic fuel inflation is expected to be only modestly lower than in FY2018. Core inflation is expected to remain stable, though higher than headline inflation as aggregate demand improves during the year. In sum, inflation will likely accelerate less than previously anticipated owing to growth and food inflation being lower than projected. The forecast for inflation is lowered from 4.3% to 3.5% for FY2019 and from 4.6% to 4.0% for FY2020, in both years staying within the central bank target range.

In its first budget, the reelected government has prioritized fiscal prudence over populism. The fiscal deficit for FY2019 is budgeted at 3.3% of GDP, down from the actual deficit of 3.4% in FY2018. Central government revenue is targeted to grow by 14.3% in FY2019, aided by strong growth in nontax revenue. Tax revenue growth is expected to remain sluggish on account of only modest growth in collections of income tax and GST. The target for personal income tax collection is nonetheless ambitious and may be difficult to achieve with a GDP growth slowdown, despite government efforts to widen and deepen the tax net and impose higher taxes on individuals with high net worth. Lower forecast GST collection has been offset by raising excise duty and taxes on petroleum products. Nontax revenue has been budgeted higher on larger dividends and profits from public enterprises, including the central bank, and higher proceeds from disinvestment.

Figure 3.3.26 International reserves

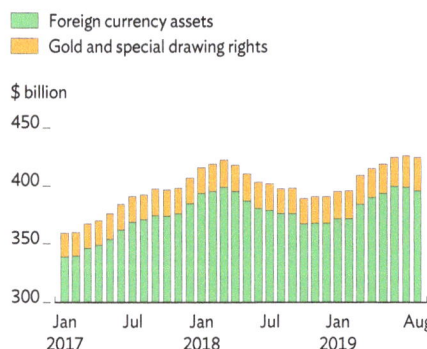

Source: Reserve Bank of India. http://www.rbi.org.in (accessed 16 September 2019).

Figure 3.3.27 Purchasing managers' index

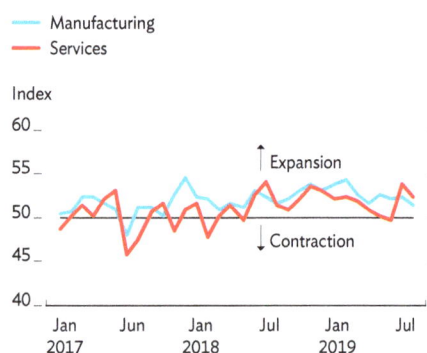

Note: Nikkei, Markit.
Source: Bloomberg (accessed 4 September 2019).

Current expenditure is set to grow by 14.3% and capital expenditure by 6.9%. Thus, while current expenditure is set to increase from the equivalent of 11.4% of GDP to 11.6%, capital expenditure will decline from 1.7% to 1.6%. Higher current expenditure will go mainly to higher outlays for committed expenditure, mainly subsidies and interest payments. Capital expenditure on defense, railways, roads, urban infrastructure, electric power, and roads is projected to increase at a healthy rate. As in the previous years, a large part of capital expenditure is shifted off-budget to state-owned entities.

Exports are likely to take a hit from subdued global demand and rising trade tensions. Petroleum exports are expected to contract in FY2019 and underperform projections in *ADO 2019*. Non-oil exports will also moderate with rising trade tensions and weak global demand, though recent weakness in the Indian rupee could provide some impetus. In sum, exports in FY2019 are expected to grow by 5.0%, revised down from 8.0% forecast in *ADO 2019*. The surplus in services is likely to shrink as global demand weakens.

A weakening currency and oil prices slightly higher than previously anticipated are likely to take oil imports higher, though the pace of expansion will be slower than in FY2018. Growth in imports other than oil and gold will fall short of the forecast in *ADO 2019* in tandem with disappointing GDP growth. On balance, overall imports are now expected to grow by 4.0%, revised down from 8.0% forecast in *ADO 2019*, but remittances above earlier expectations may cushion the trade deficit. The current account deficit is expected to equal 2.2% of GDP in FY2019, slightly smaller than forecast in *ADO 2019*.

In FY2020, export growth will likely remain muted at 6.5% as growth in the advanced economies and the PRC slows further. Stable oil prices will moderate import growth, though a pickup in aggregate demand should expand imports excluding oil and gold. All imports are expected to grow by 8.0%, and the current account deficit is expected to widen to the equivalent of 2.5% of GDP in FY2020, as forecast in *ADO 2019*. However, if higher oil prices from the drone attack are sustained, the current account deficit could widen further.

Capital inflows are expected to remain healthy in FY2019 and FY2020. With rising trade tensions between the US and the PRC, some firms may move part of their operations to India, thereby enhancing FDI inflows. However, for this to materialize, the government will have to continue its effort to improve the ease of doing business and further liberalize FDI regulations. Global monetary easing could also bolster portfolio inflows. Capital flows are expected to be sufficient to finance the current account deficit, though a shortfall is possible and may require a modest drawdown of reserves.

Table 3.3.2 Selected economic indicators, India (%)

	2019		2020	
	ADO 2019	Update	ADO 2019	Update
GDP growth	7.2	6.5	7.3	7.2
Inflation	4.3	3.5	4.6	4.0
Current acct. bal. (share of GDP)	−2.4	−2.2	−2.5	−2.5

Note: Years are fiscal year ending on 31 March of the next year.
Source: ADB estimates.

Pakistan

Growth decelerated steeply in fiscal year 2019 (FY2019, ended 30 June 2019), reflecting lower investment amid policy uncertainty and persistent macroeconomic imbalances. Sizable currency depreciation accelerated inflation but helped substantially narrow the current account deficit. Growth is expected to slow further in FY2020 as the authorities implement a comprehensive program of fiscal consolidation and monetary tightening to stabilize the economy and address structural weaknesses.

Updated assessment

Provisional estimates show GDP growth slowing from 5.5% in FY2018 to 3.3% in FY2019, below the *ADO 2019* forecast of 3.9%. On the supply side, all sectors contributed substantially less to GDP growth than a year earlier (Figure 3.3.28). Growth in agriculture decelerated from 3.9% to 0.8% as water shortages meant smaller harvests of major crops. Industry growth fell markedly from 4.9% to 1.4% as demand weakened. Large-scale manufacturing reversed 5.1% expansion to fall by 2.1% with contraction almost across the board, while construction dropped by 7.6%. Exceptional 40.5% growth in electricity production as new generation projects reached completion fully accounted for industry growth. With marked weakening in agriculture and industry, growth in services slowed from 6.2% to 4.7%.

On the demand side, private consumption, accounting for 82% of GDP, contributed 3.1 percentage points to growth despite higher inflation and borrowing costs. Public consumption, edging up to the equivalent of 12% of GDP, contributed 1.0 percentage point (Figure 3.3.29). Meanwhile, contraction in gross fixed investment trimmed growth by 1.3 percentage points, mostly reflecting significantly reduced public investment as the government cut development spending and the near completion of energy and transport projects, including those initiated under the China–Pakistan Economic Corridor. Private investment also fell markedly as progress stalled on structural reform, undermining business confidence. Net exports contributed 0.1 percentage points to growth as imports dropped substantially, mainly because of steep currency depreciation.

The Pakistan rupee depreciated against the US dollar by 24% in FY2019 as the authorities moved toward the adoption of a flexible exchange rate determined by the market, after having defended an overvalued rupee in recent years (Figure 3.3.30). Inflation trended substantially higher, from an average of 3.9% in FY2018 to 7.3%, mainly reflecting currency depreciation and a considerable increase in domestic fuel prices. Average food inflation reached 4.6%, partly because of the poor harvest, and nonfood inflation accelerated to 9.2% (Figure 3.3.31).

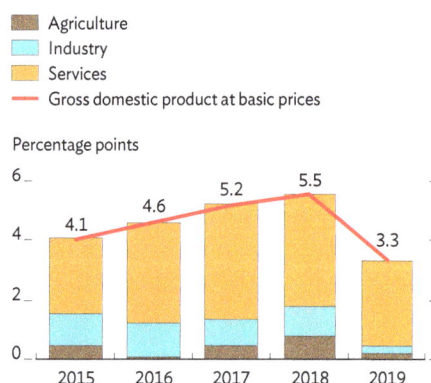

Figure 3.3.28 Supply-side contributions to growth

- Agriculture
- Industry
- Services
- Gross domestic product at basic prices

Percentage points

Note: Years are fiscal years ending on 30 June of that year.
Source: Ministry of Finance. *Pakistan Economic Survey 2018–19.* http://www.finance.gov.pk.

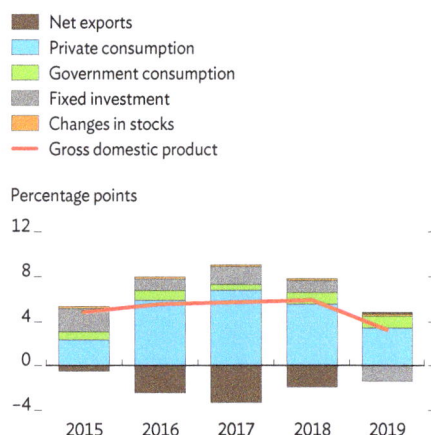

Figure 3.3.29 Demand-side contributions to growth

- Net exports
- Private consumption
- Government consumption
- Fixed investment
- Changes in stocks
- Gross domestic product

Percentage points

Note: Years are fiscal years ending on 30 June of that year.
Source: Ministry of Finance. *Pakistan Economic Survey 2018–19.* http://www.finance.gov.pk.

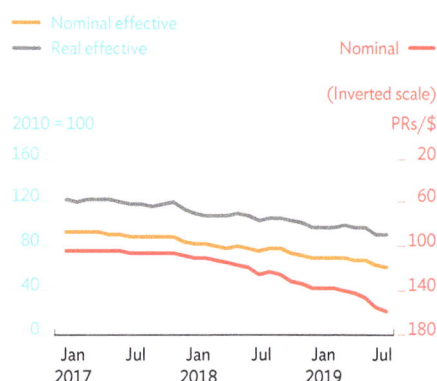

Figure 3.3.30 Exchange rates

- Nominal effective
- Real effective
- Nominal

(Inverted scale)

2010 = 100   PRs/$

Source: State Bank of Pakistan. *Economic Data.* http://www.sbp.org.pk (accessed 2 September 2019).

To keep the policy rate positive in real terms, the State Bank of Pakistan, the central bank, raised its policy rate by a cumulative 575 basis points to 12.25% at the end of FY2019, and by another 100 basis points to 13.25% in July 2019. Market rates gradually rose in line with the policy rate (Figure 3.3.32).

The deficit in the general government budget, which consolidates federal and provincial accounts, markedly surpassed a large deficit equal to 6.5% of GDP in FY2018 to reach 8.9% in FY2019 (Figure 3.3.33). Revenue declined significantly from the equivalent of 15.1% of GDP to 12.7%. Nontax revenue was halved from 2.2% of GDP to 1.1%, mainly reflecting reduced central bank profits and a sharp drop from miscellaneous sources, while tax revenue fell from 13.0% of GDP to 11.6% as income and sales tax revenues declined.

Expenditure increased by 11.5% over FY2018 to reach the equivalent of 21.6% of GDP in FY2019 despite a 33% decline in development spending and net lending, which was cut from 4.7% of GDP last year to only 3.2% in an effort to contain the budget deficit. Current expenditure increased by 17% to equal 18.4% of GDP in FY2019 with higher spending on defense and subsidies to public enterprises—and particularly on interest payments as those on external debt rose significantly because of currency depreciation and those on domestic debt rose under monetary tightening.

The significantly higher fiscal deficit was financed largely through domestic borrowing: 66% from bank sources, 22% from nonbank sources, and 12% external. As commercial banks reduced their net government position, the central bank provided all of the banking system's contribution to financing the budget deficit. Central bank financing thus more than doubled to PRs3.0 trillion in FY2019, equal to 8% of GDP.

Outstanding public debt and liabilities, domestic and external, have been markedly increasing in recent years to equal 84.8% of GDP at the end of FY2019, substantially breaching the threshold at 60% of GDP stipulated in the Fiscal Responsibility and Debt Limitation Act. Public external debt including liabilities rose from the equivalent of 27.4% of GDP at the end of FY2018 to 37.2% a year later—or by $9.9 billion to $87.9 billion—mainly because of currency depreciation (Figure 3.3.34). Domestic debt reached 53.8% of GDP in FY2019, with reprofiling reducing the share of its short-term component to 27%, nearly half the level in FY2018, thus reducing exposure to interest rate risk.

The current account deficit eased from 6.3% of GDP in FY2018 to 4.8% in FY2019 (Figure 3.3.35). The trade deficit narrowed by almost 11.5% to $28.2 billion as rupee depreciation drove down merchandise imports by 7.4%, particularly for goods other than petroleum. Despite currency depreciation in real effective terms, merchandise exports declined by 2.2%, partly because low cotton production constrained

Figure 3.3.31 Monthly inflation

- Food
- Others
- Headline
- Core

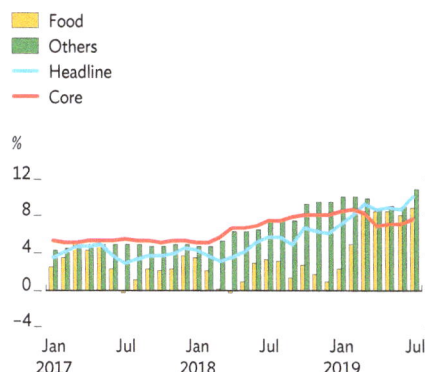

Source: State Bank of Pakistan. *Economic Data.*
http://www.sbp.org.pk (accessed 1 September 2019).

Figure 3.3.32 Interest rates and inflation

- Weighted average lending
- Policy
- Inflation

Source: State Bank of Pakistan. *Economic Data.*
http://www.sbp.org.pk (accessed 5 September 2019).

Figure 3.3.33 Government budget indicators

- Tax revenue
- Nontax revenue
- Net lending and development spending
- Current spending
- External financing
- Bank financing
- Nonbank financing

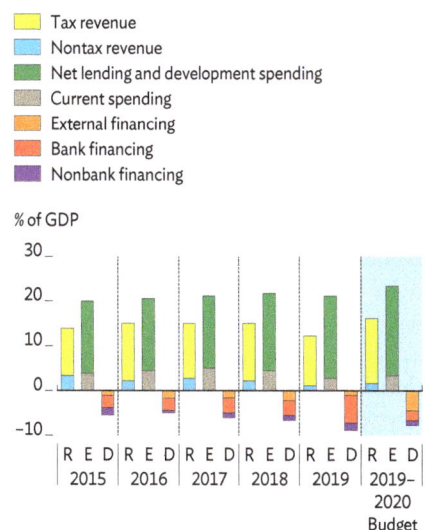

D = deficit, E = expenditure, R = revenue.
Note: Years are fiscal years ending on 30 June of that year.
Sources: Ministry of Finance, Budget in Brief FY2019–2020 and Summary of Consolidated Federal & Provincial Budgetry Operations (July–June 2018–19).

textile exports. Workers' remittances stirred from 3 years of near stagnation to grow by 9.7%, lending support to the current account.

The financial account surplus narrowed considerably in FY2019, by 16.2%, the $2.3 billion fall mostly accounted for by $1.8 billion less in foreign direct investment owing in part to policy uncertainty but also to the winding down of energy and infrastructure projects in the China–Pakistan Economic Corridor. Notwithstanding large bilateral financing received from the People's Republic of China, Saudi Arabia, and the United Arab Emirates, gross foreign exchange reserves fell by $2.5 billion to $7.3 billion at the end of June 2019, or cover for 1.7 months of imports (Figure 3.3.36).

Prospects

To restore macroeconomic stability, the government plans to catalyze significant international financial support and promote sustainable and balanced growth under a 3-year economic stabilization and reform program with the International Monetary Fund (IMF). Fiscal consolidation under the program aims to reduce the large public debt while expanding social spending, establish a flexible exchange rate regime to restore competitiveness, and rebuild official reserves.

Given the need for the authorities to address sizable fiscal and external imbalances, the economy is expected to slow further, with GDP growth projected at 2.8% in FY2020. Fiscal adjustments are expected to suppress domestic demand, and demand contraction will keep growth in manufacturing subdued. However, agriculture is expected to recover from weather-induced contraction this year, with major incentives in the government's agriculture support package included in the budget for FY2020.

Inflation remained elevated at the start of FY2020 at 9.4% in July and August. It is projected to accelerate further to average 12.0% in FY2020 because of a planned hike in domestic utility prices, taxes introduced in the FY2020 budget, and the lagged impact of currency depreciation. Pressure from inflationary expectations can be relieved by the government's commitment to refrain from directly financing the budget deficit by borrowing from the central bank as monetary policy continues to tighten.

The economic reform program supported by the IMF envisages a multiyear strategy for revenue mobilization to pare public debt to a sustainable level. The budget assumes tax revenue increased to equal 14.3% of GDP. With nontax revenue projected at 2.3% of GDP in FY2020, total revenue is expected to increase to 16.6% of GDP.

Expenditure in FY2020 is projected to equal 23.8% of GDP with an increase of 1.8 percentage points in current spending to cover larger interest payments and higher allocations

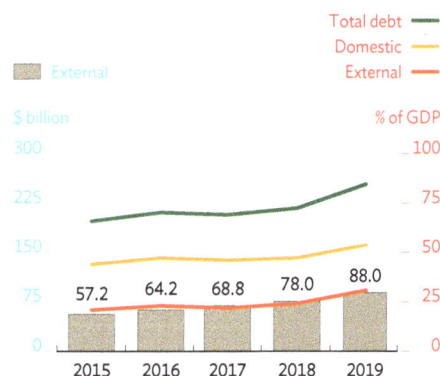

Figure 3.3.34 Public debt

Note: Years are fiscal years ending on 30 June of that year. External debt includes government and other external liabilities and public corporations.
Source: State Bank of Pakistan.

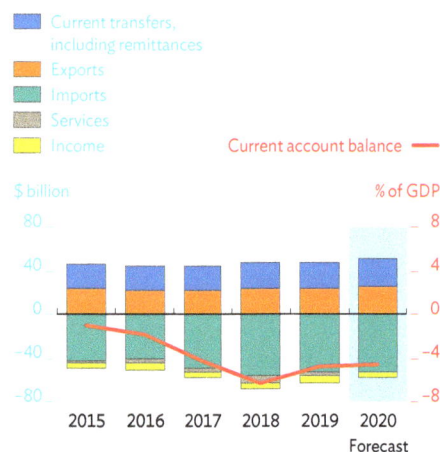

Figure 3.3.35 Current account components

Note: Years are fiscal years ending on 30 June of that year.
Source: State Bank of Pakistan. http://www.sbp.org.pk (accessed 29 August 2019).

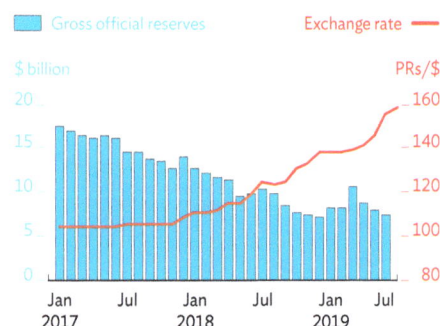

Figure 3.3.36 Gross official reserves and exchange rate

Source: State Bank of Pakistan. *Economic Data.* http://www.sbp.org.pk (accessed 5 September 2019).

for social spending to avoid hurting the poor as reform progresses. At the same time, to support adjustment efforts, the government sets federal government wage increases below the inflation rate. Development spending is projected to rise to 3.6% of GDP in FY2020 and support stronger social spending in the FY2020 budget.

The budget deficit in FY2020 is expected to equal 7.2% of GDP—still large but 1.7 percentage points lower than the FY2018 outcome (Figure 3.3.37). Financing is expected to come mostly from external and nonbank sources after the government announced that it would not borrow from the central bank toward financing the budget deficit in FY2020. Resource allocation indicates a shift toward external borrowing, with net external financing estimated at PRs1.8 trillion, or 4.2% of GDP. Financing from nonbank sources is projected at PRs833 billion, equal to 1.9% of GDP.

To strengthen fiscal discipline, the government recently adopted the Public Financial Management Act in connection with the FY2020 finance bill. Working with provincial governments, the federal government will prepare a fiscal strategy to align provincial expenditure and the annual deficit with budgetary targets that have heretofore been routinely breached. Capacity will be strengthened in the Ministry of Finance for monitoring fiscal risks and conducting cash management.

On the external front, the trade deficit shrank by nearly half in July, the first month of FY2020, from $3.4 billion a year earlier to $1.8 billion. With further narrowing of the trade deficit and a continued positive trend in workers' remittances, the current account deficit is projected to narrow further to 2.8% of GDP in FY2020. Import payments will remain subdued, reflecting weak economic activity and the pass-through of past rupee depreciation against the US dollar. The real effective exchange rate is now thought to be near equilibrium, and a lower and more stable rupee is expected to improve export competitiveness.

Foreign capital inflows are expected to increase. Foreign direct investment should revive as investors' confidence is restored with the implementation of the IMF stabilization and reform program. This should also help bring additional finance from multilateral institutions and other international partners. Along with the activation of a Saudi oil facility with potential disbursements of $1 billion in the current fiscal year, these developments are expected to raise foreign exchange reserves to more than $10 billion by the end of FY2020.

Table 3.3.3 Selected economic indicators, Pakistan (%)

	2019		2020	
	ADO 2019	Update 2019	ADO 2019	Update 2019
GDP growth	3.9	3.3	3.6	2.8
Inflation	7.5	7.3	7.0	12.0
Current acct. bal. (share of GDP)	−5.0	−4.8	−3.0	−2.8

Note: Years are fiscal year ending on 30 June of that year.
Source: ADB estimates.

Figure 3.3.37 Fiscal deficit financing

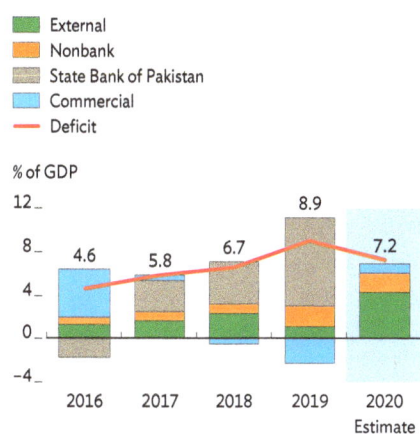

Note: Years are fiscal years ending on 30 June of that year.
Source: Ministry of Finance. Federal Budget. http://www.finance.gov.pk (accessed 2 September 2019).

Other economies

Afghanistan

Favorable weather allowed agriculture to recover from last year's drought more strongly than expected, prompting upward revisions in GDP growth projections for 2019 and 2020. However, growth in manufacturing and services continues to be constrained by heightened security risks and political uncertainty after the recent suspension of the US–Taliban peace negotiations and a presidential election scheduled for 28 September 2019. It is unclear whether an agreement for a permanent ceasefire or successful intra-Afghan talks will emerge in the near future.

With rising production in agriculture, Afghanistan's most important employer, an upturn in household income is expected to support growth in private consumption. However, continued insecurity weighs heavily on the business climate and private investment. Growth in budget expenditure in 2019 is expected to slow by 4.0% as grants decline. In the first half of the year, strengthened revenue administration helped to lift revenue by 14% over the same period in 2018 to reach 55% of the annual budget target. The development budget execution rate is reported at 41%, an improvement of 5 percentage points from a year earlier.

Average annual inflation in the first half of 2019 accelerated from 0.8% a year earlier to 2.5%. Reversing an unusual decline in the food prices in 2018, when substantial imports countered drought-induced shortages, food inflation at 3.4% pushed up the overall inflation rate in the first half of 2019. Prices for fruit, cereals, and vegetables moved higher, partly because demand rose with higher rural incomes following recovery from drought. With declining international fuel prices and afghani appreciation against the currencies of two major trade partners, Iran and Pakistan, nonfood inflation decelerated from 2.1% last year to 1.7%. Inflation is now projected to be lower than expected in *ADO 2019*, with Da Afghanistan Bank, the central bank, committed to keeping inflation in check.

The afghani continued to depreciate in the first half of 2019, falling by 6% against the US dollar amid currency speculation and smuggling, as well as political uncertainty. Gross foreign exchange reserves remained stable at $8.5 billion in August. With recovery in agriculture, exports are reported to have increased by 2.1% in the first half of the year and imports to have markedly declined by 7.7% from the same period last year. Forecasts for current account balances including grants are thus revised to modest surpluses in both 2019 and 2020.

Table 3.3.4 Selected economic indicators, Afghanistan (%)

	2019		2020	
	ADO 2019	Update	ADO 2019	Update
GDP growth	2.5	2.7	3.0	3.4
Inflation	3.0	2.0	4.5	3.5
Current acct. bal. (share of GDP)	–1.1	1.2	–0.4	0.7

Source: ADB estimates.

Bhutan

GDP growth in fiscal year 2019 (FY2019, ended June 2019) is estimated to have been slightly below the *ADO 2019* forecast in April. Official GDP data are not available, but industry growth was weaker than expected, reflecting a 5.1% decline in hydropower production in FY2019 despite high rainfall. A 17.1% curtailment of government expenditure occurred as expected as the country transitioned to a new government that formulated and adopted the Twelfth Five-Year Plan, 2018–2023.

Services continued to underpin the economy with a 7.3% rise in international tourism revenue to $87.7 million. Over the first 3 quarters, credit growth to the private sector accelerated by one-third from the year-earlier period to 15.2%. Credit remained highly concentrated in construction and services, in particular tourism. However, under continuing government programs to stimulate cottage and small industries, credit growth accelerated to 17.6% in trade and commerce, 10.6% in manufacturing, and 9.8% in agriculture.

Developments expected to boost growth in FY2020 in line with the *ADO 2019* projection are the commissioning of the 740-megawatt Mangdechhu Hydropower Plant, continued improvement in tourism with new government programs, sustained momentum in the private sector, and a marked increase in government capital expenditure under the Twelfth Five-Year Plan.

Following a marked downward trend in FY2018, inflation started to rise at midyear in FY2019 but averaged only 2.8% in the whole of it. Food inflation remained higher than overall inflation but trended lower for most of the year, averaging 3.5%, well down from 6.5% in the year-earlier period. Average nonfood inflation accelerated from 1.8% a year earlier to 2.4%. A fall in international oil prices and low import prices kept inflation subdued in FY2019 and lower than forecast in *ADO 2019*. A pay hike for civil servants in July 2019 and an anticipated upward trend in India's wholesale prices will boost inflation in FY2020 but less than projected in April.

Estimates for FY2019 show exports falling by 8.7%, mainly from a decline in hydropower production, rather than increasing moderately as expected in *ADO 2019*. Imports declined by 4.8%, somewhat less than expected as hydropower construction continued to lag and government capital expenditure slumped. The trade deficit widened to equal an estimated 15.8% of GDP, and the current account deficit widened, instead of narrowing as forecast in *ADO 2019*, on a lower secondary income surplus because of smaller budgetary grants, and on a larger service deficit, mainly reflecting maintenance services for the much-delayed Punatsangchhu I plant and higher financial, insurance, and transportation payments. The current account deficit is expected to narrow in FY2020 as exports rise with the full operation of the Mangdechhu plant, but it will remain well above the April forecast.

Table 3.3.5 Selected economic indicators, Bhutan (%)

	2019		2020	
	ADO 2019	*Update*	*ADO 2019*	*Update*
GDP growth	5.7	5.3	6.0	6.0
Inflation	3.8	2.8	4.0	3.5
Current acct. bal. (share of GDP)	−16.9	−23.4	−13.4	−19.4

Note: Years are fiscal years ending on 30 June of that year.

Source: ADB estimates.

Maldives

Forecasts of GDP growth are unchanged from those in *ADO 2019*. Tourism was strong in the first half of 2019, especially in the second quarter (Q2), with arrivals expanding by 18.7% from the year-earlier period. Growth was driven mainly by a substantial rebound from Asian markets, up by 20.4% and accounting for 37.9% of arrivals, especially from India and the People's Republic of China (PRC).

Growth in PRC tourists, the largest single national group, rebounded by 10.1% from a similar decline earlier, while Indian visitors almost doubled. European guests, about half of arrivals, grew by 16.5%. Bed-nights sold, a proxy for tourism earnings, rose by 14.7%. These results so far justify the *ADO 2019* forecast that tourism and growth would remain solid this year but less robust in 2020.

The main downside risk to the outlook is a much sharper fall in global economic growth than expected. Such a shock would, as in the past, markedly weaken tourism earnings and raise issues of fiscal and public debt sustainability, given the country's very low buffer of usable foreign exchange reserves.

Average inflation in the first half 2019 was negligible at 0.04% as prices for food, electricity, and transport fell significantly in Q1 from a year earlier, with the price index down by 1.2%. This reflected policy changes that came into effect in Q2 of 2018—reversing an earlier decision to remove blanket subsidies on staple foods and cutting electricity tariff on the atolls—as well as a 20%–25% cut in domestic air fares in January 2019. The index climbed by 1.3% in Q2 of 2019, without a notable base effect, on somewhat higher food prices, an uptick in house rentals, and price increases for restaurants and hotels. Prevailing domestic price policies and forecasts of lower global energy prices are expected to keep price pressures in check and maintain low inflation in the remainder of 2019 and in 2020. Accordingly, *ADO 2019* inflation projections are maintained.

The trade deficit narrowed by 6.1% in the first half of 2019 from the year earlier period, mainly as imports surprised on the downside with the completion of some public infrastructure projects and delays in the implementation of ongoing projects, while the formulation of new projects has slowed. Moreover, robust tourism has boosted the service balance. Given these developments, projections for current account deficits are lowered from those in *ADO 2019*.

Gross foreign reserves in the first half of 2019 fell from $712.0 million a year earlier to $677.4 million, taking into account a $100 million currency swap repayment to the Reserve Bank of India. Usable reserves (gross reserves less commercial banks' foreign currency deposits) fell slightly from $281.4 million to $276.0 million, maintaining cover for only about 1 month of imports.

Table 3.3.6 Selected economic indicators, Maldives (%)

	2019		2020	
	ADO 2019	Update	ADO 2019	Update
GDP growth	6.5	6.5	6.3	6.3
Inflation	1.0	1.0	1.5	1.5
Current acct. bal. (share of GDP)	–21.8	–18.0	–22.0	–19.0

Source: ADB estimates.

Nepal

GDP expansion in fiscal year 2019 (FY2019, ended 16 July 2019) exceeded the *ADO 2019* forecast, with growth in all sectors above expectations. Agriculture grew by 5.0% on a favorable monsoon that brought a record 8.3% increase in rice production. Industry advanced by 8.1% on increased electricity production, accelerated earthquake reconstruction, and strong consumer demand. Services grew at 7.3% as higher remittances supported retail trade and as stepped-up tourist arrivals favored hotels and restaurants.

On the demand side, growth in private consumption markedly accelerated in FY2019 on higher remittances and agricultural income, contributing two-thirds of GDP expansion. Fixed investment moderated from a year earlier. Private investment spending, mostly into energy and services, grew by 27.0% to account for 29.0% of GDP. Public investment increased by 5.5% from the high level achieved in FY2018, but construction on national pride projects suffered delays.

The *ADO 2019* growth forecast for FY2020 is retained. Floods in early July 2019 delayed rice planting, which probably means lower growth in agriculture than in FY2019, but an increase by almost half in the FY2020 budget for capital expenditure promises to offset that shortfall if realized in actual spending.

Inflation slightly exceeded the *ADO 2019* projection as food inflation accelerated from 2.8% in FY2018 to 3.1% on account of flooding and landslides in July that affected some supply channels and a delay in food supply owing to strict tests along the India–Nepal border over concern about pesticides. Strong demand drove nonfood inflation from an average of 5.3% in FY2018 to 5.9%. Inflation will likely rise in FY2020 beyond the *ADO 2019* forecast, assuming a somewhat smaller harvest, a marked pickup in government expenditure, and a moderate rise in inflation in India, the main supplier.

The current account deficit, forecast to widen in *ADO 2019*, narrowed substantially instead as large national pride projects experienced implementation delays and markedly curbed import growth. Export growth exceeded expectations, but earnings remained small, allowing the trade deficit to widen by 4.6%. Growth in workers' remittances was, at 7.7%, sufficient to keep the current account deficit stable at $2.3 billion. With financing inflows somewhat down from a year earlier, foreign exchange reserves fell by 5.8% to $9.5 billion, this second year of decline nevertheless leaving import cover for 7.8 months.

The FY2020 current account deficit is now forecast to be much narrower than projected in *ADO 2019* as it continues to shrink, however marginally from FY2019, in response to measures that curtail imports of low-priority goods, as well as higher hydroelectricity production, which will replace fuel imports for generators, and more workers going to high-income destinations like Japan.

Table 3.3.7 Selected economic indicators, Nepal (%)

	2019		2020	
	ADO 2019	Update	ADO 2019	Update
GDP growth	6.2	7.1	6.3	6.3
Inflation	4.4	4.6	5.1	5.5
Current acct. bal. (share of GDP)	-9.3	-7.7	-8.1	-7.6

Note: Years are fiscal years ending in mid-July of that year.

Source: ADB estimates.

Sri Lanka

Growth rebounded from 1.8% year on year in the fourth quarter of 2018 to 3.7% in the first quarter of 2019. The rebound reflected 4.1% growth in services, 5.5% expansion in agriculture, and recovery in industry mainly from a pickup in construction. The first quarter saw muted private consumption, continued tightening in government consumption, and a near 5.0% decline in fixed investment. Net exports contributed to growth, and contraction in inventories subtracted from it.

While growth in the first quarter aligned with the *ADO 2019* forecast, the projection for growth in 2019 is marked down to take into account terror bombings in April 2019, as is the projection for 2020. Tourist arrivals fell sharply from 4.6% growth year on year in the first quarter of 2019 to 41.4% decline in the second quarter, though arrivals have picked up month on month since May. Budget revenue declined by 4.0% year on year in the first half of 2019, which, along with growth below expectations, will likely make meeting the deficit target difficult without spending cuts.

The national consumer price index rose by an average of 2.6% in the first 7 months of 2019. Even as food prices dropped from a high base in 2018, nonfood inflation rose with higher administered prices and Sri Lanka rupee depreciation at the end of 2018. Inflation forecasts for 2019 and 2020 are reduced because inflation to date has been below expectations. The Colombo consumer price index rose by an average of 4.0% in the first 8 months of 2019 and is projected at 4.2% in 2019 and 5.0% in 2020.

The Central Bank of Sri Lanka eased monetary policy three times in 2019 in response to subdued growth, low inflation, and slowing growth in private credit. It cut the statutory reserve requirement by 100 basis points in February and standing deposit and lending facility rates by 50 basis points in May and again in August. Sovereign bond issues worth $4.4 billion helped to raise gross international reserves to $8.3 billion in July 2019. Rupee appreciation against the US dollar by 3.6% in the first 7 months of the year was offset by 2.5% depreciation induced by global volatility in August.

The trade deficit shrank by 37.0% year on year in the first half of 2019 as exports grew by 4.7% and imports declined by 16.1%. Measures introduced in 2018 to restrict imports were eased in May 2019. Despite a marked reduction in tourism earnings, as expected after the terror attacks, the current account deficit is now forecast to be less than projected in *ADO 2019*, reflecting trade developments to date. The deficit forecast for FY2020 is trimmed as well but is still projected to widen marginally.

Table 3.3.8 Selected economic indicators, Sri Lanka (%)

	2019 ADO 2019	2019 Update	2020 ADO 2019	2020 Update
GDP growth	3.6	2.6	3.8	3.5
Inflation	3.5	3.0	4.0	3.8
Current acct. bal. (share of GDP)	−2.5	−2.2	−2.6	−2.3

Source: ADB estimates.

Southeast Asia

Southeast Asia is hard hit by persistent trade friction between the People's Republic of China and the US, slowing world trade, and weakening global growth. The subregional GDP growth forecast is downgraded by 0.4 percentage points for this year and by 0.3 points for next year. With softer growth comes lower inflation but, as imports slow along with exports, little revision to an earlier forecast for a slightly narrower regional current account surplus.

Subregional assessment and prospects

The forecast for subregional GDP growth is now revised down from 4.9% in *ADO 2019* to 4.5% for this year from 5.0% to 4.7% for 2020. Growth forecasts are downgraded from April for half of the 10 economies in the subregion—Indonesia, the Lao People's Democratic Republic (Lao PDR), the Philippines, Singapore, and Thailand—and unchanged for the other half, with Brunei Darussalam, Cambodia, Malaysia, Myanmar, and Viet Nam on track to meet *ADO 2019* forecasts (Figure 3.4.1).

The factors that dim prospects include steep declines in export growth, weaker domestic investment, and agriculture subdued by drought under El Niño. Meanwhile, domestic consumption held up well across the subregion, and this cushioned the slowdown. Trade is the main problem. With escalation in the trade conflict between the People's Republic of China (PRC) and the US, weakening global economic activity and trade, and a cyclical downturn in electronics, export growth slowed significantly in the first half of the year across the subregion, except in Cambodia and Myanmar.

The downward revision to growth forecasts is accompanied by similar downward revisions for inflation, from 2.6% to 2.3% for this year and from 2.7% to 2.6% for next year.

Figure 3.4.1 GDP growth, Southeast Asia

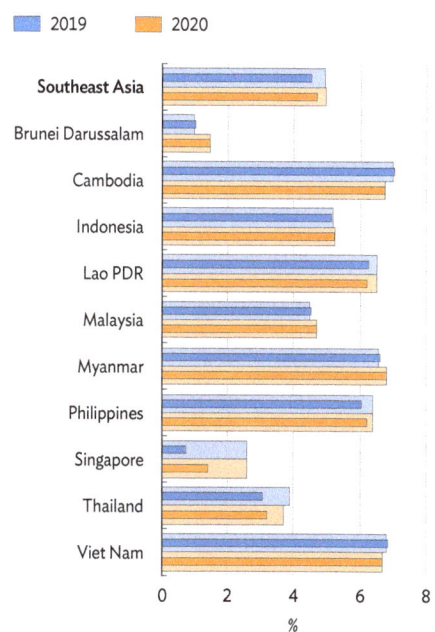

Lao PDR = Lao People's Democratic Republic.
Note: Lighter colored bars are *ADO 2019* forecasts.
Source: *Asian Development Outlook* database.

The subregional assessment and prospects were written by Thiam Hee Ng and Dulce Zara. The section on Indonesia was written by Emma Allen and Priasto Aji; Malaysia and Thailand by Thiam Hee Ng; the Philippines by Teresa Mendoza; Viet Nam by Cuong Minh Nguyen, Nguyen Luu Thuc Phuong, and Chu Hong Minh; and other economies by Poullang Doung, Soulinthone Leuangkhamsing, Rattanatay Luanglatbandith, Pilipinas Quising, Yumiko Tamura, Shu Tian, and Mai Lin Villaruel. Authors are in the Southeast Asia and Economic Research and Regional Cooperation departments of ADB.

Downgrades are made for five economies—Brunei Darussalam, Cambodia, Malaysia, the Philippines, and Viet Nam—in light of softening demand, lower forecast oil prices, prudent restraint on growth in credit and the money supply, and subdued domestic food prices. Inflation forecasts for this year are unchanged for Indonesia, Singapore, and Thailand but raised for the Lao PDR and Myanmar largely because of unexpected pressure on domestic food prices arising from lower domestic food production and logistical problems affecting inland food shipments (Figure 3.4.2).

Forecasts for the subregional current account are largely unchanged from *ADO 2019* as demand for imported raw materials and for parts and components to supply export-oriented manufacturing has declined under bleaker export prospects. Wide variation is seen across the subregion, however, in forecast adjustments to individual current account balances. Projections for current account deficits this year are narrower for the Lao PDR, Myanmar, and the Philippines; wider for Cambodia; and unchanged for Indonesia. The current account surplus in Malaysia is now seen widening much more than forecast in *ADO 2019* as its exports benefit from the resumption of exports of liquefied natural gas and from higher palm oil shipments. The forecast narrowing of Viet Nam's surplus is now expected to be steeper than foreseen in April, and Singapore's surplus will remain as forecast in *ADO 2019* (Figure 3.4.3).

With growth slowing, inflation benign, and external payments positions comfortable, the central banks of larger subregional economies cut their policy interest rates to revive lackluster domestic investment: Indonesia by a total of 50 basis points in July and August, the Philippines by a similar magnitude in May and July, and Malaysia and Thailand by 25 basis points in May and August, respectively. Fiscal policy similarly supported growth within the limits imposed by national fiscal consolidation programs—except in the Philippines, where delay in passing the national budget caused the budget deficit to trend down.

The subregional outlook is subject to significant risks, both external and domestic. Growth could be slower than currently foreseen if the US–PRC trade conflict escalates further or if global trade tensions morph into a widespread currency war, injecting volatility into international financial markets. On the domestic front, unexpected delays in implementing major infrastructure projects, particularly in the Philippines and Thailand, would pose risks to growth prospects. In the Philippines, growth prospects hinge as well on how quickly the government catches up on its public spending commitments after the delays experienced in the first half of the year.

Figure 3.4.2 Inflation, Southeast Asia

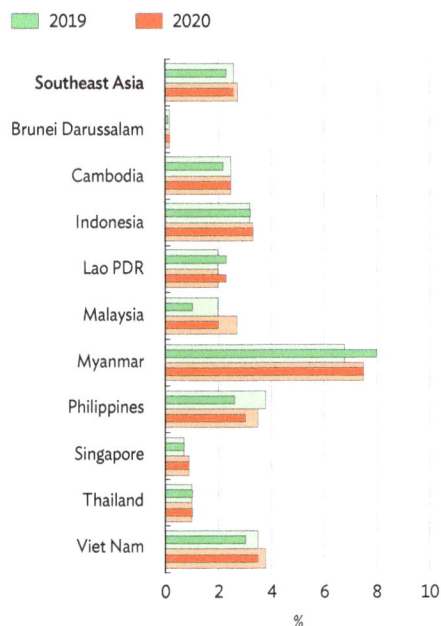

Lao PDR = Lao People's Democratic Republic.
Note: Lighter colored bars are *ADO 2019* forecasts.
Source: *Asian Development Outlook* database.

Figure 3.4.3 Current account balance, Southeast Asia

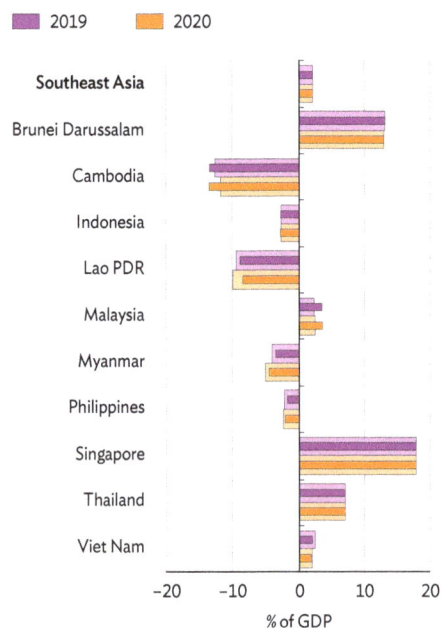

Lao PDR = Lao People's Democratic Republic.
Note: Lighter colored bars are *ADO 2019* forecasts.
Source: *Asian Development Outlook* database.

Indonesia

Growth is now seen to be marginally lower than forecast in *ADO 2019*. Slightly slower growth this year than last reflects a significant downturn in exports as growth slows in key trade partners, coupled with subdued commodity prices and domestic investment. Growth is still forecast to accelerate in 2020 but less than earlier envisaged. Inflation will likely continue at the 2018 rate this year and rise marginally next year. The current account deficit is projected to shrink in 2019, as forecast in April, but is now forecast to widen in 2020.

Updated assessment

GDP growth slowed marginally from 5.2% year on year in the first half of 2018 to 5.1% in the first half of this year. Stronger domestic consumption partly offset a worsening external environment and weakening domestic investment (Figure 3.4.4). As global trade weakened, Indonesia's exports of goods and services by volume contracted by 1.8% in the first half of the year, sharply reversing 6.8% growth a year earlier. Meanwhile, merchandise exports also shrank, by 7.7% in US dollar terms, reversing 10.2% growth. This substantial export decline dragged down GDP growth.

Domestic investment also decelerated as private investors adopted a wait-and-see approach in the run-up to a presidential election in April. Growth in fixed investment year on year in the first half moderated from 6.9% a year earlier to 5.0%, slipping more than anticipated in *ADO 2019*. The only area exempted from softening investment was plantation agriculture, where investors looked forward to the rollout of the Biodiesel 20 program, through which the government requires that diesel vehicles and heavy machinery use blends containing at least 20% biofuel.

Domestic consumption held up well in the first half of the year, countering the effect of weaker exports and subdued investment. Private consumption, accounting for about 60% of GDP, improved on 5.1% growth year on year in the first half of 2018 to grow by 5.3%. Household spending was supported by a robust labor market, scaled-up government social assistance programs, and benign inflation. Consumption received a further boost until April from election-related spending. Reflecting this, government consumption accelerated from 4.1% a year earlier to 6.9%. In the 12 months to February 2019, 2.2 million new jobs were created in the formal economy as consumer spending strengthened, and the unemployment rate declined from 5.1% to 5.0%. These developments helped trim the poverty incidence from 9.8% a year earlier to 9.4%.

By sector, growth in agriculture and industry slowed somewhat in the first half of the year as services accelerated (Figure 3.4.5). As a mild drought caused by El Niño damaged food crops, growth in agriculture slowed from 4.1% year on

Figure 3.4.4 Demand-side contributions to growth

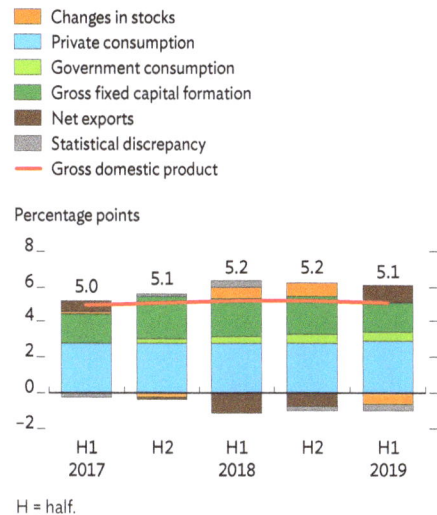

Figure 3.4.5 Supply-side contributions to growth

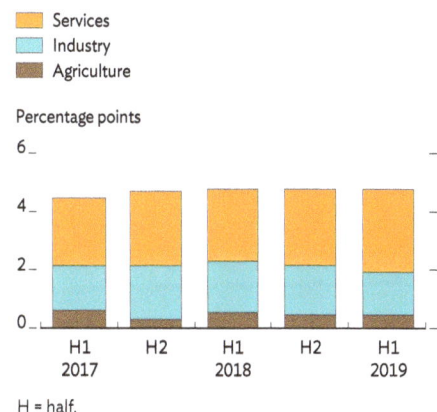

year in the first half of 2018 to 3.7%. Weaker exports and investment softened industry growth from 4.3% to 3.7%. Within industry, depreciation last year of the Indonesian rupiah against the US dollar helped expand the production of labor-intensive and export-oriented textiles and apparel, but softening demand for automobiles caused contraction in transport equipment. Strengthening domestic consumption and political parties' election spending accelerated growth in services from 5.7% to 6.5%. Within the service sector, information and communication technology registered solid growth, as did wholesale and retail commerce.

Inflation averaged 2.9% in the first half of 2019, low by historical standards and near the lower bound of the 2.5%–4.5% target range set by Bank Indonesia, the central bank (Figure 3.4.6). Despite the weather-induced damage to food production, deft supply management, including the regular monitoring of food supplies and improved logistics, kept prices stable, as did constant administered prices for fuel and only limited pass-through from rupiah depreciation. Core inflation edged down in tandem with headline inflation.

On the balance of payments, 7.7% contraction in merchandise exports was accompanied by 6.5% contraction in merchandise imports with falling imports of raw materials and components for export-oriented industries (Figure 3.4.7). Subdued domestic investment clipped imports of capital goods. The trade surplus was nevertheless nearly halved to $1.4 billion in the first half of the year from the same period in 2018. With deficits in primary income and trade in services, the current account deficit widened from the equivalent of 2.5% of GDP in the first half of 2018 to 2.8% in 2019 (Figure 3.4.8).

In the financial account of the balance of payments, foreign direct investment remained buoyant at $11.9 billion, supported by robust equity capital channeled largely to utilities, transport, telecommunications, and e-commerce. Meanwhile, portfolio investment inflows rose sharply to $9.8 billion, supported by the government's frontloading of its debt securities issues for the year (Figure 3.4.9). Foreign investors increased their holdings of Indonesian government bonds by $8.2 billion in the first 8 months of the year. In the first half of 2019, the surplus in the financial account ballooned from $5.3 billion a year earlier to $17.0 billion. This more than offset the current account deficit to add over $5 billion to Indonesia's gross international reserves in the first 8 months of the year. At $126.4 billion in August 2019, these reserves provided cover for 7.1 months of imports and government debt repayments (Figure 3.4.10).

With inflation benign and foreign exchange reserves comfortable, the central bank cut its policy interest rate, the 7-day reverse repo rate, in three installments in July, August, and September of this year by a total of 75 basis points to 5.25%.

Figure 3.4.6 Monthly inflation

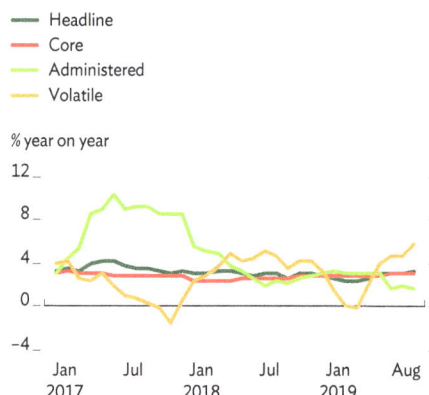

Source: CEIC Data Company (accessed 4 September 2019).

Figure 3.4.7 Merchandise trade

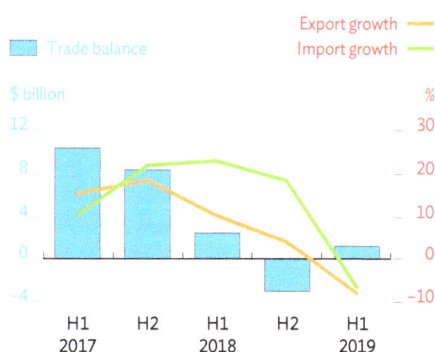

H = half.
Source: CEIC Data Company (accessed 30 August 2019).

Figure 3.4.8 Current account components

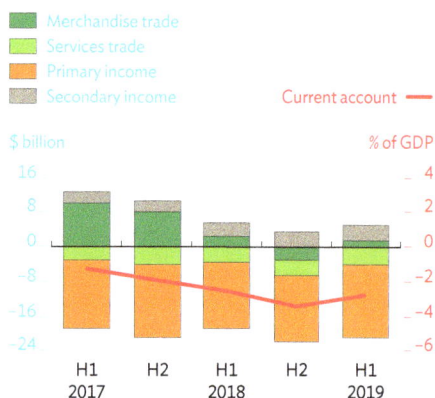

H = half.
Source: CEIC Data Company (accessed 30 August 2019).

These were the first rate cuts in almost 2 years as monetary policy was previously tightened to counter pressure on the balance of payments.

Fiscal policy too remained supportive of growth in the first half as central government expenditure and transfer payments expanded by 9.6%. Social and personnel spending picked up ahead of the April 2019 elections, while energy subsidies and capital spending declined. Despite lower export-related revenue, central government revenue and grants still grew by 7.8%. The budget deficit in the first half of 2019 expanded from the equivalent of 1.5% of GDP a year earlier to an estimated 1.8%.

Prospects

Domestic private consumption should grow both this year and next, and investment is likely to resume once the new government is installed in October and begins implementing its policies and programs. Prospects for exports are likely to remain limited in the near term. Taking these factors into account, forecasts for GDP growth this year and next are now revised down slightly from those published in *ADO 2019*. The forecast for some shrinkage in the current account deficit this year is maintained, but the size of the projected deficit next year is revised up as recovery in domestic investment drives imports higher.

Exports will likely continue to slow in the remaining months of 2019 with weakening growth among Indonesia's key trade partners and subdued commodity prices, coupled with requirements that reserve a portion of commodity production for domestic use. The slowdown will not be as steep as in the first half of the year because it will be partly offset by continuing strength in exports of manufactures such as textiles and base metal products, which have been bolstered by previous foreign and domestic investments in mining and electric power. In 2020, exports are expected to improve, though more moderately than foreseen in April in light of a weaker external environment. To counter flagging export growth, the government is supporting export diversification by strengthening the role of Indonesia's Eximbank and promoting tourism by improving amenity quality, accessibility, and the sustainable management of destinations. Indonesia is also expanding its export potential by pursuing new markets in Africa, Eastern Europe, the Middle East, and Central Asia through bilateral and multilateral trade cooperation.

Private consumption looks set to hold up in the near term, as it did in the first half of the year. Consumer spending should maintain robust growth, underpinned by rising household income, growing employment, and low and stable inflation. Consumption may be bolstered as well by rising confidence in the new administration's ability to sustain price stability, improve the investment climate, and provide and maintain

Figure 3.4.9 Financial account

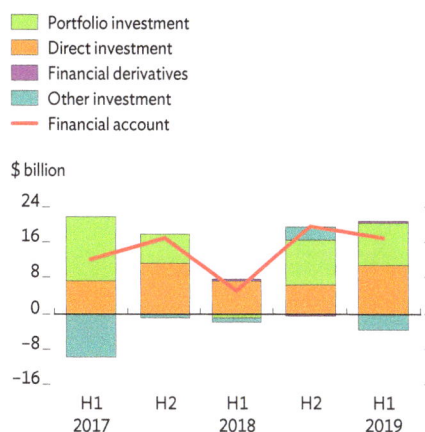

- Portfolio investment
- Direct investment
- Financial derivatives
- Other investment
- Financial account

H = half.
Source: CEIC Data Company (accessed 30 August 2019).

Figure 3.4.10 Gross international reserves

Note: Import cover is in months of imports and official external debt repayment.
Source: CEIC Data Company (accessed 30 August 2019).

public infrastructure (Figure 3.4.11). In the remaining months of 2019, growth in government consumption is expected to moderate from the first half of the year, which was bumped up partly by election-related spending. Government consumption is expected to reaccelerate next year, however, with higher outlays to improve public service delivery.

Fixed investment is expected to improve as the year draws to a close, particularly for constructing presold property units in metropolitan areas and for public infrastructure associated with more than 100 national strategic projects that were still under construction in July 2019. Recent initiatives to link regional transfers through special allocation funds to these strategic projects should make the development of infrastructure networks more efficient. With speedier project implementation, credit growth should continue to be strong (Figure 3.4.12). Public investment should remain buoyant next year as well, with infrastructure spending maintained at a high level and infrastructure planning bolstered to make expenditure more effective.

Recent cuts to the policy interest rate are likely to give a fillip to growth in credit to private borrowers. In addition, the government plans to continue expanding its subsidized credit program for micro, small, and medium-sized enterprises. In 2020, private investment should continue to improve with new reform initiatives the new administration is expected to undertake to attract export-oriented investment and accelerate the modernization of the economy.

By sector, services are expected to maintain robust growth, boosted by expanded online services and a growing youth population that is digitally savvy. Within industry, construction will likely benefit from urban property development. A sharper focus under the new administration on diversifying and upgrading manufacturing should see the sector's contribution to economic growth strengthen. Agriculture is expected to improve in 2020, assuming normal weather.

Inflation should be as forecast in *ADO 2019*, sustained at 3.2% this year and rising to 3.3% next year. Core inflation is expected to remain well contained, and continued effective supply management will keep food prices stable. Gradual adjustments to some administered energy prices are planned in 2020, with the diesel subsidy set to be halved and the electricity subsidy to rise for poor and vulnerable households as the government steps up its poverty-reduction efforts.

On the external account, the current account deficit is expected to shrink to the equivalent of 2.7% of GDP, as forecast in *ADO 2019*, with improved net exports of services and primary income receipts in the remaining months of the year. The expected pickup in investment in 2020 should boost demand for imports, which is now expected to cause the current account deficit to widen slightly to 2.9% of GDP in 2020.

Table 3.4.1 Selected economic indicators, Indonesia (%)

	2019		2020	
	ADO 2019	Update	ADO 2019	Update
GDP growth	5.2	5.1	5.3	5.2
Inflation	3.2	3.2	3.3	3.3
Current acct. bal. (share of GDP)	-2.7	-2.7	-2.7	-2.9

Source: ADB estimates.

Figure 3.4.11 Consumer confidence in the government

— Overall
— Recovery of national economy
— Stabilize the price of goods
— Provide and maintain public infrastructure

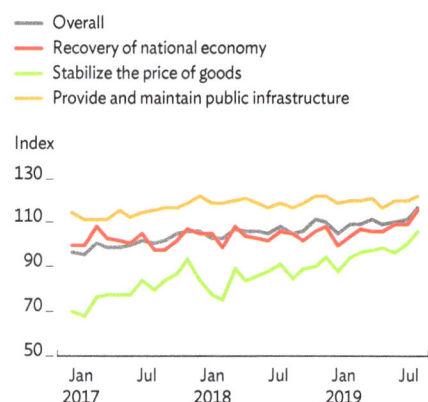

Note: Above 100 indicates optimism.
Source: Haver Analytics (accessed 4 September 2019).

The overall balance of payments is seen to remain in surplus, supported by both strong direct investment and portfolio inflows. Export-oriented foreign investment is expected to continue to strengthen, boosting tourism industries, base metal manufactures, and automobiles. Indonesia's large and growing domestic market should continue to attract foreign investment in e-commerce and the broader digital economy. The country's external payments position is thus seen to remain comfortable.

Fiscal policy is expected to remain accommodative, with 2019 likely to have a budget deficit slightly higher than the government's original target. Meanwhile, the budget proposed for next year remains prudent, keeping the deficit equal to 1.8% of GDP and prioritizing efficiency and quality in public spending.

Continued escalation in the trade conflict between the People's Republic of China and the US would further harm global trade, making it a key risk to the growth outlook above. If the trade conflict induces fresh volatility in international financial markets, it could reverse capital flows into emerging market economies like Indonesia, upsetting investment plans.

Figure 3.4.12 Contribution to total credit growth in commercial and rural banks

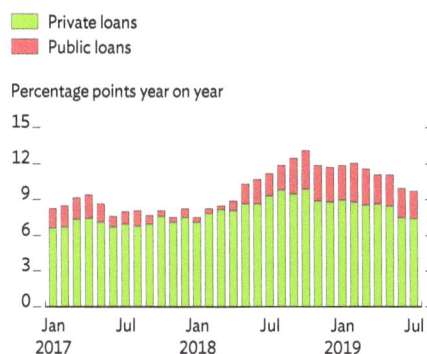

Sources: Haver Analytics (accessed 4 September 2019).

Malaysia

Developments in the first half of 2019 suggest that GDP growth in 2019 will align with the *ADO 2019* forecast in April for a slight dip this year. Inflation is no longer expected to accelerate, and the current account surplus will widen much more than earlier projected. In 2020, growth should strengthen somewhat, as forecast in *ADO 2019*. Inflation is seen picking up next year but less than forecast in April, and the wider current account surplus will persist.

Updated assessment

In the first half of 2019, GDP growth moderated from 4.9% a year earlier to 4.7% as exports weakened and investment continued to contract, more than offsetting buoyant consumption (Figure 3.4.13). After growing by 2.5% by volume in the first half of last year, exports of goods and services nearly stagnated in the first half of 2019 with weakening growth in global output and trade, especially in electronics.

Meanwhile, domestic investment deepened its declining trend from 2.6% contraction in the first half of last year to 4.7% in the corresponding period of this year. Growth in private investment slowed from 3.4% to 1.2% as firms and investors continued to wait on the sidelines for greater clarity on government policy direction. Public investment, having contracted by 5.4% in the first half of 2018, plunged by 11.3% in the first half of the same period of this year as several large infrastructure projects were put on hold.

The adverse effects of the slowdown in exports and investment were cushioned to some extent by accelerating growth in domestic consumption, both private and public. While rising incomes and buoyant employment helped private consumption to improve upon its 7.2% increase in the first half of last year to 7.7% this year, higher public spending on pensions and gratuities pushed growth in government consumption up from 1.8% to 3.2%.

By sector, slowing industry and services more than offset acceleration in agriculture (Figure 3.4.14). A slump in construction—as the government reevaluated and renegotiated many infrastructure projects agreed by the previous administration—continued to drag down industry growth, from 3.4% in the first half of 2018 to 2.8% a year later. Growth in services edged down from 6.5% to 6.3%. By contrast, agriculture recovered from near stagnation in the first half of last year to grow by 4.9% as better weather pushed up palm oil yield and output.

Slower growth and the removal last year of a goods and services tax nudged inflation down from an average of 1.5% in the first 7 months of 2018 to a scant 0.4% a year later (Figure 3.4.15). Core inflation, which excludes food and fuel, was higher but still only 0.7%.

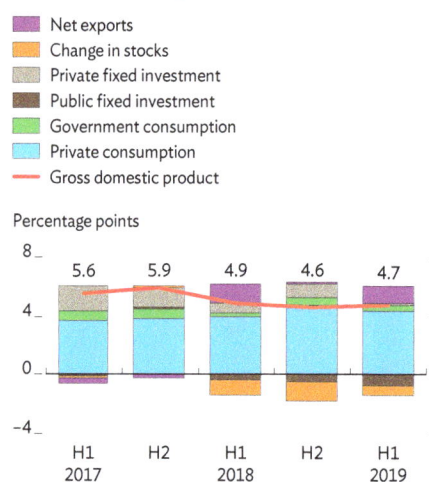

Figure 3.4.13 Demand-side contributions to growth

Net exports
Change in stocks
Private fixed investment
Public fixed investment
Government consumption
Private consumption
Gross domestic product

H = half.
Sources: Haver Analytics; Bank Negara Malaysia. 2019. Monthly Statistical Bulletin. August. http://www.bnm.gov.my (accessed 30 August 2019).

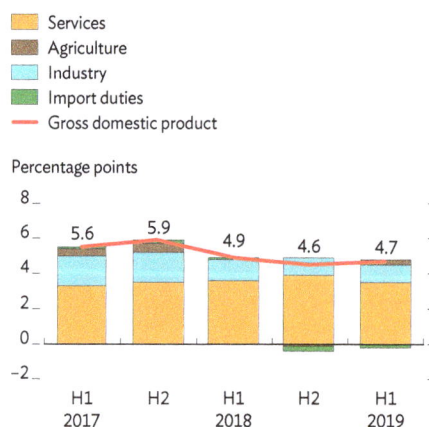

Figure 3.4.14 Supply-side contributions to growth

Services
Agriculture
Industry
Import duties
Gross domestic product

H = half.
Sources: Haver Analytics; Bank Negara Malaysia. 2019. Monthly Statistical Bulletin. August. http://www.bnm.gov.my (accessed 30 August 2019).

As global trade took a hit from persistent trade conflict between the US and the People's Republic of China (PRC), the dollar value of Malaysia's merchandise exports contracted by 4.4% in the first 6 months of 2019, reversing 15.0% growth in the year-earlier period. Merchandise imports similarly contracted by 4.9% against a 13.1% rise a year earlier (Figure 3.4.16). With a slump in domestic investment, capital goods imports contracted by 9.1% in the first half of the year from a 4.4% drop in the corresponding period a year earlier. The trade surplus fell as a result, but only slightly, from $15.3 billion in the first half of 2018 to $15.1 billion in the first half of this year.

With an improvement in net service exports, the current account surplus rose sharply from $4.2 billion in the first half of 2018 to $7.4 billon a year later, swelling as a share of GDP from 2.3% to 4.2% (Figure 3.4.17). With higher inflows of foreign direct investment (FDI) but larger portfolio capital outflows, the financial account of the balance of payments recorded a deficit of $32.4 billion, equal to 4.4% of GDP. International reserves stood at $102.7 billion at the end of June 2019, equal to 1.2 times short-term external debt and providing cover for 7.3 months imports.

With growth moderating but still robust, the government continued to pursue its recently initiated fiscal consolidation program. Trends in the first half of the year put it on track to meet its target for 2019 of a fiscal deficit equal to 3.4% of GDP. Revenue increased by 17.8% to reach 48.1% of the full-year target, and expenditure grew by 7.6% to reach 47.2% of the full-year target. While the government's operating expenditure grew by 5.9%, development expenditure was up by 17.9%, largely from higher social spending. The net result was a first-half fiscal deficit of RM22.4 billion, equal to 3.1% of GDP.

Monetary policy in the first half of the year continued to be accommodative, as envisaged in *ADO 2019*. In May 2019, Bank Negara Malaysia, the central bank, reduced its policy rate by 25 basis points to 3.00% in response to concerns about rising trade tensions, deepening uncertainty about the global and domestic economic environment, and weaker commodity prices.

Prospects

As an economy highly dependent on trade, Malaysia can expect to see its near-term growth prospects dragged down by the persistent US–PRC trade conflict. Exports will likely continue to languish, though over the longer term the country may benefit from production relocating from the PRC. In any case, domestic demand should hold up and continue to support the economy, as in the first half of this year. GDP growth is therefore likely to meet *ADO 2019* forecasts of a small dip to 4.5% this year, returning to 4.7% growth in 2020 (Figure 3.4.18).

Figure 3.4.15 Inflation and policy rate

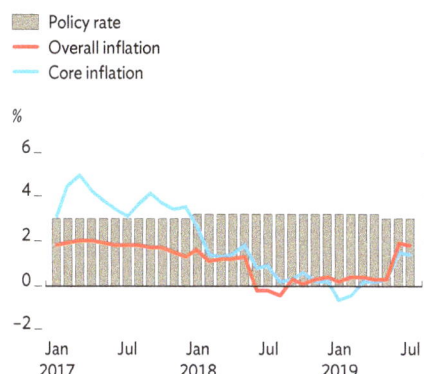

Sources: Haver Analytics; Bank Negara Malaysia. 2019. Monthly Highlights and Statistics. September. http://www.bnm.gov.my (accessed 4 September 2019).

Figure 3.4.16 Growth in imports

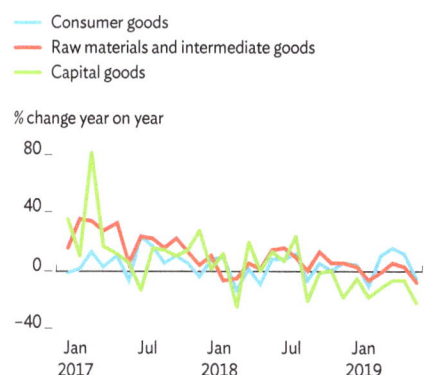

Source: Haver Analytics (accessed 3 September 2019).

Figure 3.4.17 Current account balance components

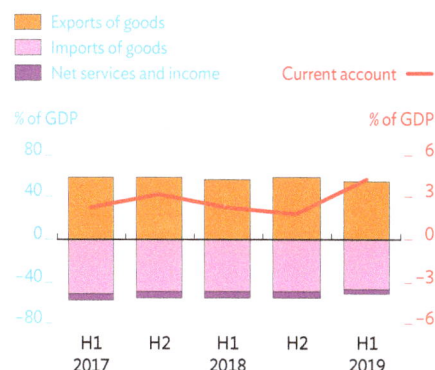

H = half.
Source: Haver Analytics (accessed 4 September 2019).

Growth in private consumption is expected to remain robust in the near term but moderate in the second half as benefits from the removal in June 2018 of the goods and services tax wane. A low unemployment rate should underpin continued consumer spending, but slower wage growth this year could start to constrain consumption. Consumer sentiment has been on a downward trend, which could further weaken private consumption. Growth in domestic investment will likely be weak this year but pick up in 2020 from the resumption of large public infrastructure projects such as the East Coast Railway Link. Although the cost of this project has been brought down from RM65.5 billion to RM44.0 billion through renegotiation with the PRC, it is still a large infrastructure project with potential to significantly lift the economy. Malaysia is also embarking on its $5.2 billion National Fiberization and Connection Plan, which will improve the quality of high-speed internet throughout the country and may spur the development of new industries. The resumption of infrastructure spending promises to attract more private investment. Investment should benefit as well from a pickup in FDI disbursement in the near term following a near doubling of FDI approvals in the first half of this year over a year earlier, to $6.1 billion. Interest was particularly strong from US manufacturers. In the first half of 2019, FDI manufacturing approvals from the US jumped to $2.8 billion from just $0.8 billion in the whole of 2018.

By sector, growth in agriculture should pick up in the near term as palm oil yields and production return to trend following last year's huge downturn. Industry should achieve slightly higher growth this year than was foreseen in *ADO 2019* from improved mining and quarrying output as liquified natural gas production normalizes after supply disruption last year. The large Refinery and Petrochemical Integrated Development project is expected to become operational next year, and its designed refining capacity of 300,000 barrels per day should help industry expand. Services will likely fall a bit short of 5.8% growth envisaged earlier but nevertheless continue to post robust growth. Strong domestic consumption should keep demand healthy for services in a range of business lines, from hotels and restaurants to transport and communications.

Because consumer prices hardly rose at all in the first half of the year, inflation for the whole of 2019 is no longer seen doubling from 2018, as was forecast in *ADO 2019*. In the second half of the year, some upward inflationary pressure is likely to come from the removal of a price ceiling on domestic fuel. Inflation forecasts are now revised down to a steady 1.0% in 2019, rising to 2.0% next year (Figure 3.4.19).

Table 3.4.2 Selected economic indicators, Malaysia (%)

	2019		2020	
	ADO 2019	Update	ADO 2019	Update
GDP growth	4.5	4.5	4.7	4.7
Inflation	2.0	1.0	2.7	2.0
Current acct. bal. (share of GDP)	2.4	3.5	2.4	3.5

Source: ADB estimates.

Figure 3.4.18 GDP growth

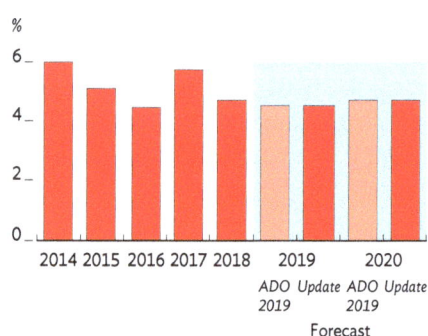

Source: *Asian Development Outlook* database.

Figure 3.4.19 Inflation

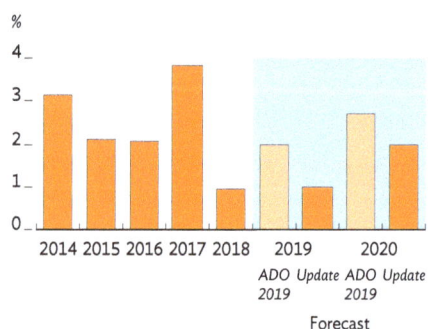

Source: *Asian Development Outlook* database.

The weakening global environment threatens to continue to weigh on exports, as it did in the first half of the year, though the effects will likely be cushioned somewhat by the resumption of liquefied natural gas exports after last year's supply disruption and higher palm oil shipments (Figure 3.4.20). As exports retreat, imports will decelerate as well, widening the current account surplus. The surplus is now seen rising this year to the equivalent of 3.5% of GDP, well above 2.4% as forecast in *ADO 2019*, and staying that high in 2020.

Modest inflation and a continued healthy current account surplus should enable the central bank to pursue an accommodative monetary policy even as the government pursues fiscal consolidation. In May 2019, the central bank cut its policy interest rate by 25 basis points to 3.00%, which was seen as a preemptive move to keep a deteriorating global economic environment from undermining growth in Malaysia. With little upward pressure on prices, room exists for further policy rate cuts.

The economic outlook over the near term is clouded by external risks stemming from the US–PRC trade conflict and the possibility of further escalation. That risk would be magnified if regional and international financial markets become much more volatile. Over the longer term, though, Malaysia could actually benefit from the trade conflict as production relocates from the PRC to other economies in the region. A key domestic risk over the short term is persistent weakening in domestic investment.

Figure 3.4.20 Growth in exports

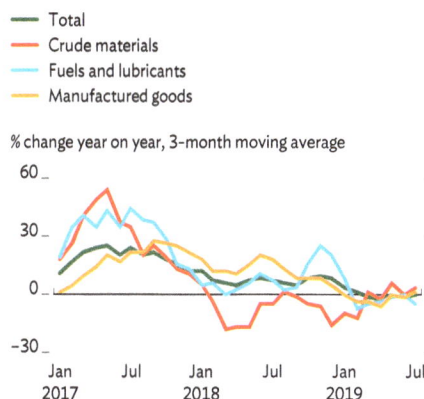

Source: Haver Analytics (accessed 3 September 2019).

Philippines

Economic growth is now seen to be slightly lower than foreseen in *ADO 2019*, reflecting a slowdown in the global economy and in domestic investment. With domestic private consumption holding up well and accommodative fiscal and monetary policies, economic growth should recover in the near term. Moderating growth is also seen to be accompanied by lower inflation and narrower current account deficits than forecast in *ADO 2019*.

Updated assessment

GDP growth moderated from 6.3% year on year in the first half of 2018 to 5.5% in the first half of 2019, indicating that the Philippine economy may have entered a phase in its business cycle when growth is expected to temporarily ease (Figure 3.4.21). Although private consumption continued to expand robustly, it was more than offset by a slowdown in domestic investment and weakening exports.

Private consumption sustained strong 5.8% growth, the same rate as in the first half of 2018, and made the largest demand-side contribution to GDP growth. Higher wage employment and remittances from overseas workers sustained consumption. The unemployment rate was low at 5.4% in July 2019, unchanged from a year earlier, but with about 700,000 jobs for wage workers added in the 12-month period. Remittances rose by 2.9% in the first half to reach $16.2 billion, equal to 9.6% of GDP. Meanwhile, real growth in government consumption slowed from 12.6% in the first half of 2018 to 7.1% a year later, largely because of a delay in passing the 2019 budget (Figure 3.4.22).

Domestic investment, after rising by a hefty annual average rate of 14.0% in the 5 years from 2014 to 2018, and by 14.9% year on year in the first half of last year, plateaued in the first half of this year. Public construction plunged by 22.1%, reversing double-digit expansion in recent years. Private construction accelerated by 16.7%, while investment in machinery and equipment declined by 2.9% mainly because of falling investment in transport equipment. These factors caused overall investment to fall by 0.1% in the first half, with contraction deepening to 8.5% in the second quarter.

Weaker external demand trimmed real growth in exports of goods and services in the first half of the year from 12.6% a year earlier to 5.0%. As export growth slowed, so did import growth. Real growth in imports of goods and services decelerated from 16.1% to 4.2%, partly reflecting subdued demand for raw materials and components for export-oriented manufacturing, as well as for capital goods at a time of weak domestic investment.

Figure 3.4.21 Demand-side contributions to growth

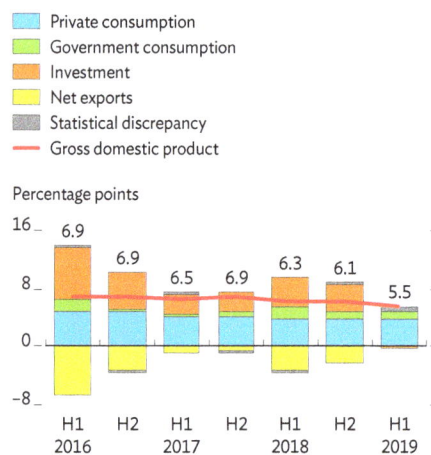

Sources: *Asian Development Outlook* database; CEIC Data Company (accessed 6 September 2019).

Figure 3.4.22 Growth in government spending

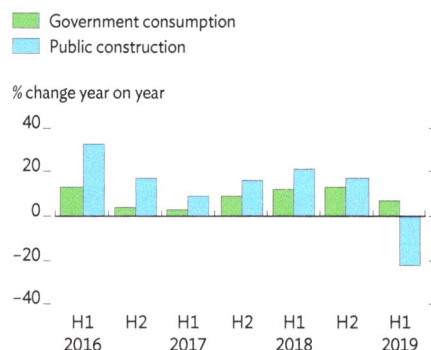

Source: CEIC Data Company (accessed 6 September 2019).

The plateauing of domestic investment was caused mainly by contraction in public spending on infrastructure in the first half and relatively high interest rates. The delayed passage of the 2019 national budget and a ban on public infrastructure spending in the run-up to midterm elections in May 2019 held back public expenditure, narrowing the fiscal deficit from the equivalent of 2.3% of GDP in the first half of 2018 to 0.5%. Excluding interest payments, the primary fiscal balance reversed from a deficit equal to 0.3% of GDP a year earlier to a surplus of 1.6% in the first half of 2019.

Growth acceleration in services was offset by a slowdown in industry. Service output growth rose from 6.7% in the first half of 2018 to 7.0% in the first half of this year and contributed nearly three-fourths of GDP growth (Figure 3.4.23). Expansion was broadly based across service segments, including retail trade, financial and real estate services, and business process outsourcing. Hotels and transport gained from buoyant tourism.

Industry growth slowed from 7.1% to 4.2% with moderation in manufacturing and falling public construction (Figure 3.4.24). Manufacturing growth was, at 4.4%, the slowest recorded in several years, weighed down by sluggish external demand, though it still contributed nearly a fifth of GDP growth. Communications equipment, the largest segment after food processing, declined. Other segments such as food and beverages, chemicals, metal products, and electrical machinery posted gains thanks to domestic demand. Private construction accelerated by 16.7%, more than double the pace a year earlier, partly countering the decline in public construction. Overall, industry contributed one-fourth of GDP expansion. Meanwhile, agriculture was again nearly stagnant with 0.7% growth, as drought under El Niño compounded long-term structural impediments to sector productivity and growth.

Moderating growth was accompanied by lower inflation as the effects of monetary tightening last year lowered inflation expectations and better domestic rice supplies brought lower rice prices. Average inflation in the first 8 months of the year decelerated from 4.7% a year earlier to 3.0% (Figure 3.4.25). By August of this year, inflation year on year had fallen further to 1.7%. Rice prices have declined on improved supply since the lifting of quantitative restrictions on rice imports in February of this year. Domestic fuel prices also softened in line with global oil prices. Meanwhile, core inflation averaged 3.6% in the first 8 months of the year and decelerated to 2.9% year on year in August, indicating that inflation expectations were easing, thanks in part to measures to improve domestic supplies of rice and other agricultural commodities. Monetary tightening in 2018, as Bangko Sentral ng Pilipinas, the central bank, raised its policy interest rate by a cumulative 175 basis points, also eased inflationary pressure by reining in credit expansion.

Figure 3.4.23 Supply-side contributions to growth

Agriculture
Industry
Services
Gross domestic product

Percentage points

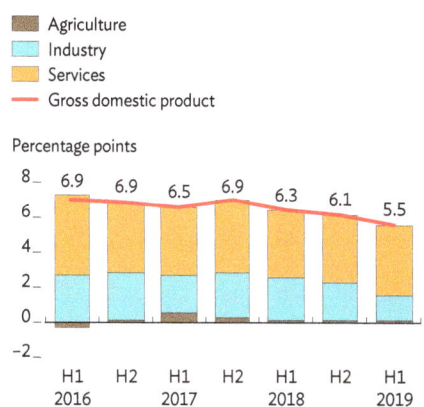

H = half.
Source: CEIC Data Company (accessed 6 September 2019).

Figure 3.4.24 Growth in construction

Public
Private

% change year on year

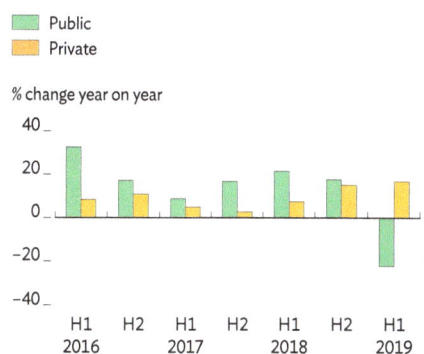

H = half.
Source: CEIC Data Company (accessed 6 September 2019).

Figure 3.4.25 Inflation and interest rate

Overnight reverse repurchase rate
Headline inflation
Core inflation

%

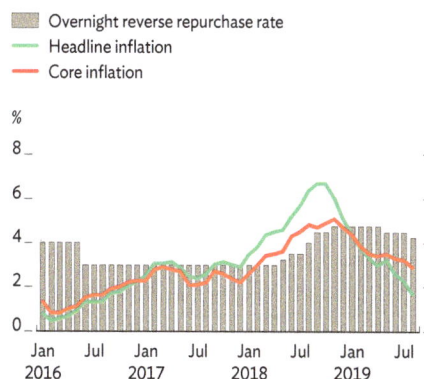

Source: CEIC Data Company (accessed 6 September 2019).

Domestic liquidity (M3) grew by 6.7% year on year in July, sharply down from 11.1% in July 2018, while growth in credit to the private sector slowed from 16.8% a year earlier to 6.8% (Figure 3.4.26).

Delayed passage of the 2019 budget and a ban on public spending during midterm elections in May caused public expenditure excluding interest to contract by 1.9% in the first half of the year. This fell short of the budget allocation by 8.2%, with spending on public infrastructure projects below the budget by 20.7%. Revenue, on the other hand, rose by 9.7% in large part through higher tax collection. These trends in revenue and expenditure narrowed the fiscal deficit in the first half of the year to the equivalent of 0.5% of GDP, well below the 3.2% deficit ceiling for the full year.

The current account deficit in the first half of 2019 narrowed sharply from the equivalent of 2.4% of GDP a year earlier to 1.0%. Merchandise exports and imports both remained nearly flat as exports declined by 0.1% and imports rose by 0.3%. With GDP growth, the merchandise trade deficit narrowed from the equivalent of 14.7% of GDP to 13.9%. Higher remittances and earnings from exports of services partly cushioned the merchandise trade deficit. In the financial account, foreign direct investment net inflow amounted to $3.6 billion in the first half of the year, but this was 38.8% down from a year earlier. Meanwhile, portfolio investment posted net inflow, reversing net outflow a year earlier. The overall balance of payments surplus was $4.8 billion, turning around a $3.3 billion deficit in the first half of 2018.

Foreign exchange reserves stood at $84.9 billion in June, providing cover for more than 7 months of imports of goods and services and income payments. With external debt equal to 23.8% of GDP as of June 2019, most of it with medium- to long-term maturity, the external payments position remained strong.

Prospects

Against the backdrop of weakening global economic outlook, forecasts for GDP growth are revised down from 6.4% for both years in *ADO 2019* to 6.0% for this year and 6.2% for 2020 (Figure 3.4.27). The revised forecasts are premised on recovery in investment, both public and private. This requires that fiscal and monetary policies become more accommodative.

After delays in the first half of the year, government spending should rebound beginning in the second half. Expenditure under the 2020 budget is 12.0% higher than in the 2019 budget, with higher spending in particular on infrastructure, social services, and income transfers to poor households. Public and private investment should regain traction as new and larger infrastructure projects get under way. The government is mobilizing more revenue to support

Figure 3.4.26 Monetary indicators

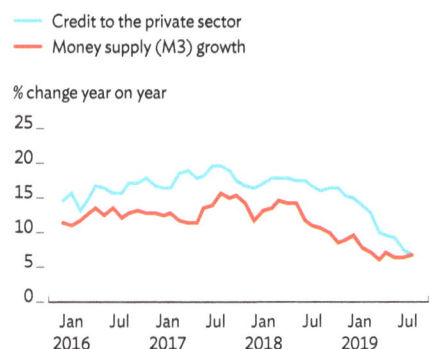

— Credit to the private sector
— Money supply (M3) growth

Source: CEIC Data Company (accessed 6 September 2019).

Table 3.4.3 Selected economic indicators, Philippines (%)

	2019		2020	
	ADO 2019	Update	ADO 2019	Update
GDP growth	6.4	6.0	6.4	6.2
Inflation	3.8	2.6	3.5	3.0
Current acct. bal. (share of GDP)	−2.3	−1.7	−2.4	−2.0

Source: ADB estimates.

Figure 3.4.27 GDP growth

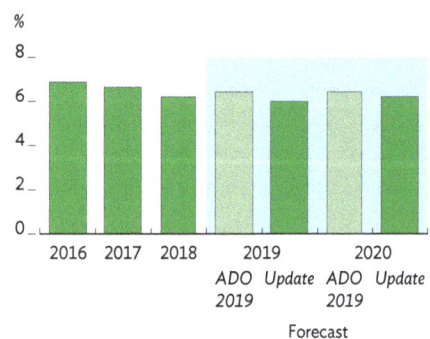

Source: *Asian Development Outlook* database.

public investment, while at the same time keeping the fiscal deficit within its fiscal program for 2020–2022, equal to 3.2% of GDP. The ratio of tax revenue to GDP improved from 14.2% in 2017 to 14.7% in 2018, helped by incremental revenue from the Tax Reform for Acceleration and Inclusion law enacted in December 2017. Another law passed in July 2019 imposes higher taxes on cigarettes. The government is pushing as well for higher taxes on alcoholic products and for other measures under its comprehensive program of tax reform.

Private consumption should continue to hold up well in the near term, helped by low unemployment, sustained growth in jobs in the formal sector, and moderate inflation. Also important to consumption are steady remittances from Philippine workers overseas, which continued to grow well in the year to July by 7.2% year on year. Recovery in government consumption could also reinforce private consumption.

Investor sentiment remains broadly positive. Bank lending to businesses continued to grow by 9.8% year on year in July. Private construction is sustained by continued strength in demand for homes and for office and retail space. Building permit approvals rose by 10.4% year on year in the first quarter of 2019. The latest central bank survey of business confidence showed business and consumer sentiment picking up.

By sector, the near term prospects for agriculture remain subdued by uncertain weather and longstanding structural impediments. Manufacturing, while drawing support from domestic consumption, is being buffeted by a slowdown in global trade and economic growth that is proving to be deeper than earlier projected. The Markit manufacturing purchasing managers' index was in the range of 51–52 in July and August, indicating a modest increase in production in the near term. A rebound in public infrastructure spending should lift construction.

Services should maintain the strong growth they showed in the first half of 2019. Buoyant private consumption will underpin retail trade, while growing international tourist arrivals, up by 11.4% year on year in the first half of 2019, should continue to benefit a range of service segments such as hotels and restaurants, transport, and communication.

Trends in the first half suggest that inflation is likely to average 2.6% in 2019 and 3.0% in 2020, both projections lower than *ADO 2019* forecasts and well within the central bank target range of 2%–4% (Figure 3.4.28). Stable global food and fuel prices should keep a lid on inflation.

The outlook for exports remains weak in light of lackluster economic prospects in major trade partners, including Japan, which accounts for 15% of exports, and the European Union, which accounts for 12%. As exports remain sluggish, imports of raw materials and of parts and components used mainly to manufacture exports should remain subdued too.

Figure 3.4.28 Inflation

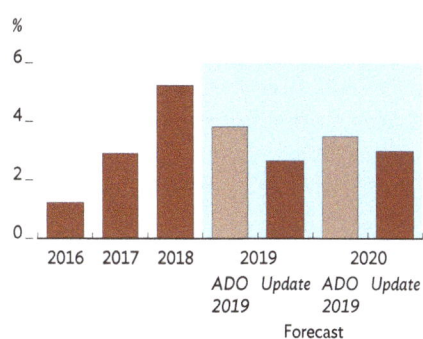

Source: *Asian Development Outlook* database.

However, continued strength in domestic consumption and a recovery in investment could accelerate imports of both consumer and capital goods. Strength in net service exports and remittances from overseas workers should continue to cushion the trade deficit somewhat (Figure 3.4.29). The current account deficit is expected to be narrower than foreseen earlier, equal to 1.7% of GDP in 2019 and 2.0% in 2020.

Fiscal and monetary policies are likely to be accommodative in light of moderating trends for both economic growth and inflation, as well as a strong external payments position. Ample room exists to further reduce policy interest rates and ease monetary and credit conditions in the near term. The proposed budget for 2020 targets a fiscal deficit equal to 3.2% of GDP, with expenditure budgeted at 19.9% of GDP and revenue at 16.7%. The planned deficit is likely to be higher than what will be realized this year following the delay in passing the 2019 budget.

Downside risks to the outlook stem from growth below expectations in the major industrial economies, which are among the Philippines' main sources of remittances and foreign direct investment, as well as its largest export markets. This risk is magnified by continued escalation in trade tensions between the US and the People's Republic of China. On the domestic front, growth prospects will hinge on how quickly the government can catch up on its public spending on infrastructure after the delays suffered in the first half of the year. Relaxing restrictions on foreign direct investment would help lift investment and economic growth over the longer term, as would developing a national competition policy to lower barriers to entry into the domestic market and to curtail anticompetitive practices.

Figure 3.4.29 Current account components

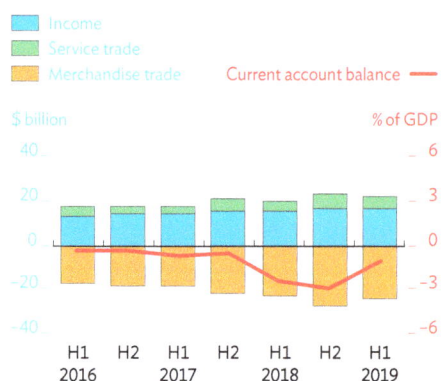

H = half.
Source: CEIC Data Company (accessed 15 September 2019).

Thailand

The economy is slowing more than anticipated in *ADO 2019*. Although domestic consumption is holding up well, unexpectedly weak exports and domestic fixed investment are now seen to drag down GDP growth this year and next, much more than what was foreseen in April. Meanwhile, trends in the first half suggest that inflation and the current account surplus are likely to align with *ADO 2019* forecasts.

Updated assessment

Shrinking exports and slowing fixed investment more than offset strengthening domestic consumption to drag down GDP growth from 4.8% year on year in the first half of 2018 to 2.6% in the same period of this year (Figure 3.4.30). Exports of goods and services contracted by 6.1% in volume terms, reversing 8.8% growth a year earlier as escalation in the trade conflict between the US and the People's Republic of China (PRC) slowed trade worldwide. Merchandise exports shrank by 4.1% in US dollar terms, down from 12.4% growth a year earlier. Exports contracted across the board, with electronics declining by 10.4%, machinery and equipment by 4.5%, and automobiles by 3.7%. Even earnings from agricultural exports declined with lower exports of rice, rubber, and tapioca.

Adding to the economic woes of export contraction, growth in domestic fixed investment weakened from 3.5% in the first half of 2018 to 2.6% in the first half of this year. While private fixed investment maintained robust growth at 3.3%, public investment increased by a paltry 0.6% (Figure 3.4.31). Contracting exports and weakening fixed investment were partly offset, however, by strengthening domestic consumption. Supported by rising wages, low inflation, and government welfare programs, growth in private consumption accelerated from 4.0% a year earlier to 4.6%. Government consumption held up well thanks mainly to higher spending on social transfers and a continuing rise in government employee compensation.

Growth slowed across sectors in the first half of the year. Agriculture stagnated as drought and erratic rainfall reduced rice and sugarcane harvests. Falling export demand and weakening fixed investment dragged down growth in industry from 2.9% year on year in the first half of 2018 to 1.2%. Export-oriented industry saw a bigger drop than did industry producing goods mainly for the domestic market. A significant slowdown in international tourist arrivals cut growth in services from 5.7% to 4.0% (Figure 3.4.32).

Slowing growth and stable international oil prices kept a lid on already low inflation. In the first 7 months of 2019, headline inflation edged down from an average of 1.0% a year earlier to 0.9%, and core inflation fell from 0.7% at 0.6% (Figure 3.4.33).

Figure 3.4.30 Demand-side contributions to growth

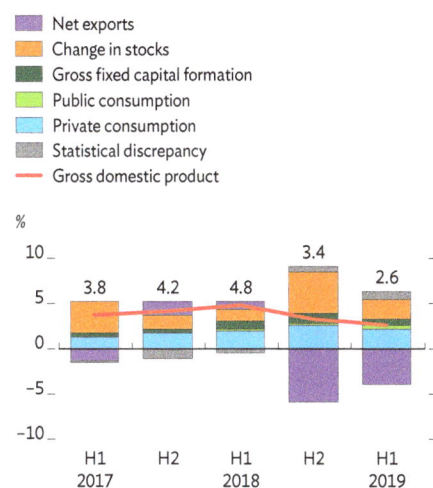

Net exports
Change in stocks
Gross fixed capital formation
Public consumption
Private consumption
Statistical discrepancy
Gross domestic product

H = half.
Source: Office of the National Economic and Social Development Council, http://www.nesdb.go.th (accessed 22 August 2019).

Figure 3.4.31 Fixed investment growth

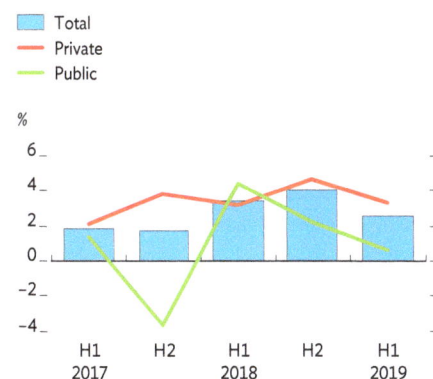

Total
Private
Public

H = half.
Source: Office of the National Economic and Social Development Council, http://www.nesdb.go.th (accessed 22 August 2019).

Inflation thus fell short of the lower bound of the target range of 1.0%–4.0% set by the Bank of Thailand, the central bank.

Imports of goods and services declined by 1.4% in the first half of 2019, reversing 9.0% expansion a year earlier as imports of raw materials and intermediate goods for export-oriented production were held back by export contraction, and as imports of capital goods stalled under weakening fixed investment. Merchandise imports fell by 3.1% in US dollar terms, marking a steep plunge from 16.7% growth a year earlier. The trade surplus thus moderated in the first half of the year from $13.8 billion a year earlier to $12.2 billion (Figure 3.4.34). With lower net service and primary income receipts, the current account surplus narrowed from $20.9 billion at the end of June 2018, equal 8.2% of GDP, to $17.4 billion a year later, or 6.6% of GDP.

The capital and financial accounts of the balance of payments dropped from net inflow of $13.2 billion in the first half of 2018 to net outflow of $8.4 billion in the first half of this year as domestic firms boosted their investment abroad. The surplus in the overall balance of payments slipped from $7.6 billion to $5.6 billion. Foreign exchange reserves at the end of June 2019 nevertheless stood at a healthy $215.8 billion, cover for nearly 12 months of imports, or 3.5 times Thailand's short-term foreign debt.

With the external payments position still comfortable, the central bank cut its policy rate, the 1-day bilateral repurchase rate, by 25 basis points to 1.50% in August 2019. Meanwhile, the government ran a fiscal deficit equal to 3.3% of GDP in the first 9 months of fiscal year 2019 (ending 30 September 2019), which was much lower than the 4.1% deficit a year earlier despite slowing growth and low and stable inflation. Government revenue collection in the first 9 months of the fiscal year was 3.3% above the official target, and expenditure was 2.3% higher. Public debt remained low at the equivalent of 40.5% of GDP at the end of June 2019, almost all of it domestic.

Prospects

Although growth is expected to pick up somewhat in the second half of 2019, the forecast for the whole year is for growth to fall from 4.1% in 2018 to 3.0% (Figure 3.4.35). It should recover to 3.2% next year, which is still half a percentage point lower than forecast in April. Subdued growth will be accompanied by tepid annual inflation at 1.0% this year and next, the forecast unchanged from *ADO 2019*. Forecasts for the current account surplus are also unchanged.

Weak external demand will continue in the near term as the US–PRC trade conflict drags on and perhaps even escalates, damaging global trade. Thailand's exports of goods and services, forecast in *ADO 2019* to grow by 5.0% annually to the forecast horizon, are now expected to contract by 3.5% this year

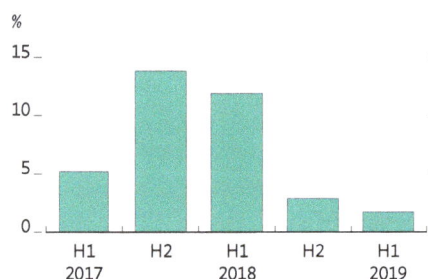

Figure 3.4.32 Growth in tourist arrivals

H = half.
Source: CEIC Data Company (accessed 4 September 2019).

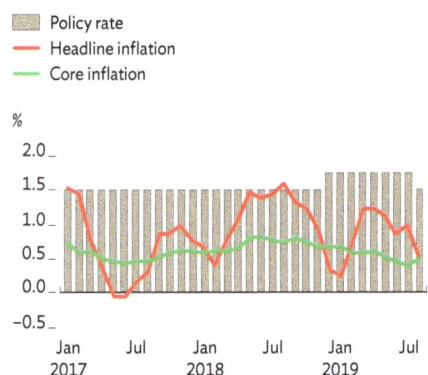

Figure 3.4.33 Inflation and policy interest rate

Source: CEIC Data Company (accessed 4 September 2019).

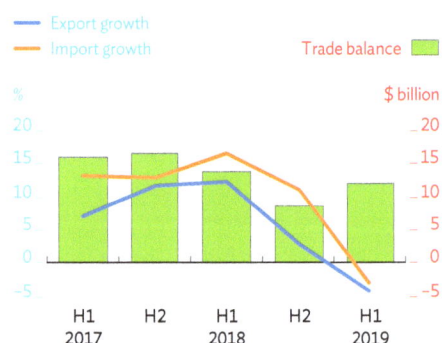

Figure 3.4.34 Trade indicators

H = half.
Source: Bank of Thailand. http://www.bot.or.th (accessed 4 September 2019).

and 3.0% next year. Merchandise exports, likewise previously expected to grow by 5.0% annually, are now seen to remain nearly stagnant in US dollar terms both this year and next.

Fixed investment should, as in the first half, sustain growth for the rest of this year, before accelerating somewhat in 2020. Public investment is expected to pick up next year as public infrastructure projects now being proposed reach the construction stage next year. Headwinds from the global economic slowdown are likely to reduce firms' capacity utilization in the rest of this year and limit the need for new investment to raise capacity. That said, private investment should pick up gradually beginning late this year or early next year, as foreshadowed by a jump in investment approvals in the first half of 2019 and suggested by the possibility of multinational firms relocating their production facilities from the PRC to countries not targeted by US tariff hikes, including Thailand. Indeed, in the first half of 2019, the value of foreign applications for investment promotion under the Board of Investment more than doubled year on year to nearly B150 billion, led by a strong increase for projects located in the Eastern Economic Corridor, a massive government-led development program in the provinces of Chachoengsao, Chonburi, and Rayong.

Private consumption is forecast to sustain annual growth at 5.0% this year and next, supported by low unemployment and inflation, easy monetary and credit conditions, and recently announced policy measures to shore up domestic consumption. In August 2019, the government announced additional allowances worth B20 billion to holders of state welfare smartcards. In addition, an estimated 4.6 million welfare recipients and 5.0 million elderly will receive an additional B500 allowance monthly in August and September. Parents who care for children will receive an extra B300 for each child in each month.

By sector, agriculture is expected to show a strong increase in 2020 as it recovers from the unfavorable weather this year. Manufacturing will continue to be hampered by weak global demand, though domestic-oriented industries are expected to do better as domestic demand holds up well in the face of weakening external demand. The service sector is now expected to grow by about 4% annually this year and next. Recently announced government measures to provide Thai domestic travelers with B1,000 in spending money and a 15% cash rebate on tourism-related spending, up to B30,000, can help offset the adverse effects of softening international tourist arrivals.

As growth weakens, inflation will remain low at 1.0% this year and next, as forecast in *ADO 2019*, skirting the lower bound of the central bank's target range (Figure 3.4.36).

Figure 3.4.35 GDP growth

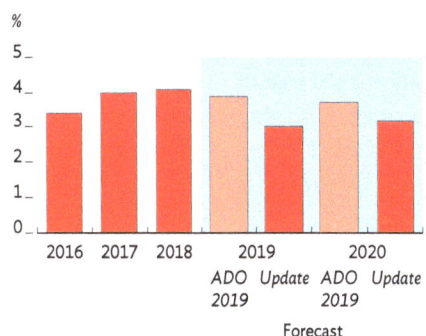

Source: *Asian Development Outlook* database.

Table 3.4.4 Selected economic indicators, Thailand (%)

	2019		2020	
	ADO 2019	Update	ADO 2019	Update
GDP growth	3.9	3.0	3.7	3.2
Inflation	1.0	1.0	1.0	1.0
Current acct. bal. (share of GDP)	7.0	7.0	7.0	7.0

Source: ADB estimates.

Figure 3.4.36 Inflation

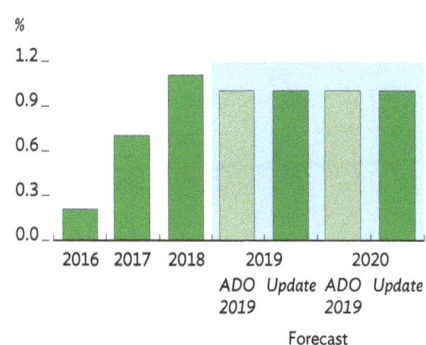

Source: *Asian Development Outlook* database.

With global commodity prices stable, little upward pressure on inflation is likely to arise from the supply side.

As imports soften alongside contracting exports, the current account surplus is expected to remain in line with the *ADO 2019* forecasts, equal to 7.0% of GDP both this year and next (Figure 3.4.37). Add the possibility of production facilities relocating from the PRC to Thailand, foreign direct investment could pick up gradually. The outlook for portfolio inflows is also positive, as Thailand is seen as a safe haven in Southeast Asia. The overall balance of payments should therefore improve, adding to the country's already large foreign exchange reserves.

Slow growth and inflation leave room for a further easing of monetary policy. As the government has recently shown itself to be a proactive supporter of economic growth, further fiscal stimulus can be expected if the global economy takes an unexpected turn for the worse. Public infrastructure spending is expected to gather momentum with project implementation speeding up. The fiscal deficit for 2019 is forecast to be slightly above the government's original target, equal to 3.0% of GDP.

Continued escalation of the US–PRC trade conflict is a major external risk to the outlook in the near term because it could further damage global trade and Thailand's highly trade-dependent economy. A domestic risk to the outlook would be unexpected delays in implementing planned big-ticket infrastructure projects.

Figure 3.4.37 Current account balance

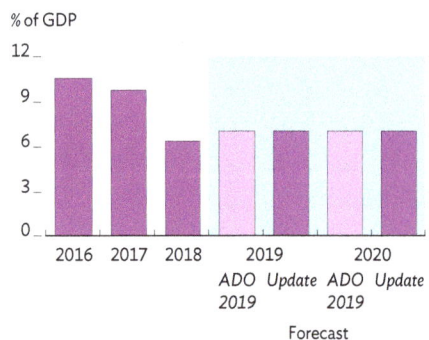

Source: *Asian Development Outlook* database.

Viet Nam

Trends in the first half of the year support *ADO 2019* forecasts for moderate deceleration this year and next following exceptionally high growth in 2018. However, inflation is now projected to slow in 2019, and the projection for 2020 is also revised down. The current account surplus is now forecast to narrow in both years more than projected in April. Despite a slowdown in exports, the economy remains broadly healthy thanks to resilient domestic demand and sustained inflows of foreign direct investment (FDI).

Updated assessment

GDP growth moderated from 7.0% in the first half of 2018 to 6.8% in the corresponding period of this year. On the demand side, as external demand weakened, volume growth in exports of goods and services slowed by more than half, from 15.7% in the first 6 months of 2018 to 7.1% a year later. The adverse effect of the export slowdown on GDP growth was well cushioned, however, by continued strength in domestic demand (Figure 3.4.38).

In the first half of the year, private consumption held up well as it expanded by 7.2%, the same rate as a year earlier, supported largely by rising incomes, buoyant employment, and moderate inflation. Meanwhile, domestic investment posted 7.1% growth, also matching the year-earlier rate as it was bolstered by a strengthening business environment, continued investor confidence, and strong inflows of FDI. The first 6 months of 2019 witnessed the establishment of 67,000 new companies, the highest half-yearly number recorded in 5 years. FDI disbursement is estimated to have risen by 8.1% in the first half of 2019 to reach $9.1 billion, equal 8.4% of GDP. Reflecting improved business sentiment, foreign equity investment nearly doubled in the first half of this year over the corresponding period in 2018, reaching $8.1 billion.

Growth moderated across the board in agriculture, industry, and services, but to varying degrees (Figure 3.4.39). Prolonged drought and a fresh outbreak of African swine fever dragged growth in agriculture down from 3.8% in the first half of 2018 to 2.4% a year later. Within agriculture, growth in farm production dropped sharply from 3.1% to 1.3%, and forestry output growth eased from 5.5% to 4.2%, while fisheries sustained strong 6.4% expansion.

Industry and construction performed well in the first half of the year, slipping only marginally from 9.1% growth in the first half of 2018 to 8.9%. Within industry, manufacturing growth slowed slightly to a still robust 11.2% as mining reversed 1.3% contraction in the first half of 2018 to grow by 1.8%. Construction sustained growth at a brisk 7.9%. Services similarly sustained growth at 6.7% as strong domestic demand offset a slowdown in international tourist arrivals from a whopping 27.2% rise in the first half of 2018 to 7.5% a year later (Figure 3.4.40). Banking and financial services posted impressive 8.0% growth in the first half of 2019.

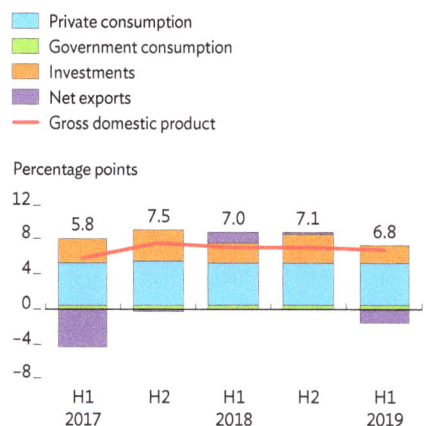

Figure 3.4.38 Demand-side contributions to growth

Private consumption
Government consumption
Investments
Net exports
Gross domestic product

Percentage points

H = half.
Source: General Statistics Office of Viet Nam.

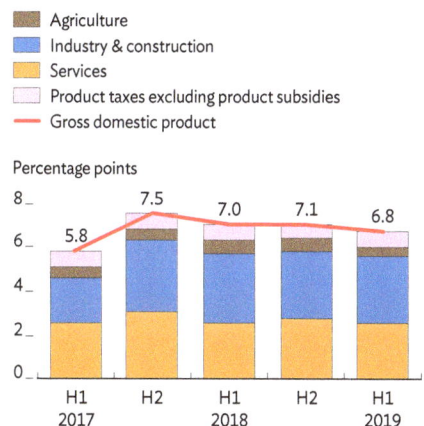

Figure 3.4.39 Supply-side contributions to growth

Agriculture
Industry & construction
Services
Product taxes excluding product subsidies
Gross domestic product

Percentage points

H = half.
Source: General Statistics Office of Viet Nam.

Figure 3.4.40 Visitor arrivals

Number   Growth

Million visitors   %

Source: General Statistics Office of Viet Nam.

Average inflation slowed from 3.3% in the first half of 2018 to 2.6% in the first half of this year, the lowest half-yearly average in 3 years (Figure 3.4.41). Subdued petroleum prices, slower monetary and credit growth, and a relatively stable exchange rate offset some of the inflationary pressure from a hike in administered prices for electricity and a rise in food prices.

In the external account, growth in merchandise exports slowed from 17.1% year on year in the first half of 2018 to 7.2% a year later. Growth in merchandise imports decelerated as well, but only from 10.7% to an estimated 8.9%, leaving the current account surplus to narrow by half, from the equivalent of 3.5% of GDP a year earlier to an estimated 1.7%. Meanwhile, the capital account posted a surplus estimated at 7.9% of GDP, bolstered by a rise in net FDI and net portfolio capital inflows. The overall balance of payments surplus, equal to 8.5% of GDP, was only slightly higher than 8.4% a year earlier (Figure 3.4.42). Foreign exchange reserves edged up in June 2019, providing cover for an estimated 3 months of imports.

Fiscal consolidation continued in the first half of 2019. Government revenues climbed from the equivalent of 28.7% of GDP in the first 6 months of last year to 30.0% in the corresponding period of 2019, while the ratio of expenditure to GDP dropped from 28.6% to 26.8%. As a result, the budget recorded a surplus equal to 3.2% of GDP in the first half of the year, sharply up from a marginal surplus of 0.1% in the corresponding months of 2018. Meanwhile, progress in reforming state-owned enterprises continued to lag. Against a government target to equitize 127 such enterprises from 2017 to 2020, only 34 had been equitized by May of this year.

Monetary and credit conditions remained prudent in the first half of the year as growth year on year in the money supply (M2) slowed from 16.6% a year earlier to an estimated 10.6%, and as growth in bank credit slowed from 15.7% to an estimated 14.2% (Figure 3.4.43).

The first half of this year witnessed progress in bank reform. The officially reported ratio of nonperforming loans (NPLs) to all loans on bank balance sheets declined from 2.1% in June 2018 to 1.9% in June 2019. At the same time, the ratio of all NPLs—adding to NPLs still held by banks those warehoused at the Viet Nam Assets Management Company and loans held by banks and considered at high risk of becoming troubled—declined from 6.9% in the middle of 2018 to 5.9% a year later. Moreover, modest progress was made toward a government target of all banks satisfying Basel II capital adequacy requirements by 2020. In July 2019, nine of 35 local banks already met them.

Figure 3.4.41 Monthly headline inflation

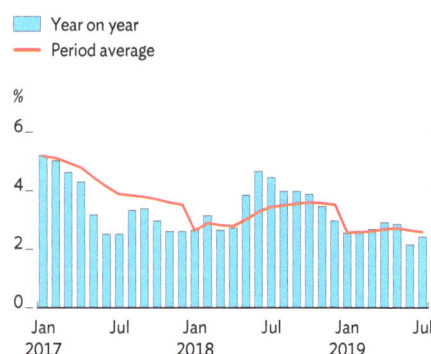

Source: General Statistics Office of Viet Nam.

Figure 3.4.42 Balance of payments indicators

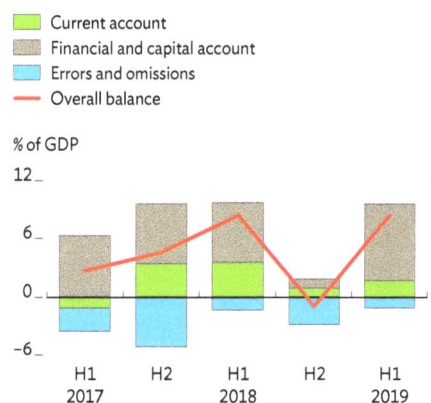

H = half.
Sources: State Bank of Viet Nam; International Monetary Fund; ADB estimates.

Figure 3.4.43 Credit and money supply growth

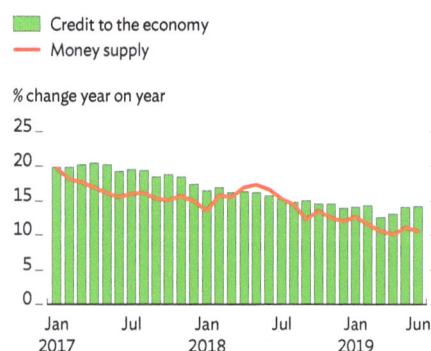

Sources: State Bank of Viet Nam; ADB estimates.

Prospects

As trade conflict persists between the People's Republic of China (PRC) and the US, and with the consequent weakening of global trade, export growth is forecast to slow in the near term. However, stronger domestic demand should offset weakening exports. GDP growth is thus expected to align with *ADO 2019* forecasts of 6.8% for this year and 6.7% for 2020 (Figure 3.4.44).

On the demand side, prospects for domestic consumption continue to be positive. Private consumption should benefit from moderate inflation, robust employment, and strong growth despite moderation. Continued government efforts to improve the business environment could, along with recent upward revisions to sovereign credit ratings, spur private investment. If the US–PRC trade conflict continues to escalate, more manufacturers may consider Viet Nam as an alternative base, providing fresh impetus to FDI inflows. The recent signing of a free trade agreement with the European Union promises to further open market access for trade and investment, as does the regional Comprehensive and Progressive Agreement for Trans-Pacific Partnership. FDI inflows should therefore continue to be strong in the near term, as evidenced by $13.1 billion in FDI commitments made in the first 8 months of 2019 (Figure 3.4.45). A recent amendment to the law governing public investment should improve public investment by accelerating processes and procedures and enabling faster disbursement of public investment.

By sector, the outlook for industry and services remains positive, but agriculture will likely continue to be sluggish. The manufacturing purchasing managers' index remained in the first 8 months of the year above 50, which bodes well for that industry (Figure 3.4.46). Mining output will continue to recover, and construction is forecast to sustain growth despite tightening credit for real estate. Services are seen to continue growing with further expansion in retail and wholesale trade to meet buoyant domestic demand, and with higher tourist arrivals, assuming they reach a target of 15 million by end of the year.

Forecasts for average inflation are revised down to 3.0% for 2019 and 3.5% for 2020 (Figure 3.4.47). Average inflation was contained at 2.6% year on year in the first 8 months of 2019, the lowest in 3 years. Inflationary pressure in the near term may come from upward adjustments to administered prices, buoyant domestic demand, higher minimum wages, and a possible increase in food prices caused by African swine fever and severe drought. This pressure may be countered, however, by slower money supply and credit growth.

Figure 3.4.44 Gross domestic product growth

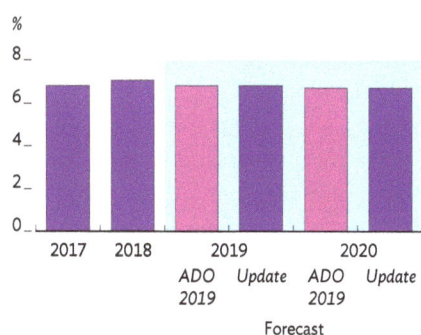

Source: *Asian Development Outlook* database.

Figure 3.4.45 Foreign direct investment

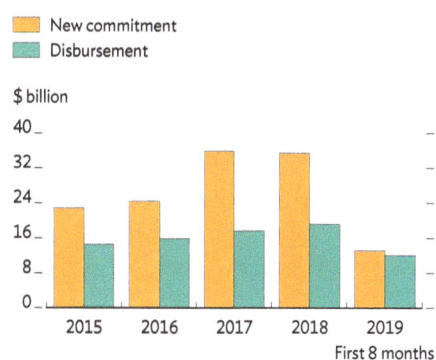

Source: General Statistics Office of Viet Nam.

Table 3.4.5 Selected economic indicators, Viet Nam (%)

	2019		2020	
	ADO 2019	*Update*	*ADO 2019*	*Update*
GDP growth	6.8	6.8	6.7	6.7
Inflation	3.5	3.0	3.8	3.5
Current acct. bal. (share of GDP)	2.5	2.0	2.0	1.8

Source: ADB estimates.

The current account surplus is now forecast to narrow more than projected in *ADO 2019* both this year and next. Export earnings are seen slowing more than earlier expected, even as imports slow less than foreseen because of robust domestic consumption and investment—especially with the prospect of some production facilities relocating from the PRC to Viet Nam. Remittances may suffer from the global economic slowdown, further undermining the surplus. The forecast for the current account surplus is revised down to the equivalent of 2.0% of GDP this year and 1.8% in 2020.

The government will continue to pursue fiscal consolidation. While disbursement on capital expenditure should speed up, the government is continuing its effort to strengthen revenue collection and impose much tighter controls on nonessential spending to contain the budget deficit and improve public debt sustainability. Despite only moderate inflation, prudent monetary policy will continue in 2019 and is foreseen holding credit growth within the government target of 14%. Banks are under continued pressure to meet Basel II requirements by 2020. Credit will thus continue to be discouraged for high-risk investments such as real estate.

Risks to the forecasts are significant. The major external risk would be further escalation of the US–PRC trade conflict and consequent shrinkage in global trade. If the trade conflict, heretofore waged mainly through tariff hikes, morphed into competitive currency devaluation, it would have broader repercussions on international financial markets and pose fresh risks to the Viet Nam economy.

Figure 3.4.46 Manufacturing purchasing managers' index

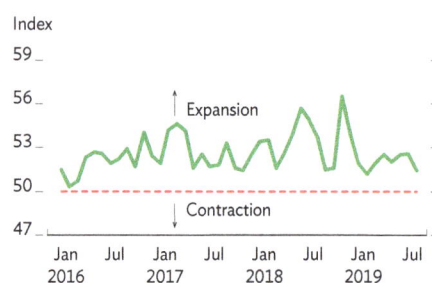

Note: Nikkei, Markit.
Source: Bloomberg (accessed 23 August 2019).

Figure 3.4.47 Inflation

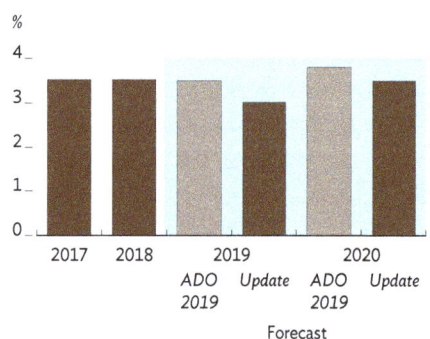

Source: *Asian Development Outlook* database.

Other economies

Brunei Darussalam

In the first quarter (Q1) of 2019, GDP contracted by 0.5% year on year as weaker domestic investment and exports more than offset consumption that exceeded expectations. Exports of goods and services declined by 3.2% by volume, disappointing earlier hopes for a major turnaround, while investment, having risen by a whopping 28.0% in 2018, grew by only 1.0% in Q1 of 2019. Private consumption was a bright spot in an otherwise gloomy view from the demand side, rising by 4.9% in Q1.

By sector, significant recovery in services in Q1 of 2019 was overwhelmed by declines in agriculture, continuing a trend from 2016, and industry, which contracted by 2.3%, largely reflecting a 2.5% decline in oil and gas and 3.3% shrinkage in construction. Within the oil and gas industry, liquefied natural gas and methanol output was down by 6.5%, and oil and gas mining contracted by 1.0%. Economic activity aside from petroleum and construction rose by 2.8%, lifted by 9.4% growth in financial services and wholesale and retail trade.

Unexpected strength in domestic consumption in Q1 should continue for the rest of the year. Further, Q1 weakness in domestic investment may reverse as the government continues to pursue economic diversification through a program of investment in priority areas like information and communication technology and downstream petroleum industries. Export volume should recover, especially in Q3 and Q4. Encouragingly, some major repairs to oil refineries begun in 2018 have recently reached completion, which should allow a steady rise in oil and natural gas production and exports. The newly built Hengyi refinery recently purchased a second batch of crude oil for production trials, suggesting that the facility may officially come online in Q3 of 2019, as long anticipated. In sum, the growth slowdown suffered in Q1 is likely to reverse in the remaining 3 quarters, yielding 1.0% GDP growth in 2019 as a whole, as forecast in *ADO 2019*.

Consumer prices declined by 0.5% year on year on average in the first 7 months of 2019, confounding an assertion in April that 0.1% inflation in 2018 signaled the country's emergence from a multiyear deflationary trend. Lower prices stemmed largely from unexpected weakness in international food prices, as Brunei Darussalam is a net food importer. The inflation forecast for 2019 is therefore lowered from 0.2% in *ADO 2019* to 0.1%.

In the first 6 months of the year, exports rose by 8.4% in US dollar terms, while imports rose by 11.1%. These trends materialized largely as foreseen in April. This *Update* therefore retains the *ADO 2019* forecast for a current account surplus equal to 13.0% of GDP this year and next.

Table 3.4.6 Selected economic indicators, Brunei Darussalam (%)

	2019		2020	
	ADO 2019	Update	ADO 2019	Update
GDP growth	1.0	1.0	1.5	1.5
Inflation	0.2	0.1	0.2	0.2
Current acct. bal. (share of GDP)	13.0	13.0	13.0	13.0

Source: ADB estimates.

Cambodia

The economy is on track to achieve growth forecasts made in *ADO 2019* in April, despite disappointing growth in agriculture. Inflation is even more subdued, but the current account deficit is no longer expected to narrow significantly either this year or next.

Drought in the first half of the year hindered crop and fishery output, prompting a downward revision to the forecast for growth in agriculture from 1.7% to 1.1% in 2019. Meanwhile, a surge in production of garments, footwear, and travel goods prompts forecast growth in industry to be upgraded from 10.1% in *ADO 2019* to 10.6%. Continued strength in tourism and in wholesale and retail trade should sustain recent buoyancy in services.

Cambodia has bucked a trend of slowing exports in Southeast Asia. Growth in merchandise exports rose from 14.3% in the first 5 months of 2018 to 21.8% in the same period this year. While exports to Europe rose by only 1.3%, exports to the US grew by 41.2%. Growth in international tourist arrivals moderated but was still strong at 11.2% in the first half of the year. Expansionary monetary and credit conditions should help services grow by 6.7% in 2019.

Despite strong growth, inflation slowed with lower fuel prices, domestic food price increases below expectations, and continuing high dollarization, with average consumer price inflation decelerating from 2.5% at the end of 2018 to 2.2% at the end of June 2019.

A surge in exports drove up imports of parts and components for export-oriented production, while strong growth and rising incomes fueled higher imports of consumer goods, and buoyant construction pushed up imports of materials. Merchandise imports therefore rose by a hefty 21.5% by dollar value in the first 5 months of the year, nearly matching a 24.5% increase a year earlier, with growth in imports of construction materials soaring by 68.2%.

The current account deficit likely widened in the first half of the year, despite the surge in exports and strong tourism receipts. Forecasts for current account deficits excluding official transfers are thus revised up, all but erasing previously forecast narrowing in both 2019 and 2020. Buoyed by solid foreign direct investment, the financial account should stay in surplus. Gross international reserves are expected to reach $12.3 billion by year-end, providing cover for 6 months of imports.

Trends in the first half of the year suggest that the fiscal deficit will be close to the budget target for the year, equal to 4.5% of GDP. Meanwhile, credit to the private sector was up by 26.4% year on year in June 2019, when bank lending for real estate was up by 37.2%, mortgages by 39.4%, and construction by 32.1%.

An external risk to the growth outlook in the near term is the possibility that the European Union will suspend, in part or in full, Cambodia's preferential trade status under the

Table 3.4.7 Selected economic indicators, Cambodia (%)

	2019		2020	
	ADO 2019	Update	ADO 2019	Update
GDP growth	7.0	7.0	6.8	6.8
Inflation	2.5	2.2	2.5	2.5
Current acct. bal. (share of GDP)	–12.7	–13.5	–11.8	–13.5

Source: ADB estimates.

Everything But Arms arrangement that it extends to least-developed economies. A domestic risk is a continued buildup of credit to real estate and related businesses.

Lao People's Democratic Republic

The economy likely slowed in the first half of 2019. Although agriculture may have recovered somewhat from last year's flood-induced slowdown, slowing growth in international tourist arrivals and near stagnation in exports, electricity generation, money supply, and credit suggest that industry and services both softened in the half.

In the first 4 months of the year, merchandise exports, having soared by 20.5% in dollar terms in the same months of 2018, essentially stagnated as annual growth in electricity generation, a key export, slowed from 7.0% a year earlier to a paltry 2.3%. These trends indicate that industry growth slowed in the first half of the year, and contraction in mining output is thought to have deepened. Meanwhile, growth in international tourist arrivals, a proxy for the service sector, slowed from 6.1% in the first 6 months of 2018 to 5.0% in the same period this year. Monetary and credit conditions remained tight, as shown by growth in money supply by only 3.9% in the first quarter and credit growth at 3.1%.

Inflation averaged 2.1% in the first 7 months of the year, driven largely by a 4.3% increase in food prices. In the external account, lower growth and weakening domestic demand caused imports to contract by 4.7% in the first 5 months of the year. In the same period, the trade deficit shrank from $671.4 million a year earlier to $548.6 million, likely narrowing the current account deficit.

As growth prospects for the Lao People's Democratic Republic (Lao PDR) are unlikely to improve significantly in the near term, forecasts for GDP growth are lowered for 2019 and 2020. Inflation, on the other hand, is now seen slightly higher than the *ADO 2019* forecast for both years because of continued pressure on food prices. The current account deficit is now considered likely to be somewhat narrower than *ADO 2019* forecasts for this year and next.

The key risk to the outlook in the near term stems from the country's vulnerability to external financial shocks. The external payments situation is precarious, as the Lao PDR holds less than $1 billion in official foreign exchange reserves, barely enough to cover perhaps a single month of imports. The Lao kip appears to be overvalued, considering the significant premium over the official exchange rate paid on the parallel market for hard currency. In light of this, the International Monetary Fund reiterated in its August 2019 *Article IV Consultation Report* that the Lao PDR continues to be at risk of high debt distress.

Table 3.4.8 Selected economic indicators, Lao People's Democratic Republic (%)

	2019		2020	
	ADO 2019	Update 2019	ADO 2019	Update 2019
GDP growth	6.5	6.2	6.5	6.2
Inflation	2.0	2.3	2.0	2.3
Current acct. bal. (share of GDP)	-9.5	-8.9	-10.0	-8.4

Source: ADB estimates.

Myanmar

Trends in the first half of fiscal year 2019 (FY2019, ending 30 September 2019) suggest that economic growth will likely align with the *ADO 2019* forecast. Inflation is now seen to be higher than expected in April, and the current account deficit narrower than expected.

GDP growth in the first half of FY2019 was likely strong, though official GDP data are not yet available for these months. Trends in export earnings, international tourist arrivals, and foreign direct investment (FDI) inflows support an estimate of growth at 6.6% year on year.

Despite a slowdown in the global economy and in the People's Republic of China (PRC), merchandise exports rose by 7.7% in US dollar terms in the first 10 months of FY2019, while imports contracted by 5.9%. The contraction in imports reflected mainly the government's tighter screening of imports of luxury goods in 2018. Myanmar thus posted a small trade surplus of $54.6 million in the period.

Meanwhile, international tourist arrivals and FDI inflows accelerated. In the first 7 months of FY2019, international tourist arrivals accelerated sharply from 4.0% a year earlier to 17.9%. Similarly, in the first 5 months of FY2019, FDI inflows increased by a whopping 45.3%, reversing a 75.6% decline in the corresponding months of the previous year. While Western investors shunned Myanmar because of concerns over continued unrest in some conflict-affected areas, higher investment flowed from Asian investors, in particular from Hong Kong, China; the PRC; and Singapore. These foreign investments seem to have gone largely into transport, communications, and manufacturing.

GDP growth should therefore meet *ADO 2019* forecasts for both this year and next, as prospects for exports, international tourist arrivals, and FDI look positive in the near term. Reflecting this, the Nikkei's manufacturing purchasing managers' index for Myanmar rose to 54.2 in May 2019, well above the threshold of 50 indicating future growth. New orders were particularly strong for construction and other goods related to infrastructure development.

With the economy posting strong growth, inflationary pressure intensified even though the local currency largely held its own value against the US dollar. In the first 9 months of FY2019, average inflation accelerated from 5.2% a year earlier to 8.1%, which was well above the *ADO 2019* forecast for the whole fiscal year. Food prices rose by an average of 9.0%, reflecting lower domestic food production and food shortages in several parts of the country caused by transportation and other logistical constraints. The forecast for inflation is thus revised significantly up for this year. It is left unchanged for 2020.

Table 3.4.9 Selected economic indicators, Myanmar (%)

	2019		2020	
	ADO 2019	*Update*	*ADO 2019*	*Update*
GDP growth	6.6	6.6	6.8	6.8
Inflation	6.8	8.0	7.5	7.5
Current acct. bal. (share of GDP)	−4.0	−3.5	−5.0	−4.5

Source: ADB estimates.

With the country posting a trade surplus, the current account deficit likely narrowed in the first 9 months of FY2019. In addition, strengthening inbound tourism pushed up net service exports to make a significant contribution to the narrowing of current account deficit. Forecasts for a widening current account deficit are now reined in by half a percentage point of GDP for 2019 and 2020.

Singapore

Economic growth is slowing much more than foreseen in *ADO 2019*. With plummeting exports, GDP expansion collapsed from 4.4% year on year in the first half of 2018 to a paltry 0.6% in the same period of 2019.

In the 6 months to June 2019, exports of goods and services contracted year on year by 1.8% by volume, reversing 7.6% growth in the corresponding period of 2018. Having grown by 9.5% in the first half of 2018, net exports contracted by 3.5%. This decline was marginally offset by growth in domestic demand, which accelerated from 2.1% year on year in the first half of 2018 to 3.1% a year later, with growth in domestic consumption improving from 3.7% to 4.1%. Domestic investment recovered from mild contraction in the first half of 2018 to grow by 1.4%, but most of this turnaround was inventory buildup in response to weakening external demand, not recovery in fixed investment.

Weakening exports and investment slowed growth across the board. Services decelerated from 3.6% growth year on year in the first half of 2018 to a meager 1.2% a year later, and growth in industry braked even more sharply, from 7.1% growth to 0.9% contraction.

Inflation was tepid, averaging 0.6% in the first 7 months of this year. Reflecting subdued demand for imports of raw materials and intermediate goods for export production, and of capital goods for fixed investment, imports of goods and services contracted year on year by 1.5% by volume, reversing 7.3% growth a year earlier.

Growth prospects look bleak over the near term as uncertainty caused by persistent trade conflict between the US and the People's Republic of China bedevils global growth. Reflecting this, the purchasing managers' index—an early indicator that foretells growth when above a threshold of 50— fell to 49.8 in July 2019 for manufacturing and to 49.3 for electronics. Recent surveys of business expectations show a dimming view of the next 6 months.

GDP growth forecasts are marked down to the forecast horizon, more steeply for this year than for 2020. Weak growth will keep inflation low, and simultaneous slowdowns in exports and imports should sustain a high current account surplus. Forecasts for both economic indicators are unchanged from *ADO 2019*.

Table 3.4.10 Selected economic indicators, Singapore (%)

	2019		2020	
	ADO 2019	Update	ADO 2019	Update
GDP growth	2.6	0.7	2.6	1.4
Inflation	0.7	0.7	0.9	0.9
Current acct. bal. (share of GDP)	17.8	17.8	17.8	17.8

Source: ADB estimates.

The Pacific

Higher growth is projected for the subregion in 2019 with improved prospects for Papua New Guinea, Samoa, and Solomon Islands. In contrast, forecasts for the Cook Islands, Fiji, Palau, and Tonga are lowered. The 2020 projection is downgraded in expectation of delayed mining projects in Papua New Guinea and fiscal consolidation in Fiji. Inflation forecasts are trimmed in line with declining food prices this year and lower growth next year. Increased foreign revenues in Timor-Leste will boost the current account surplus.

Subregional assessment and prospects

GDP growth in the Pacific is projected to average 4.2% in 2019, or 0.7 percentage points higher than projected in *ADO 2019* as economic activity strengthens in Papua New Guinea (PNG) and Solomon Islands, two of the subregion's largest economies, and in Samoa (Figure 3.5.1). If realized, this will be the first significant acceleration in subregional expansion since 2014. The forecast improvement follows historically low growth at 0.4% in 2018.

In PNG, recovery from an earthquake in February 2018 has been stronger than anticipated, and liquefied natural gas production and exports in 2019 have outpaced projections. A higher growth forecast for PNG in 2019 also reflects revised national accounts data that now show the economy contracting slightly in 2018, in the wake of an earthquake. However, growth outside of the dominant mineral industry remains low. In Solomon Islands, higher infrastructure spending financed by development partners is seen to boost growth more than previously anticipated. Construction in preparation for hosting the 2019 Pacific Games in July likewise stimulated growth in Samoa, as did rising inbound tourism.

By contrast, an ongoing tourism downturn has deepened in Palau, where the economy is now expected to contract in fiscal year 2019, and a dramatic slowdown in visitor arrivals has constrained economic growth in the Cook Islands. The 2019 growth projection for Fiji is adjusted downward as key sectors outside of tourism are performing below expectations.

Figure 3.5.1 GDP growth, the Pacific

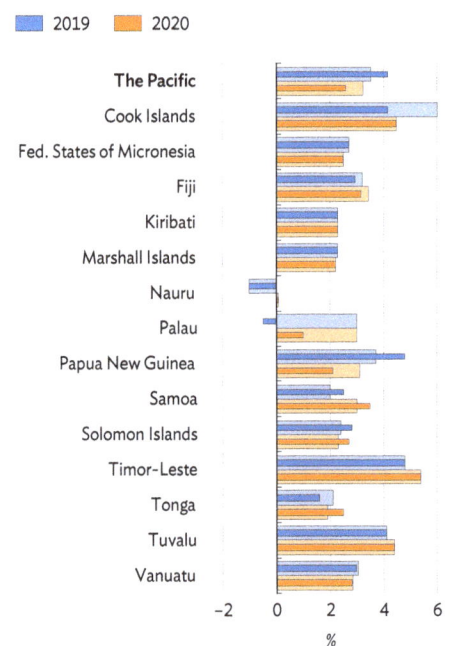

Note: Lighter colored bars are *ADO 2019* forecasts.
Source: *Asian Development Outlook* database.

The writeup on the Pacific economies was prepared by Jacqueline Connell, Edward Faber, David Freedman, Lily Anne Homasi, Rommel Rabanal, and Cara Tinio of the Pacific Department of ADB, and by Prince Cruz and Noel Del Castillo, consultants to the Pacific Department.

In Tonga, delays affecting major reconstruction projects after Cyclone Gita in 2018 have limited growth this year.

Elsewhere in the Pacific, growth forecasts are maintained. The impacts of the ongoing trade conflict and intensifying global risks have so far been minimal but could worsen if disputes persist and begin to affect other partner economies, particularly Australia and New Zealand. Economic developments in Timor-Leste, Vanuatu, and the small island economies of Kiribati, Nauru, and Tuvalu remain broadly in line with the outlook presented in *ADO 2019*.

The subregional growth projection for 2020 is adjusted down from 3.2% in *ADO 2019* to 2.6%. This comes largely from a downgrade for PNG in view of the delayed commencement of two large mining projects. The 2020 outlook for Fiji is likewise cut, reflecting plans for fiscal consolidation contained in the latest annual budget. The fiscal 2020 growth forecast for Palau is also reduced as uncertainty continues in the vital tourism industry. By contrast, projections for Samoa and Solomon Islands are upgraded in expectation of continuing momentum from 2019, while growth in Tonga is likewise seen to accelerate as more reconstruction projects are implemented.

Average inflation in the subregion is now expected to ease further to 3.4% in 2019, 0.3 percentage points lower than projected in April (Figure 3.5.2). Although fuel prices were higher than projected early in the year, they were offset in most Pacific economies by lower prices for imported food. In Solomon Islands, Timor-Leste, and Tonga, inflation in 2019 is now likely to be below earlier forecasts. More benign price pressures are seen to persist into next year, likely muted further by weaker economic growth in PNG. The subregional 2020 inflation projection is therefore reduced from 4.0% in *ADO 2019* to 3.4%.

The current account surplus for the Pacific as a whole, as a percentage of subregional GDP, is expected to be 1.4 percentage points higher than projected in *ADO 2019*, mainly as earnings exceed expectations in Timor-Leste, both from offshore oil and gas production and from sovereign wealth fund investments (Figure 3.5.3). However, current account deficits this year are now expected to be wider in Fiji, Solomon Islands, and Vanuatu from higher import bills. In 2020, the aggregate current account surplus is projected to be 2.5 percentage points higher than forecast in *ADO 2019* as the PNG surplus expands with imports undermined by the delayed construction of new mining projects and liquefied natural gas exports continuing unabated.

Figure 3.5.2 Inflation, the Pacific

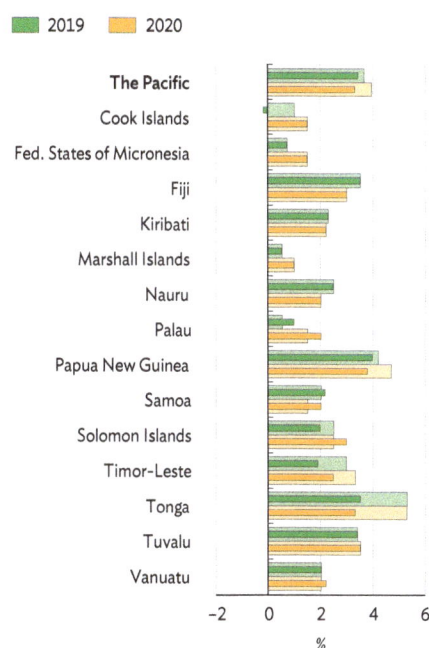

Note: Lighter colored bars are *ADO 2019* forecasts.
Source: *Asian Development Outlook* database.

Figure 3.5.3 Current account balance, the Pacific

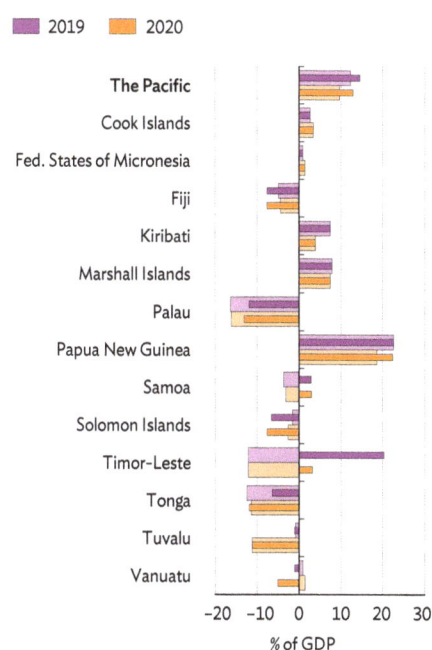

Note: Lighter colored bars are *ADO 2019* forecasts.
Source: *Asian Development Outlook* database.

Fiji

The 2019 growth projection is adjusted downward for a deeper slowdown than foreseen in *ADO 2019* and to accommodate a change in base year. GDP is now calculated using 2014 prices, no longer 2011 prices, which changes growth estimates from 2015. Although tourism grew strongly by 6.1% in the first half of 2019, as forecast, other industries have performed below expectations. Sugar and timber output, which had previously been expected to contribute substantially to growth, fell in the first 5 months of 2019 as transport issues compounded the effects of unfavorable weather. Meanwhile, commercial bank credit for investment declined, affecting lending for land and building purchase as well as for construction.

As projected in *ADO 2019*, tourism is expected to continue to perform well in 2020, buoyed by the acquisition of two new Airbus 350s by Fiji Airways in late 2019 and by Tourism Fiji's efforts to further expand the meetings, conferences, and exhibitions market. Nonetheless, a projected growth recovery in 2020 is downgraded slightly on account of plans for fiscal consolidation reflected in the June 2019 budget, with the deficit for fiscal year 2020 (FY2020, ending 31 July 2020) being reduced to the equivalent of 2.6% of GDP from 3.3% in FY2019.

As of July 2019, inflation was running 0.7 percentage points below the full-year forecast in *ADO 2019*, but trends still align with projections in April. No major shifts in commodity prices justify changing the forecast for slowing inflation in 2019 and 2020.

The current account deficit still looks likely to shrink in both years. However, with revised estimates showing a much larger current account deficit in 2018 than initially reported, deficit forecasts for 2019 and 2020 are now wider than in *ADO 2019*. Wider deficit forecasts also reflect rising imports for consumption and higher prices for imported fuel than earlier anticipated.

Extreme weather events are a perennial risk to forecasts for Fiji as they can reverse strong growth in tourist arrivals and shrink the tourist industry's contribution to the current account balance and to economic growth in general. Extreme weather events can also damage agriculture and thereby diminish growth prospects.

Table 3.5.1 Selected economic indicators, Fiji (%)

	2019		2020	
	ADO 2019	Update	ADO 2019	Update
GDP growth	3.2	2.9	3.5	3.2
Inflation	3.5	3.5	3.0	3.0
Current acct. bal. (share of GDP)	−4.7	−7.7	−4.2	−7.6

Source: ADB estimates.

Papua New Guinea

As forecast in *ADO 2019*, growth is driven this year primarily by a rebound in mineral production, including liquefied natural gas (LNG), oil, condensate, and gold. The increase in LNG production is greater than earlier forecast partly because 2018 production was less than initially estimated, lowering the base for growth in 2019, but also because production is now expected to be higher than projected earlier.

Meanwhile, growth in the economy outside of mineral extraction was weaker than expected in the first half of the year. This is reflected in credit to the private sector growing by only 3.7% year on year to May 2019, and by government tax revenue below expectations. There has been some improvement in the availability of foreign currency, but this has been insufficient to significantly spur the private sector, which continues to face delays in accessing it. In addition, a change of government in May 2019 temporarily unsettled business confidence. Agricultural output is expected to be weaker in 2019 than earlier forecast. World prices for palm oil have been declining, and production in the first quarter was the lowest in 2 years. Projected growth in construction is revised down as well because government capital expenditure fell below target in the first half of the year.

The 2020 growth forecast is revised down as oil production is projected to decline and with delays experienced to the start of two large projects: Papua LNG and the Wafi-Golpu gold and copper mine. Some work may commence on these projects in 2020, but significant activities are not expected to commence until 2021.

The forecast for inflation is revised down for 2019 in line with slower growth outside mineral extraction and following 5.3% contraction in broad money supply in the year to May 2019. Consumer prices rose in the first 3 months of 2019 by just 0.7% quarter on quarter, the lowest quarterly increase in 5 years. Prices fell for health care, clothing and footwear, alcoholic beverages, and betelnut but crept higher for education and for hotels and restaurants. Lower projected growth in 2020 prompts a steeper forecast downgrade for inflation next year.

The current account surplus equaled 22.3% of GDP in the 12 months ending March 2019, driven by exports of LNG equal to 15.8% of GDP and of gold at 9.6%. The forecast for the 2020 current account surplus is revised higher because the delayed start of new projects will keep imports below earlier projections. Foreign exchange reserves fell from a high of $2.3 billion in December 2018 to $1.9 billion in May 2019 as the Bank of Papua New Guinea, the central bank, injected foreign currency into banks for distribution to private enterprises.

The government has revised its budget deficit forecast for 2019 from the equivalent of 2.1% of GDP, as targeted under its medium-term fiscal strategy, to 2.7%, as outlined in its *Mid-Year Economic and Fiscal Outlook*. Expenditure tracked above target in the first 6 months as utility and rental arrears were carried over from 2018 and as the public sector wage bill continued to grow. Further, the revenue trend in the first 6 months of the year was weaker than expected as tax collection fell short of its target, partly because of less buoyant economic conditions. The government plans to cut the 2019 capital expenditure budget to meet its revised fiscal deficit target. A number of external financing sources are under consideration to finance the fiscal deficit.

Table 3.5.2 Selected economic indicators, Papua New Guinea (%)

	2019		2020	
	ADO 2019	Update	ADO 2019	Update
GDP growth	3.7	4.8	3.1	2.1
Inflation	4.2	4.0	4.7	3.8
Current acct. bal. (share of GDP)	22.5	22.6	18.5	22.3

Source: ADB estimates.

Solomon Islands

Growth forecasts for both 2019 and 2020 are revised up by 0.4 percentage points from forecasts published in *ADO 2019*. This largely reflects similar upward revision to the growth estimate for 2018 from 3.0% to 3.8%, mainly because of a higher contribution from construction. Growth is still seen decelerating to the forecast horizon. While infrastructure projects are expected to sustain their support, weaker logging output and crop production will weigh on growth.

Construction is now expected to be more robust than earlier forecast as work continues on road projects, water supply and sanitation upgrades, airport rehabilitation, preparations for the Tina River hydroelectricity project, and the 2023 Pacific Games. This is expected to provide flow-on benefits to businesses such as wholesale and retail trade and transport. Growth in agriculture so far this year has been mixed. While the fish catch strengthened, the output of key agricultural products including palm oil and copra was estimated lower than expected in the first half of 2019. The value of mineral exports dropped by half in the first quarter.

Following a caretaker period in the first quarter of 2019, a new government was sworn in following national elections in April.

The *ADO 2019* forecast for lower inflation in 2019 is adjusted downward in light of inflation below expectations in the first 5 months of the year and a decision in March by the Central Bank of Solomon Islands to moderately tighten monetary policy. Several factors are likely to stir inflation in the remainder of the year, though, notably the government's decision in August to double the minimum wage, the first rate change in more than 10 years. Further, the government implemented in September an import duty and goods tax on white rice. As price pressures are seen to persist into next year, inflation is now forecast to accelerate in 2020. Private sector credit was 7% higher year on year in the first quarter of 2019.

The current account deficit is expected to widen in both 2019 and 2020 as imports rise to supply infrastructure projects and as export earnings fall with easing logging output and crop production. Foreign exchange reserves provided cover for 12.4 months of imports in July, unchanged from the end of 2018.

Timor-Leste

Growth forecasts for 2019 and 2020 are unchanged from *ADO 2019*. Fiscal stimulus is helping the economy return to growth after contracting in 2017 and 2018. Although delays in approving the 2019 budget and bottlenecks in budget execution saw public spending fall in the first quarter (Q1), these problems were resolved in Q2.

Table 3.5.3 Selected economic indicators, Solomon Islands (%)

	2019		2020	
	ADO 2019	Update	ADO 2019	Update
GDP growth	2.4	2.8	2.3	2.7
Inflation	2.5	2.0	2.5	3.0
Current acct. bal. (share of GDP)	-1.4	-6.5	-2.6	-7.4

Source: ADB estimates.

Table 3.5.4 Selected economic indicators, Timor-Leste (%)

	2019		2020	
	ADO 2019	Update	ADO 2019	Update
GDP growth	4.8	4.8	5.4	5.4
Inflation	3.0	1.9	3.3	2.5
Current acct. bal. (share of GDP)	-12.0	10.1	-12.0	-3.2

Source: ADB estimates.

Public spending to the end of July was up by 31.3% with increased recurrent expenditure. This was partly offset by weak execution of public capital investment. Only 19% of the budget for infrastructure was executed in the first half of 2019, but spending is expected to pick up in the second half of the year in line with past experience.

Rising public expenditure contributed to a 4.3% increase in merchandise imports in the first half of 2019. Service imports are projected to rise in the whole of 2019 to handle increased construction, but they declined slightly in Q1 along with lower travel services. International visitor arrivals at Dili's international airport rose by 17.3% year on year in Q1 of 2019, but total passenger numbers were down by 23.9%, indicating greatly reduced domestic and international air travel by residents of Timor-Leste.

Other economic indicators are consistent with increased economic activity and rising private consumption. Motorbike and private car registration rose by 51.6% year on year in Q1, and electricity consumption by businesses was up by 9.7%. Credit to the private sector increased by 4.5% year on year in the first half of 2019, with Q1 data showing a 10.8% increase in lending to individuals.

Inflation forecasts for 2019 and 2020 are cut in response to inflation below expectations in the first half of 2019 and a revised outlook for international food prices. Consumer price inflation across Timor-Leste decelerated to 0.9% year on year in June, with average annual inflation to that month standing at 1.8%. Driving down inflation were lower prices for food—both locally produced and imported, including rice, bread, and meat—which offset higher costs for housing, clothing, education, alcohol, and tobacco. Inflation fell more rapidly in Dili than in the rest of the country, perhaps because lower import prices pass through to consumers in the capital more quickly than further afield.

Earnings from offshore oil and gas production and sovereign wealth fund investments were exceptionally high in the first half of 2019. Instead of a slight widening of the current account deficit in 2019, a substantial surplus is now forecast. Production from the offshore Bayu-Undan field increased by 11.2% year on year following the drilling of additional wells at the end of 2018. Strong production and rising oil prices saw Timor-Leste receive $432.7 million in production taxes and royalties in the first half of 2019. This exceeds the budget forecast for the whole of 2019 and equals 26.3% of GDP. The current account is projected to return to modest deficit in 2020.

Petroleum Fund investments earned $218.5 million in dividends and interest in January–June and posted a further $1.3 billion in asset gains from rising equity and bond markets. High inflows and strong investment returns saw the Petroleum Fund balance rise to a new record of $17.4 billion at the end of Q2.

The portfolio now includes a $650 million loan to Timor Gap, the national oil company, to finance the acquisition of equity in a joint venture to develop Greater Sunrise, a large offshore gas field. A newly ratified treaty between Australia and Timor-Leste paves the way for the eventual development of Greater Sunrise. The new treaty also increases the Timor-Leste share of taxes and royalties from the Bayu-Undan field from 90% to 100%, further boosting government revenue and the current account balance.

Vanuatu

The forecast for GDP growth in 2019 is unchanged. Although construction is likely to grow more than earlier forecast, this will be offset by visitor arrivals and agricultural output below expectations.

In contrast with an earlier projection that construction would wind down with the completion of reconstruction projects, construction is set to continue in 2019 and beyond but at a slower pace than in 2018. While imports of construction materials were 21.3% lower year on year in the first half of 2019, several projects to rehabilitate and upgrade roads are expected to commence in the second half of this year.

Visitor arrivals were lower than expected in early 2019. Air arrivals were down by 2.5% year on year in the first half of 2019. Although arrivals increased slightly from Australia, they fell from other major markets, notably New Caledonia, New Zealand, and other Pacific countries. Visitor arrivals by cruise ship more than halved in the same period as fewer cruise ships visited. Tourism prospects remain positive, however, with the renovated Bauerfield International Airport expected to catalyze visitor arrivals.

Export performance has been mainly flat in 2019, rising by just 2.7% in the first half of the year. Exports of kava, which overtook copra in 2018 as the highest-value merchandise export, increased by 15.7% year on year in the first half of 2019 and more than offset a fall in the value of other commodity exports including copra, coconut oil, and beef. A rhinoceros beetle infestation found on Efate poses a challenge to Vanuatu's coconut industry. The infestation prompted the government to declare a state of emergency and establish restricted zones in July 2019.

Although the consumer price index rose by 2.3% year on year in the first half of 2019 on higher food and transportation prices, the inflation forecast for 2019 is maintained as consumer price increases are expected to slow in the second half. The forecast for 2020 is adjusted slightly upward in line with global food and oil prices. The Reserve Bank of Vanuatu, the central bank, has maintained an accommodative monetary policy.

Table 3.5.5 Selected economic indicators, Vanuatu (%)

	2019		2020	
	ADO 2019	Update	ADO 2019	Update
GDP growth	3.0	3.0	2.8	2.8
Inflation	2.0	2.0	2.0	2.2
Current acct. bal. (share of GDP)	1.0	–1.0	1.5	–5.0

Source: ADB estimates.

Current account forecasts are revised down. *ADO 2019* projected surpluses this year and next from higher tourism and lower imports with the completion of infrastructure projects. Now, though, the current account is expected to return to deficit, following a small surplus in 2018, as imports to supply construction continue, and with weaker exports of goods and services. From 2020, the current account deficit is expected to widen considerably as Air Vanuatu imports aircraft under a plan called Shared Vision 2030 to boost air travel and tourism.

North Pacific economies

The near-term outlook is maintained for the Federated States of Micronesia (FSM) and the Marshall Islands. However, GDP growth projections for Palau are downgraded as it struggles to reverse a tourism downturn. Dependent as the North Pacific economies are on external developments, their medium- and long-term prospects hinge as well on how successfully current efforts strengthen project implementation capacity.

Federated States of Micronesia

Economic stimulus from capital spending has been weaker than anticipated. Hopes were high that the involvement of the US Army Corps of Engineers would facilitate the implementation of projects funded through the Compact of Free Association the FSM has with the US. However, delays have stemmed from issues affecting project selection and coordination between the government and the corps. Revised GDP estimates show growth in fiscal year 2018 (FY2018, ended 30 September 2018 in all North Pacific economies) was much lower than previously reported.

The FSM continues to benefit from high corporate income tax revenue paid by foreign companies domiciled in the country after they liquidate offshore investments. Collections from these one-off windfalls exceeded expectations in the first 3 quarters of FY2019, pushing the fiscal surplus for the year substantially higher than projected earlier. The surplus will be deposited in the FSM Trust Fund.

Delays in implementing capital projects are now seen to persist in the near term, but high spending ahead of the recent national election and greater clarity on policy directions have been mitigating factors. On balance, GDP forecasts for FY2019 and FY2020 are unchanged. Inflationary pressure remains low and broadly in line with expectations. As higher international prices for petroleum products are seen offsetting lower prices for imported food, this *Update* retains *ADO 2019* projections for inflation and current account surpluses in FY2019 and FY2020.

Table 3.5.6 Selected economic indicators, Federated States of Micronesia (%)

	2019		2020	
	ADO 2019	Update	ADO 2019	Update
GDP growth	2.7	2.7	2.5	2.5
Inflation	0.7	0.7	1.5	1.5
Current acct. bal. (share of GDP)	1.0	1.0	1.5	1.5

Note: Years are fiscal years ending on 30 September of the same calendar year.
Source: ADB estimates.

Marshall Islands

Economic growth projections for this year and next are maintained from *ADO 2019*. Delays in project completion, and project implementation constraints, continue to dampen stimulus from public investment funded by development partners and US compact grants. Although FY2019 is expected to be a record year for copra production, this upside is countered by reports that fish caught near Kwajelein Atoll are contaminated with high concentrations of toxic chemicals from industrial vessels and local landfills. In addition, concerns remain regarding the government's plan to issue a cryptocurrency and the possible implications.

Another concern arises from doubts that the Marshall Islands can achieve fiscal self-sufficiency by 2023, when compact grants expire. Although the government continues to realize fiscal surpluses, largely thanks to high revenue from fishing license fees, these surpluses are gradually being squeezed by increases in public spending. Further, resources from the country's Compact Trust Fund are not expected to sustainably offset the elimination of compact grants after 2023. A July 2019 report by the US Government Accountability Office predicts that disbursements from the trust fund can replace compact grants in the first 10 years, but not subsequently. Meanwhile, the possibility exists that the trust fund will be unable to disburse any money at all in some years, with this risk worsening after the first decade.

A recent rebasing of the country's real GDP series suggests that historical growth estimates may be higher than previously reported, but information currently available does not justify revising any projections.

Inflation and current account surplus projections are unchanged from *ADO 2019*. Annual inflation at 0.4% in the first half of FY2019 suggests that inflation is on track to meet forecasts for the whole fiscal year, with some acceleration seen for FY2020. The current account surplus is still expected to widen somewhat in FY2019 as project completion causes merchandise imports to fall and then narrow again in FY2020 with higher international prices for food imports.

Palau

A recovery in tourist arrivals projected earlier in the year has not materialized, so tourism in Palau will likely record a fourth consecutive year of decline. Arrivals in October 2018–June 2019 were about 20% lower than in the same period a year earlier. The two largest markets for tourists to Palau recorded the steepest declines, with reduced flight connections through Hong Kong, China for tourists from the People's Republic of China and through Tokyo for visitors from Japan. Plans for Skymark, a low-cost airline in Tokyo, to reintroduce regular flights to Palau have yet to be realized.

Table 3.5.7 Selected economic indicators, Marshall Islands (%)

	2019		2020	
	ADO 2019	Update	ADO 2019	Update
GDP growth	2.3	2.3	2.2	2.2
Inflation	0.5	0.5	1.0	1.0
Current acct. bal. (share of GDP)	8.0	8.0	7.5	7.5

Note: Years are fiscal years ending on 30 September of the same calendar year.
Source: ADB estimates.

Table 3.5.8 Selected economic indicators, Palau (%)

	2019		2020	
	ADO 2019	Update	ADO 2019	Update
GDP growth	3.0	−0.5	3.0	1.0
Inflation	0.5	1.0	1.5	2.0
Current acct. bal. (share of GDP)	−16.3	−11.9	−16.0	−13.0

Note: Years are fiscal years ending on 30 September of the same calendar year.
Source: ADB estimates.

Taipei,China remains the lone bright spot among Palau's main tourist markets, registering 37.6% growth in arrivals in the first 6 months of 2019.

The GDP growth outlook for FY2019 is therefore downgraded to a slight contraction. Although higher government expenditure with greater financial assistance from the US will provide some economic stimulus, it will not fully offset the continuing downturn in tourism. A September 2018 amendment to the Compact of Free Association between Palau and the US allows capital spending to increase by up to a quarter in FY2019, and boosts provision for infrastructure maintenance. Growth in FY2020 is nevertheless now seen to be lower than projected in *ADO 2019*, reflecting persistent malaise in Palau's vital tourism industry.

Despite weak economic activity, inflation has been slightly higher than anticipated. Consumer price inflation in the first 3 quarters of FY2019 averaged 0.9%, driven up by rising prices for imports. As international prices for key commodities, particularly petroleum products, are expected to continue to rise, inflation projections are raised for both FY2019 and FY2020.

Revised estimates show much smaller current account deficits in recent years, which prompts lower deficit forecasts for FY2019 and FY2020 than in *ADO 2019*. However, deficits are now seen wider in both years than in FY2018 as tourism languishes and import bills rise.

South Pacific economies

The growth outlook is mixed, with projections downgraded for the Cook Islands in light of slower growth in visitor arrivals, and upward adjustments for Samoa. In Tonga, the delayed implementation of rehabilitation and reconstruction projects following Cyclone Gita in February 2018 pushed anticipated growth stimulus from fiscal year 2019 (FY2019, ended 30 June 2019) in all South Pacific economies into the new fiscal year.

Cook Islands

Economic growth in FY2019 is estimated to have slowed more than projected in *ADO 2019*. Available data show the economy growing at less than half the rate in FY2018, supported mainly by tourist businesses like retail, hotels, and transportation as visitor arrivals grew by 1.3%, albeit less than earlier projected. Steady increases in visitor arrivals in the first half of FY2019 came courtesy of annual events, both national and international, such as the Te Maeva Nui Festival, which showcases Cook Islands culture and heritage usually in August, and Vaka Eiva, an international paddling competition usually in November. These events offer special package deals that attract tourists.

Table 3.5.9 Selected economic indicators, Cook Islands (%)

	2019		2020	
	ADO 2019	Update	ADO 2019	Update
GDP growth	6.0	4.2	4.5	4.5
Inflation	1.0	-0.2	1.5	1.5
Current acct. bal. (share of GDP)	2.8	2.8	3.4	3.4

Note: Years are fiscal years ending on 30 June of that year.

Source: ADB estimates.

The outlook for growth in FY2020 is unchanged from *ADO 2019*. Growth will continue to be driven by tourism, with continued expansion in visitor arrivals, and by capital investment.

Recent government estimates showed a fiscal surplus equal to 1.7% of GDP in FY2019, narrower than the 4.0% surplus realized in FY2018 as a drop in grant inflows reduced fiscal resources. Net external debt remains well below the government's official threshold equal to 35.0% of GDP, as foreseen in *ADO 2019*. A fiscal deficit equal to 1.4% of GDP is budgeted for FY2020, reflecting the government's continued commitment to investing in infrastructure projects.

Deflation returned in FY2019, though *ADO 2019* had forecast a second year of inflation. Price declines hit housing, utilities, and transport, with food prices remaining stable. The forecast for somewhat stronger inflation in FY2020 is unchanged from *ADO 2019*, predicated on the expectation of higher global food prices.

Earlier forecasts for small but widening current account surpluses are retained for FY2019 and FY2020.

Samoa

Economic recovery in FY2019 is estimated to have outperformed the forecast in *ADO 2019*. Data available for the first 3 quarters of the fiscal year show growth exceeding initial expectations in trade, transport, accommodation, and restaurants. Also expanding were construction, partly in preparation for the 2019 Pacific Games in Apia in July, and financial services. A 9.3% increase year on year in visitor arrivals in FY2019 suggests that growth in tourism-related businesses continued to exceed expectations in the last quarter.

The growth projection for FY2020 is revised up in anticipation of stimulus from public infrastructure projects. Visitor arrivals are expected to continue to climb, buoyed by the Pacific Games and other regional events.

The government estimates that it incurred a fiscal deficit equal to 0.2% of GDP in FY2019, as growth in both recurrent and capital spending outpaced that of revenues. The deficit remained well within the mandated threshold of 2.0% of GDP. Public debt stood at the equivalent of 48.0% of GDP at the end of FY2019. A fiscal deficit equal to 1.2% of GDP is budgeted for FY2020.

Inflation in FY2019 was higher than projected in *ADO 2019*. Prices for both imported and locally produced goods rose faster than expected, affecting food, beverages, utilities, and transport, but inflation was still well down from FY2018. The FY2020 projection is adjusted upward but remains a slight deceleration.

Table 3.5.10 Selected economic indicators, Samoa (%)

	2019		2020	
	ADO 2019	Update	ADO 2019	Update
GDP growth	2.0	2.5	3.0	3.5
Inflation	2.0	2.2	1.5	2.0
Current acct. bal. (share of GDP)	–3.5	3.0	–3.0	3.0

Note: Years are fiscal years ending on 30 June of that year.

Source: ADB estimates.

Samoa is estimated to have widened its small current account surplus in FY2019, not incurred the deficit projected in *ADO 2019*. Although imports increased as expected to supply construction tied to the Pacific Games, earnings from tourism rose by 13.2% year on year in FY2019, and remittances rose by 11.4%, both sources substantially higher than forecast. Earnings increased as well from merchandise exports, particularly fish and manufactured food. These trends in exports, tourism, and remittances are seen to continue in FY2020, sustaining the current account surplus.

Tonga

After the onslaught of Cyclone Gita in February 2018, rehabilitation and reconstruction have been important drivers of growth. However, with major construction projects idled by delays, the growth estimate for FY2019 is lower than the projection in *ADO 2019*.

The growth projection for FY2020 is consequently upgraded to reflect reconstruction stimulus delayed into the new fiscal year. A continuing downside risk to the growth forecast is the persistence of bottlenecks affecting the government receipt of external funding to support reconstruction.

The latest fiscal data mean downward revision of earlier revenue projections to the forecast horizon, but expected declines in expenditure are greater. Earlier forecasts of fiscal deficits are thus reversed to surpluses equal to 1.4% of GDP in FY2019 and 0.9% in FY2020.

With the slowdown in construction projects, and as domestic prices normalized following cyclone-related supply disruption, estimated inflation in FY2019 stayed below the projection in *ADO 2019*. With international crude oil prices seen to moderate next year, further deceleration is expected in FY2020.

The current account deficit in FY2019 is estimated to be little more than half of the projection in *ADO 2019* as slow project implementation meant lower imports. Higher imports of capital goods will widen the deficit in FY2020 somewhat more than earlier forecast.

Small island economies

Projections are maintained from *ADO 2019* for steady growth in Kiribati to the forecast horizon and for slightly slower growth this year in Tuvalu. Contraction in Nauru in the recently closed fiscal year is now estimated to be slightly less severe than forecast in April. Inflation forecasts for all three small island economies are unchanged. Projected current account balances for Kiribati and Tuvalu are also retained.

Table 3.5.11 Selected economic indicators, Tonga (%)

	2019		2020	
	ADO 2019	*Update*	*ADO 2019*	*Update*
GDP growth	2.1	1.6	1.9	2.5
Inflation	5.3	3.5	5.3	3.3
Current acct. bal. (share of GDP)	–12.2	–6.4	–11.2	–11.7

Note: Years are fiscal years ending on 30 June of that year.

Source: ADB estimates.

Kiribati

Growth forecasts for Kiribati in 2019 and 2020 are unchanged from *ADO 2019*, as the economy is expected to continue to enjoy support from sustained government spending and infrastructure projects financed by development partners.

The fiscal balance is projected to remain in deficit in the next 2 years as government spending climbs but revenue falls. Revenue from fishing licenses is forecast to decline, as foreseen in *ADO 2019*, partly because of variation in the migratory patterns of pelagic tuna. Meanwhile, expenditure is likely to be flat in the short term, but capital spending will rise in the medium term with the anticipated purchase of new passenger aircraft. Delivery is expected late in 2019 and early in 2020.

As forecast in *ADO 2019*, inflation is seen to accelerate slightly this year and settle down again in 2020. A projected decline in global food prices has not been reflected in the overall inflation rate in Kiribati because prices for fuel above expectations have added to shipping costs.

Kiribati is still projected to post a shrinking surplus in its current account in 2019 and 2020, in line with *ADO 2019*. Although fishing revenue fell slightly in the first half of 2019, there have been no changes to imports sufficient to revise projections.

Table 3.5.12 Selected economic indicators, Kiribati (%)

	2019		2020	
	ADO 2019	*Update*	*ADO 2019*	*Update*
GDP growth	2.3	2.3	2.3	2.3
Inflation	2.3	2.3	2.2	2.2
Current acct. bal. (share of GDP)	7.6	7.6	4.0	4.0

Source: ADB estimates.

Nauru

The economy is now estimated to have contracted by less than forecast in fiscal year 2019 (FY2019, ended 30 June 2019) mainly because revenue from fishing licenses exceeded expectations, as did employment taxes and service fees from the Regional Processing Centre, an Australian-funded facility for asylum seekers. This has allowed government expenditure to rise above earlier projections. The fiscal surplus is estimated to equal 5.1% of GDP, higher than projected, and the government has continued to contribute to the Nauru Intergenerational Trust Fund.

The forecast is maintained for marginal growth in FY2020. The FY2020 budget projects a small surplus equal to 0.3% of GDP, down from FY2019 with the absence of one-off windfall fishing revenue. The economy remains narrowly based, and any changes in contract arrangements for the Regional Processing Centre could significantly affect both government revenue and economic activity.

Inflation is estimated to have slowed in FY2019 as forecast in April and is still projected to slow further in FY2020.

Table 3.5.13 Selected economic indicators, Nauru (%)

	2019		2020	
	ADO 2019	*Update*	*ADO 2019*	*Update*
GDP growth	–1.0	–0.5	0.1	0.1
Inflation	2.5	2.5	2.0	2.0
Current acct. bal. (share of GDP)	...	...	...	...

Source: ADB estimates.

Tuvalu

Growth forecasts are retained for both 2019 and 2020 with a slight dip this year. Infrastructure projects supported by development partners continue to be the main drivers of economic growth.

While much of the infrastructure spending was focused on preparations for a Pacific Islands Forum summit in August 2019, the government has also allotted spending to construct and upgrade schools, improve health services, and build other facilities needed on outer islands. Continued spending on infrastructure and an expected decline in fishing license revenue will likely spell a fiscal deficit in 2019, as forecast in *ADO 2019*. With the latest government data indicating a projected funding gap, Tuvalu is now expected to post a fiscal deficit in 2020 as well.

Projections for higher inflation in 2019 and 2020 are unchanged, with rising public sector wages and infrastructure projects still the major causes.

Forecasts for the current account balance in the next 2 years are unchanged from those in *ADO 2019*. Weaker fishing license revenue in the next 2 years and sustained growth in imports of goods will continue to be the main drivers of change in the current account balance, which is expected to slip into a slight deficit in 2019 and fall a good bit deeper in 2020. The vagaries of weather may translate into fishing revenue shortfalls, creating much wider current account deficits and necessitating fiscal tightening, which could hobble growth prospects.

Table 3.5.14 Selected economic indicators, Tuvalu (%)

	2019		2020	
	ADO 2019	Update	ADO 2019	Update
GDP growth	4.1	4.1	4.4	4.4
Inflation	3.4	3.4	3.5	3.5
Current acct. bal. (share of GDP)	−0.9	−0.9	−11.0	−11.0

Source: ADB estimates.

STATISTICAL APPENDIX

Statistical notes

This statistical appendix presents selected economic indicators for the 45 developing member economies of the Asian Development Bank (ADB) in three tables: gross domestic product (GDP) growth, inflation, and current account balance as a percentage of GDP. The economies are grouped into five subregions: Central Asia, East Asia, South Asia, Southeast Asia, and the Pacific. The tables contain historical data for 2016–2018 and forecasts for 2019 and 2020.

The data are standardized to the degree possible to allow comparability over time and across economies, but differences in statistical methodology, definitions, coverage, and practice make full comparability impossible. The national income accounts section is based on the United Nations System of National Accounts, while the data on balance of payments use International Monetary Fund accounting standards. Historical data are ADB estimates variously based on official sources, statistical publications and databases, and documents from ADB, the International Monetary Fund, and the World Bank. Projections for 2019 and 2020 are generally ADB estimates made on the bases of available quarterly or monthly data, though some projections are from governments.

Most economies report by calendar year. The following record their government finance data by fiscal year: Brunei Darussalam; Fiji; Hong Kong, China; the Kyrgyz Republic; Singapore; Tajikistan; Thailand; and Uzbekistan. The following report all variables by fiscal year: the Cook Islands, the Federated States of Micronesia, Myanmar, Nauru, Palau, the Republic of Marshall Islands, Samoa, Tonga, and all South Asian countries except Maldives and Sri Lanka. Since 2018, fiscal years in Myanmar end in September of that calendar year, having earlier ended in March of the following calendar year; Myanmar's fiscal years 2017 and 2018 thus overlap from October 2017 to March 2018.

Regional and subregional averages are provided in the three tables. The averages are computed using weights derived from gross national income (GNI) in current US dollars following the World Bank Atlas method. The GNI data for 2016–2017 are obtained from the World Bank's World Development Indicators Online. Weights for 2017 are carried over through 2020. The GNI data for the Cook Islands and Taipei,China are estimated using the Atlas conversion factor.

The following paragraphs discuss the three tables in greater detail.

Table A1: Growth rate of GDP (% per year). The table shows annual growth rates of GDP valued at constant market price, factor cost, or basic price. GDP at market price is the aggregation of value added by all resident producers at producers' prices including taxes less subsidies on imports plus all nondeductible value-added or similar taxes. Constant factor cost measures differ from market price measures in that they exclude taxes on production and include subsidies. Basic price valuation is the factor cost plus some taxes on production, such as those on property and payroll taxes, and less some subsidies, such as those on labor-related subsidies but not product-related subsidies. Most countries use constant market price valuation. Pakistan, Fiji, and Maldives use basic prices. To 2015, Singapore calculated real GDP using annually reweighted chain volume measures of GDP reference years.

Table A2: Inflation (% per year). Data on inflation rates are period averages. The inflation rates presented are based on consumer price indexes. The consumer price indexes of the following economies are for a given city or group of consumers only: in Cambodia for Phnom Penh, in the Marshall Islands for Majuro, and in Solomon Islands for Honiara.

Table A3: Current account balance (% of GDP). The current account balance is the sum of the balance of trade in merchandise, net trade in services and factor income, and net transfers. The sums are divided by GDP at current prices in US dollars. Official transfers to Cambodia, the Lao People's Democratic Republic, and Viet Nam are excluded from their current account balances.

Table A1 Growth rate of GDP (% per year)

	2016	2017	2018	2019 ADO2019	2019 Update	2020 ADO2019	2020 Update
Central Asia	2.4	4.2	4.3	4.2	4.4	4.2	4.3
Armenia	0.2	7.5	5.2	4.3	4.8	4.5	4.5
Azerbaijan	–3.1	0.1	1.4	2.5	2.6	2.7	2.4
Georgia	2.8	4.8	4.7	5.0	4.7	4.9	4.6
Kazakhstan	1.1	4.1	4.1	3.5	3.7	3.3	3.4
Kyrgyz Republic	4.3	4.7	3.5	4.0	4.0	4.4	4.4
Tajikistan	6.9	7.1	7.3	7.0	7.0	6.5	7.0
Turkmenistan	6.2	6.5	6.2	6.0	6.0	5.8	5.8
Uzbekistan	6.1	4.5	5.1	5.2	5.8	5.5	6.0
East Asia	6.0	6.2	6.0	5.7	5.5	5.5	5.4
Hong Kong, China	2.2	3.8	3.0	2.5	0.3	2.5	1.5
Mongolia	1.4	5.4	6.8	6.7	6.7	6.3	6.1
People's Republic of China	6.7	6.8	6.6	6.3	6.2	6.1	6.0
Republic of Korea	2.9	3.2	2.7	2.5	2.1	2.5	2.4
Taipei,China	1.5	3.1	2.6	2.2	2.2	2.0	2.0
South Asia	7.5	6.9	6.6	6.8	6.2	6.9	6.7
Afghanistan	2.2	2.7	2.7	2.5	2.7	3.0	3.4
Bangladesh	7.1	7.3	7.9	8.0	8.1	8.0	8.0
Bhutan	7.4	6.3	5.5	5.7	5.3	6.0	6.0
India	8.2	7.2	6.8	7.2	6.5	7.3	7.2
Maldives	7.3	6.9	7.6	6.5	6.5	6.3	6.3
Nepal	0.6	8.2	6.7	6.2	7.1	6.3	6.3
Pakistan	4.6	5.2	5.5	3.9	3.3	3.6	2.8
Sri Lanka	4.5	3.4	3.2	3.6	2.6	3.8	3.5
Southeast Asia	4.8	5.2	5.1	4.9	4.5	5.0	4.7
Brunei Darussalam	–2.5	1.3	0.1	1.0	1.0	1.5	1.5
Cambodia	7.0	7.0	7.5	7.0	7.0	6.8	6.8
Indonesia	5.0	5.1	5.2	5.2	5.1	5.3	5.2
Lao People's Dem. Rep.	7.0	6.9	6.3	6.5	6.2	6.5	6.2
Malaysia	4.5	5.7	4.7	4.5	4.5	4.7	4.7
Myanmar	5.9	6.8	6.8	6.6	6.6	6.8	6.8
Philippines	6.9	6.7	6.2	6.4	6.0	6.4	6.2
Singapore	3.0	3.7	3.1	2.6	0.7	2.6	1.4
Thailand	3.4	4.0	4.1	3.9	3.0	3.7	3.2
Viet Nam	6.2	6.8	7.1	6.8	6.8	6.7	6.7
The Pacific	2.7	2.8	0.4	3.5	4.2	3.2	2.6
Cook Islands	6.0	6.8	8.9	6.0	4.2	4.5	4.5
Federated States of Micronesia	0.9	2.7	0.4	2.7	2.7	2.5	2.5
Fiji	2.5	5.4	3.5	3.2	2.9	3.5	3.2
Kiribati	5.1	0.3	2.3	2.3	2.3	2.3	2.3
Marshall Islands	1.8	3.6	2.5	2.3	2.3	2.2	2.2
Nauru	10.4	4.0	–2.4	–1.0	–0.5	0.1	0.1
Palau	0.6	–3.8	1.5	3.0	–0.5	3.0	1.0
Papua New Guinea	2.0	3.0	–0.6	3.7	4.8	3.1	2.1
Samoa	8.1	1.0	–2.2	2.0	2.5	3.0	3.5
Solomon Islands	3.4	3.4	3.8	2.4	2.8	2.3	2.7
Timor-Leste	5.1	–3.5	–0.5	4.8	4.8	5.4	5.4
Tonga	3.1	2.8	0.4	2.1	1.6	1.9	2.5
Tuvalu	3.0	3.2	4.3	4.1	4.1	4.4	4.4
Vanuatu	3.5	4.4	3.2	3.0	3.0	2.8	2.8
Developing Asia	6.0	6.2	5.9	5.7	5.4	5.6	5.5
Developing Asia excluding the NIEs	6.5	6.6	6.4	6.2	6.0	6.1	6.0

Note: The newly industrialized economies (NIEs) are Hong Kong, China; the Republic of Korea; Singapore; and Taipei,China.

Table A2 Inflation (% per year)

	2016	2017	2018	2019 ADO2019	2019 Update	2020 ADO2019	2020 Update
Central Asia	10.4	9.0	8.3	7.8	8.0	7.2	7.4
Armenia	−1.4	1.0	2.5	3.5	3.0	3.2	3.2
Azerbaijan	12.4	12.9	2.3	4.0	3.7	5.0	3.8
Georgia	2.1	6.0	2.6	3.2	4.3	3.0	3.5
Kazakhstan	14.6	7.4	6.0	6.0	5.8	5.5	5.2
Kyrgyz Republic	0.4	3.2	1.5	3.0	2.0	3.5	3.5
Tajikistan	6.1	6.7	5.4	7.5	8.0	7.0	7.5
Turkmenistan	3.6	8.0	13.6	9.0	13.4	8.2	13.0
Uzbekistan	8.8	13.9	17.5	16.0	15.0	14.0	13.0
East Asia	1.9	1.6	2.0	1.8	2.3	1.8	2.1
Hong Kong, China	2.4	1.5	2.4	2.3	2.3	2.3	2.3
Mongolia	1.1	4.3	6.8	8.5	8.5	7.5	7.5
People's Republic of China	2.0	1.6	2.1	1.9	2.6	1.8	2.2
Republic of Korea	1.0	1.9	1.5	1.4	0.7	1.4	1.4
Taipei,China	1.4	0.6	1.3	1.1	0.9	1.2	0.9
South Asia	4.5	3.9	3.6	4.7	4.0	4.9	4.9
Afghanistan	4.4	5.0	0.6	3.0	2.0	4.5	3.5
Bangladesh	5.9	5.4	5.8	5.5	5.5	5.8	5.8
Bhutan	3.3	4.3	3.6	3.8	2.8	4.0	3.5
India	4.5	3.6	3.4	4.3	3.5	4.6	4.0
Maldives	0.5	2.8	−0.1	1.0	1.0	1.5	1.5
Nepal	9.9	4.5	4.2	4.4	4.6	5.1	5.5
Pakistan	2.9	4.2	3.9	7.5	7.3	7.0	12.0
Sri Lanka	4.0	7.7	2.1	3.5	3.0	4.0	3.8
Southeast Asia	2.0	2.8	2.7	2.6	2.3	2.7	2.6
Brunei Darussalam	−0.7	−0.2	0.1	0.2	0.1	0.2	0.2
Cambodia	3.0	2.9	2.5	2.5	2.2	2.5	2.5
Indonesia	3.5	3.8	3.2	3.2	3.2	3.3	3.3
Lao People's Dem. Rep.	1.6	0.8	2.0	2.0	2.3	2.0	2.3
Malaysia	2.1	3.8	1.0	2.0	1.0	2.7	2.0
Myanmar	6.8	4.0	5.9	6.8	8.0	7.5	7.5
Philippines	1.3	2.9	5.2	3.8	2.6	3.5	3.0
Singapore	−0.5	0.6	0.4	0.7	0.7	0.9	0.9
Thailand	0.2	0.7	1.1	1.0	1.0	1.0	1.0
Viet Nam	2.7	3.5	3.5	3.5	3.0	3.8	3.5
The Pacific	4.7	4.2	4.2	3.7	3.4	4.0	3.4
Cook Islands	−0.1	−0.1	0.4	1.0	−0.2	1.5	1.5
Federated States of Micronesia	−0.9	0.1	1.4	0.7	0.7	1.5	1.5
Fiji	3.9	3.3	4.1	3.5	3.5	3.0	3.0
Kiribati	1.9	0.4	2.1	2.3	2.3	2.2	2.2
Marshall Islands	−1.5	0.0	0.8	0.5	0.5	1.0	1.0
Nauru	8.2	5.1	3.8	2.5	2.5	2.0	2.0
Palau	−1.3	0.9	2.0	0.5	1.0	1.5	2.0
Papua New Guinea	6.7	5.4	4.7	4.2	4.0	4.7	3.8
Samoa	0.1	1.4	3.7	2.0	2.2	1.5	2.0
Solomon Islands	0.6	0.5	3.5	2.5	2.0	2.5	3.0
Timor–Leste	−1.3	0.6	2.2	3.0	1.9	3.3	2.5
Tonga	2.6	7.4	5.3	5.3	3.5	5.3	3.3
Tuvalu	2.6	4.4	1.8	3.4	3.4	3.5	3.5
Vanuatu	0.8	3.1	2.3	2.0	2.0	2.0	2.2
Developing Asia	2.4	2.2	2.4	2.5	2.7	2.5	2.7
Developing Asia excluding the NIEs	2.6	2.3	2.6	2.6	2.9	2.6	2.9

Note: The newly industrialized economies (NIEs) are Hong Kong, China; the Republic of Korea; Singapore; and Taipei,China.

Table A3 Current account balance (% of GDP)

	2016	2017	2018	2019 ADO2019	2019 Update	2020 ADO2019	2020 Update
Central Asia	−6.4	−2.4	−1.8	−1.7	−1.3	−1.8	−1.7
Armenia	−2.1	−3.0	−9.4	−6.9	−7.5	−6.1	−6.5
Azerbaijan	−3.6	4.1	12.9	13.6	13.9	10.8	11.6
Georgia	−13.1	−8.8	−7.7	−7.9	−7.3	−7.8	−7.1
Kazakhstan	−6.5	−3.3	0.0	−0.8	−1.0	−1.2	−1.4
Kyrgyz Republic	−11.6	−6.5	−10.0	−12.0	−12.0	−12.0	−12.0
Tajikistan	−4.2	2.2	−5.0	−4.0	−4.5	−3.8	−4.3
Turkmenistan	−19.9	−11.5	−8.2	−5.7	−2.3	−3.4	−3.2
Uzbekistan	0.4	2.5	−7.1	−7.0	−7.0	−6.5	−6.5
East Asia	2.8	2.5	1.3	0.8	1.6	0.6	1.1
Hong Kong, China	4.0	4.7	4.3	3.5	3.3	3.3	3.1
Mongolia	−6.3	−10.1	−16.9	−9.6	−10.7	−13.0	−16.1
People's Republic of China	1.8	1.6	0.4	0.0	1.0	−0.1	0.4
Republic of Korea	6.5	4.6	4.4	4.1	3.9	3.9	3.8
Taipei,China	13.7	14.4	11.6	6.0	8.0	6.0	8.0
South Asia	−0.5	−2.0	−2.7	−2.7	−2.5	−2.6	−2.5
Afghanistan	7.6	3.4	6.9	−1.1	1.2	−0.4	0.7
Bangladesh	1.9	−0.5	−3.5	−2.3	−1.7	−2.5	−1.8
Bhutan	−31.1	−23.2	−18.2	−16.9	−23.4	−13.4	−19.4
India	−0.6	−1.9	−2.1	−2.4	−2.2	−2.5	−2.5
Maldives	−23.5	−21.8	−25.0	−21.8	−18.0	−22.0	−19.0
Nepal	6.2	−0.4	−8.2	−9.3	−7.7	−8.1	−7.6
Pakistan	−1.7	−4.1	−6.3	−5.0	−4.8	−3.0	−2.8
Sri Lanka	−2.1	−2.6	−3.0	−2.5	−2.2	−2.6	−2.3
Southeast Asia	3.2	3.1	1.8	2.1	2.3	2.1	2.2
Brunei Darussalam	12.9	16.4	7.9	13.0	13.0	13.0	13.0
Cambodia	−10.9	−10.5	−13.1	−12.7	−13.5	−11.8	−13.5
Indonesia	−1.8	−1.6	−3.0	−2.7	−2.7	−2.7	−2.9
Lao People's Dem. Rep.	−15.7	−13.5	−12.2	−9.5	−8.9	−10.0	−8.4
Malaysia	2.4	2.8	2.1	2.4	3.5	2.4	3.5
Myanmar	−4.3	−4.7	−3.7	−4.0	−3.5	−5.0	−4.5
Philippines	−0.4	−0.7	−2.6	−2.3	−1.7	−2.4	−2.0
Singapore	17.5	16.4	17.9	17.8	17.8	17.8	17.8
Thailand	10.5	9.7	6.4	7.0	7.0	7.0	7.0
Viet Nam	2.9	2.9	2.4	2.5	2.0	2.0	1.8
The Pacific	11.7	11.7	11.6	12.3	13.7	9.8	12.3
Cook Islands	7.1	1.6	2.2	2.8	2.8	3.4	3.4
Federated States of Micronesia	3.9	7.5	2.0	1.0	1.0	1.5	1.5
Fiji	−3.9	−7.0	−8.9	−4.7	−7.7	−4.2	−7.6
Kiribati	20.4	14.5	13.4	7.6	7.6	4.0	4.0
Marshall Islands	9.7	4.8	7.0	8.0	8.0	7.5	7.5
Nauru	1.7	0.5	1.0	...	...	...	...
Palau	−6.6	−11.4	−8.7	−16.3	−11.9	−16.0	−13.0
Papua New Guinea	24.0	22.5	21.7	22.5	22.6	18.5	22.3
Samoa	−4.5	−1.8	1.2	−3.5	3.0	−3.0	3.0
Solomon Islands	−4.6	−5.3	−5.1	−1.4	−6.5	−2.6	−7.4
Timor−Leste	−31.1	−17.8	−11.8	−12.0	10.1	−12.0	−3.2
Tonga	−13.8	3.1	1.8	−12.2	−6.4	−11.2	−11.7
Tuvalu	24.0	6.7	4.8	−0.9	−0.9	−11.0	−11.0
Vanuatu	0.8	−6.4	3.4	1.0	−1.0	1.5	−5.0
Developing Asia	2.2	1.8	0.8	0.4	1.1	0.3	0.7
Developing Asia excluding the NIEs	1.2	0.9	−0.2	−0.5	0.3	−0.5	−0.2

... = data not available.

Note: The newly industrialized economies (NIEs) are Hong Kong, China; the Republic of Korea; Singapore; and Taipei,China.

www.ingramcontent.com/pod-product-compliance
Lightning Source LLC
Chambersburg PA
CBHW061234270326
41929CB00031B/3486